O9-BTM-738

American Literature
1764–1789
The Revolutionary Years

American Literature

1764—1789

The Revolutionary Years

Everett Emerson

EDITOR

The University of Wisconsin Press

MIDDLEBURY COLLEGE LIBRARY

PS
193
A4

Published 1977
The University of Wisconsin Press
Box 1379, Madison, Wisconsin 53701

The University of Wisconsin Press, Ltd.
70 Great Russell Street, London

Copyright © 1977
The Regents of the University of Wisconsin System
All rights reserved

FIRST PRINTING

Printed in the United States of America

For LC CIP information see the colophon

ISBN 0–299–07270–3

Contents

Preface

No one needs to be reminded of the importance of the years 1764–89 in American history. These same years produced a substantial body of literature, much of which can be described as the literature of the Revolution: it urges either American independence or loyalty to the British crown, celebrates the American cause, or employs the Revolution and persons and events associated with it as its inspiration and its subject. These years also saw the composition of a body of literature not so closely associated with military and political affairs but coexistent with them, works still full of interest both as literature and as history. In these pages we have undertaken to examine both kinds: literature directly concerning the American Revolution and American literature written in the epoch of the Revolution.

Even a partial listing of our men and women of letters should suggest that these were vintage years. Benjamin Franklin heads the roll, followed at no great distance by Thomas Jefferson, then St. John de Crèvecoeur and Thomas Paine. Here too are Philip Freneau, Phillis Wheatley, Royall Tyler, John Woolman, William Bartram, Mercy Otis Warren, Joel Barlow, Jonathan Mayhew—and the list goes on and on. Contemplating such a distinguished roster, one must ask, why? What explanation can be found for the flourishing of literature during the years when the United States was achieving independence and nationhood? Circumstances do not seem to have been auspicious. The strand of towns and agricultural communities along the Atlantic from Georgia to what is now Maine was thinly populated, at least from the perspective of two hundred years. The phenomenal literary productivity is striking, especially when the achievements of the Founding Fathers and their contemporaries is compared with the much less impressive body of literature of the next twenty-five years.

The cause of independence aroused not only the martial but also the literary arts of Americans. Literary talents were called for, since Americans put real trust in rational and persuasive argument, written or spoken, and literacy was high. In the years leading up to the Declaration of Independence, especially after the Stamp Act, there was a vast outpouring of publications, mostly pamphlets, debating what Americans should do. And what resulted, among other things, was that Americans developed a new self-consciousness, a new awareness of who they were, of who they had become. Literature helped Americans to understand their new situation. After the Declaration of Independence, literature was useful in rallying the citizens of the new nation to support the cause of independence. And after the war, literature was greatly needed: the young nation must have a national literature. That literature contributed significantly to shaping history during these years is indisputable. Works such as *Common Sense*, the *Federalist Papers*, and the Declaration of Independence did much to determine what was to happen in America. The present reinterpretation of the literature of the revolutionary years should help Americans of two hundred years later to understand their history and their heritage.

This undertaking has required much cooperation and good will. I am grateful to those who helped plan the book with me, to my friends J. A. Leo Lemay and Kenneth Silverman for advice and assistance, to Sargent Bush, whose close reading of the manuscript improved it greatly, and to my capable co-workers in this project.

The headnotes, which connect and introduce the chapters, were prepared by the editor.

EVERETT EMERSON

July 1976
Amherst, Massachusetts

Chronology, 1764-1789

1764

With British government in debt, Parliament passes Revenue Act ("Sugar Act") to raise funds to pay for recent wars against the French and Spanish.

James Otis, *The Rights of the British Colonies Asserted and Proved.*
John Dickinson, *An Address to the Committee of Correspondence.*
Anonymous, *The Paxton Boys.*

1765

Parliament adopts Stamp Act, providing tax on newspapers and documents. Widely opposed in America, notably in the Virginia House of Burgesses and by the Boston Sons of Liberty. Stamp Act Congress meets in New York City in October, with representatives from Massachusetts, Rhode Island, Connecticut, New York, New Jersey, Pennsylvania, Delaware, Maryland, and South Carolina; it questions the legality of the Stamp Act. Sons of Liberty are organized and force royal collection agents to resign. Quartering Act requires colonial authorities to provide for British troops.

John Adams, "Dissertation on the Canon and Feudal Law."
John Dickinson, *The Late Regulations Respecting the British Colonies.*
Thomas Godfrey, *The Prince of Parthia.*

1766

The Stamp Act repealed. New York Assembly refuses to support Quartering Act; clashes between colonials and British troops result.

The Examination of Dr. Franklin.
Jonathan Mayhew, *The Snare Broken.*
Charles Chauncy, *A Discourse on "The Good News from a Far Country."*
Southwark Theatre built in Philadelphia, first permanent American playhouse.
Robert Rogers, *Ponteach.*

1767

Parliament adopts Townshend Revenue Acts, placing duties on glass, paper, and tea (three pence a pound). Nonconsumption movement spreads through colonies.

1768

Massachusetts House of Representatives adopts circular letter of Samuel Adams addressed to other colonies against Townshend Acts. Endorsed by New Hampshire, Virginia, Maryland, Connecticut, Rhode Island, Georgia, South Carolina. Boston, focal point of American opposition, occupied by British troops.

John Dickinson, *Letters from a Farmer in Pennsylvania.*

1769

Nonconsumption policies damage British trade.

Samuel Adams (and others), *Appeal to the World.*

1770

Townshend Acts repealed, but tea
duty remains. British guard kills
Crispus Attucks, runaway slave,
and four others in hostile crowd
(the Boston Massacre). British
troops removed. Nonconsumption
agreements abandoned.

1771

Philip Freneau and Hugh Henry
Brackenridge, *The Rising Glory of
America*.
Benjamin Franklin begins *Auto-
biography*.

1772

Committee of Correspondence created in Massachusetts.

Joseph Warren, *An Oration*.
John Trumbull, *The Progress of
Dulness*.

1773

Parliament adopts Tea Act. Boston
Tea Party enacted in protest.

Slaves petition for freedom in New
England.
Benjamin Church, *An Oration to
Commemorate the Bloody Tragedy*.
Mercy Otis Warren, *The Adulateur*.
Benjamin Franklin, "An Edict by
the King of Prussia" and "Rules by
Which a Great Empire may be Re-
duced to a Small One."
Phillis Wheatley, *Poems*.

1774

"Intolerable [or Coercive] Acts" (including Boston Port Bill, closing the port) adopted by Parliament. Burke's speech on reconciliation. Continental Congress, representing all thirteen states except Georgia, meets in Philadelphia. Plan of Union introduced. Trade Association created, and Declaration of Rights (calling for repeal of all colonial legislation passed since 1763) adopted.

Thomas Jefferson, *A Summary View of the Rights of British America.*
Alexander Hamilton, *A Full Vindication.*
Daniel Leonard's essays signed "Massachusettenis" begin to appear.
Samuel Seabury, *Free Thoughts; The Congress Canvassed;* and *A View of the Controversy.*
Isaac Wilkins, *Short Advice.*
Charles Lee, *Strictures On A Pamphlet.*
John Woolman, *Journal.*
Francis Hopkinson, *A Pretty Story.*

1775

Parliament declares Massachusetts in a state of rebellion. British government seeks to put down Americans with force. Troops march to Concord, Massachusetts, to seize American arms. Battle of Concord and Lexington. Second Continental Congress meets, to serve for five years. Washington made commander-in-chief of American forces. British holding Boston attack Bunker Hill. Parliament adopts prohibitory bill, blockading the American colonies and authorizing the seizure of American goods on salt water. British hire German mercenaries and promise freedom to blacks who fight for the crown.

Joseph Galloway, *A Candid Examination of the Mutual Claims of Great-Britain and the Colonies.*
John Zubly, *The Law of Liberty.*
Jonathan Sewall, *A Cure for the Spleen.*
Samuel Langdon, *Government Corrupted by Vice, and recovered by Righteousness.*
Alexander Hamilton, *The Farmer Refuted.*
John Trumbull, *M'Fingal.*
Phillis Wheatley coins term *Columbia* to refer to America in "To His Excellency George Washington."
Mercy Otis Warren, *The Group.*

1776

British evacuate Boston. July 2, Independence declared. July 4, Declaration of Independence adopted. British defeat Washington on Long Island and take New York City. Washington leads troops to victory at Trenton and Princeton.

Thomas Paine, *Common Sense;* first of *The American Crisis* pamphlets.
Charles Inglis, *The True Interest of America.*
John Adams, *Thoughts on Government.*
John Witherspoon, *The Dominion of Providence.*
Robert Munford, *The Patriots.*
Hugh Henry Brackenridge's *The Battle of Bunkers-Hill* performed at Southwark Theatre.
General John Burgoyne's *The Boston Blockade* staged in Boston.
Anonymous, *The Blockheads: or The Affrighted Officers.*
Anonymous, *The Battle of Brooklyn.*
Anonymous, *The Fall of British Tyranny.*

1777

British take Philadelphia. Americans defeat British at Saratoga. Articles of Confederation adopted by Continental Congress.

Benjamin Franklin, "The Sale of the Hessians."
Hugh Henry Brackenridge's *The Death of General Montgomery* performed at Southwark Theatre.

1778

France recognizes United States. Franco-American treaty of friendship adopted. British leave Philadelphia. Indecisive battle of Monmouth, New Jersey.

Francis Hopkinson, "The Battle of the Kegs."
Jonathan Carver, *Travels.*

1779

Spain declares war on Britain.   Joel Barlow, *The Prospect of Peace*.
                                        Philip Freneau, *The House of Night*.
                                        Mercy Otis Warren, *The Motley Assembly*.

1780

British capture Charleston. Ameri-   Thomas Paine, *Public Good*.
cans defeated at Camden, South
Carolina.

1781

Articles of Confederation ratified.   Philip Freneau, "The British Prison
Cornwallis defeated at Yorktown.   Ship."

1782

British abandon southern ports.   Benjamin Franklin, "Supplement
                                        to the *Boston Independent Chronicle*."
                                        John Trumbull, final verson of
                                        M'Fingal.
                                        Thomas Paine, *Letter to the Abbé Raynal*.
                                        St. John de Crèvecoeur, *Letters from an American Farmer*.
                                        Anonymous, *The Blockheads; or, Fortunate Contractor*.

1783

Treaty of Paris signed, ending the
war.

1784

"State of Franklin" created in east-
ern Tennessee.

Benjamin Franklin, "Information
for those Who Would Remove to
America"; composition of part 2 of
Autobiography.

1785

Land ordinance adopted by Congress.

Timothy Dwight, *The Conquest of
Canäan*.

1786

Serious commercial depression.
Shays's rebellion.

Philip Freneau, *Poems*.
The Anarchiad, first parts.

1787

Northwest Ordinance adopted, preparing the way for government
there. Constitutional Convention
meets in Philadelphia in spring and
summer, with Washington as presiding officer.

Joel Barlow, *The Vision of Columbus*.
First of *Federalist Papers* published.
Royall Tyler, *The Contrast*.

1788

The Constitution ratified.

Franklin resumes composition of *Autobiography*.
Timothy Dwight, *The Triumph of Infidelity*.

1789

Federal government established with Washington as president.

William Dunlap, *The Father,* and *Darby's Return.*

American Literature
1764–1789
The Revolutionary Years

1

The Cultural Context
of the American Revolution

EVERETT EMERSON

What was America at the time of the Revolution? It could be described as a collection of semiseparate colonies along the Atlantic coast emerging into unity and independence. For an understanding of the context of the literature of the revolutionary years, however, such an answer will not suffice, for the question implies other questions. Who were the Americans? How many were there? Where did they live? How did they make their living? What ideas did they hold? What vehicles existed for the dissemination of ideas and information? To what extent did literature perform a function in their lives? What literary inheritance did they claim?

I

Because the revolutionary years, as conceived here, span nearly a generation, the answer to the questions offered must be somewhat oversimple. The United States in 1789 was dramatically different from the American colonies in 1764, both because of the Revolution and because of forces at work independent of its cataclysmic events. One of these forces was population growth: in the eighteenth century the American population doubled every twenty-five years. The areas of greatest growth were interior Massachusetts, New Hampshire, Vermont, the upper Hudson Valley, New York City, the Pennsylvania-Maryland border area, Baltimore, Frederick, the Virginia Piedmont, the Shenandoah Valley, and the Caroline backcountry. Early marriage was common, and families averaged about eight children, though mortality claimed one-third to one-half of them before the age of five.

The greater part of the Americans lived in rural areas, and there were no cities at all in the modern sense of the word, for in 1776 Bostonians were only 16,000 in number and New Yorkers only 25,000. Philadelphia was the largest population center, with 40,000 people. The only other towns with more than 10,000 residents were Newport and Charleston. Some present-day American cities were in their infancy: Savannah had about 3,000 citizens, Norfolk 6,000, Albany 4,000. When the first census was taken in 1790, about 75 percent of white Americans were of English, Scotch, or Scotch-Irish origin, with the next largest white group being those of German origin, about 9 percent. Most Americans were Protestants or Anglicans; there were fewer than 25,000 Catholics at the beginning of the Revolution. The black population, nearly all slaves, was about 18 percent of the total; the Indian population, not counted in the census, was less than 8,000 in the thirteen original states. These facts are important in a consideration of the cultural contributions of early America: Americans were few in number and lived mostly away from urban centers. Moreover, many of them were occupied with the tasks of surviving and creating a new way of life in a new land.

On the eve of the Revolution, the American frontier was not far inland, beginning in the South some seventy-five miles below Savannah and in the North at Penobscot Bay in what is now central Maine. Only in Virginia and sourthern Pennsylvania was the area as far west as the Appalachians settled, and little of inland New York, except for the Hudson River Valley, had inhabitants other than Indians. (St. John de Crèvecoeur, who describes vividly life on the frontier, lived less than seventy-five miles from New York City.) Though distances were not great by modern standards, travel by land was very difficult. It was a considerable accomplishment for a stage company to offer transportation from New York to Philadelphia in only two days; the journey from New Haven to New York took as long. Among the hazards that could put a halt to travel were rain, snow, and forest fires.

Though public education was commonly available only in New England, most white Americans could read, and most possessed a few books, at least a Bible and the current almanac. Education was prized. In the late 1760s Philadelphians enjoyed the benefits of at least sixteen evening schools that taught writing, arithmetic, and bookkeeping. Charles Thomson observed, "In this Country almost every man is fond of reading, and seems to have a Thirst for knowledge." Higher education was for the privileged few, however, with only about three thousand men (and no women) having been graduated from college in the thirty years before the Revolution. There were eight American colleges in 1776. Most Americans accepted traditional religion, but after the war deism and rationalism became more popular, as is suggested by the publication in 1788 of Timothy Dwight's *Triumph of Infidelity*, an attack on deism. Jackson Turner Main describes the social structure of revolutionary

America as follows: The proletariat constituted about 30 percent of the population, of which some two-thirds were slaves and the rest indentured servants and wage laborers. About 60 percent were of the "middling sort": farmers, artisans, craftsmen, and such professional people as teachers, ministers, and doctors. About seventy-five to one hundred pounds a year enabled one to live at the standards of this class. The "better sort," consisting of large landowners, some lawyers, and office holders, constituted about 10 percent of the population and controlled about 45 percent of the country's wealth. To live as a gentleman required about four hundred pounds a year (pluss food grown on one's own land or the equivalent in income). To improve one's economic status, a man's best opportunity was to move westward: on the frontier, most people could, through hard work, enjoy middle-class standards.

Travelers' accounts provide a good idea of what American life was like during the revolutionary years. When Lord Adam Gordon, a British infantry officer, visited New York City in 1765 he described it as having about three thousand houses,

> about 300 stores, 12 churches and places of worship and perhaps 20,000 inhabitants,—here are more Negroes than in any Northern province, and by being the seat of government, civil and military, and the place to which all the money for the exigencies of America is sent from Britain is rich. . . . Over against the town to the eastward lies a part of Long Island, which has long been peopled; the soil of it is naturally light and sandy, and almost wore out, yet the inhabitants are loth to quit this hold, on account of its remarkable healthiness and pleasantness . . . .[1]

Nine years later another visitor to New York, Patrick M'Robert, commented on its many fine buildings, public and private, then observed that "the streets are in general ill-paved, irregular, and too narrow. There are four market places, as well supplied with all kinds of provisions." Water came from pumps, but "tea water" was brought "in carts thro' the streets from the suburbs." New York's industries consisted of "several large roperies, distilleries, breweries, and a large iron works." He found "plenty of mechanicks of all kinds, by whom every thing that is made . . . in Britain is made to as great perfection here." He admired the inhabitants, who were "in general brisk and lively, kind to strangers, dress very gay; the fair sex are in general handsome, and said to be very obliging. Above 500 ladies of pleasure keep lodgings contiguous within the consecrated liberties of St. Paul's [church]."[2]

Gordon found the people of Hartford "uncommonly stiff and formal and as

1. "Journal of Lord Adam Gordon," in *Travels in the American Colonies,* ed. Newton D. Mereness (New York: Antiquarian Press, 1961), pp. 414–15.

2. Carl Bridenbaugh, ed., "Patrick M'Robert's Tour Through Part of the North Provinces of America," *Pennsylvania Magazine of History and Biography* 59 (1935): 140–42.

industrious as in any one province.'' Boston he found ''more like an English old town than any in America. The language and manners of the people very much resemble the old country, and all the neighboring lands and villages carry with them the same idea.'' Among the southern colonies, Gordon preferred Virginia, for

> the houses are larger, better and more commodious than those to the Southward, their Breed of Horses extremely good, and in particular those they run in their Carriages, which are mostly thorough bred Horses and country Mares,—they all drive Six horses, and travel generally 8 to 9 Miles an hour—going frequently Sixty Miles to dinner—you may conclude from this their Roads are extremely good—they live in such agreement, that the Ferries, which would retard in another Country, rather accelerate their meeting here, for they assist one another, and all Strangers with their Equipages in so easy and kind a manner, as must deeply touch a person of any feeling and convince them that in this Country, Hospitality is every where practiced. (p. 405)

Before they were united by the Revolution, the inhabitants of the thirteen colonies usually felt closer to Britain than to their fellow Americans in other colonies. Boundary disputes, such as those over what was to become Vermont, were among the factors that divided the colonists. There New Yorkers disputed with men of Connecticut, Massachusetts, and New Hampshire. Life styles varied greatly among the colonists, with three major styles observable, those of the South, the middle colonies, and New England. Though regional differences did much to separate, the colonists also had many points of contact. Trade was of major importance. Many American families had dispersed, especially among the northern towns, and a good deal of travel took place, even for pleasure despite its difficulties. South Carolinians and Philadelphians summered in Newport in considerable numbers in the late 1760s. Churches and masonic lodges provided an important web of relationships. A particularly striking example of intercolonial cooperation was the creation of the college that is now Princeton. It was strongly supported by New York Presbyterians, and the people of Connecticut contributed over thirteen thousand pounds. In 1757 Jonathan Edwards, the famous Massachusetts preacher and theologian, succeeded to its presidency, to be followed in 1759 by the Virginia revivalist, Samuel Davies. Nor were the southern colonies so separate as may be supposed. In 1775 North Carolina's three delegates to the Continental Congress consisted of a 1760 graduate of Harvard, a former Marylander, and a man from New Jersey who still maintained a business in Philadelphia. The war experience brought the colonists much closer, as men fought together and deliberated together. They kept informed, as best they could, on the progress of the war in the South and the North. The Revolution gave America its first national hero, George Washington, who was admired from Cambridge to Charleston, though not universally. His appearance, his dignity, his surrender of his commission at Annapolis, as well as his military success, provided Americans with a symbol of unity and a rallying point.

II

The most important means of intercolonial contact was the newspaper, and it was especially important during the Revolution. At the time of the battles of Concord and Lexington thirty-seven newspapers were being published in the colonies, and many had wide circulation. Publishers drew substantially on other newspapers in preparing their own. Newspapers were of tabloid size, usually consisting of four pages; most were published weekly. In preparing the American people for the Revolution, newspapers played a vital role. Newspaper editors widely opposed the Stamp Act of 1765 because it provided that newspapers should be printed only on special paper that was stamped and taxed. No American newspaper was ever printed on stamped paper. The *Pennsylvania Journal* of October 31, 1765, protested the Stamp Act by printing a large tombstone on its first page. The lead article reads:

> I am sorry to be obliged to acquaint my Readers, that as The Stamp Act, is feared to be obligatory upon us after the *First of November* ensuing, (the *fatal To-morrow*) The Publisher of this paper unable to bear the Burthen, has thought it expedient to stop a while, in order to deliberate whether any Methods can be found to elude the chains forged for us, and escape the insupportable Slavery; which it is hoped, from the just Representations now made against the Act, may be effected.

Accounts of protests against British taxes filled American papers. The nonimportation and nonconsumption agreements that angry Americans adopted after the Townshend Acts that taxed glass, paper, tea, and other imports were especially taken up by newspaper editors. Few newspapers served as Loyalist, pro-British organs in the years before 1774. In fact pro-British forces in America were slow to organize a propaganda campaign.

In the 1760s and 1770s the *Boston Gazette* carried the writings of the Caucus Club that included James Otis, Sam and John Adams, Samuel Cooper, and John Hancock. John Adams reports how he devoted Sunday afternoons to preparing the next day's issue, "a curious employment, cooking up paragraphs, articles, occurrences, etc., working the political engine." John Dickinson's *Letters from a Farmer in Pennsylvania,* among the most effective prorevolutionary statements, were published in the *Pennsylvania Chronicle*, and the first of Paine's *Crisis* papers ("These are the times that try men's souls") was published in the *Pennsylvania Journal* and read to Washington's army before the battle of Trenton. Its propaganda was unusally effective. The editor of the *South Carolina Gazette* corresponded with Sam Adams and published a great deal of Boston material, including a full page on the Boston Massacre. In 1775 he printed Joseph Warren's fiery speech recalling the Massacre and including the words, "if the only way to safety is through fields of blood, you will not hesitate until tyranny be trodden under foot."

Because of the lack of any well-organized system of reporting, the battles of the war itself were much less well treated in newspapers. What happened close to a population center could be described with some ease, but coverage of fighting in such remote areas as North Carolina was much more sketchy. The *Essex Gazette* of Salem, Massachusetts, provided the best account of the outbreak of hostilities, the battles of Concord and Lexington. It begins:

> Last Wednesday, the 19th of April, the Troops of his *Brittanick* Majesty commenced Hostilities upon the People of this Province, attended with Circumstances of Cruelty not less brutal than what our venerable Ancestors received from the vilest Savages of the Wilderness. The Particulars relative to this interesting Event, by which we are involved in the Horrors of a Civil War, we have endeavored to collect as well as the present confused State of Affairs will permit.

Newspapers were more literary in revolutionary days than they are today. The *Georgia Gazette* of Savannah, the *Connecticut Courant* of Hartford, and the *Maryland Gazette* of Annapolis were among the many newspapers that regularly published poetry, often in celebration of America. Even more literary were the magazines, which performed a special function in the beginnings of the American nation, as George Washington himself recognized. In a letter written June 25, 1788, he declared, "I consider such easy vehicles of knowledge [as the magazine] as more highly calculated to preserve the liberty, stimulate the industry, and meliorate the morals of an enlightened and free people." Magazines were published in great numbers, but almost all were early failures because of problems with distribution, manufacturing, and finding contributors. American magazines imitated and borrowed from British magazines but some were attractive and informative. (British magazines were also regular borrowers.)

A good example is the *Royal American Magazine*, edited by Isaiah Thomas, who was later the author of an important history of printing in America and founder of the American Antiquarian Society. Highly miscellaneous in nature, Thomas's monthly magazine published in 1774 and 1775 numerous letters, really short essays, communicating both information and opinion; a department of poetical essays on such topics as "Tobacco" ("vile weed, in ev're shape thou art bad") and "A Prophecy of the Future Glory of

America"; and, separately numbered, pages from Thomas Hutchinson's classic *History of Massachusetts Bay*. The first issue addressed "the Literati of America" to praise the English language. "Its highest perfection, with every other branch of human knowledge, is perhaps reserved for this LAND of light and freedom." Later issues contain arguments for and against the education of women, beginning with a writer who questions, "How many female minds, rich with native genius and noble sentiments, have been lost to the world, and all their mental treasures lost in oblivion." The May issue published "An Act for BLOCKADING the Port of BOSTON," and the July issue reported among its "Domestic Intelligence," "There is not a town of any consequence on the continent of North America, but is justly alarmed with the proceedings of the British Parliament, and taking necessary steps to strengthen the Union of the colonies, and thereby defeat the cruel designs of arbitrary power."

The dramatic change in the attitudes of the American people during the 1760s and 1770s has often been remarked. In 1816 John Adams wrote, "The Revolution was in the minds and hearts of the people . . . . This radical change in the principles, opinions, sentiments, and affections of the people was the real American Revolution," and David Ramsey, in his *History of the American Revolution* (1789), wrote, "In establishing American independence, the pen and the press had a merit equal to that of the sword." The fact that many crises occurred during the years of the Revolution and the forming of the republic gave the newspaper very great power. Newspapers sprang up in great numbers in response to need. For example, Isaiah Thomas's patriotic *Massachusetts Spy*, founded in 1770, had 3500 subscribers in 1775. The radical change that Adams referred to was brought about by a variety of forces, but the function of newspapers and magazines in creating change was among the most important. They of course reflected changing attitudes, but they also crystallized people's thinking and hastened wholesale change. A quantitative study of colonial newspapers shows that during the years 1735–75 increasing attention was paid to American place names and decreasing attention to others. A dramatic shift can be detected in 1763, when references to the colonies and the colonists as a single unit increased substantially: before the 1760s few colonists had thought of themselves as Americans. During the years 1765–75 newspapers came to adopt similar patters of terminology. This phenomenon was obviously an effect of such events as the Royal Proclamation of 1763 that denied the western land claims of the colonies and asserted their obligation to pay for defense measures. But it also affected the Americans' view of themselves. The colonists swiftly began to recognize the fact of the American continent and the fact that they constituted a community, and they thereby became much more sensitive to interference from Britain.

I I I

In the years before the Revolution many of the best American minds were attracted to religion and the ministry; the struggle between good and evil was to be found within men's souls. As the movement for independence grew, ministers lost power, for even if they identified themselves with the movement, they could not readily exchange their religious responsibilities for political ones. They had taught their people to see sin and evil as dominant forces in life; now many Americans saw as their greatest danger the British campaign to tax them, an effort that they feared would extend British political corruption to American shores. The Townshend Acts that reorganized the custom services created a new set of royal officials, paid from the taxes they collected in a system that—so Americans thought—bred corruption. The nonimportation and nonconsumption agreements that Americans adopted to combat the new taxation soon were looked upon as part of the struggle between good and evil, in which denial and frugality were pitted against luxury and dissipation.

This shift in attention to politics was facilitated by the investiture of the new interests with the emotional associations of traditional religion. Thus Abigail Adams wrote in 1774 to her husband John, "If we expect to inherit the blessings of our Fathers, we should return a little more to their primitive Simplicity of Manners, and not sink into inglorious ease." A writer for the *Newport Mercury* in 1773 invoked the Puritan ethic on behalf of the developing movement leading to revolution when he declared, "The Americans have plentifully enjoyed the delights and comforts, as well as the necessaries of life, and it is well known that an increase of wealth and affluence paves the way to an increase of luxury, immortality, and profaneness, and here kind providence interposes; and as it were, obliges them to forsake the use of one of their delights, to preserve their liberty." Americans asserted their independence of Britain in part to save themselves from what they saw as the evils of luxury and political corruption.

I V

In eighteenth-century America, in literary efforts and in writings on political affairs, the qualities of decorum, formality, and dignity are to be found everywhere. Especially in the revolutionary years, educated Americans, like their English contemporaries, were admirers of the classics in literature and art, and they consciously imitated the grand style of ancient Greece and Rome. In education the Renaissance tradition was continued; at King's College (later Columbia) in 1754, for instance, beginning students were required to know Cicero's orations and the first books of Vergil's *Aeneid*. The framers of the Constitution studied Aristotle, Cicero, and Polybius; even the largely self-educated Benjamin Franklin freely quoted Vergil, Horace, and Xenophon. The father of his country, George Washington, upon retirement from military service, ordered for himself busts of Alexander, Ceasar, Sallust, Terence, and Horace.

Classical antiquity was most important in the birth of the new nation as a source of republican aspiration. Such classical writers as Cicero, Tacitus, Plutarch, and Sallust considered the society in which they lived disordered and corrupt, and they looked back to an earlier age of republican virtue, patriotism, justice, and simplicity. Feeding on this literature, patriot leaders almost from the first coupled the ideal of independence with the ideal of republicanism. As early as 1775 Samuel Adams, writing to Elbridge Gerry, declared, "It is now in the power of our assembly to establish wholesome laws and regulations, which could not be done under the former administration of government." Republicanism, according to John Adams in 1776, "introduces knowledge among the people, inspires them with a conscious dignity becoming freemen; a general emulation takes place, which causes good humor, sociability, good manners, and good morals to be generals." Americans could become eighteenth-century Catos and Brutuses.

The new republican ideal dramatically affected how Americans thought about their land and themselves. In the middle years of the century Americans usually had looked upon themselves as provincials. They were far from culturally self-sufficient. Just as a good deal of the contents of American magazines were borrowed from London magazines, similarly American booksellers sold chiefly English books. In both literature and politics English ideals were accepted as standard. A characteristic American literary subservience was demonstrated by Mather Byles, the mid-century Boston preacher, wit, and poet. Byles established his sense of worth as a poet by soliciting what he considered a letter of approval from Alexander Pope and as a clergyman by obtaining a degree of doctorate of divinity from Aberdeen University. Americans judged themselves inferior to their countrymen across the water because they lacked the culture and social life of the mother country. But the most admired English writers of the day, such as Jonathan Swift and Pope in his Horatian satires that compared Britain and Rome, were devastating critics of English life. Sensitive Englishmen saw their society declining, through luxury and corruption, just as Rome had. Americans, who were not in a position to judge this criticism, tended to accept it more fully than did Englishment and believed that their new, unsophisticated society was potentially superior. Although they saw degeneration in their own midst, they considered that it was caused by British political corruption reaching across the Atlantic. Independence offered greater dignity to Americans, no longer to be second-class citizens of the British empire, taxed but not represented in Parliament. They were confident that they could create a new nation with special virtue, and they believed that the world fully expected them to do so.

In formulating their views about the new republic that they were to enjoy, the Founding Fathers could and did make use of widely held Whig political ideas. These had been set forth in England a hundred years before in the political writings of John Milton; of Algernon Sidney, whose *Discourses Concerning Government* (1698) has been called a "textbook of revolution" for Americans; and of John Locke. More especially this political philosophy had been disseminated in the eighteenth century through *Cato's Letters*, originally published as a series of newspaper essays by John Trenchard and Thomas Gordon, and in the writings of Bishop Benjamin Hoadly. Widely reprinted in American newspapers, these were the political works best known to such men as Jonathan Mayhew and John Adams. What they taught was simple and is now familiar: the contract theory of government; the people's right to resist authority unresponsive to public needs and even to rise up against their rulers; the natural rights doctrine set forth in the Declaration of Independence; the virtues of mixed government that distributed power; the dangers of political power and corruption; and the rule of law over ruler as well as ruled. These writers taught the value of the individual, the people's right to decide what is the public good, and the dangers of powerful government. Though their ideas had little impact in eighteenth-century Britain, in America they were in the air everywhere in the mid-century and later. When the propagandists for the revolution organized, shaped, and clarified them in the 1760s and 1770s, their appeals found acceptance because the ideas on which they were based were already part of the Americans' political thinking.

Hoadly's influence has been identified in the writings of Jonathan Mayhew, John Dickinson, and John Allen, among others. In his autobiography John Adams explains that before 1775 he had read "Harrington, Hobbs, Nedham, and Lock, but with little Application to any particular Views: till these Debates in Congress and these Interrogations in public and private, turned my thoughts to those Researches, which produced the Thoughts on Government, the Constitution of Massachusetts, and at length the Defence of the Constitution of the United States and the Discourses of Davila." The same ideas, in a somewhat more radical and simpler form, had reached large numbers of Americans through their newspapers.

The eighteenth-century pamphleteers who called themselves "Cato" had written, "It is certain that the whole People, who are the Publick, are the best Judges, whether things go ill or well with the public." These sentiments were more immediately meaningful from the mouth of the Boston minister Andrew Eliot, who in 1765 preached, "Men cannot but perceive when they enjoy their rights and privileges; when they sit at quiet under their own vines and fig-trees, and there is none to make them afraid.'' The process of resistance culminating in the Revolution rested on the principles of the English ''Real Whigs'' who taught the need for constant resistance to the tendency of politi-cal authority to extend its power. Gordon had warned that if the abuse of power ''is suffered once, it will be apt to be repeated often; a few repetitions create a habit; habit claims proscription and right.'' Since the reason that men abuse power is that they are selfish, political corruption is the most obvious danger sign. The wide adoption of this political philosophy in America— before the adoption of the Townshend Acts—determined the manner in which the acts were to be viewed.

V

It has been said that there is no such thing as the ''American Enlightenment,'' that ideas in America should be described as originating from experience rather than from reading in European philosophy. Students of literature are especially prone to describe a society in terms of the books that it reads and produces and to conjure up an ''American Revolutionary Mind'' from the best thoughts of a few intellectuals such as Jefferson and Adams. Admittedly it is a mistake to suppose that the thought of Newton and Voltaire and belief in the unlimited ability of human reason to right all the world's wrongs dominated the thought of Americans in the eighteenth century. But one can ascertain the strong influence of English political thought and of English poets in America. One can detect, too, a growing interest in science, sufficient to identify America with the European scientific revolution. Science must be recognized as a factor in the mix of ideas surrounding the Revolution.

Franklin is of course the great name in early American science. Besides his own scientific work (most notably with electricity), in 1743 he founded the American Philosophical Society, which interested itself in both natural phi-losophy, especially botany. The society's members included New En-glanders, Georgians, even West Indians. Closer to its Philadelphia home were John Bartram and his son William, who looked for botanical specimens both to the west and to the south, and David Rittenhouse, a self-taught astronomer. But there were men in some numbers all up and down the coast who closely observed the Indians, earthquakes, electricity, and alligators. Whether or not they had read Newton, they saw the world to be governed by knowable laws that created harmony. Professor John Winthrop of Harvard thanked Newton for discovering the law of attraction and repulsion, ''the fundamental law which the alwise CREATOR has established for regulating the several movements in this giant machine.'' In the dissemination of the new science the almanac was of especial influence. A devotion to science, to the laws of nature, significantly contributed to belief in such political ideas as the doctrine of natural law and the Whig principle of balanced government. The connection between the new political ideas and the new science is suggested by the poems published in the famous Ames almanacs in celebration of the accomplishments of Newton and of Locke.

VI

In the mid- and late eighteenth century literature was integrated into American culture and society in a way that specialist Americans of two hundred years later may have difficulty recognizing. In quantity if not in quality, imported if not domestic, literature was to be found everywhere, in almanacs, newspapers, magazines. But one should not exaggerate the extent of imaginative literary production. Without a cultural center, there was little native drama till late in the century. Though Franklin had reprinted what is usually considered the first English novel, Richardson's *Pamela*, as early as 1744, the first American novel was not published till 1789. A good deal of poetry, or at least verse, was produced, but not much of it appeared in book form. American book production and the creation of a native American literature were slight for a number of reasons. Print was scarce. Until after the Revolution paper produced in America was of such poor quantity that it was suitable only for broadsides, newspapers, and other matter whose anticipated life was short. Moreover, as Timothy Dwight explained, ''books of almost every kind, on almost every subject, are already written to our hands. Our situation in this respect is singular. As we speak the same language with the people of Great Britain, . . . our commerce with it brings to us, regularly not a small part of the books with which it is deluged. In every art, science, and part of literature, we obtain those, which to a great extent supply our wants. Hence book-making is a business, less necessary to us than to any nation in the world; and this is a reason, powerfully operative, why comparatively few books are written.''

After the Revolution Philip Freneau jokingly proposed that ''all imported authors'' ''should be taxed'' to encourage ''real American writers.'' American writers needed far more encouragement than they received. Freneau himself, perhaps the most talented imaginative writer of the revolutionary years, made his living as secretary to a West Indian planter, in the Philadelphia post office, as a shipmaster, and as a journalist. Many men and some women wrote, but as Jefferson noted as late as 1813, ''We have no distinct class of literati in our country.'' Since ''every man is engaged in some industrious pursuit,'' ''few therefore of those who are qualified, have leisure to write.'' Benjamin Franklin recognized the same phenomenon. ''All things have their season,'' declared the greatest American man of letters of his day, ''and with young countries as with young men, you must curb their fancy to strengthen their judgment.'' Franklin observed, sympathetically, ''To America, one schoolmaster is worth a dozen poets, and the invention of a machine or the improvement of an implement is of more importance than a masterpiece of Raphael. . . . Nothing is good or beautiful but in the measure that it is useful; yet all things have a utility under particular circumstances. Thus poetry painting, music (and the stage as their embodiment) are all necessary and proper gratifications of a refined state of society but objectionable at an earlier period, since their cultivation would make a taste for their enjoyment precede its means.'' The three greatest writers of early America, Edward Taylor, Benjamin Franklin, and Jonathan Edwards, were not chiefly men of letters, though each wrote a great deal.

One peculiar problem was that the neoclassical literature imported from England did not provide a useful model for those who wished to create literature in America. David Humphreys observed, ''Every poet who aspires to celebrity strives to approach the perfection of Pope.'' The special character of London pervades the writings of Addison and Steele, Swift, Pope, and Samuel Johnson, and though American poets might initate their manner, the American scene did not supply comparable matter. One English critic complained that American literature did not reflect that here ''nature sets before the eye of the poet the most luxuriant and the most terrific scenes.'' Perhaps it was inevitable that the work of such poets as Thomas Godfrey, Benjamin Church, and William Livingston would be painfully derivative; the currently fashionable London models and the highly individualistic example of Milton inspired little of value. The poetry of Richard Lewis (1700–1734) is a notable exception, but there was no American of Lewis's ability working in the English Augustan tradition late in the century.

The written word, as we have seen, was a major factor in the creation of an atmosphere in which the American Revolution could take place. In time the fact of American independence was to create a felt need for an American literature. But even during the revolutionary years a new literary subject was widely recognized as the view spread that America was created as a refuge from tyranny with a common hereitage of freedom. American poets began to develop the shared theme of the rising glory of America, where men could begin the world anew, where humanity could realize its age-old dreams of a full and rich life. The theme can be found in John Trumbull's 1770 Yale commencement poem, *Prospect of the Future Glory of America*, in Joel Barlow's ''Poem, Spoken at the Public Commencement'' (1781), in David Humphreys's ''The Glory of America'' (1783), and most notably in Philip

Freneau's *A Poem on the Rising Glory of America* (1771), which begins:

> NO more of Memphis and her mighty kings,
> Or Alexandria, where the Ptolomies
> Taught golden commerce to unfurl her sails,
> And bid fair science smile: No more of Greece
> Where learning next her early visit paid,
> And spread her glories to illume the world,
> No more of Athens, where she flourished,
> And saw her sons of mighty genius rise
>
> . . . .
>
> No more of Britain, and her kings renown'd,
>
> . . . .
>
> A Theme more new, tho' not less noble, claims
> Our ev'ry thought on this auspicious day;
> The rising glory of this western world,
> Where now the dawning light of science spreads
> Her orient ray, and wakes the muse's song;
> Where freedom holds here sacred standards high,
> And commerce rolls her golden tides profuse
> Of elegance and ev'ry joy of life.

The rising glory of America was delayed by the departure from these shores of 75,000 Loyalists, including many educated people (two hundred were Harvard graduates). Without these and without a leisure class, early American culture was inevitably thin. But America's literary inheritance from the revolutionary years is rich, as the pages that follow demonstrate. The *Federalist Papers*, the great propaganda of Thomas Paine, the writings of Crèvecoeur, the extraordinary urbanity of Franklin, the genius of Thomas Jefferson—these and much more make these years ones that deserve celebration, now and as the years pass.

SUGGESTIONS FOR FURTHER READING

Editions

The Boston Gazette 1774. Barre, Mass.: Imprint Society, 1972. [Attractive facsimile edition of this important newspaper during a crucial year.]

Clough, Wilson Ober, ed. *Intellectual Origins of American National Thought: Pages from the Books Our Founding Fathers Read*. 2d ed., revised. New York: Corinth Books, 1961.

Commager, Henry Steele, and Richard B. Morris, eds. *The Spirit of 'Seventy-Six. The*

Story of the American Revolution as Told by Participants. 2 vols. Indianapolis, Ind. Bobbs-Merrill, 1958.

Pickering, James H., ed. *The World Turned Upside Down: Prose and Poetry of the American Revolution*. Port Washington, N.Y.: Kennikat Press, 1975.

Vaughan, Alden T., ed. *America Before the Revolution, 1725–1775*. Englewood Cliffs, N.J.: Prentice-Hall, 1967. [A composite portrait of American life.]

Scholarship and Criticism

Bailyn, Bernard. *The Ideological Origins of the American Revolution*. Cambridge, Mass.: Harvard University Press, 1967.

Boorstin, Daniel J. *The Americans: The Colonial Experience*. New York: Alfred A. Knopf, 1964.

Davidson, Phillip. *Propaganda and the American Revolution, 1763–1783*. Chapel Hill: University of North Carolina Press, 1941.

Greene, Evarts Boutell. *The Revolutionary Generation, 1763–1790*. New York: Macmillan, 1943.

Greene, Jack P., ed. *The Reinterpretation of the American Revolution, 1776–1789*. New York: Harper and Row, 1969. [See especially the essays by Edmund S. Morgan and Perry Miller.]

Jones, Howard Mumford. *O Strange New World. American Culture: The Formative Years*. New York: The Viking Press, 1964.

Kraus, Michael. *Intercolonial Aspects of American Culture on the Eve of the Revolution With Special Reference to the Northern Towns*. New York: Columbia University Press, 1928.

Maier, Pauline. *From Resistance to Revolution: Colonial Radicals and the Development of American Opposition to Britain, 1765–1776*. New York: Alfred A. Knopf, 1972.

Main, Jackson Turner. *The Social Structure of Revolutionary America*. Princeton, N.J.: Princeton University Press, 1965.

Merritt, Richard L. *Symbols of American Community 1735–1775*. New Haven, Conn.: Yale University Press, 1966.

Wood, Gordon S. *The Creation of the American Republic, 1776–1787*. Chapel Hill: University of North Carolina Press, 1969.

2

The Patriot Pamphleteers

ELAINE K. GINSBERG

[*The writings most closely associated with the American Revolution are of course those that helped to create it—the pamphlets published in the dozen or so years before the actual declaration of American independence. Profoundly influential in shaping American opinion as disaffection with British policies grew, the pamphleteers included Thomas Jefferson and Thomas Paine, both the subjects of individual chapters in this volume. The essay that follows provides an overview of the work of the patriot pamphleteers.*]

In the political arena the eighteenth century was the age of pamphleteering. Thus it is no surprise that, during the long period of verbal sparring between England and her American colonies that preceded the Declaration of Independence, pamphlets were a major literary weapon of the American patriots. An important reason for the influence of the patriot pamphleteers was the versatility of their medium. Pamphlets were usually from ten to fifty quarto or octavo pages, loosely stitched and unbound, although they could contain as few as eight or as many as eighty pages. Inexpensive and relatively easy to produce, they sold for a few pence or, at most, two shillings, making them readily available to a large portion of the colonial population. Their circulation was extensive, the more so because parts of the most popular pamphlets were often reprinted in newspapers throughout the colonies. The reverse was also true; frequently a series of newspaper essays or letters was subsequently printed and sold as a pamphlet. Too, pamphlets were, on many occasions, read aloud to groups of freeholders at meetings, militiamen at muster, or citizens at less formal gatherings. Many speeches and sermons of the period were printed as pamphlets, often at the request of the group to which they were first delivered. The authors of these published orations were known, of course; for the most part, however, the patriot pamphleteers wrote anonymously, although many people discovered who the anonymous authors were. More adaptable than the newspaper essay or the broadside, pamphlets could be used to develop lengthy, carefully reasoned constitutional arguments or brief, highly emotional diatribes against British tyranny. They could be written in the form of treatises, exhortations, letters, poems, fables, or dramatic dialogues. They could be directed to a sophisticated intellectual group or to the general public.

Though not so skilled as their English counterparts, the American pamphleteers were prolific nevertheless. Over four hundred pamphlets related to the Anglo-American controversy were published in the colonies before July 4, 1776. In most of these the patriots argued the issues and developed the themes that were eventually to lead to the establishment of an independent America. It is these pamphlets that will be the major subject of this study, for they best reveal what was in the hearts and minds of the patriots who led the Revolution. Approximately eleven hundred more pamphlets were published between the Declaration of Independence and the end of the war, but this latter group of pamphlets is of a different sort than the former. Perhaps because the patriots saw no need to argue for rights for which they were now engaging in armed combat, more likely because they were busy attending to the progress of the war and the establishment of the federal and state governments, far fewer pamphlets of an expository nature were published between 1776 and 1783. Rather, one finds that proceedings, acts, and resolutions of the state and national assemblies constitute a large portion of the publications.

Generally, the pamphlets written by the American patriots before the Declaration were of three kinds. The greatest number were written in response to particular events: the Stamp Act precipitated the first barrage of pamphlets from the American colonists, followed by the passage of the Townshend Acts, the Boston Massacre, and the Intolerable Acts, to name just a few events. These pamphlets were most often written by a single individual but occasionally were group efforts. The latter includes such pamphlets as *A Short Narrative of the Horrid Massacre* (1770), published at the order of the town of Boston, and *A Narrative of the Excursion and Ravages of the King's Troops Under the Command of General Gage, on the Nineteenth of April, 1775* (1775), published at the order of the Massachusetts Provincial Congress, both designed to prove that, in each case, British soldiers had attacked the Americans without provocation.

A second category is the pamphlet exchange, a series of pamphlets rebutting, defending, or attacking each other. These were sometimes bitter personal attacks, sometimes theoretical disputations, and sometimes a combination. Such an exchange is illustrated by a series which began with Governor Stephen Hopkins's *The Rights of the Colonies Examined*, published in Providence in 1765. Martin Howard, Jr., answered Hopkins with *A Letter From A Gentleman at Halifax* (1765). Both Hopkins and James Otis then replied to Howard, who defended himself in a second pamphlet, which was again answered by both Hopkins and Otis. In all, seven pamphlets are included in this series. Nineteen such series published from 1764 to 1776 have been identified.

A third category is the occasional pamphlet, most often a printing of a sermon or speech delivered to commemorate a special occasion. From the early days of the colonies, the Americans had published thanksgiving and election day sermons and orations in order that these might be read by people who had not heard them and preserved by people who had. The patriots of the revolutionary era added several new special occasions: ceremonies dedicating Liberty Trees, ceremonial addresses to artillery companies, and the anniversaries of such events as the repeal of the Stamp Act and the Boston Massacre. The latter especially prompted some of the most emotional, exaggerated rhetoric of the period.

In addition to the foregoing types of pamphlets, which encompassed the great majority of those published by the American patriots, there were at times printed proceedings of town meetings, proclamations of colonial legislatures, and an occasional odd piece such as *The Examination of Doctor Benjamin Franklin* (1766), a transcript (though not an accurate one) of Franklin's oral testimony before the House of Commons relating to the repeal of the Stamp Act. Most important, the pamphleteers left no subject untouched: they dealt with history, politics, economics, government, philosophy, and religion. The themes they reiterated included the philosophical questions of natural law and natural rights, the political and economic issues of the relationship between the colonies and the mother country, and the patriotic themes of the unique heritage of the American people and the "rising glory of America."

I

In examining these reiterated themes of the pamphlets before 1776, one notes that the theme of independence, rather than dominating as might be expected, was notably absent. Until Thomas Paine boldly called for independence in *Common Sense* in January 1776, the idea of independence was not favorably proposed by an American pamphleteer, despite the fact that it had been hinted at in newspapers and discussed by political leaders. Nearly all the American pamphleteers who mentioned the idea did so in the context of denying that independence was their goal. Indeed, most protested their strong desire to return to the relationship which had existed between the colonies and the mother country prior to 1763. There was, moreover, at least at the beginning of the controversy, the strong belief that Americans needed only to air their grievances rationally and these grievances would, by rational men, be redressed. John Dickinson, author of the *Letters from a Farmer in Pennsylvania* (1768), while firmly denying the right of Parliament to impose taxes on the colonists without their consent, wrote to his fellow Americans that he hoped they would guard against those who would "under pretences of patriotism" endeavor to stir them to "any measure disrespectful to our Sovereign and our mother country." He generously conceded that "every government at some time or other falls into wrong measures. These may proceed from mistake or passion. But every such measure does not dissolve the obligation between governors and governed." Dickinson, probably the most widely read pamphleteer in the colonies before Thomas Paine, continued: "In truth—the prosperity of these provinces is founded in their dependence on *Great Britain*; and when she returns to her 'old good humour, and her old good nature,' . . . I hope they will always think it their duty and interest, as it most certainly will be, to promote her welfare by all the means in their power."

The same theme was expressed, though more rhapsodically (and perhaps with more fervor than his countrymen would have shared) by James Otis in *The Rights of the British Colonies Asserted and Proved* (1764). Otis wrote that the colonists, happy under Great Britain, "love, esteem, and reverence our mother country, and adore our King. And could the choice of independency be offered the colonies, or subjection to Great-Britain upon any terms above absolute slavery, I am convinced they would accept the latter." In 1774 Philip Livingston, a delegate to the Continental Congress from New York, considered "the thoughts of establishing a republic in America, blocking off her connection with Great Britain, and becoming independent . . . the most vain, empty, shallow, and ridiculous project that could possibly enter into the heart of man." And Boston radical Joseph Warren, three months before he was killed at the battle of Bunker Hill in June 1775, assured his audience that "an independence on Great Britain is not our aim. No, our wish is, that Britain and the Colonies may like the oak and ivy, grow and increase in strength together."

Despite these protestations of loyalty, patriot pamphleteers recognized the possibility of the colonies being pushed to independence by the actions of the mother country. Dickinson himself, three years before his *Farmer's Letters*, warned with admirable foresight that "we can never be made an independent people, except it be by *Great Britain* herself; and the only way for her to do it, is to make us frugal, ingenious, united and discontented." The same conclusions were still being drawn by some patriots as late as 1776. Pennsylvania delegate James Wilson, shortly before he signed, albeit reluctantly, the Declaration of Independence, made a final plea for reconciliation but concluded: "Though an independent Empire is not our *Wish*: it may . . . be the Fate of our Countrymen and ourselves. It is in the Power of your enemies to render Independency or Slavery your and our Alternative. . . . That the Colonies may continue connected, as they have been, with Britain, is our second Wish: Our first is—THAT AMERICA MAY BE FREE.''

II

If not independence, then what were the pamphleteers agitating for? In the words of John Adams, *"Rights,* that cannot be repealed or restrained by human laws—*Rights* derived from the great Legislator of the universe.'' The disagreement between the colonies and Great Britain that began over the issue of taxation quickly turned to a philosophical discussion of what the rights of the colonists were. John Dickinson, like Adams, identified these as the acknowledged rights of human nature. He reaffirmed that they are not the gifts or grants of kings or parliaments. "We claim them,'' he wrote, "from a higher source—from the King of Kings, and Lord of all the earth. They are not annexed to us by parchments and seals. They are created in us by the decrees of Providence, which establish the laws of our nature. They are born with us; exist with us; and cannot be taken from us by any human power, without taking our lives.'' In 1775 the young Alexander Hamilton proclaimed ecstatically: "THE SACRED RIGHTS OF MANKIND ARE NOT TO BE RUMMAGED FOR AMONG OLD PARCHMENTS OR MUSTY RECORDS. THEY ARE WRITTEN, AS WITH A SUNBEAM, IN THE WHOLE VOLUME OF HUMAN NATURE, BY THE HAND OF DIVINITY ITSELF, AND CAN NEVER BE ERASED OR OBSCURED BY MORTAL POWER.''

The sources of the patriots' philosophical position concerning these natural rights were the ideas and writings of the leading thinkers of the European Enlightenment: Voltaire, Rousseau, Beccaria, Grotius, Pufendorf, Burlamaqui, Vattel, and Locke. Foremost among the ideas which formed the foundation of the colonists' thought was the state of nature, as described by Locke, in which man once lived and to which he might at any time return. In this state of nature, Locke theorized, man is governed by natural law and possesses certain natural rights, including the rights to life, liberty, property, conscience, and happiness. To better secure these rights, men who are free and equal compact among themselves to institute a government which then must "promote the welfare'' of the people. Whenever any form of government fails to do so, the compact may be dissolved and the people may return to the state of nature, free to form a government that *will* promote their welfare.

The pervasiveness of Lockean philosophy in America in the eighteenth century should not be underestimated. Almost every argument, every petition to Parliament or the king began with Lockean principles. A good illustration is a statement presented to the Boston town meeting on November 20, 1772. Probably written by Samuel Adams, the statement first concerns itself with "the *Rights* of the Colonists." Among these natural rights are "First, a Right to *Life*; Secondly to *Liberty*; thirdly to *Property*." Furthermore,

> All Men have a Right to remain in a State of Nature as long as they please; And in Case of intollerable Oppression, civil or religious, to leave the Society they belong to, and enter into another.
>
> When Men enter into Society, it is by voluntary Consent; and they have a Right to demand and insist upon the Performance of such Conditions, and previous Limitations as form an equitable *original Compact*.
>
> Every natural Right, not expressly given up, or from the Nature of a social Compact necessarily ceded, remains. . . .
>
> The natural Liberty of Man, by entering into Society, is abridg'd or restrain'd so far only as is necessary for the great End of Society, the best Good of the Whole.[1]

The patriot pamphleteers insisted that the colonists were entitled not only to those rights that were their natural heritage, but also to those that derived from their heritage as British citizens. Governor Stephen Hopkins of Rhode Island, among others, pointed out that "the British subjects in America, have equal rights with those in Britain; that they do not hold these rights as a privilege, granted them, nor enjoy them as a grace and favor bestowed; but possess them as an inherent indefeasible right; as they, and their ancestors, were freeborn subjects, justly and naturally entitled to all the rights and advantages of the British constitution." The American colonists' insistence that they were entitled to all the rights and privileges possessed by British citizens in England was accompanied on occasion by expressions of indignation and resentment. The Americans seemed to feel that, in addition to being persecuted by the British government, they were being unjustly patronized by their British cousins. Silas Downer, for one, complained that "the language of every paultry scribbler, even of those who pretend friendship for us in some things, is after this lordly stile, *our colonies—our western dominions—our plantations—our islands—our subjects in America* . . . . Strange doctrine that we should be the subjects of subjects, and liable to be controuled at their will!" Paradoxically, then, the Americans were fighting to defend the spirit of the British constitution, not to establish new rights never before enjoyed by the colonial people, but to assert their claim to old rights recently (they felt) denied.

The political ideas expressed by the patriot pamphleteers were largely derived from the English Whig tradition. Their long treatises introduced no new

1. *The Votes and Proceedings of the Freeholders and other Inhabitants of the Town of Boston* (Boston: Edes and Gill and T. and J. Fleet, [1772?]), pp. 2–3, 4–5.

political theories, no daring philosophies; they merely recapitulated what they had read and studied. Quoted everywhere in the colonies, in addition to Locke, were such theorists and writers as Algernon Sidney, Henry St. John (Viscount Bolingbroke), John Somers, Benjamin Care, James Burgh, Joseph Addison, Alexander Pope, and, more than any others, Thomas Gordon and John Trenchard, authors of the *Independent Whig* and *Cato's Letters*. Most important among the principles which the colonists drew from the English Whigs was the right of a people not to be governed by any laws to which neither they nor their representatives had given consent. On this the colonists based their resistance to attempts by Parliament to tax the colonies. Joseph Warren affirmed this principle in a 1772 oration commemorating the Boston Massacre: "The greatest and most important right of a British subject is, that *he shall be governed by no laws but those to which he either in person or by his representative hath given his consent*: And this I will venture to assert, is the grand basis of British freedom; it is interwoven with the constitution, and whenever this is lost, the constitution must be destroyed."

Nevertheless, the cry "No taxation without representation" did not mean for most of the colonists that they wished to be represented in Parliament. America was too far from England, communication too slow, and the interests of the people too different from those in the mother country for American representation in Parliament to be a satisfactory solution. The powers, the Americans argued, "which the House of Commons receives from its constituents are entrusted by the Colonies to their assemblies in the several Provinces." Thus the power and the right to tax the colonists should remain solely in the hands of the colonial legislatures. Nor was the issue of taxation without representation merely an economic consideration. Repeatedly the colonists associated their fight against taxes with the more abstract values of happiness, freedom, and security. John Dickinson, for example, exhorted his readers: "Let these *truths* be indelibly impressed on our minds—*that we cannot be* HAPPY, *without being* FREE—that we cannot be free, *without being secure in our property*—that *we* cannot be secure in our property, *if, without our consent, others may, as by right, take it away*—that *taxes imposed on us by parliament*, do thus take it away...."

In Parliament's attempt to tax the colonies the American patriots also saw evidence of a conspiracy to limit their freedom. In this attitude they were encouraged by the earlier writings of the English Whigs which had, since the end of the seventeenth century, warned of the corrupting influence of power. American newspapers and pamphlets had for many years echoed these warnings, borrowing not only the arguments of the English Whigs, but their words as well. Consequently, because the Americans were already in the habit of looking for abuse of power wherever power existed, the Stamp Act and the events that followed served only to reinforce already existing fears. John

Dickinson's eleventh letter cautioned his countrymen that "every free state should incessantly watch, and instantly take alarm on any addition being made to the power exercised over them." He indicated two pertinent instances in British history from which Americans might learn: Henry VII's establishment of a standing army and James II's creation of an excise tax. "'Tis true," Dickinson continued, "that all the mischiefs apprehended by our ancestors from a *standing army* and *excise*, have not *yet happened*: But it does not follow from thence, that they *will not happen*. The inside of a house may catch fire, and the most valuable apartments be ruined, before the flames burst out. The question in these cases is not, what evil *has actually attended* particular measures—but, what evil, in the nature of things, *is likely to attend* them."

Other patriots were moved to exaggerate even further the possible dire consequences of these two precedents. John Allen, a fiery Baptist preacher whose *Oration, on the Beauties of Liberty* (1773) was reprinted seven times in four cities, warned eloquently of the possible dangers ahead:

> You think it hard to pay duties for *teas*, imports, clearances, *entries*, &c., &c. But what will you farmers and landholders think, of paying a fixed tax for every acre of land you enjoy, for every apple tree you rear, for every barrel of cyder you make, for every pound of candles you burn, for every pound of soap you use, for every pair of shoes you wear, for the light of the morning, and the sun, that a kind heaven gives you, what do you think of paying a continual tax for all these, this is contain'd in the mischievous design, stand alarm'd, O ye Americans—[2]

Allen's *Oration* was originally delivered on the annual Thanksgiving Day, December 3, 1772. On March 5, 1773, Benjamin Church delivered *An Oration*, also subsequently printed as a pamphlet, on the anniversary of the Boston Massacre. That massacre, Church asserted in impassioned prose, taught the dangers of a standing army: "Defenceless, prostrate, bleeding countrymen—the piercing, agonizing groans—the mangled moan of weeping relatives and friends:—These best can speak; to rouse the luke-warm into noble zeal, to fire the zealous into manly rage, against the *foul oppression, of quartering troops, in populous cities, in times of peace*."

The extent to which the American patriots saw evidence in every action of Parliament, the ministry, and, eventually, the king of a plot to enslave the Americans is demonstrated by the repeated cries of "conspiracy" and "tyranny" which appear as major themes in the pamphlets. As early as 1765 John Adams sensed that "there seems to be a direct and formal design on foot, to enslave all America." Silas Downer, in *A Discourse Delivered in Provi-*

2. John Allen, *An Oration, on the Beauties of Liberty* (Boston: Kneeland and Davis, 1773), p. 30.

dence (1768) at the dedication of a Tree of Liberty, warned: "upon the whole, the conduct of *Great Britain* shows us that they have formed a plan to subject us so effectually to their absolute commands, that even the freedom of speech will be taken from us." John Allen wrote of a "mischievous design," and Oliver Noble, commemorating the Boston Massacre in 1775, seemed certain that a conspiracy existed: "Can it be any longer a secret, that a PLAN has been *systematically* laid, and persued by the British *ministry*, near twelve years, for enslaving *America*; as the STIRRUP by which they design to *mount* the RED HORSE of TYRANNY and DESPOTISM at home?" If final evidence of this widespread belief in a conspiracy is needed, it is contained in the Declaration of Independence, which speaks of "a long train of abuses and usurpations" evincing "a design to reduce [the colonists] under absolute despotism."

If the patriot pamphleteers were vehement in their accusations of conspiracy, they were more so in their denunciations of British tyranny. These often took the form of verbal attacks on British troops, which were described by one writer as being composed of "the most debauched Weavers 'prentices, the scum of Irish Roman Catholics, who desert upon every occasion, and a few, very few, Scotch, who are not strong enough to carry packs." John Hancock, in his 1774 oration commemorating the Boston Massacre, had a whole host of accusations to make against the British troops quartered in Boston:

> As though they thought it not enough to violate our Civil Rights, they endeavoured to deprive us of the enjoyment of our religious privileges, to viciate our morals, and thereby render us deserving of destruction. Hence the rude din of arms which broke in upon your solemn devotions in your temples, on that day hallowed by Heaven, and set apart by God himself for his peculiar worship. Hence impious oaths and blasphemies so often tortur'd your unaccustomed ears. Hence all the arts which idleness and luxury could invent, were used, to betray our youth of one sex into extravagance and effeminancy, and of the other into infamy and ruin; and did they not succeed but too well? Did not a reverence for religion forcibly decay? Did not our infants almost learn to lisp out curses before they knew their horrid import? Did not our youth forget they were Americans, and regardless of the admonitions of the wise and aged, servilely copy from their tyrants those vices which finally must overthrow the empire of Great Britain?[3]

Quite naturally, the closer the colonies and Britain came to open and unrestrained warfare, the more violent the patriot pamphleteers became in their verbal attacks. Perez Morton, moved by the death of Joseph Warren at Bunker Hill, asked:

> And can we, my Countrymen, with Indifference behold so much Worth and Valor laid prostrate by the hand of *British Tyranny*! . . . —Are we not yet

3. John Hancock, *An Oration* (Boston: Edes and GIll, 1774), pp. 8–9.

convinced "that he who hunts the Woods for Prey, the naked and untutored
Indian, is less a savage than the *King of Britain*"! Have we not Proofs, wrote
in Blood, that the corrupted Nation, from whence we sprang (tho' there may
be some traces of their ancient Virtue left) are stubbornly fixed on our
Destruction! And shall we still court a *Dependence* on such a State? Still
contend for a Connection with those, who have forfeited every kindred
Claim, but even their Title to Humanity![4]

III

Most of the pamphlets written by the Americans before July 1776, whether
conservative or radical, were devoted to lengthy, detailed, repetitive, and
often tedious discussions of the philosophical, political, and economic questions involved in the dispute between the colonies and the mother country. In
a more positive tone, however, the patriot pamphletters echoed the providential view of the founding of America, emphasizing the unique heritage of
America and the American people and the future "rising glory of America."

The American colonists at the time of the Revolution accepted as their
special inheritance the unique place of America in the history of the world.
This special destiny was expressed early in the American experience by John
Winthrop in his sermon delivered on the *Arbella* in 1630 as it carried the
Puritan settlers to Massachusetts Bay. When Winthrop prophesied that they
would be "as a City upon a Hill, the eyes of all people" upon them as they
carried out God's work, he sounded a keynote which remained a theme in
American life and literature through the twentieth century. Governor Hopkins, for example, like many other pamphleteers, reminded his readers that
"the first planters of these colonies were pious Christians; were faithful subjects; who, with a fortitude and perseverance little known, and less considered, settled these wild countries, by God's goodness and their own amazing
labours." Oliver Noble, using the Book of Esther as his text for a sermon
commemorating the Boston Massacre, expressed this theme as ringingly as
any pamphleteer. Noble assured his audience that God was on the side of the
Americans, just as He was on the side of Esther, Mordecai, and the Jews.
"Are not the people of *America*," Nobel asked, "also God's covenant
people? And is not the Lord of Hosts *their* covenant GOD?... The cause of
America ... is the Cause of GOD, never did Man struggle in a greater, or more
glorious CAUSE." The Americans, Noble continued, hold their property and
possessions in this land "under God alone." "Our fathers fled to this wilderness, in an arbitrary reign; and from the iron hand of oppression at home, that

---

4. Perez Morton, *An Oration Delivered April Eighth, 1776* (Boston: J. Gill, 1776), p. 12.

they might enjoy civil and religious *Liberty*, here undisturbed, and hand down
the invaluable treasure to the latest posterity.''

In his "Dissertation on the Canon and Feudal Law" John Adams emphasized that the "great struggle which peopled America" was "not religion
alone, as is commonly supposed; but it was a love of universal liberty." As a
result, Americans have the most habitual, radical sense of liberty. Joseph
Warren expressed with much passion the American heritage of love and
liberty:

> None but they who set a just value upon the blessings of Liberty are worthy
> to enjoy her—Your illustrious fathers were her zealous votaries—When the
> blasting frowns of tyranny drove her from public view, they clasped her in
> their arms, they cherished her in their generous bosoms, they brought her
> safe over the rough ocean, and fixed her seat in this then dreary wilderness;
> they nursed her infant age with the most tender care; for her sake, they
> patiently bore the severest hardships; for her support, they underwent the
> most rugged toils: In her defence, they boldly encountered the most alarming
> dangers; neither the ravenous beasts that ranged the woods for prey; nor the
> furious savages of the wilderness, could damp their ardor![5]

God's special providence and the Americans' liberty-loving heritage together created the fertile soil upon which a glorious nation, dedicated to the
freedom and equality of all men, could prosper and serve as an asylum for the
oppressed of all lands. Samuel Mather demonstrated that "America must be
known to the ancients," and concluded that "these Parts of the World seem to
have been designed of Heaven for an *Asylum*, a Place of Rest and Refresh-
ment, to those, who have been oppressed and groaning under the Tyranny of
Political and Ecclesiastical Power." Samuel Williams echoed this theme on
the annual Thanksgiving Day in 1774: "For while the greatest part of the
nations of the earth are held together under the yoke of universal slavery, the
North American provinces yet remain *the country of free men*: The *Asylum*
and the last, to which such may yet flee from the common deluge." The
Reverend William Smith saw an even greater role for America in the world.
"Heaven," he wrote, "has great and gracious purposes towards this continent." This country will be for "ages to come, a chosen seat of *Freedom,
Arts,* and *heavenly Knowledge*."

It is interesting to note that most of the pamphleteers who discussed the
heritage of America seemed to identify that heritage with the Puritan colonization of New England. Perhaps this is because most of the pamphleteers were
New Englanders; over 40 percent of the pamphlets published during the
period of the American Revolution were published in Massachusetts. Nevertheless, very few of the pamphleteers recognized the diverse minority groups

5. Joseph Warren, *An Oration* (Boston: Edes and Gill, 1772), pp. 16–17.

in the colonial population. They ignored such citizens as the Germans in Pennsylvania, the Dutch in New York, and the Scots, Irish, and Welsh scattered throughout the colonies. Only on rare occasions, when a writer wished to make the point that England was not really the "mother country" of all the colonists, were the non-English colonists mentioned. Almost as infrequent was mention of the Negro slave population of the colonies, although a few patriot pamphleteers included the continued encouragement of the slave trade among their accusations against the British ministry, and Jefferson, in his original draft of the Declaration of Independence, denounced the "execrable commerce" of slavery.

I V

With an army to be raised and outfitted, an active war to be waged, and state governments to be constituted, the patriot leaders found themselves too occupied to publish lengthy philosophical disquisitions after 1776. Instead, printed sermons and occasional orations carried the rhetorical burden of the patriot cause until the peace treaty of 1783. Several new themes and some variations upon former themes were expressed in these pamphlets. That the Revolution was a defensive war, justified by "reason and religion," was a point consistently made. In *A Sermon, Preached before His Excellency John Hancock, Esq.* (1780) Samuel Cooper repeated what many others before him had said when he assured the Massachusetts legislature that "Heaven and *earth* can bear witness that these States are innocent of the blood that hath been shed, and the miseries diffused by this unrighteous war. We have stood upon the ground of justice, honor, and liberty, and acted merely a defensive part." Even more than they had in the years before 1776, the patriots insisted upon America's innocence in the controversy with Great Britain and blamed the war on Britain's decadence and decay. Corruption in England had bred the difficulties, asserted Timothy Dwight in 1781 when he wrote that "the sins of Great Britain are in degree enormous and in multitude innumerable." David Ramsay explained that "artificial manners always prevail in kingly governments; and royal courts are reservoirs, from whence insincerity, hypocrisy, dissimulation, pride, luxury, and extravagance, deluge and overwhelm the body of the people." In contrast, Ramsay continued, the new republican state governments will never breed the corruption of the British system, since "Republics are favorable to truth, sincerity, industry, and simplicity of manners." Furthermore, the new governments will "fan the sparks of genius in every breast"; they will produce "poets, orators, criticks, and historians, equal to the most celebrated of the ancient commonwealths of Greece and

Italy." Upon the ratification of the peace treaty in 1783 David Tappan foresaw an even greater future for this new republic; he saw "this immense northern continent" converted into "a seat of knowledge and freedom, of agriculture and commerce, of useful arts and manufactures, of Christian piety and virtue, . . . the delight of God and good men, the joy and praise of the whole earth soaring on the Wings of literature, wealth, population, religion, virtue, and everything that is excellent and happy, to a greater height of perfection and glory than the world has ever yet seen."

American patriots after 1776 also repeated the related theme that "God has ever been the friend and patron of the American Israel." James Madison, president of William and Mary College and cousin of the future president of the United States, wrote that "America has become the theater, whereon the providence of God is now manifested. —America is now holding forth that display of divine power, which shall excite the wonder and gratitude of posterity." And David Tappan concluded that the American Revolution was the "principle link" in a great chain of Providence leading to the "Millenial State." In addition to planning and directing the American Revolution, the Lord, the patriots felt, had chosen as their leader a new American Moses. Like the early New England historians who identified their leaders—Bradford, Winthrop, and Cotton—with the Old Testament patriarchs, the American pamphleteers saw their "exalted General," George Washington, as their Mosaic counterpart. Nathan Strong preached on the annual Thanksgiving Day in Hartford in 1780 that "it was the Lord who raised up and inspired the country with confidence in a commander, who was formed by His own infinite wisdom, on purpose for the great design of vindicating American freedom." James Madison also asserted that the Lord had called forth Washington to be "the guide, the protector, the deliverer of America!" Contributing to the growing heroic legend of Washington, Madison rhetorically asked "in whom else could we have found those virtues—a fortitude which fears God alone, a prudence which baffles the designs of his enemies, a foresight which outruns time itself at every emergency . . . that love of justice, that spirit of benevolence which mitigates the horrors of war, and which has almost taught the proud Britain the practice of humanity."

V

The pamphleteers who developed the philosophical, political, and economic arguments and reiterated the patriotic themes of the American Revolution were lawyers, merchants, ministers, and farmers. Although they were highly literate, they were not professional men of letters. Nowhere in the colonies was there a pamphleteer with the wit or literary skill of a Swift, a Defoe, or an Addison. In fact, the most skilled and effective writers of the period did not publish many pamphlets. Samuel Adams, whom John Adams considered the moving force behind the Revolution, did his writing anonymously in the pages of Boston newspapers, in the petitions of the Boston town council, in the letters of the Boston Committee of Correspondence, and in a voluminous correspondence with other leaders in both England and America. Although his "Dissertation on the Canon and Feudal Law" was published in the *Boston Gazette* in 1765, and as a pamphlet in London in 1768, John Adams did not publish any pamphlets in America until his *Thoughts on Government* in April 1776. The "Novanglus" essays, Adams's best statement of the colonial position, were written as separate pieces for the *Boston Gazette*. Although Benjamin Franklin facilitated the publication and circulation of a number of pamphlets written by others, he too mainly devoted his writing energies to the newspaper.

Except perhaps for Thomas Paine, John Dickinson was probably the most widely read and widely quoted American pamphleteer. His best known work, *Letters from a Farmer in Pennsylvania,* appeared originally in *The Pennsylvania Chronicle* from December 1767 to February 1768. The letters were so popular that they were reprinted in almost all the colonial newspapers published at that time. Within a month after the appearance of the last letter, they were collected and printed as a pamphlet which then went through six more editions in the colonies, plus several in England. As a member of the Pennsylvania Assembly, Dickinson's writing talents were often called upon to draft petitions, acts, and declarations of that body. A lawyer who had been educated at the Inns of Court, his initial publication in the national cause.was a pamphlet entitled *The Late Regulations Respecting the British Colonies on the Continent of America Considered* (1765). This pamphlet is written in Dickinson's favorite form, as a letter "from a Gentleman in Philadelphia to his Friend in London." The epistolary form, however, is merely conventional; one is conscious of no specific audience other than the general public. In *An Address to the Committee of Correspondence in Barbados* (1766), however, Dickinson continually addresses the committee as "*gentlemen.*" Although he begins by assuring the committee that he is certain they are men of "sense, spirit, and virtue," as he develops his argument the repeatedly italicized *gentlemen* takes on an increasingly ironic tone despite his disclaimer at the end that he means "no personal reflections." A strong sense of the real audience, the American colonists, is also present, especially when he chastises the committee for censuring those (the North Americans) who merit "their highest esteem,—their warmest praise."

In the *Address* Dickinson identifies himself simply as "a North American"; in the *Farmer's Letters* he assumes a pastoral pose. He does not, however, develop this persona, either by adopting the diction of the farmer or by emphasizing the interests of the agrarian class. Dickinson's farmer is more akin to Horace's Sabine farmer, a gentleman of leisure who spends a "good deal" of time in his library. He is an educated, humane, and rational man who nevertheless asserts his reluctance to request the attention of the public. He has acquired "a greater knowledge in history, and the laws and constitution" of his country than most men of his class and he displays this knowledge throughout his letters: he cites precedents in classical, English, and European history and refers to works by Plutarch, Cicero, Machiavelli, Montesquieu, Hume, and Locke, to name just a few; he ends each letter with a Latin phrase. The Farmer appeals to the more noble and rational impulses of his country-men, and throughout he retains a tone of calm dignity and restraint. He writes in his first letter, "the cause of *liberty* is a cause of too much dignity to be sullied by turbulence and tumult. It ought to be maintained in a manner suitable to her nature. Those who engage in it, should breathe a sedate, yet fervent spirit, animating them to actions of prudence, justice, modesty, brav-ery, humanity and magnanimity." When the reader observes the restraint and dignity of the persona of the *Farmer's Letters*, he has less difficulty in under-standing why John Dickinson, whose strong arguments against the exercise of Parliamentary powers and in favor of American liberty were so influential in leading the colonists toward their declaration of independence, did himself balk at that final step.

In his pamphlets Dickinson's prose style is generally plain, perhaps reflect-ing his Quaker sympathies. On occasion, however, he could overwhelm his readers with ponderous footnotes. He was at ease with the classics and with the best of English literature, and these influences are readily apparent. Fur-thermore, there are occasional noteworthy passages of vivid prose. He writes, concerning the colonies' debts and taxes, that "the last sinks our paper cur-rency very fast. The former sweeps off our silver and gold in a torrent to *Great-Britain*, and leaves us continually toiling to supply from a number of distant springs the continually wasting stream." To the accusation that the colonies are rebellious Dickinson replies: "If my father, deceived and urged on by bad or weak men, should offer me a draught of poison, and tell me it would be of service to me, should I be undutiful if, knowing what it is, I should refuse to drink it? or if inflamed by passion, he should aim a dagger at my heart, should I be undutiful, if I refuse to bare my breast for the blow?" Dickinson is also capable of an occasional passionate exhortation, calling upon his countrymen at times to heed the role assigned to them by divine providence to protect the "unborn ages" whose fate depends upon the virtue of the present generation.

Among the pamphleteers who wrote in the patriot cause, the Massachusetts lawyer and political leader James Otis was perhaps the strangest figure. According to John Adams, Otis was "well versed in Greek and Roman history, philosophy, oratory, poetry, and mythology." He had, in 1760, published a treatise on Latin prosody and had probably also written one on Greek prosody. He was a student of the history, the common law, and the statute laws of England. Although his position was at times in jeopardy, he remained in the forefront of Massachusetts politics until an injury sustained in 1769 precipitated a gradual decline into insanity. Otis was the author of *A Vindication of the Conduct of the House of Representatives of . . . Massachusetts* (1762), *A Vindication of the British Colonies* (1765), and *Brief Remarks on the Defense of the Halifax Libel* (1765). He is best known, however, for his pamphlet *The Rights of the British Colonies Asserted and Proved* (1764), the most widely read statement in the period between the passage of the Sugar Act and that of the Stamp Act (from April 1764 to March 1765). The pamphlet was praised and condemned, both in the colonies and in England, but it was also misunderstood. This misunderstanding arose from Otis's attempt to claim, at the same time, that Parliament was the supreme legislature of the colonies and that it had no right to tax them. Formally, the pamphlet appears to have a logical structure. Otis discusses first the nature of government, then the rights of colonies in general, the natural rights of colonists, and finally the rights, both political and civil, of the British colonies in particular. The four sections, however, are not evenly balanced, with the first and fourth being greatly emphasized. In addition, there are digressions, apparent irrelevancies, and sections of ponderous documentation. Occasionally the writing seems to have no logic or coherence. In this, Otis's classical training failed him. On the other hand, at times he could write rhythmic prose. In discussing the origin of government he writes that it "has an everlasting foundation in the *unchangeable will of* GOD, the author of nature, whose laws never vary." He continues:

> The same omniscient, omnipotent, infinitely good and gracious Creator of the universe who has pleased to make it necessary that what we call matter should *gravitate* for the celestial bodies to roll around their axes, dance their orbits, and perform their various revolutions in that beautiful order and concert which we all admire has made it *equally* necessary that from *Adam* and *Eve* to these degenerate days the different sexes should sweetly *attract* each other, from societies of single families, of which *larger* bodies and communities are as naturally, mechanically, and necessarily combined as the dew of heaven and the soft distilling rain is collected by the all-enlivening heat of the sun.[6]

Otis's next pamphlet, *A Vindication of the British Colonies* (1765), was written in defense of his friend Stephen Hopkins, who had been attacked by Martin Howard, Jr., in *A Letter From A Gentleman at Halifax* (1765). In his

6. James Otis, *The Rights of the British Colonies Asserted and Proved* (Boston: Edes and Gill, 1764), p. 8.

Vindication Otis repeats many of the arguments of his previous pamphlet but is, at the same time, more polemic. He attacks *ad hominem*, finding in the *Halifax Letter* "inaccuracies in abundance, declamation and false logic without end; *verse* is retailed in the shape of *prose*, solecisms are attempted to be passed off for good grammar, and the most indelicate fustian for the fine taste." About one of Howard's statements Otis remarks: "If I mistake not, there is in the air of this period the quintessence of a mere martial legislator, the insolence of a haughty and imperious minister, the indolence and half-thought of a *petit-maître*, the flutter of a coxcomb, and the nonsense of a pettifogger."

Perhaps the least known among the popular patriot pamphleteers was, and still is, John Allen, an itinerant Baptist preacher. Like Thomas Paine, Allen was a transplanted English radical who arrived in the colonies, probably in 1770, with a hatred of British tyranny already smoldering within him. Allen published at least three pamphlets in New England before the Revolution: *An Oration, on the Beauties of Liberty* (1773), *The American Alarm* (1773), and *The Watchman's Alarm* (1774). The *Oration*, originally delivered at the Second Baptist Church of Boston, passed through seven editions in four cities between 1773 and 1775. Allen's prose is stirring and impassioned. In the *Oration* he combines rhetorical questions and exhortations as he asks:

> Has not the voice of your father's blood cry'd yet loud enough in your ears, in your hearts? "ye sons of America scorn to be slaves." Have you not heard the voice of blood in your own streets, louder than that which reached to Heaven, that cry'd for vengeance, that was, saith the Lord to Cain, the voice of thy brother's blood, of only one, but this of many brethren. Therefore, if there be any vein, any nerve, any soul, any life or spirit of liberty in the Sons of *America*, shew your love for it; guard your freedom, prevent your chains, stand up as one man for your liberty; for none but those, who set a just value upon this blessing, are worthy the enjoyment of it.[7]

The Watchman's Alarm to Lord N—h . . ., written in response to the order closing the Port of Boston in 1774, is the most poetic and most sermonlike of Allen's pamphlets. Allen works throughout this essay with the figure of a watchman overlooking the city through the dark night. From Isaiah 21:11, 13 he takes the repeated refrain "Watchman what of the night? Watchman what of the night?," which lends poetic unity to his exhortation. For most of the essay "night" suggests sorrow, the loss of rights, the loss of liberty, and suffering under tyrannical rulers. The watchman closes, however, with assurance; he foretells in a stirring anaphora that the "dark night" will end and the morning will come, "the morning of hope, the morning of help, the morning of mercies."

Several other patriot pamphleteers are notable for the literary quality of

7. John Allen, *An Oration, on the Beauties of Liberty*, pp. 27–28.

their work. Colonel Richard Bland, a prominent Virginia planter, developed an elaborate conceit in a pamphlet entitled *The Colonel Dismounted: Or, The Rector Vindicated* (1764). Bland attacked his opponent in a local controversy, the Reverend John Camm, by posing as a defender of Camm and using his own words to condemn him. The supposed author, who signs himself "Common Sense," begins with elaborate and ridiculous praise of the rector and then reports a public debate between himself and the colonel in which the latter speaks forcefully and eloquently against Camm and the defender answers only weakly or not at all.

Whereas Bland used ridicule, Charles Lee produced, in *Strictures On A Pamphlet, Entitled A "Friendly Address . . ."* (1774), one of the most notable examples of the use of invective in the revolutionary period. Like Paine and Allen, Lee was late to arrive in the colonies, but he quickly employed his pen in the colonial cause. Answering a pamphlet by Thomas Bradbury Chandler, Lee challenges the world "to produce so many wicked sentiments, stupid principles, audaciously false assertions, and monstrous absurdities crowded together into so small a compass." Refuting Chandler's argument that the colonists can avoid the tea tax by not drinking tea, Lee employs *reductio ad absurdum*: "The same logic would demonstrate that a duty on beer, candles, or soap would be no tax, as we are not obliged to drink beer; we may drink water, we may go to bed before it is dark, and we are not forced to wash our shirts." Chandler's pamphlet was also answered by Philip Livingston in *The Other Side Of The Question* (1774). Livingston, however, used ironic ridicule, cleverly imitating *Tristram Shandy* and including scatological passages which fit naturally into his sophisticated style.

Among the other patriot pamphlets, those which were originally orations commemorating the Boston Massacre are deserving of mention as they contain some of the most impassioned and effective rhetoric of the period. Joseph Warren, for example, was a master of vivid imagery, as shown by the following passage recalling the fatal fifth of March:

> Approach we then the melancholy walk of death. Hither let me call the gay companion, here let him drop a farewell tear upon that body which so late he saw vigorous and warm with social mirth—Hither let me lead the tender mother to weep over her beloved son—Come widowed mourner, here satiate thy grief; behold thy murdered husband gasping on the ground, . . . bring in each hand thy infant children to bewail thy father's fate—Take heed, ye orphan babes, lest while your streaming eyes are fixed upon the ghastly corpse, *your feet slide on the stone bespattered with your father's brains.*[8]

8. Joseph Warren, *An Oration, Delivered March Sixth, 1775* (Boston: Edes and Gill and Joseph Greenleaf, 1775), p. 15.

In addition to those discussed here, the patriot pamphleteers produced many works of a more literary nature, such as John Trumbull's *M'Fingal,* Francis Hopkinson's *A Pretty Story*, the writings of Mercy Otis Warren, several dramatic dialogues, and a good deal of poetry. All of these are discussed elsewhere in this volume, as is the work of the greatest of all the pamphleteers of the American Revolution, Thomas Paine. All together, the pamphlets of the American patriots are noteworthy accomplishments although the pamphleteers were not literary men primarily; they were educated, articulate political and religious leaders who found themselves caught in circumstances which demanded, and to which they gave, their utmost talents and energies. Thus they deserve a prominent place, not only in the political history, but also in the literary history of America, for they reflected the minds and hearts of a generation of patriots who saw themselves as bringing to fruition John Winthrop's dream and laying the foundation for the "rising glory of America."

SUGGESTIONS FOR FURTHER READING

Editions

Early American Imprints 1639–1800. Edited by Clifford K. Shipton. Worcester, Mass.: The American Antiquarian Society, 1955–64, with supplements, 1966–68. [All American imprints of pamphlets are available in this Readex Microprint series, which is indexed according to the numbers in Charles Evans's *American Bibliography*.]

Pamphlets of the American Revolution, 1750–1776. Edited by Bernard Bailyn and Jane Garrett. 1 vol. to date. Cambridge, Mass.: Belknap Press of Harvard University Press, 1965—.

Tracts of the American Revolution 1763–1766. Edited by Merrill Jensen. Indianapolis, Ind.: The Bobbs-Merrill Company, 1967.

Scholarship and Criticism

Adams, Thomas R. *American Independence, The Growth of An Idea: A Bibliographical Study of the American Political Pamphlets Printed Between 1764 and 1776 Dealing with the Dispute Between Great Britain and Her Colonies.* Providence, R.I.: Brown University Press, 1965.

Bailyn, Bernard. *The Ideological Origins of the American Revolution.* Cambridge, Mass.: Belknap Press of Harvard University Press, 1967.

Boorstin, Daniel. *The Americans: The Colonial Experience.* New York: Random House, 1958.

Calkin, Homer L. "Pamphlets and Public Opinion during the American Revolution." *Pennsylvania Magazine of History and Biography* 64 (1940): 22–42.

Davidson, Philip. *Propaganda and the American Revolution, 1763–1783*. Chapel Hill: University of North Carolina Press, 1941.

Granger, Bruce I. *Political Satire in the American Revolution, 1763–1783*. Ithaca, N.Y.: Cornell University Press, 1960.

Rossiter, Clinton. *Seedtime of the Republic: The Origin of the American Tradition of Political Liberty*. New York: Harcourt, Brace and Co., 1953.

Schlesinger, Arthur M. *Prelude to Independence: The Newspaper War on Britain, 1764–1776*. New York: Alfred A. Knopf, 1958.

3

Thomas Paine

EVELYN J. HINZ

[*Thomas Paine deserves special treatment as the most influential of the patriot pamphleteers. An immigrant to America, Paine was one of the last of the pamphleteers to take up his pen on behalf of the American cause. While the work that he did both in America and in France is well known, not so well understood is the relationship between his writings and his own personality and needs, the focus of the essay that follows.*]

Nothing, perhaps, points so forcibly to the importance of a humanistic consideration of the causes and significance of the American Revolution as the role played by Thomas Paine, since Paine, the most brilliant propagandist of the patriotic cause, was not a native-born American but an Englishman, an uneducated Englishman who began his career as a champion of independence with only the briefest acquaintance with American affairs. Unfortunately, the usual moral drawn is that Paine was an altruistic genius, a naturally "enlightened" man, a political visionary, whereas what Paine's case so beautifully illustrates is the universality of those resentments and aspirations which motivated the founding of the American republic as the legitimate offspring of colonial America and which will always pertain to the idea of America, regardless of her geographical and historical identity.

What Paine articulated in his propaganda was his own sense of the injustice he had experienced in the Old World and his dream of a future in the New World, and what makes his propaganda American and accounts at the same time for its impact is that these feelings are the common denominator of one aspect of the American experience. Hence Paine's commitment to the American Revolution is less dramatically messianic than it might appear or has been made to appear; the American Revolution was for him not a new and objective cause but an objective correlative for his own cause, and it was because of the coincidence of his own interests with those of the patriots that he was able so quickly to grasp and so eloquently to articulate American sentiments.

Paine himself repeatedly protested that there was nothing personal in his attraction to the American cause and that he wrote with total objectivity; but significantly it was also Paine who warned us, in his critique of the Abbé Raynal's interpretation of the American Revolution: "He is a weak politician who does not understand human nature." If we ourselves are not to merit his scorn of this kind of naiveté, we must be tough enough to see past Paine's own protestations of altruism and humanistic enough not to be disturbed by the fact that ultimately the American cause was furthered by a cantankerous dreamer who used it to vent his personal grievances and naively utopian visions. "The cause of America is in a great measure the cause of all mankind," Paine wrote in the introduction to *Common Sense*; to appreciate Paine's literary contribution to the American Revolution we must realize the extent to which that "great measure" is essentially a psychological one and to begin we must recognize the extent to which the cause of America was the cause of Tom Paine.

I

Paine was born in the small town of Thetford in 1737; when he left England thirty-seven years later he had literally failed in or abandoned everything he had attempted. The son of a Quaker staymaker, Paine was given the rather unusual opportunity for a boy of his class to go to grammar school. When he was thirteen, however, he was recalled to the normal routine and became an apprentice in his father's shop. After an abortive attempt to run away to sea when he was sixteen, he finally, at nineteen, enlisted aboard the privateer *King of Prussia*. He returned to London a year later, having given up the life of a sailor; in 1757 he was employed as a journeyman staymaker, but a year later left the city for Dover; the subsequent year he left Dover for Sandwich, where, with a loan from his former employer, he set up his own shop as a master staymaker. In 1759, with his shop heading toward bankruptcy, he married Mary Lambert, the daughter of an excise official, and a few months later, ridden with debt, he escaped to Margate, where less than a year later his wife died.

In 1761 he returned to his parents' home in Thetford and began preparing himself for a job in the excise service, which he managed to obtain in 1762. In July 1765, however, he was dismissed for violation of trust when it was discovered that he had approved goods without actually having examined them. Following his dismissal he fell back upon staymaking once more, shifting from town to town, until finally, in 1766, virtually destitute, he moved to London and found employment as a teacher in a private academy, but only for a short period. In 1767 he moved to another school for only three months. Destitute, he wrote a letter in July of that year to the Excise Board "humbly" petitioning to be reinstated. The petition was granted, though it was not until February 1768 that he was finally given a post at Lewes—after having rejected the first opening offered him.

In Lewes Paine lodged with the family of Samuel Ollive, a tobacconist, and following the death of the father he effected a "marriage of prudence" with the daughter, Elizabeth. The marriage was never consummated, and shortly after Paine's second discharge from the excise service the couple separated legally. This second discharge, in April 1774, was the result of Paine's having been absent without leave from his job, though as Paine himself saw it, it was the nature of the business he was absent upon which was the real motive for his dismissal: he was in London distributing a brief he had prepared (in 1772) agitating for an increase in the excisemen's salary.

Paine was later to ignore this first piece of political writing, arguing that he had never published anything prior to his coming to America and that it was the cause of America which made him an author. Nothing, however, better prepares us for an understanding of Paine's commitment to the American Revolution or for the type of propaganda he would write than this small and abortive pamphlet; for behind his impassioned, statistical presentation of the plight of the officers of excise is Paine's solipsistic rationalization of his own failures and failings. Being an exciseman, he argues, deprives one of the advantages of a fixed abode; the poor pay of excisemen encourages them to be lax in their duties; the pride of being an officer rather than a mechanic or laborer forces excisemen to conceal their poverty, while the poor pay makes the excise the refuge of those unfitted for the better paying jobs in the trades. To the crucial question of why, since it is their own choice of occupation, excisemen complain rather than search for a more congenial employment, Paine's answer is that it is *too late*: "The Time limited for an admission into an Excise Employment, is between twenty-one and thirty Years of Age—the very Flower of Life. Every other Hope and Consideration is then given up, and the Chance of establishing themselves in any other Business becomes in a few Years not only lost to them, but they become lost to it. 'There is a Tide in the Affairs of Men,' which if embraced, leads on to Fortune—*That neglected*, all beyond is Misery or Want." Paine was neither in misery nor in want when he undertook to write *The Case of the Officers of Excise*; actually he seems to have been more comfortable and secure than he had ever been; he was, however, thirty-five years old, and certainly not riding any tide of fortune. To make himself the spokesman for unionizing excisemen was to invite disaster, but it was also a way to escape heroically from a job in which he had little interest.

Where Paine's interest did lie was in declamation on the one hand and in science (or natural philosophy, as it was called) on the other. The former he had found some opportunity to pursue at the White Hart Tavern in Lewes, where members of an informal men's club met to discuss politics, exchange ideas, and entertain each other with literary efforts and the odd pot of ale. Paine contributed several poems, among them an elegy on the death of General Wolfe; he was also frequently awarded the title, "General of the Headstrong War," an accolade bestowed upon the debater who defended his position the most vociferously, and in Paine's case, as we might gather, the most obstinately. Paine's interest in science was sparked during his first sojourn in London when he attended the lectures of Benjamin Martin and James Ferguson, two deistic popularizers of Newtonian principles, and he subsequently met the distinguished astronomer, Dr. John Bevis. During his residence in Lewes his interest in science also brought him the friendship of George Lewis Scott, a science enthusiast and commissioner of the Excise Board; and finally it was because of his interest in science and through Scott that Paine, when he was in London promoting the *Case of the Officers of Excise*, met the great American experimenter, Benjamin Franklin.

In October of 1774, armed with letters of introduction from Franklin, Paine set sail for America. With his uncanny perspicacity Franklin introduced Paine as an "ingenious worthy young man," and while at thirty-seven Paine could not realistically have been described as young, he may well have seemed so to a person of Franklin's sophistication. Ingeniousness and worthiness are often better defined by the writer of such letters than by the recipient. Bearing in mind Ben Franklin's sometimes ironic humanity, let it be sufficient to say that in October of that year there sailed for America a defeated and discontented Englishman hoping to make a new start—a ready-made patriot.

II

In his letter of introduction Franklin had suggested that Paine be found employment as "a clerk, or assistant tutor in a school, or assistant surveyor," so that he might support himself until he was able to "make acquaintance and obtain a knowledge of the country." Paine, however, did not seem to need any acclimatization, for on January 4, 1775, only a month after his arrival, he published in a local paper "A Dialogue Between General Wolfe and General Gage in a Wood Near Boston," the drift of which was not only that Americans were displeased with British measures and ministers but that the Massachusetts colonists "are disaffected to the British Crown." Even among patriots, few at that date contemplated the complete break which Paine's phrase implied, but Paine had cut his ties with England and America must therefore be similarly "disaffected."

In mid-January Paine introduced himself to Franklin's son-in-law, who in turn introduced him to Robert Aitken, proprietor of Philadelphia's largest book store. About to put out a new periodical, the *Pennsylvania Magazine*, Aitken employed Paine first as an assistant and then with the second issue engaged him as editor. In addition to his contributions to this magazine, Paine also published a small article entitled "African Slavery in America" in another journal, as a result of which he made the acquaintance of Dr. Benjamin Rush, a prominent physician and early abolitionist. Rush was also an avid patriot, and he encouraged Paine to undertake the writing of what became *Common Sense*; with its publication on January 10, 1776, the fortunes of Paine and America were semiofficially launched.

Following the official launching with the Declaration of Independence in July, Paine sought to get closer to the action, and first offered his services as secretary to Daniel Roberdeau, commander of a group of volunteers, and then as aide-de-camp to General Nathanael Greene. Following Greene's much-faulted retreat to Newark, Paine wrote the first number of his "Crisis" essays.

In January 1777, he was appointed secretary to a commission sent by Congress to answer questions which the new status of America posed for the Indians, and in April, as a kind of token for his services as a propagandist, he was elected secretary to a newly established Committee for Foreign Affairs. As a man whose personal passions often took priority over political considerations, Paine was a bad choice for the job, and in January 1778, he was forced to resign, having committed a double indiscretion in his determination to prove his case against Silas Deane, an American agent sent to procure supplies from France. First, he based his case upon documents to which he had access in his position as confidential secretary; second, he inadvertently made it seem that France had aided the colonies while she was still at peace with England, thereby undoing the cover-up job designed to make the whole affair look like a commercial transaction.

Appointed clerk to the Pennsylvania Assembly in the fall of 1779, a position he was given mainly to subsidize a collection of his works he proposed to prepare, Paine in the following year concerned himself with the financial plight of the army, and after quixotically suggesting voluntary subscription, he worked with Robert Morris in the establishment of what became the Bank of North America. In December 1780 Paine published *Public Good*, and then in 1781 resigned his position as clerk in order to accompany Colonel Laurens to France to negotiate a loan. Paine's initial plan was to go from France to England, where he believed that he could convince his erstwhile countrymen of the stupidity of continuing the war, but he was persuaded to give up the idea and in August 1781 he returned with Laurens in a ship bringing the sought-for economic and military supplies.

Arguing that the original idea for a French loan had been his, upon his return he requested some financial recognition of his services; in February

1782 a year's salary of $800 was arranged, the money deriving from a secret service fund, the rationale being the remaining need for his pen. Paine complied, and during the closing years of the Revolution occupied himself with replying to the Abbé Raynal's criticism of America, with more "Crises," and with supporting the right of the federal government to impose an import tax on Rhode Island in a series of six letters comparable in theme to *Public Good*.

After the war New York awarded Paine a confiscated Loyalist estate, New Rochelle; Pennsylvania gave him £500, and Congress $3000. He was not, however, proposed for the honored task which he would undoubtedly have considered as the best reward: membership in the convention elected in 1787 to frame the Constitution of the United States. Even before the end of the war he had been working upon another dream—his plans for the construction of an iron bridge, and in 1787, having despaired of seeing it erected in America, Paine decided to seek support in the Old World and set sail for Europe.

In 1802 he returned to America, but this time to a people who were largely "disaffected" from him. And this not because during his sojourn abroad he may have seemed to be an opportunist in becoming so quickly involved in translating the cause of America into the cause of France nor because he had extended the "Rights of Man" to England, but basically because to Bible-oriented Americans he had carried common sense too far in applying it to an investigation of the nature of the Divine King (*The Age of Reason*) and because he had accused George Washington of aspiring to be an American king (*Letter to Washington*). He still retained the friendship of Jefferson, but as president, Jefferson had to be wary of seeming on too friendly terms with a man most of the country now despised. So Paine's last seven years were spent in social ostracism; he continued to write, but mainly embittered, nostalgic, and repetitive things, and—final irony—in an 1806 election for members of Congress and the state assembly he was denied the vote on the grounds that he was not an American citizen. Paine died on June 8, 1809, and was buried on his farm in New Rochelle, consecrated ground having also been denied to this well-known infidel.

III

Most of Paine's contributions to the *Pennsylvania Magazine* are important only insofar as they reflect his inability to write well when he was not personally primed for an issue or when he tried to write like a gentleman. After reading such pieces as "Duelling" or "Cupid and Hymen" one understands why it was rumored that the writer was a Grub Street hack. Those instances in which he does write relatively well are either when he is eulogizing science and the New World or when he is denouncing England and those in high places. Considered chronologically, a number of the essays are also important for the index which they provide to Paine's initial attitude toward America and to the development of his involvement in the American Revolution.

In the introductory essay which he wrote for the first number of the *Magazine*, January 1775, it was the opportunity which he believed America provided for the scientific mentality which fired his imagination and it is as a vehicle for the dissemination of new ideas that he sees the function of the "Magazine in America," as the essay is entitled. America, he declares, is a country whose "reigning character is the love of science," and the *Magazine* will be the "nursery of genius." Similarly, a February essay, "Useful and Entertaining Hints," is a plea for respect for experimentation and for the cessation of ridicule when experiments prove unsuccessful; he also expresses a fear that Americans may be content with their world, and he urges them not to rest in achievement but ever to seek for improvement. Another February article, "New Anecdotes of Alexander the Great," is a rather playful allegory upon the end awaiting tyrants, but one in which Paine the giant-slayer makes his appearance both in the form of the speaker who holds the emperor—reduced to a bug—between his finger and thumb, and in the form of a "Tom Tit" who "chopped him up with as little ceremony as he put whole kingdoms to the sword."

In a March essay Paine similarly moralizes on the fate awaiting the high and mighty; this time, however, he uses a figure closer to home, the allegory being directed toward the fate awaiting England. Entitled "Reflections on the Life and Death of Lord Clive," the essay condemns Clive for his imperialistic activities in India, but it is so structured that for Clive and India one can read Gage and America: "Resolved on accumulating an unbounded fortune he enters into all the schemes of war, treaty, and intrigue.... The Wretched inhabitants are glad to compound for offences never committed, and to purchase at any rate the privilege to breathe."

On April 19 there was fired at Lexington the "shot heard round the world," as Emerson was to memorialize the event, and with his May contribution to the *Magazine*, Paine began practicing for *Common Sense*. "Reflections on Titles" is an indignant and generalized criticism of reverence for titles as a "sacrifice of common sense" unless the title is one which derives from the public and is consistent with the character of the person to whom it is applied. Hence to apply the title of "Right Honourable" to the "plunderer of his country" or the "murderer of mankind" is an absurdity not to be countenanced, while it is with pleasure that one sees it applied to a group of public-spirited citizens: "The Honourable Continental Congress."

By June Paine was no longer content merely to reflect upon absurdities but began musing upon ways to put an end to them. In "The Dream Interpreted" he sees a most pleasing landscape changed into a wasteland; but then, after a tempest, which he dreaded as something which would further destroy the land, there emerges a country more beautiful and healthy than before. The message is too obvious to require interpretation, but what might be pointed out is that in the essay Paine nicely presents himself as the dreamer only, not the interpreter, as the spectator of the dream, not its creator, while he begins the essay by observing that the wiser the man, the more wildly will he dream: "While those who are unable to wander out of the track of common thinking when awake, never exceed the boundaries of common nature when asleep."

In "The Dream" Paine had emphasized that "America has not sought the quarrel, but has been driven into it," and in "Thoughts on Defensive War," published in July, he expands upon this theme, arguing that Americans are not a warlike people but a people who are merely fighting to protect their property and political rights (and by extension their religious liberty), since these go hand in hand. A strategic argument, because he had thus provided the most justifiable reason for rebellion, had turned the revolution into a crusade, and in the process justified his own anomalous position as a Quaker calling for war.

How instrumental Paine's contributions to the *Pennsylvania Magazine* were in shaping public opinion it is difficult to say. He boasted to Franklin that when he assumed the editorship the subscription rate jumped phenomenally, and though most of his essays were published pseudonymously, they do seem to have attracted a fair amount of attention. But the most important thing to observe of these essays is that they prepared the way for *Common Sense*, and about the impact of that pamphlet there can be little dispute.

I V

Common Sense is without doubt *the* classic in the propaganda literature of the American Revolution. Published anonymously, the pamphlet was first attributed to a variety of patriots, including Franklin and the two Adamses. Those who did so, however, not only overlooked the byline, "Written by an Englishman," but also the style and tone of the work; for if it expressed ideas that were common to the leading radicals it did so in a way that no politically astute or established American would have dared—and not through lack of courage but because of a sense of public responsibility. *Common Sense* is not merely the first open declaration for independence; it is a howl of defiance against everything British and an unqualified proclamation of America's readiness to stand on her own. It could not have been written by anyone who took a "commonsensical" look at America's situation at the beginning of 1776 nor by anyone with any reverence and sense of tradition; it could only have been written by a personally disenchanted Britisher who neither knew nor cared about the actualities of America's position and who was driven instead by a desire to avenge himself and who saw in America's independence a vision of his own apotheosis.

Though structured as a four-part political and philosophical inquiry into the "Origin and Design of Government, Monarchy and Hereditary Succession, the Present State of American Affairs, and the Present Ability of America," *Common Sense* is an erratic harangue with variations on two essentially psychological themes. The first is that in rebelling against Britain Americans are not being disloyal to the mother that nurtured them. Paine's major tactic here is to argue that if Britain had acted like a mother no American would have dreamed of such an action and, furthermore, that it is this very kind of loyalty which Britain is relying upon in order to maintain her control of America: "But Britain is the parent country, say some. Then the more shame upon her conduct. Even brutes do not devour their young, nor savages make war upon their families; Wherefore, the assertion, if true, turns to her reproach; but it happens not to be true, or only partly so, and the phrase *parent* or *mother country* hath been jesuitically adopted by the King and his parasites, with a low papistical design of gaining an unfair bias on the credulous weakness of our minds." Hence to be loyal to Britain is not to be a dutiful son but a servile imbecile. It is also to reveal *oneself* an unfit parent, Paine then conversely argues; for sooner or later Britain's authority over America must come to an end and, as "parents, we can have no joy knowing that *this government* is not sufficiently lasting to insure anything which we may bequeath to posterity." Significantly, when debunking reverence for the British constitution, Paine with characteristic expediency and inconsistency uses as one of his main arguments against hereditary succession that it is "an insult and imposition on posterity."

Paine's second major problem in converting Americans to his way of thinking was to overcome their fears that they had more to lose than to gain from separating themselves from Britain. Here his method perforce consists basically of bravado, loud ringing assertions deduced from generalized examples in which apparent disadvantages are shown really to be advantages: "The infant state of the colonies, as it is called, so far from being against, is an argument in favor of independence. We are sufficiently numerous, and were we more so we might be less united." Or the financial aspect: "Debts we have none; and whatever we may contract on this account will serve as a glorious memento of our virtue. . . . No nation ought to be without a national debt. A national debt is a national bond." Conversely and rather ironically, Paine's method is to shame those who believe that reconciliation is the better course as armchair commentators either ignorant of the cruelties which Britain has perpetrated in America or untouched because they have not personally experienced any:

> Hath your house been burnt? Hath your property been destroyed before your face? Are your wife and children destitute of a bed to lie on, or bread to live

on? Have you lost a parent or child by their hands, and yourself the ruined and wretched survivor? If you have not, then are you not the judge of those who have. But if you have, and can still shake hands with the murderers, then are you unworthy the name of husband, father, friend, or lover, and whatever may be your rank or title in life, you have the heart of a coward, and the spirit of a sycophant. (1: 91[1])

Paine, a man without family ties and living in Philadelphia, had experienced none of these atrocities—not in America, that is—but he had had a wife— indeed two—in England, and in some ways he was a "ruined and wretched survivor."

What seems to constitute a point of objective and realistic relief in *Common Sense* is Paine's proposal of a plan for the governing of the states—the lack of which, he argues, is the only admissible cause of fear about independence. But if it has a constitutional ring, the plan is also as simple-minded as the image Paine conjured up of the origins of government, while in advancing the plan Paine clearly envisioned himself as the godfather of the government of the United States, since he concludes his observations with the divine *fiat*: "Amen."

Circumstances in part help to account for the tremendous impact of *Common Sense*. It was on August 23, 1775, that England issued her declaration that Massachusetts was in a state of rebellion, in October the Americans witnessed the British burning of Falmouth, in November British warships fired on Norfolk and the proclamation declaring freedom for slaves who would attack their masters was issued, while in New England tensions and tempers increasingly flared, and on January 6, 1776, Howe ordered the destruction of the Old North Church and numerous residences to supply firewood to his troops. But perhaps most important of all was the coincidence of the appearance of *Common Sense* with the arrival of news of the king's opening speech to Parliament, a violently intransigent speech calling for the suppression of the rebellion. In January 1776 Americans were angry but in a state of confusion as well as rebellion; Paine clarified the confusion by justifying the anger and giving it a glorious name.

V

Inciting a discontented people to revolt is one thing; maintaining morale when men are tired and the cause seems hopeless is another. The purpose of *The*

---

1. All quotations are taken from the Moncure D. Conway edition of *The Writings of Thomas Paine*.

American Crisis, the collective title given to a series of essays which Paine wrote between 1776 and 1783, was to keep the fight going and to bring it to a victorious conclusion. There are sixteen "Crisis" essays in all, thirteen titled by number, plus a "Crisis Extraordinary" and two called "Supernumerary Crisis." The reason for this rather awkward labeling procedure was Paine's desire to make the series correspond to the number of the American colonies and the spans in his iron bridge.

It is impossible here to deal with each "Crisis" essay individually, and in some ways it is unnecessary; for while each was written in response to a specific critical issue and hence when read chronologically they provide an interesting history of the Revolution, in point of theme they generally reflect the sentiments Paine expressed in *Common Sense*, while the style is more or less consistent throughout. An examination of a representative "Crisis" essay should then suffice, and since the first is probably also the most memorable this would seem to be the best choice.

"Crisis 1" begins with the oft-quoted statement: "These are the times that try men's souls." As he was writing in December 1776, Paine was for once not exaggerating. In August, in the first real test of strength, the Battle of Long Island, Washington had been badly defeated; in November, Greene was forced to retreat from Fort Lee and Congress had fled to Baltimore. These disconcerting facts could not be denied, but they could be positively interpreted; this Paine sought to do by resorting on the one hand to the cliché that "the harder the conflict, the more glorious the triumph," and on the other hand by providing an "on the spot" description of Greene's retreat which glossed over the blunders which had occasioned it and instead focused on the fortitude of the army: "suffice it for the present to say, that both officers and men, though greatly harassed and fatigued, frequently without rest, covering, or provision, the inevitable consequences of a long retreat, bore it with a manly and martial spirit. All their wishes centred in one, which was, that the country would turn out and help them drive the enemy back." If the army was defeated, in other words, it was not because Paine had been wrong in asserting that America was militarily ready to wage a war of independence but because the public had not kept up their end of the bargain.

In addition to this use of shame tactics, Paine also employs a fair amount of scare tactics. Arguing that with God and Washington on their side the patriots are sure to win out before long, he then envisions what will be the fate of the Loyalists and those on the side of Howe: "should the tories give him encouragement to come or assistance if he come, I as sincerely wish that our next year's arms may expel them from the continent, and the congress appropriate their possessions to the relief of those who have suffered in well-doing. A single successful battle next year will settle the whole. America could carry on a two years war by the confiscation of the property of disaffected persons, and be made happy by their expulsion.'' Conversely, he concludes the essay by speculating on the fate of the rebels and America in general if, having incurred the wrath of Britain by rebelling, they should not succeed: ''a ravaged country—a depopulated city—habitations without safety, and slavery without hope—our homes turned into barracks and bawdy-houses for Hessians, and a future race to provide for, whose fathers we shall doubt of.'' If ''time makes more converts than reason,'' as Paine himself put it in *Common Sense*, effective propaganda makes even more.

''Crisis 1'' was first published in the *Pennsylvania Journal* on December 19, and on December 23 it was reprinted in pamphlet form. Washington is reported to have ordered it read by all his corporals to their troops, and legend has it that it was largely responsible for his successful movement on Trenton on Christmas Day 1776, which victory in turn was a morale booster for the population at large. Paine himself, of course, believed that the impact of this essay had been decisive, and in his thirteenth ''Crisis,'' published on April 19, 1783, he draws attention to the fact by footnoting the first ''Crisis'' after beginning: '' 'The times that tried men's souls,' are over.'' Significantly it is given to Paine's editor to observe that this was the eighth anniversary of Lexington.

V I

Paine had envisioned himself writing the history of the American Revolution from his entrance into American affairs, a project toward which he had directed his attention, in thought at least, whenever he was not immediately involved in shaping America's future. In 1781, however, there appeared in English translation a volume entitled *The Revolution in America*; a French historian, the Abbé Raynal, had anticipated him and had addressed himself to what Paine had staked out as his special territory. Furthermore, the Abbé had amused himself with the triviality of the incidents which had sparked the American Revolution and had criticized the Franco-American alliance as an unnatural union. He had, in other words, called into question the two events in which Paine believed himself to have been the chief agent. To engage Paine's interest a subject had to be personally relevant and contemporary—which is why he would never write his history of the Revolution and why instead he wrote it vicariously under the guise of a critique entitled *Letter to the Abbé Raynal*.

The *Letter* begins with a rather lengthy introduction in which, curiously, instead of attacking the Abbé for his errors Paine seems to be concerned with excusing him for them. First he suggests that undoubtedly the Abbé's errors result from his lack of first-hand acquaintance with the American arena, and second, he observes that the book was "unfairly purloined" from the Abbé by an unscrupulous Englishman and hence published before the Abbé had an opportunity to reconsider and revise what he had written. But the first excuse, of course, is Paine's way of emphasizing that only one who had been there, such as himself, was qualified to write the history of the Revolution. The second, in addition to allowing him to make of the English pirate a general example of the avariciousness of the English mentality, enables him to comment upon the unusualness of the writer, again Paine himself, who can "at once, and without the aid of reflection and revisal, combine warm passions with a cool temper, and the full expansion of the imagination with the natural and necessary gravity of judgement, so as to be rightly balanced within themselves, and to make a reader feel, fancy, and understand justly at the same time."

In the body of the *Letter*, Paine first takes issue with Raynal's observation that the American Revolution originated in a simple dispute over whether Britain had the right to levy a tax on tea; according to Paine, the tea tax was a symbolic gesture by which Britain sought to determine how far she could go, and which Americans, recognizing it as such, rejected on principle. Though Britain's motives were political and commercial, those of America were ideological and moral; it was their long-standing attachment to the ideals of liberty and the dignity of man which made them rebel: "Nothing of personality was incorporated with their cause"; they saw that the "cause of America" was the "cause of mankind." And this being the case, Paine argues, the Abbé is totally wrong when he contends that had not France signed the treaty with America in the spring of 1778, Congress would have accepted the proposals of the British ministry at that time; the Americans would have refused even if word had not been received of forthcoming aid, and, furthermore, as Paine attempts to prove through an examination of dates and documents, Congress did refuse before they were aware that the treaty had been signed. Unfortunately the two documents which he appends do not quite bear him out; in the one written prior to the news of the alliance Congress does express a willingness to negotiate, and it is only in the one written after and in which the treaty is referred to that adamancy is expressed.

As far as the alliance itself is concerned, Paine argues, it derived from America's recognition of the benefits which her independence and prosperity would bring to all mankind; she proposed to enter into the treaty as "the best effectual method of extending and securing happiness." And like the Revolution the alliance was a symbolic act, indicative of a revolution in thinking, a change from thinking in terms of nationalism to thinking in terms of internationalism. A man with no ties to any land, Paine had finally found a justification for his rootlessness, and he signed himself at the end of the *Letter* as ''a universal citizen.''

VII

Though similar in its basic premises, *Public Good* is stylistically very different from Paine's previous publications. It is a curiously objective piece of work, relatively devoid of passionate outbursts, wild analogies, and unscrupulous invective; instead it consists of a closely reasoned argument based upon analysis of historical documents. The purpose for which it was designed partly helps to explain why.

Congress had adopted the Articles of Confederation on November 17, 1777, and had submitted them to the individual states for ratification. Maryland, however, had refused to comply, insisting that she would do so only if Virginia and other boundary states would surrender their claims to the unsettled western lands to federal control. Paine's purpose was to persuade Virginia to cede her claims, but he had to do so tactfully if he was not in turn to compound the problem by alienating her, and his Virginia friends, chief among them Thomas Jefferson. He could not, therefore, write with his usual flamboyancy. Significantly he excuses himself for the prosaic quality of *Public Good* by drawing attention to his dilemma in the preface: ''I freely confess that the respect I had conceived, and still preserve, for the character of Virginia, was a constant check upon those sallies of imagination, which are fairly and advantageously indulged in against an enemy, but ungenerous when against a friend.''

Consequently, instead of denouncing Virginia as a selfish, greedy, profiteering state, his method is to question the legitimacy of her claim through an exploration of the validity of the various British documents upon which they were based, and then to appeal to the great example which Virginians set in questioning the assumed rights of Britain in America at the beginning of the revolutionary contest. He attempts finally to convince Virginia that it is in her own best interests to surrender her claims. On the positive side, the lands she would cede will become a frontier state, providing her with protection against incursions by the Indians, and the new state would double her trade since imports will have to come via Chesapeake Bay. On the negative side, if she persists in her expansive territorial claims, her quota for the expense of carrying on the war will have to be computed accordingly, while the sale of such land by Congress would produce a fund which would reduce the taxation upon the individual states for the cost of the war. By way of conclusion, regarding the issue as now a *fait accompli*, Paine then goes on to envision the way new states will be brought into the union and, finally, ironically but characteristically, to call for a national convention to formulate a new constitution, the as yet unratified Articles of Confederation seeming already too much of a thing of the past to his futuristic eyes.

Public Good had no immediate effect upon the public or upon Congress, though in March 1781 Maryland did ratify the Articles; it did, however, enrage Virginians and had a rather long-range effect upon Paine's fortunes for in June 1784, when a bill was introduced into the Virginia legislature to bestow upon Paine an honorarium for his services during the Revolution, the vote was negative. Also, as a result of writing *Public Good*, Paine was given a voter's share in the Indiana Company, controlled by a group of speculators in land west of the Alleghenies. When he applied for a deed two years later, rumor quickly circulated that *Public Good* had been written for Paine's private good, especially when it became known that the documents for undermining Virginia's claim had been provided by the stockholders of that very company. In the sense that the basic argument of *Public Good* is that western lands belong to the confederation, the pamphlet does not seem to have a partisan objective, and on these grounds Paine has been defended from the charge that he was a hireling. Still, the fact that he never referred to *Public Good* in his later years suggests that he was not particularly proud of it, but whether he felt it not to be of the quality of his other propaganda or because its disinterested objectivity was necessitated to disguise private motives is hard to say.

VIII

Paine's writings, subsequent to the conclusion of the revolutionary period, are necessarily beyond the scope of this essay. No discussion of Paine, however, can afford to be without at least a brief commentary upon *The Rights of Man* and *The Age of Reason*, while a quick look at his *Letter to George Washington* provides an excellent way of preparing for a summation of his contribution to the American Revolution.

The Rights of Man is a two-part work published in 1791 and 1792. It is best described as an attempt to do for Englishmen what Paine believed *Common Sense* had done for the Americans, and as such it is a plea for Englishmen to overthrow the monarchy and establish a republic along the lines which Paine had drawn in *Common Sense* and elsewhere; its basic premise is Paine's old argument that government exists to guarantee the "natural rights" of the individual. *The Rights of Man* is also Paine's attempt, comparable to his *Letter to the Abbé Raynal*, to correct the errors which he believed Burke to have made in his *Reflections on the Revolution in France*. Just as in the *Letter* Paine had spent a great deal of time explaining what it takes to make a good historian, so in this work he attempts to refute Burke's arguments by ridiculing his aristocratic style. *The Rights of Man* was quite popular among English radicals, but Paine himself was tried for treason, and, since he happened to be in France at the time, the sentence took the form of his being outlawed from England.

The Age of Reason, Paine's most controversial work, is also in two parts: the first was written just prior to and published upon his release in November 1794 from Luxembourg Prison, the arrest ironically having been made on the charge that he was a citizen of a country at war with France; the second part was composed during his confinement and published in 1796. In general Paine's objective in the work is to assert the right of every man to his own opinion and to suggest that while religions come and go the theology manifested through the study of nature remains a constant. Hence in point of substance *The Age of Reason* is not that outrageous; stylistically, however, it is. For Paine is not content merely to demonstrate that man's traditional knowledge of God does not square with the knowledge acquired through a contemplation of the universe (the burden of the first part) or to prove that the Bible is inconsistent and therefore not infallible (the argument of the second part). Instead, he is not satisfied until he has demolished received religion through the agency of ridicule and set himself up as the new Son of God: "My mind is my own church."

Finally, whatever *The Age of Reason* left undone by way of preparing for a hostile American reaction, his *Letter to George Washington* completed. As we recall, Paine was sent to prison on the grounds that he was an Englishman, and during his incarceration he appealed to American officials to come to his aid and, by declaring him an American citizen, to procure his release. His final release resulted from efforts of James Monroe when he took over as American minister, but George Washington and others in America had remained silent on the issue. This lack of response seemed to Paine the worst kind of ingratitude and occasioned the retaliatory *Letter*. "The part I acted in the American revolution is well known," Paine observes; "I shall not repeat it here." But of course he does, and in the process implies that his pen and not Washington's sword was the key factor in the victory: "You slept away your time in the field, till the finances of the country were completely exhausted, and you have but little share in the glory of the event. It is time, sir, to speak the undisguised language of historical truth. Elevated to the chair of the Presidency, you assumed the merit of every thing to yourself, and the natural ingratitude of your constitution began to appear.'' John Adams also comes under attack as ''a speller after places and offices, [who] never thought his little services were highly enough paid'' and as ''one of those men who never contemplated the origin of government, or comprehended any thing of first principles.'' That one man who had so contemplated and comprehended was, in Paine's eyes, of course, none other than Paine himself, and all the honors bestowed upon Washington should have been given to him, including, it is almost not too much to say, the presidency itself.

I X

To understand the character and role played by most of the leading figures in the American Revolution requires an exercise of the historical imagination; to understand Paine and the role he played requires rather what might be called an exercise in humanistic recognition. It is not how different things were then that we have to bear in mind: it is how little human nature changes in a couple of centuries that we have to accept.

The best studies of Paine—and happily this includes the majority of recent interpretations—have recognized that he was not an original thinker but rather a popularizer of contemporary ideas; the ideas he articulated were a layman's version of Newtonian thought, deistic principles, Lockean concepts, and Rousseauistic sentiments, and these he garbled as much as he simplified. What further requires emphasis, however, is that ideas are not the important thing in Paine's propaganda; the important thing is his uncanny ability to articulate the emotions of the mob, personal emotions which are American because America is structured upon a dream.

Similarly, most objective commentatiors have realized that it is not through his avowed reasonable arguments but rather through psychological strategy that Paine's propaganda operates to persuade. But what also needs to be recognized is that this is less a deliberate technique or clever application of human psychology than an offshoot of Paine's subjectivity. Paine is not a master psychologist who can see through political protestations to their personal motivations; he is a man who imputes to others his own motivations. It is his own arrogance, for example, which lies behind his analyses of King George, Washington, and others above him, while it is his own egotistical ambitions which perversely manifest themselves in his analysis of Britain's lust for power.

Moreover, Paine's marvelously concrete and homely style is likewise a virtue essentially forced upon him. He is not a master stylist who deliberately uses plain language and domestic metaphor to clarify abstract political issues: Paine thought in these simplistic terms. And frequently also, what appears to be a perfectly poetical way of capping off an argument is really a personal *cri de coeur*. "Ye that tell us of harmony and reconciliation, can ye restore to us the time that is past?," expostulates the thirty-nine-year-old Paine, who has nothing to show for the first thirty-seven; "O! receive the fugitive, and prepare in time an asylum for mankind," pleads the man who was a constitutional wanderer.

What we have now to ask, then, is what we learn about the American patriots that they rallied to the words of this all-too-human being. And I think the best answer is that they too were human beings. In Paine's articulation of his own resentments, fears, and dreams, they read an articulation of their own, just as some of us today do. It is in this context that Paine's influence upon the American Revolution is best summarized. Americans would not have responded to Paine's propaganda if they had not been psychologically disposed to do so; and to the extent that this is the case, the Revolution was inevitable and Paine's influence secondary but ancillary. At the same time, to burn with resentment is not to fight with patriotic fervor; for the latter the resentment has to be objectified and given a name. This is where Paine's main contribution lies.

SUGGESTIONS FOR FURTHER READING

Editions

The Complete Writings of Thomas Paine. Edited by Philip S. Foner. 2 vols. New York: Citadel Press, 1945.
The Writings of Thomas Paine. Edited by Moncure D. Conway. 4 vols. New York: G. P. Putnam's Sons, 1894–96.

Scholarship and Criticism

Aldridge, Alfred Owen. *Man of Reason: The Life of Thomas Paine*. Philadelphia: J. B. Lippincott, 1959.
Bailyn, Bernard. *"Common Sense."* In *Fundamental Testaments of the American Revolution*, pp. 7–23. Washington, D.C.: Library of Congress, 1973.
Boulton, James T. "Literature and Politics I. Tom Paine and the Vulgar Style." *Essays in Criticism* 12 (1962): 18–33.
Derry, John W. *The Radical Tradition: Tom Paine to Lloyd George*. New York: St. Martin's Press, 1967.

Foner, Eric. *Tom Paine and Revolutionary America*. New York: Oxford University Press, 1976.

Hawke, David Freeman. *Paine*. New York: Harper & Rowe, 1974.

Jordan, Winthrop D. "Familial Politics: Thomas Paine and the Killing of the King, 1776." *Journal of American History* 60 (1973): 294–308.

Kenyon, Cecilia M. "Where Paine Went Wrong." *American Political Science Review* 45 (1951): 1086–99.

Williamson, Audrey. *Thomas Paine: His Life, Work and Times*. London: George Allen & Unwin, 1973.

4

The Loyalists' Reply

CHARLES E. MODLIN

[*The pamphlet writers were successful, and the Revolution was undertaken, successfully. The triumph, the subsequent creation of a new nation, and the development of that nation into a great world power have often obscured the fact that for many Americans the Revolution was a defeat. The Loyalists did not readily retreat but argued eloquently that as British citizens Americans enjoyed enormous benefits. Their contribution to American literature, still emerging from neglect, is examined in the chapter that follows.*]

Loyalists—those Americans sympathetic to the British cause in the years immediately prior to and during the Revolutionary War—comprised about a third of the American population according to the venerable formula of John Adams. More recent studies have revised the figure downward to around 20 percent or less, but the fact remains that, especially in some areas, they were a sizable, even predominant, part of the population. As a group they represent a complex mixture of national origins, occupations, and religions. Their geographical distribution was mostly in assorted pockets of strength along the coastal and frontier areas of all but the New England colonies, especially in areas where trading interests were strong and where religious and cultural minorities felt threatened by independence.

The literature of the Loyalists is mostly in the form of essays, letters, verse, drama, and sermons. Virtually all political pamphlets and newspaper articles were published anonymously, and the authorship of many of these works is uncertain, but the known Loyalist writers were an assortment of lawyers, public officials, businessmen, and Anglican clergymen. During the pamphlet wars of 1774 and 1775, most significant Loyalist publications appeared in Boston, Philadelphia, and especially New York, where the foremost publisher of Loyalist pamphlets, James Rivington, also edited *Rivington's Royal Gazette*, the leading Loyalist newspaper of the revolutionary period. Other prominent papers receptive to Loyalist writings were the *Massachusetts Gazette* in Boston and the *Pennsylvania Gazette* in Philadelphia.

Loyalism was, in effect, created by its opposition; it had no real political entity until the very premise of loyalty itself became an issue. Such an issue arose most dramatically with the convening of the First Continental Congress and its adoption in October 1774 of the Suffolk Resolves, prohibitions on imports, exports, and consumption, and the creation of the Continental Association. A flurry of reaction in pamphlets, newspapers, and broadsides expressed the shock of realization on the part of many conservative Americans that Congress had committed the colonies to a policy of serious confrontation rather than reconciliation.

I

One of the members of Congress was Joseph Galloway, a delegate from Pennsylvania whose plan for a new Anglo-American union was defeated by a one-vote margin. In accordance with the policy of consensus, the motion was expunged from the record, and never again was the opposition to independence so close to official acceptance. Galloway's plan, loosely based on the 1754 Albany Plan of Benjamin Franklin, called for continued alliance with England but also for the right of self-governance through the establishment of an American legislature to pass on all laws affecting Americans. Galloway quotes the text of his plan and attacks the work of the Continental Congress in *A Candid Examination of the Mutual Claims of Great-Britain and the Colonies* (1775), in which he charges that the tyrannical policies adopted by Congress were the work of conspirators inexorably leading the colonies "into the blackest rebellion, and all the horrors of an unnatural civil war." Galloway allows that America has lost rights but asserts that petition rather than independence is the way to recover them.

A similar statement of the Loyalist position is that of Daniel Leonard, a lawyer living in Boston under British protection after he was forced from his home in Taunton, Massachusetts. Writing under the name of "Massachusettensis," he engaged in a running newspaper debate with John Adams, publishing seventeen essays in the *Massachusetts Gazette* from December 1774 to April 1775. Leonard, like Galloway, interprets the movement toward revolution as a cleverly planned conspiracy that can lead only to disaster. Leonard holds that the British government has been and remains receptive to reasonable petitions for redress of grievances but points to a radical shift in the American attitude that has made reconciliation virtually impossible: "It is one thing to complain of the inutility or hardship of a particular act of parliament, and quite another to deny the authority of parliament to make any act."

The largest and most significant contributions to the prewar Loyalist literature were those of a group of Anglican clergymen, notably Thomas Chandler,
Jonathan Boucher, and Samuel Seabury. Combining an unflagging allegiance
to Great Britain and a native conservatism, they provided a formidable defense of Loyalism until they were all effectively silenced by exile in 1775.

Several pamphlets published in 1774–75 are ascribed to Thomas Chandler,
rector of a church in Elizabethtown, New Jersey. The best of these, *A
Friendly Address to All Reasonable Americans* (1774), pleads for reconciliation lest such belligerent acts as the Boston Tea Party and the Suffolk
Resolves should lead to war: "O all-pitying Heaven! Preserve me! Preserve
my friends! Preserve my country!" *American Queries* (1774) consists of one
hundred leading questions and answers pointing up the great advantages of
continued union with Great Britain and the dire consequences of rebellion.
What Think Ye of the Congress Now? (1775) is a spirited if futile effort to
discredit the Continental Congress and its actions. Carefully reviewing the
instructions to each colony's delegation, Chandler shows that the Congress
exceeded its authority in adopting measures hostile to Great Britain, and thus
those measures are not binding. *The Patriots of North America* (1775), a
Hudibrastic verse satire, is another harsh attack upon the Congress:

> Will Raggamuffins bold like these,
> Protect our Freedom, Peace, or Ease?
> Ah! surely no, it cannot be,
> These are false Sons of Liberty.
>
> (p. 6)

In May of 1775 Chandler sought refuge in England and remained there ten
years before returning to his church in New Jersey.

Jonathan Boucher, perhaps the ablest theoretician of the Anglican
Loyalists, served parishes in Virginia and Maryland from 1763 to September
1775 when, under extreme political pressure, he also sailed for England.
Some of the dramatic events leading up to his departure are recounted in
Reminiscences of an American Loyalist, a volume edited from his manuscripts
and first published in 1925. Much of the book is sketchy and unrelated to his
American experience, but he shows a skillful and engaging style in narrating
scenes at times when what he calls "the fermentation and conflict of human
passions" became so intense that he preached with loaded pistols beside him.
At one point, he writes, he was called before the Provincial Committee at
Annapolis on an accusation of disloyalty when an Irish militia sergeant whis-
pered to him that "I [Boucher] had more friends among those who bore arms
than enemies, *and by Jasus if he lived he would die with me*. A message in my
favour from the Congress itself would not have inspired me with more courage than I felt on this declaration of this honest Teague." In another incident
Boucher describes his defiance of two hundred armed men—twenty of them

specifically assigned to shoot him—who file into his church to keep him from speaking. He escapes by seizing the group's leader as a hostage, "and we marched together upwards of a hundred yards, I with one hand fastened in his collar and a pistol in the other, guarded by his whole company, whom he had the meanness to order to play on their drums the Rogues' March all the way we went, which they did."

In 1797 Boucher published *A View of the Causes and Consequences of the American Revolution*, a rewriting of his sermons in America, with a long preface, appendix, and footnotes taking into account subsequent historical developments. The plan of the book is to analyze the "causes and consequences" of the Revolution from the perspective of his sermons of the period. The sermons are arranged to give a sense of the developing circumstances leading to war, beginning with the Peace of 1763 and proceeding to such signs of the rebellious times as the church-and-state controversies over the American episcopate and public support of the Anglican church: "A levelling republican spirit in the Church naturally leads to republicanism in the State. . . ."

All of the sermons draw upon one basic assumption about government— that it is inviolable and derived from the patriarchal system ordained by God, a doctrine Boucher drew from Sir Robert Filmer's *Patriarcha* (1680), a work tracing the divine right of kings to the primacy of Adam in the Garden of Eden. The degeneracy of the times, Boucher charges, is a result of the pernicious idea of government at the consent of the governed which, used by demagogues to stir up public resentment of the established government, results in rebellion, the sin of Lucifer, and "it was thus the people once were cunningly led on to depose a Charles, and make a Cromwell their protector; to intercede for a thief, and to crucify the Saviour of the world."

While allowing that the English government may have been rash in its taxing policies, Boucher dismisses the duty on tea as a triviality and insists upon constitutional means for the redress of all grievances. "On the Character of Ahitophel" refers to the Stamp Act and its subsequent repeal as a model for such redress, although "it certainly reflects some dishonour on the *Ahitophels* now among us, who have profited so little by so excellent an example." Applying the same Scriptures (2 Samuel 13–16) that had proven such a rich resource for John Dryden's 1681 treatment of political rebellion in England, "Absalom and Achitophel," Boucher terms Ahitophel an Old Testament type of Judas Iscariot, and, thus, "the guilt of exciting a rebellion would stand upon a footing with that of betraying the Lord of life himself." To the leaders of present-day insurrections Boucher completes the scriptural application with the taunt to "come and shew us, if ye can, in what your conduct differs from that of the faithless incendiary whose history we have just been reviewing." That the implications of Boucher's sermon were not lost upon his audience is indicated in an appendix in which he denies the popular assumption that

George Washington and Benjamin Franklin were the respective models for his portraits of Absalom and Ahitophel, although he allows that the Franklin parallels are "striking." Despite such harsh judgments upon the Revolution and its leaders, Boucher, in a spirit of conciliation, dedicated *A View* to Washington upon his retirement as president.

The most effective prose stylist of all the Loyalist writers was Samuel Seabury, secretary of the Anglican Convention in New York, who in 1784 became the first Episcopal bishop in America. He published four pamphlets between November 1774 and January 1775, each addressed to a specific audience. *Free Thoughts on the Proceedings of the Continental Congress* (1774) and *The Congress Canvassed* (1774) are warnings to American farmers and New York merchants, respectively, on the tyranny of Congress and the Association. *A View of the Controversy Between Great-Britain and Her Colonies* (1774) is a reply to his pamphlet adversary, Alexander Hamilton. *An Alarm to the Legislature of the Province of New York* (1775) is an appeal to that body to dissociate the colony from the rebellious activities of Congress.

Seabury presents the Loyalist case from the point of view and in the blunt expression of a Westchester farmer, "plain English, from a plain countryman" who calls "a fig, —a Fig; an egg, —an Egg." This persona is most effective in *Free Thoughts* as he renders the congressional prohibitions on exports and imports in vigorous colloquialisms and concrete examples well calculated to bring the issue home to fellow farmers:

> The deuce take them for a set of gundy gutted fellows—will they let us export nothing? Do they intend to eat all our wheat, and rye, and corn, and beef, and pork, and mutton, and butter, and cheese, and turkeys, and geese, and ducks, and fowls, and chickens and eggs, &c? the devil is in't if their bellies are not filled. And yet see their ill-nature and malice against us farmers.—After having furnished them with all this good cheer, which they must have at their own price too, they will not in return let us have a dish of tea to please our wives nor a glass of Madeira to cheer our spirits, nor even a spoonful of Molasses to sweeten our butter-milk.[1]

As a consequence of such policies, "the laborious farmers, the grand support of every well-regulated country, must all go to the dogs together."

Although the Westchester Farmer became infamous as an enemy of the Revolution, Seabury's authorship of the pamphlets was a well-concealed secret. A rebel soldier passing through Westchester, Seabury notes, offered one hundred dollars to learn the identity of "that vilest of all Miscreants" so "that he might plunge his Bayonet into his Heart; another would crawl 50 miles to see him roasted." A final pamphlet was advertised in April 1775 but not

---

1. *Letters of a Westchester Farmer*, ed. Clarence H. Vance, pp. 63–64.

published, a casualty of the furor following the skirmishes at Lexington and Concord.

II

After the outbreak of war, the time for polemics was over. With no issues left to be resolved but the outcome of the war itself, the lines of hostility were drawn, and the Loyalist writings became more alien and detached, no longer an integral part of the American experience. An early example of this wartime literature is a satiric drama, *The Battle of Brooklyn*, anonymously published in 1776, soon after the Americans had suffered a crushing defeat at Brooklyn. The American forces are represented in disarray with each leader and his staff revealing ulterior motives for their participation in the Revolution. The colonels are busy collecting cattle and horses as spoils of war. General Putnam, also active in horse thefts, is anxiously inventing ruses for hanging Tories in order to confiscate their estates. Snuffle the chaplain looks upon the war as a crusade against the Anglican church. A servant, Betty, brags of selling her favors to Benjamin Harrison and George Washington. Washington is portrayed as a victim of his own ambition and now a pawn of an ill-fated revolutionary conspiracy: "To behold myself, against my principle and better judgment, made the tool of their diabolical determinations, to entail a war upon my fellow-subjects of America." Loyalist sympathies are maintained by two servants of the generals who at the end of the play reaffirm their allegiance to the king and the British constitution.

The full extreme of Loyalist rage during the war is expressed in a sermon by Simeon Baxter, an Anglican priest who was imprisoned in an abandoned copper mine in Simsbury, Connecticut. "Tyrannicide Proved Lawful," delivered to fellow prisoners in 1781, calls for the extermination of the American rebels: "Nothing is more absurd than to kill thieves, vipers, and bears, to prevent their cruel designs, and at the same time preserve Congress for acting much worse than the others intended. No one can any longer doubt of the lawfulness of destroying public robbers, whenever prudence points out the way, since the laws of God and men make it lawful to extirpate private robbers." Publishing the sermon in London the following year, Baxter included a letter to George Washington and Congress calling for their suicide in the manner of Judas, who "was not a patriot till he hanged himself for betraying his Saviour and his God—*Go and do thou likewise*; and you will prove yourselves real Saviours of America, and, like him, hold a place in the temple of everlasting Fame."

The war years also produced two outstanding Loyalist poets, Jonathan Odell and Joseph Stansbury. Odell, a physician and Anglican priest in Burlington, New Jersey, was accused of sedition in 1776 and fled to New York, where he worked with the British army and published verse in *Rivington's Royal Gazette*. He left for England during the British evacuation of New York and after the war settled in New Brunswick, Canada. Stansbury, a businessman in Philadelphia, like Odell fled to New York during the war. After a brief exile in Nova Scotia after the war, he tried to return to his old business in Philadelphia but was unsuccessful and eventually resettled in New York. The works of both poets, consisting mainly of satires, songs, odes, and occasional verse, are preserved in two nineteenth-century collections edited by Winthrop Sargent, *The Loyalist Poetry of the Revolution* and *The Loyal Verses of Joseph Stansbury and Doctor Jonathan Odell*.[2]

Odell vigorously expresses the bitterness of wartime. In a long satire, "The American Times" (1779), the "times" are bad, "almost too bad to paint." The poem consists largely of indictments of the chief conspirators in the rebellion, including Washington, "Patron of villainy, of villains chief." It concludes with a vision of Saint George exacting vengeance and prophesying a new order:

> 'America, from dire pollution clear'd,
> 'Shall flourish yet again, belov'd, rever'd:
> 'In duty's lap her growing sons be nurs'd,
> 'And her last days be happier than her first.'
>
> *(LP, p. 37)*

"The Word of Congress," published in *Rivington's Royal Gazette*, September 18, 1779, is another forceful attack upon the leaders of rebellion: "Some ars'nic verse, to poison with the pen / These rats, who nestle in the Lion's den!"

Other poems anticipate British military victory, such as "The Congratulation" (1779) with its taunting refrain, "Joy to great Congress, joy an hundred fold; / The grand cajolers are themselves cajol'd!" "The Feu de Joie" (1779) calls for an American surrender as the ultimate joy:

> O save yourselves before it is too late!
> O save your Country from impending Fate!
> Leave those, whom Justice must at length destroy.
> Repent, come over, and partake our joy.
>
> *(LV, p. 58)*

Perhaps the most effective of Odell's personal satires, originally published in the British *Gentleman's Magazine* and quoted in Boucher's *A View* and Peter Oliver's *Origin and Progress of the American Revolution*, is "Inscription for a Curious Chamber-Stove, in the Form of an Urn, So Contrived as to Make

---

2. Quotations from Odell and Stansbury are taken from these editions, hereafter cited as *LP* and *LV*.

the Flame Descend, Instead of Rise, From the Fire: Invented by Doctor Franklin'' (1776). The title is lengthy but necessary to explain the imagery of the poem, which uses the invention to satirize Franklin's political ambition, a "Spark" from Lucifer that "kindled the blaze of *Sedition*."

> Let Candor, then, write on his Urn—
> Here lies the renowned Inventor,
> Whose flame to the Skies ought to burn,
> But, inverted, descends to the Center!
> (*LV*, p. 6)

Like Odell, Stansbury was an adept satirist. Poems such as "A New Song," "The Town Meeting," "Liberty," and "Freedom" satirize the political oppression, economic chaos, civil disorder, and public disillusionment brought on by the Revolution. Other poems written late in the war effectively express a sense of melancholy at the prospect of British defeat, as in the *carpe diem* theme of "Let Us Be Happy as Long as We Can" (1783?):

> Since no one can tell what tomorrow may bring,
> Or which side shall triumph, the Congress or King;
> Since Fate must o'errule us and carry her plan,
> Why, let us be happy as long as we can.
> (*LV*, p. 87)

After the war Stansbury wrote "The United States," a graceful plea for reconciliation:

> Now this War at length is o'er;
> Let us think of it no more.
> Every Party Lie or Name,
> Cancel as our mutual Shame.
> Bid each wound of Faction close,
> Blushing we were ever Foes.
> (*LV*, p. 89)

Adjustment to postwar America was not an easy process for Loyalists, however, and a final poem, "To Cordelia" (1783), expresses to his wife the pain of exile in Nova Scotia: "So the lone hermit yields to slow decay: / Unfriended lives—unheeded glides away."

III

The Loyalists approached the American Revolution with the premise that revolution was wrong in principle. No specious claims of broken contracts could alter for Loyalists the basic fact that order is the very foundation of civilization; and order demands obedience to civil authority. In *A Friendly Address* Thomas Chandler warns: "The bands of society would be dissolved, the harmony of the world confounded, and the order of nature subverted, if reverence, respect, and obedience, might be refused to those whom the constitution has vested with the highest authority. The ill consequences of open disrespect to government are so great, that no misconduct of the administration can justify or excuse it." Civil protest, writes Jonathan Boucher, is justified only within the limits of the system and may turn out to be no more than an exercise in stoic forbearance: "If you think the duty of threepence a pound upon tea, laid on by the British Parliament, a grievance, it is your duty to instruct your members to take all the constitutional means in their power to obtain redress: if those means fail of success, you cannot but be sorry and grieved; but you will better bear your disappointment, by being able to reflect that it was not owing to any misconduct of your own. And, what is the whole history of human life, public or private, but a series of disappointments?"

Beyond their theoretical objections to revolution, Loyalists considered separation from Great Britain unthinkable in practical terms. Insisting that Americans were already the envy of the world, Loyalists dreamed of an even brighter future for America that was possible only within the secure confines of the British empire. In *Short Advice to the Counties of New-York* (1774) Isaac Wilkins argued that, united with England, "we may rise superior to the rest of the world, and set all the kingdoms of the earth at defiance. But if by our ungrateful treatment of her, she should be induced to withdraw her protection, and give us over to our own imaginations, nothing but anarchy and confusion must ensue...." In *The True Interest of America Impartially Stated* (1776) Charles Inglis offered the alluring prospect that even a loyal America might not always continue in its colonial status, for "some dreadful convulsion in Great Britain, may transfer the seat of empire to this western hemisphere—where the British constitution, like the Phoenix from its parent's ashes, shall rise with youthful vigour and shine with redoubled splendor." The Revolution put an end to the prospects of an Anglo-American empire, but the idea was persistent. Jonathan Boucher, for example, proposed a new alliance between the two nations in 1797.

In explaining the origins of a revolution they abhorred, Loyalists generally placed the primary responsibility upon a seditious faction, based in New England, which, never intending to reach any accommodation with England, had plotted rebellion from the beginning. Loyalists charged that the conspirators, after successfully corrupting the Continental Congress, implemented their designs with provocative and unlawful edicts enforced—especially upon their enemies—by mob action. Especially ironic to Loyalists was the justification of such conditions in the name of liberty and freedom, as

Joseph Stansbury observes in "The Town Meeting" (1779):

> The Mob tumultuous instant seize
> With venom'd rage on whom they please;
> 　The People cannot err!
> Can it be wrong, in Freedom's cause,
> To tread down justice, order, laws,
> 　When all the mob concur?
>
> 　　　　　　　　　　(*LV*, p. 41)

Samuel Seabury describes the fate of those who, in asserting their British freedom, violate the decrees of Congress: "They shall be considered as Outlaws, unworthy of the protection of civil society, and delivered over to the vengeance of a lawless, outrageous mob, to be *tarred, feathered, hanged, drawn, quartered, and burnt*—O rare American Freedom!"

Loyalists acknowledged with dismay that their cause was weakened not only by their own suppression but also by the effective propaganda of the Whigs and the will of the people to believe it. In his last published pamphlet, Seabury complained that "the most *detestable libels* against the *King*, the *British parliament*, and *Ministry*, have been *eagerly read*, and *extravagantly commended*, as the *matchless productions* of some *heaven-born genius*, glowing with the *pure flame* of civil liberty." *A Letter from a Virginian* (1774), a pamphlet ascribed to Boucher, laments the gullibility of the American reading public: "Hand Bills, News Papers, party Pamphlets, are the shallow and turbid Sources from whence they derive their Notions of Government; these they pronounce as confidently and dogmatically, as if . . . a bold Assertion amounted to a Demonstration." Odell analyzed the extraordinary appeal of *Common Sense* simply: "Bad as it was, it pleas'd; and that's enough." In thus allowing for their loss of public support, Loyalists could only revert in frustration to their essential distrust of public opinion. Independence, Daniel Leonard observed, is more attractive to the popular imagination than the sober virtues of humility and obedience; moreover, "there is a propensity in men to believe themselves injured and oppressed whenever they are told so."

I V

For many Loyalists the greatest evils of the Revolution were the personal hardships forced upon them by exile from their homeland. For some, such experiences only intensified their hostility to the revolutionary regime, and they made their adjustment to a new life abroad with few regrets. Jonathan Sewall claimed that virtually none of the Loyalists refugees in England that he knew—himself included—had any desire to return to America. He wrote to a correspondent in 1783 that, despite missing many of his American Friends, "such are my ideas of the disunion & and the consequent troubles which are yet to come before regular government can be firmly established, and such my abhorrence of the form which must, if any, finally prevail, that, I assure you, if my estate was now to be offered me upon condition of my returning to take possession of it, I would not accept it." Others, however, reveal in their writings a sense of American identity that their loyalty to Britain could not erase. Thomas Hutchinson, former governor of Massachusetts, laments that, though he has enjoyed honors and freedom in England, "absence from home is nevertheless a punishment at my time of life, and the society of old friends at home, is much more desirable than that of my new friends abroad."

The anguish of the American in exile is best seen in the journal and letters of Samuel Curwen, a Loyalist merchant from Salem, Massachusetts, who fled to England in 1775 and lived their eighteen years before his final return home. Following the sketchy and often inaccurate news of the war, Curwen expresses in his journal a growing resentment of the exaggerated accounts of British successes spread by "these conceited islanders" who belittle the American military capabilities. Moreover, "It picques my pride (I confess it) to hear us called *our colonies* and *our plantations*, as if our property and persons were absolutely theirs, like the Villains and their cottages in the old feudal system long since abolished though the spirit or leaven is not totally gone, it seems." He later resolves: "Adieu England as soon as I can, and welcome America as soon as I can with all its faults and follies. Home is home be it ever so homely."

Suffering from poverty and a sense of isolation, Curwen in a letter to Jonathan Sewall in 1777 regrets that he followed "what now appears to me a chimera" and wishes, instead, that he had stayed at home to bear "the comparative trifling condition of insults, reproaches, and perhaps a dress of tar and feathers . . . ." Or better yet, he later suggests, he should have kept his political opinions to himself and thus avoided all retribution.

V

The Loyalists bore the consequences of their commitment to a losing cause. After the war their writings were to appear as only a last vestige of the colonial mentality in America. Yet if their devotion to the British monarchy was out of place in the new republic, their basic conservatism was not. While the Loyalists exerted no direct influence upon the times succeeding the Revolution, they provided a precedent for future watchdogs of public order. Once

American independence was accomplished, many of its supporters regrouped into a conservative position much like that of their old Loyalist adversaries. By the end of the century such former revolutionaries as George Washington, John Adams, and Alexander Hamilton, in their efforts to stabilize a shaky national government, revealed a temperament akin to the Loyalists in their reactions to such threats to public order as the Whiskey Rebellion and the seditious activities of the Democratic Societies. Literary productions of this period, including *The Anarchiad* and many other satires of the Connecticut Wits, condemn the rampant mobocracy and demagoguery in American politics much on the order of the earlier jeremiads of Seabury, Odell, and Stansbury. Federalists pamphlets and newspapers denounce the democratic excesses of those, notably Thomas Jefferson, Philip Freneau, and Thomas Paine, whose writings a few years earlier had spurred on the Revolution.

Despite the development of a conservative tradition in American politics, the Loyalists were treated with suspicion and neglect long after their own lifetimes. Consequently, studies of their literature proceeded slowly and lagged far behind those of other aspects of the revolutionary period. An unprecedented outpouring of books and articles in recent years has considerably changed that situation, however, and the study of Loyalism is flourishing. An international Program for Loyalist Studies and Publications is now helping to advance the accessibility of Loyalist materials. Thus, the way seems clear in the future for a better understanding of the Loyalists and their share in the American experience.

SUGGESTIONS FOR FURTHER READING

Editions

Anonymous. "The Battle of Brooklyn," In *Trumpets Sounding*. Edited by Norman Philbrick. New York: Benjamin Blom, 1972.

Boucher, Jonathan. *Reminiscences of an American Loyalist*. Edited by Jonathan Bouchier. Port Washington, N.Y.: Kennikat Press, 1967.

———. *A View of the Causes and Consequences of the American Revolution*. New York: Russell and Russell, 1967.

Curwen, Samuel. *Journal and Letters of the Late Samuel Curwen*. New York: C. S. Francis, 1842.

———. *The Journal of Samuel Curwen Loyalist*. Edited by Andrew Oliver. 2 vols. Cambridge, Mass.: Harvard University Press, 1972.

The Loyalist Poetry of the Revolution. Edited by Winthrop Sargent. Philadelphia: [Collins], 1857. Reprinted, Boston: Milford House, 1972.

The Loyal Verses of Joseph Stansbury and Doctor Jonathan Odell. Edited by Winthrop
Sargent. Albany, N.Y.: J. Munsell, 1860.
The Price of Loyalty: Tory Writings from the Revolutionary Era. Edited by Catherine
S. Crary. New York: McGraw-Hill, 1973.
Seabury, Samuel. *Letters of a Westchester Farmer 1774–1775*. Edited by Clarence H.
Vance. White Plains, N.Y.: Westchester County Historical Society, 1930. Re-
printed, New York: Da Capo Press, 1970.

Scholarship and Criticism

Bailyn, Bernard. *The Ideological Origins of the American Revolution*. Cambridge,
Mass.: Belknap Press of Harvard University Press, 1967.
Calhoon, Robert McCluer. *The Loyalists in Revolutionary America 1760–1781*. New
York: Harcourt Brace Jovanovich, 1973.
Davidson, Philip. *Propaganda and the American Revolution 1763–1783*. Chapel Hill:
University of North Carolina Press, 1941.
Nelson, William. *The American Tory*. Oxford: Oxford University Press, 1961. Re-
printed, Boston: Beacon Press, 1968.
Norton, Mary Beth. *The British-Americans: The Loyalist Exiles in England 1774–
1789*. Boston: Little, Brown, 1972.

5

The Preachers

ROBERT M. BENTON

[*Some of the most articulate Loyalists were preachers, but there were patriot preachers as well, and their role was perhaps as important as that of the patriot pamphleteers. The distinction between the two can, however, be overstated, since sermons frequently were published as propaganda pamphlets. Most sermons are of course ephemeral, but sermons by outstanding clergymen were printed and thereby gained a wide audience and achieved something like permanence. The topic of the role of the pulpit in the Revolution is too large to be examined thoroughly here. The following chapter provides an overview, with special attention given to a few particularly significant preachers.*]

Most modern readers must exercise their historical imaginations to think of sermons as literature. The effort will be less great, however, if one remembers that such major writers as John Donne and Jeremy Taylor were preachers whose sermons are among the valued works they left behind. Donne's and Taylor's contemporaries in America also included some great preachers, and the extant sermons of Thomas Hooker and Thomas Shepard have been accorded a permanent place in American literature. In the days of the American Revolution the sermon continued to be valued both because it offered moral and religious guidance and also because it was a traditional form of eloquence. As men of influence in their communities, ministers inevitably played an important role in the preparation of the people for revolution. The best of their sermons have secured and maintained a significant place in the American literary inheritance.

Americans were accustomed to ministers who exerted influence in the political arena. During the Seven Years' War such clergymen as Samuel Davies, leader of the Virginia Presbyterians, and Gilbert Tennent, active in the middle colonies, had preached patriotic sermons intended to continue the religious fervor of the revivals of the 1740s. In the process they gave an increasingly political orientation to the pulpit. Farther north, ninety-eight pre-1775 election day sermons survive from Massachusetts; they reveal how religious and secular concerns were combined there. In addition to sermons such as these, officially designated thanksgiving and fast day sermons were delivered and published, and secular occasions, such as the repeal of the Stamp Act, were accompanied by sermons later published as pamphlets.

I

More than any other single group of documents, the election day sermons reveal the meaning of the Revolution for the colonists. The titles often give an indication of the political stance of the clergymen: in 1764 Stephen White called his sermon *Civil Rulers Gods by Office*, and in the following year Edward Dorr explicated *The Duty of Civil Rulers*. In 1766, the year of the repeal of the Stamp Act, discourses were published revealing the joy of the ministers for what they considered a British reprieve: Nathaniel Appleton titled his *A Thanksgiving Sermon on the Total Repeal of the Stamp Act*, and Samuel Stillman proclaimed *Good News From a Far Country*. As the years passed and the controversy became more heated, sermon titles became increasingly inflammatory, with Jonas Clark's *The Fate of Blood-Thirsty Oppressors* (1776) a typical example. Also noteworthy is the frequent title-page description of a sermon as one delivered "At the Freemen's Meeting."

What caused the New England clergy, especially the Calvinists, to become increasingly militant in the political arena was the Great Awakening, the religious revival that had swept the country some thirty-five years earlier. The Awakening was a general American phenomenon, as the work of George Whitefield, who journeyed up and down the colonies preaching from New England to Georgia, indicates. As a result, Americans became more aware of their membership in a community larger than New England, or Pennsylvania, or Virginia. They were Americans in the New World, where spiritual values might flourish, as they did not in the Old, then perceived as suffering a religious decline. Joseph Perry proclaimed in 1775 before the Connecticut General Assembly, "By the best accounts, we are assured, that in England, at this day, prevails a most awful prostration of all public, social virtue, and the peculiar graces of Christianity, and a fearful prevalence of all kinds of immorality, neglect of GOD, contempt of sacred things, and the vilest abuse of divine mercy and patience;—a growing debauchery, dissipation and veniality." A prominent belief of the advocates of the Awakening was that the millennium would begin in America, and it was thought that Americans were

already achieving the social goals the Awakening promised. The liberal or
Arminian clergy who opposed the Awakening also prepared the way for the
Revolution; they increasingly expounded the ideas of the social contract and
natural law in such a manner as to encourage popular political activity.

Some historians believe that the evangelical clergy played the primary role
in the development of American political thought during the years of prerevolutionary debate. It is true that ministers were indeed very influential, and the
Calvinists or religious conservatives were definitely more instrumental in the
cause of American liberty than were the Liberals because Calvinist political
philosophy urged action as well as thought. Although the Liberals encouraged
the intellectual acceptance of the American rights to freedom and independence, it was the Calvinists who attempted to inspire the colonists to fight for
those rights.

It was a Calvinist, David Jones of Philadelphia, who declared in 1775,
"We have no choice left to us, but to submit to absolute slavery and despotism, or as free-men to stand in our own defence, and endeavor a noble
resistance. Matters are at last brought to this deplorable extremity;—every
reasonable method of reconciliation has been tried in vain;—our addresses to
our king have been treated with neglect or contempt.'' In his sermon Jones
demonstrated the typical Calvinistic stance: "Come then, my countrymen, we
have no other remedy, but under GOD, to fight for our brethren, our sons and
our daughters, our wives and our houses.''

It was a supporter of the Awakening, the Calvinist John Cleaveland of
Ipswich, Massachusetts, who declared after the battles of Concord and
Lexington, "Great Britain, Adieu! No longer shall we honor you as our
mother; you are become cruel; you have not such bowels as the sea monsters
towards their young . . . King George III, adieu!'' The Calvinists saw America
as a land where God's purposes could be realized, if British rule, strongly
identified with luxury and corruption, could be thrown off. Eventually, as
Alan Heimert has noted, "whole Calvinist congregations, often in response to
a single sermon, followed their preachers into battle.''

The role of the Liberal clergy, important but in the long run limited, can be
seen in the work of the leading spokesman, the Reverend Jonathan Mayhew.
A product of the Great Awakening who became its most effective antagonist,
Mayhew is often characterized as America's leader in civil and religious
liberty and the foremost pioneer of liberal Christianity. From the beginning a
controversial figure, Mayhew had become an Arminian by the time of his
ordination and acceptance of the call of the West Church in Boston. In one of
his early published sermons, *A Discourse Concerning Unlimited Submission
and Non-Resistance to the Higher Powers* (1750), Mayhew delivers the most
thoroughgoing defense of the right of revolution made before the Declaration
of Independence. In it he asserts that "A people, really oppressed in a great

degree by their sovereign, cannot well be insensible when they are so oppressed; and such a people—if I may allude to an ancient fable—have, like the
hesperian fruit, a dragon for their protector and guardian.'' In this sermon,
preached on the anniversary of the death of Charles I, Mayhew urges his
auditory to be free and loyal, but in his justification of previous English
revolutions and his utilization of history as if it had the authority of Scripture,
Mayhew clearly articulated those principles basic to American revolutionary
activity.

In sermon after sermon Mayhew quotes biblical authority to support the
principle of the social contract. In his 1754 election day sermon Mayhew cites
Romans 13:4 to show that the civil magistrate ''is the minister of God to us for
good,'' and he suggests a concept of government consistent with divine ordinance: ''It being founded in, and supported by, common consent, it is impossible the design of it should be any other, since we cannot suppose that men
would voluntarily enter into society and set up and maintain a common authority upon any other principles than those of mutual security and common
good.''

The English liberal tradition of Locke and others contributed significantly
to such systematic defenses of freedom as these of Mayhew. Another factor
was the general suspicion in the colonies that there was a British conspiracy of
power against liberty and that the Church of England was acting as an arm of
the crown to force conformity. The Church of England's Society for the
Propagation of the Gospel in Foreign Parts (SPG), an arm of the church
explicitly designed to promote the conversion of Indian Americans and
blacks, was considered by many colonists to have as one of its goals the
rooting out of Presbyterianism and the establishment of the episcopacy in
America. Nothing could have done more to bring Presbyterians to the side of
the Revolution than the fear that the SPG was determined to destroy their
power and influence in the colonies. These fears, as well as those of other
clergymen like Mayhew, were realized when the SPG established a mission in
Cambridge, Massachusetts. Since there were no Indians in Cambridge, but
many orthodox clergymen, Mayhew and the majority of Congregational and
Presbyterian ministers knew that the threat was real.

In 1763 Mayhew attacked the SPG in *Observations on the Charter and
Conduct of the Society for the Propagation of the Gospel*, accusing it of
violating its charter by directing its efforts toward development of the Church
of England in areas where other churches were well established. Mayhew also
accused the Anglican hierarchy of sympathy toward Catholicism, a charge
which ensured Mayhew of Presbyterian support. Once he had taken up the
banner, Mayhew could not be restrained. Asked to deliver Harvard's Dud-
leian Lecture in 1765, Mayhew gave a discourse titled *Popish Idolatry*, in
which he continued the assault he had started in *Observations*. His attack upon

the SPG did not go unchallenged. East Apthorp, the Anglican clergyman in charge of the SPG's Cambridge mission, attempted to refute the *Observations*, but he was no match for the clever Mayhew. The most significant result of the Mayhew-Apthorp controversy, however, was not the resolution of the basic issue. It was the domination of the controversy by a viewpoint in which religious and secular life were inextricably united.

The Great Awakening had created a growing challenge to established churches—Congregational as well as Anglican. But with the Mayhew-Apthorp controversy, a movement began that would eventually result in the disestablishment of religion in the United States, for the church leaders who joined Mayhew in his attack upon the established Church of England soon found their own arguments being used against them by dissenters in their midst. The Mayhew controversy had merged with the revenue question, and dissenters suggested that English taxation was no more unjust than a tax on dissenters to support established churches. Thus the opposition of Liberals and Calvinists to the Anglican Church and English taxation contributed toward the erosion of the power they had enjoyed for a century and a half.

Jonathan Mayhew's 1763 decision to attack the SPG was not one he made lightly, and he assumed responsibility for it. Committed to the concept of freedom for the colonists, Mayhew preached in August 1765 a sermon on the text Galations 5:12–13: "I would that they were even cut off which trouble you. For, brethren, ye have been called unto liberty; only use not liberty for an occasion to the flesh, but by love serve one another." The sermon, filled with Lockean rhetoric, must have impressed his auditory more with the necessity for overt action than did his call for caution against unbridled liberty. The following day a mob attacked the homes of customs officials and destroyed records, much to Mayhew's sorrow.

In May 1766, shortly before his early death, Mayhew preached his most famous sermon, a thanksgiving mediation upon the repeal of the Stamp Act, delivered at the request of his congregation. *The Snare Broken* extols liberty in language so specific and charged that it has become the prime example of the Liberal position. Explaining that the doctrines of civil liberty articulated by Locke and others had seemed to him "rational," Mayhew expresses his great joy in discovering that they are also scriptural. His "passion" for liberty then produces his most celebrated paean of praise: "Once more then, hail! celestial maid, the daughter of God, and, excepting his Son, the first-born of heaven! Welcome to these shores again; welcome to every expanding heart! Long mayest thou reside among us, the delight of the wise, good and brave; the protectress of innocent from wrongs and oppression, the patroness of learning, arts, eloquence, virtue, rational loyalty, religion." This passage, so like Crèvecoeur's "Welcome to my shores, distressed European" from his celebrated essay "What Is an American?," reflects the growing tendency of the colonists to visualize the Grand American Experiment as a beacon to the world.

Although Mayhew's brilliant career was virtually over by the time he had delivered *The Snare Broken*, the effect of his work is an accurate barometer of the importance of the pulpit in the Revolution. When Mayhew praised liberty, he did so in the belief that finally liberty had been granted the colonists, and he was not alone. In sermon after sermon preached in 1766, Liberals praised themselves for their success and, in effect, retreated. The predominant purpose of their Stamp Act sermons was to urge Americans to return to law and duty as citizens of the British Empire; consequently, the Liberals found themselves in the position of attempting to preserve the status quo rather than to lead away from it.

Similar to Mayhew's Stamp Act sermon was one by his Liberal colleague Charles Chauncy, the pastor of the First Church in Boston, whose noted 1766 sermon was titled *A Discourse on "The Good News from a Far Country."* As a first article in Chauncy's good news, he praised "the kind and righteous regard the supreme authority in England, to which we inviolably owe submission, has paid to the 'commercial good' of the nation at home, and its dependent provinces and islands." He expressed sublime confidence that all grievances would be redressed, and he celebrated the joy of the colonists who were under a king and Parliament "who can repeal as well as enact a law, upon a view of it as tending to the public happiness."

Chauncy's enthusiasm could not be restrained. He likens the repeal of the Stamp Act to the Jews' deliverance from bondage in Egypt, and he asserts that "it has made way for the return of our love, in all its genuine exercises, towards those on the other side of the Atlantic who, in common with ourselves, profess subjection to the same most gracious sovereign. The affectionate regard of the American inhabitants for their mother country was never exceeded by any colonists in any part or age of the world." Chauncy therefore urges each colonist to be content with his condition and mind his own business so as not to "prove ourselves a factious, turbulent people." The substance of this discourse, echoed by other Liberal clergy, was to identify political non-partisanship with Christian virtue.

A subtle difference in response to the repeal of the Stamp Act can be seen in public utterances of Calvinistic clergy. In a pastoral letter of May 30, 1766, Elihu Spencer, then moderator of the Presbyterian Church, also urges church members to give thanks for the repeal of the act. He calls upon them to honor the king and, while they enjoy their liberty, "not be the servants of sin and Satan." For Spencer, however, it was God who had brought the punishment, and it was He who effected the deliverance. Consequently, the colonists' allegiance is primarily to God and not to England.

In his letter Spencer utilized the jeremiad, a traditional Puritan sermon form, through which he could suggest that punishment was the result of sin and that only sincere repentance would remove affliction. As Liberal clergy began to employ the jeremiad, they did so to equate political agitation with man's disobedience of God's commands. Mayhew, Chauncy, and their colleagues expressed gratitude for the kindness of the king and Parliament to the colonies and suggested that virtue was to be found in submission. Such a stance did not long remain popular with zealous Americans who witnessed growing British tyranny.

The conservatives continued to be much more effective in employing the jeremiad. For example, in his 1775 election day sermon, Samuel Langdon, then the president of Harvard, proclaimed that it was the sins of Americans that had brought Divine judgment upon them, and he made a general call for repentance: "Would not a reverend regard to the authority of divine revelation, a hearty belief of the gospel of the grace of God, and a general reformation of all those vices which bring misery and ruin upon individuals, families, and kingdoms, and which have provoked Heaven to bring the nation into such perplexed and dangerous circumstances, be the surest way to recover the sinking state, and make it again rich and flourishing?" Here he is specifically concerned with the country's profanity, unchastity, and avarice.

Langdon does not suggest that repentance would manifest itself in conformity to British laws, nor does he urge reformation in the hope that it might turn away British wrath. He proclaims religious revival as the only sure course toward victory: "If true religion is revived . . . we may hope for the direction and blessing of the Most High, while we are using our best endeavors to preserve and restore the civil government of this colony, and defend America from slavery." He calls British tyranny "the vilest slavery, and worse than death," and he praises God who "has given us, as men, natural rights, independent on all human laws whatever," rights which support the colonies' attempt to "form themselves into a civil society, according to their best prudence, and so provide for their common safety and advantage." He specifically grants to the majority by common consent the right to end one government and set up another in its place, using language so similar to that of the Declaration of Independence that one might believe Jefferson had written the sermon.

Here Langdon, like other Calvinists, utilized the terminology of covenant theology, generously supplemented with natural rights political theory, to explain British tyranny. Influenced as they were by the Great Awakening, wherein they saw God pouring out his spirit on America, Calvinists saw the American Revolution as the beginning of the millennium. For Langdon only true repentance was lacking. With it, victory would be assured:

> Then the Lord will be our refuge and strength, a very present help in trouble,
> and we shall have no reason to be afraid though thousands of enemies set

themselves against us round about,—though all nature should be thrown into tumults and convulsions. He can command the stars in their courses to fight his battles, and all the elements to wage war with his enemies. He can work salvation for us, as He did for His people in ancient days . . . .[1]

In the hands of Calvinists the jeremiad was not a tool to subdue unruly passions but a sword to lead in a holy war.

II

Although most clergymen supported the movement toward independence, many Anglican clergymen remained loyal to the English crown. Probably the most eminent was the Reverend Jonathan Boucher of Annapolis (discussed in the chapter on Loyalist writings). Less resolute was another Anglican, the eloquent preacher Jacob Duché, who was born and educated in the colonies. The rector of Christ Church, Philadelphia, he wrote *Observations on a Variety of Subjects* (1774), wherein through his spokesman, the young Englishman Tamoc Caspipina, he describes America pleasantly and with considerable hope for its cultural future, if without any penetrating analysis. In 1775 he preached an impassioned sermon on *The Duty of Standing Fast in Our Spiritual and Temporal Liberties*, and largely as a consequence he was named in 1776 chaplain to the Continental Congress. A man of refinement, one of America's finest orators, he seemed in all respects single-minded in his support of the colonies and in his opposition to the British cause. He gave dignity to the revolutionaries, and he was greatly admired by both John and Samuel Adams. Following the British victories in the New York area, however, Duché made an about-face and wrote George Washington to urge him to resign his command and force the Congress to rescind the Declaration of Independence. Perhaps Duché believed that such an action would enhance his and the colonies' chances for survival. In 1777 he left America for England.

The non-Anglican clergy were less prone to dramatic reversals. A chief spokesman and defender of the dissenting groups against "Episcopal oppression" was John Joachim Zubly, who in 1760 had become pastor of the Independent Presbyterian Church in Savannah, Georgia. As a member of the Continental Congress Zubly kept the colonists in Georgia apprised of the political ideas current in the more populous northern settlements. Because he feared the establishment of a republic, Zubly could not support the growing demand for independence. In a 1775 sermon, *The Law of Liberty*, Zubly proposed methods of opposition to oppressive acts that might lead to war.

1. *The Pulpit of the American Revolution*, ed. John Wingate Thornton, p. 257.

Preached at the beginning of the Provincial Congress of Georgia, Zubly's sermon begins on a cautionary note: "It is easy to extinguish a spark; it is folly to blow up discontent into a blaze; the beginning of strife is like the letting out of waters, and no man may know where it will end."

Zubly clearly expressed his opposition to independence while sustaining a tone of moderation:

> Never let us lose out of sight that our interest lies in a perpetual connection with our mother country . . . let us convince our enemies that the struggles of America have not their rise in a desire of independency, but from a warm regard to our common constitution, that we esteem the name of Britons, as being the same with freemen; let every step we take afford proof how greatly we esteem our mother country, and that, to the wise of a perpetual connection, we prefer this only consideration, that we may be virtuous and free.[2]

For maintaining such a position, Zubly was denounced and banished from Georgia. Although he returned and resumed his pastoral work in 1779 when royal government had been reestablished, he had lost all political influence.

Also in the Presbyterian-Reformed tradition, but unlike Zubly in conviction, was Dr. John Witherspoon. Born in Scotland, Witherspoon crossed the Atlantic to become president of the College of New Jersey (Princeton) in 1768, and although he had opposed the participation of the clergy in politics, he soon became a leader in what some would call this "Scotch-Irish Presbyterian rebellion." By 1775 he was proclaiming the necessity of maintaining the union of the colonies, and in 1776, one month after delivering a sermon on a congressionally appointed fast day, he was chosen a delegate to the Continental Congress. Although Witherspoon was not known for his eloquence, his fast day sermon was a powerful presentation of *The Dominion of Providence over the Passions of Men*. In part it was designed to show how British oppression would eventually be used by God to promote his glory. In this widely read sermon, Witherspoon proclaims, "If your cause is just,—if your principles are pure,—and if your conduct is prudent, you need not fear the multitude of opposing hosts." He notes that this is the first time he has introduced any political subject into the pulpit, but he asserts that "it is not only lawful but necessary, and I willingly embrace the opportunity of declaring my opinion without any hesitation, that the cause in which America is now in arms, is the cause of justice, of liberty, and of human nature." Witherspoon ended his sermon with a supplication: "God grant that in America true religion and civil liberty may be inseparable, and that the unjust attempts to destroy the one, may in the issue tend to the support and establishment of both." Although he had entered the political arena with great hesitancy, once involved he was committed to the justice of the cause and urged the Congress

2. *The Patriot Preachers of the American Revolution*, ed. Frank Moore, p. 138.

to adopt the Declaration of Independence. Witherspoon was the only clergyman to sign that document. In addition to his sermons, Witherspoon wrote
many patriotic pieces for magazines and newspapers, and he was a strong
supporter of the Articles of Confederation.

Another preacher advocating the revolutionary cause was Hugh Henry
Brackenridge, who in 1777 joined the American troops in the field as an army
chaplain. In "The Bloody Vestiges of Tyranny" Brackenridge directly ac-
cuses the king of England of having determined "with himself, to drench with
slaughter, and imbrue the continent in blood." In his depiction of the Boston
Massacre of 1770 Brackenridge describes the streets as running with blood
that cries for vengeance, like the blood of Abel crying from the hostile
ground. Drawing historical and biblical parallels to American efforts, Brackenridge encourages all classes of men "to execrate the tyrant and the
tyranny; and to rank the George of England with the Cains, and the murders of
Mankind." After asserting the degenerate name and nature of Englishmen,
Brackenridge proclaims the Revolution to be a holy war in which "Duty,
honour, and the love of virtue calls to battle."

III

Not only did the pulpit play an important role in the Revolution; the Revolution played a vital role in the history of the ministry in America. The more
involved the country became in legal discussions relating to the constitution of
the emerging new nation, the less significant was the role of the clergy in
shaping opinion. The issue of slavery produced profound disagreement within
the ministerial ranks, especially in Virginia where Calvinists openly questioned the concept that all men were born free. As dissension and disestablishment grew, religious unity became more fragmented. Among those religious groups maintaining a pacifist stance, dissension was common. While
the "Fighting Quakers" renounced the religious ideal of nonviolence in favor
of patriotism, the main body of the Society of Friends adhered to the principle
and suffered severe persecution. The Baptists claimed to be pacifists, but they
vigorously espoused the cause of freedom and took up arms under their own
officers.

Many denominations with strong religious affiliations to England or Europe
found themselves compromised, especially the Methodists, who many colonists assumed were unpatriotic, since in 1775 John Wesley urged the colonists to lay down their arms and support England. Lutherans took no official position, while the Dutch and German Reformed churches vacillated.
Many groups were too small to exert influence and were either bewildered by

the conflict or simply let their individual members make their own decisions. The struggle for independence did not bring to the colonies a wave of religious enthusiasm. Despite the Calvinists' effective utilization of the jeremiad, the Revolution remained a battle fought to sever a political bond. Although a second "awakening" occurred in the early 1800s, the war did not make the colonists more religious. The postwar years were truly an "Age of Reason."

Three election day sermons preached in the decade following the Declaration of Independence deserve special note because of what they reveal of the function of the pulpit then. In a 1778 sermon Phillips Payson celebrates the future glory of America. He calls the American colonists "God's chosen," and he wishes that "the whole world may learn the worth of liberty." In a 1780 sermon Simeon Howard, Mayhew's successor at the West Church, Boston, urges continued support for the American cause which he deems "so just in the sight of God and man, which Heaven has so remarkably owned, and all wise and good men approved,—a cause which not only directly involves in it the rights and liberties of America, but in which the happiness of mankind is so nearly concerned,—for in this extensive light I have always considered the cause in which we are contending." In like manner President Ezra Stiles of Yale in 1783 sees the effects of the Revolution as being instrumental in "the liberties of the world itself." Stiles characterizes Americans as missionaries to the world: "And thus the American Republic, by illuminating the world with truth and liberty, would be exalted and made high among the nations, in praise, and in name, and in honor. I doubt not this is the honor reserved for us; I had almost said, in the spirit of prophecy, the zeal of the Lord of Hosts will accomplish this."

These three sermons suggest the role of the pulpit following the Declaration. Americans were characterized as a special people, chosen by God for a unique mission to the world. More than a group of colonists striving for political independence, Americans were told they were divinely ordained ambassadors called to usher in a new era in world history. Thus the idea of a covenant between God and his people underwent a transformation as a result of the Revolution. The traditional concept of New England's covenant with God grew weaker and was replaced by the new sense of national mission which the country felt in the nineteenth century, a concept which remains crucial in America's twentieth-century foreign policy.

The pulpit, so dominant in the early years of American colonization, lost its position as a result of the Revolution. Most denominations found themselves faced with the necessity of reorganization and the formulation of new identities. The Church of England in America became the Protestant Episcopal Church in the United States. The Methodist Episcopal Church was organized following the Revolution, and the Congregationalists found that a lack of strong unity inhibited their continued growth. Although the Presbyterians seemed most in accord with the spirit of the times, old theological disagreements and the debate over slavery created a disharmony which persists to the present time.

Fragmentation in religion was not the only result of the Revolution. As the impact of science and the concepts of natural law permeated political and social thought, so did they influence religious thought. The doctrine of universal salvation and departures from the old Calvinism led to the development of Unitarian and Universalist churches. The man of the Revolution could no longer believe himself to be the utterly helpless, thoroughly contemptible creature the Calvinists had proclaimed him to be. He saw himself as a rational human being, capable of choosing between good and evil, and directing his own destiny.

The major contribution of the pulpit to the Revolution occurred in the years of prerevolutionary debate when Liberals and Calvinists alike helped Americans formulate and articulate a basic political philosophy with their sermons, many of substantial literary merit. Doctrinal disputes and growing religious disunity, however, inhibited the power of the pulpit once the Revolution began. The disestablishment of religion and the acceptance of the principles of religious toleration eventually resulted in the First Amendment to the Constitution, which proclaims that Congress ''shall make no law respecting the establishment of religion, or prohibit the free exercise thereof.'' The amendment made certain that the pulpit would never reclaim its former power. Thus, while the pulpit was primarily responsible for the erosion of its own power, it helped sever the chains that could bind men's minds and granted to them the freedom that has continuously characterized the American spirit.

SUGGESTIONS FOR FURTHER READING

Editions

American Bibliography. Edited by Charles Evans and others. 14 vols. New York: Peter Smith, 1941. [The full text of all Evans entries which are extant may be found in the Readex Microprint Corporation's *Early American Imprints*.]

The Patriot Preachers of the American Revolution. Edited by Frank Moore. New York: Charles T. Evans, 1862.

The Pulpit of the American Revolution. Edited by John Wingate Thornton. Boston: Gould and Lincoln, 1860.

Religion and the Coming of the American Revolution. Edited by Peter N. Carroll. Waltham, Mass.: Ginn-Blaisdell, 1970.

The Wall And The Garden. Edited by A. W. Plumstead. Minneapolis: University of Minnesota Press, 1968.

Scholarship and Criticism

Akers, Charles W. *Called Unto Liberty: A Life of Jonathan Mayhew 1720–1766.* Cambridge, Mass.: Harvard University Press, 1964.

Bailyn, Bernard. *The Ideological Origins of the American Revolution.* Cambridge, Mass.: Harvard University Press, 1967.

Bridenbaugh, Carl. *Mitre and Sceptre: Transatlantic Faiths, Ideas, Personalities, and Politics, 1689–1775.* New York: Oxford, 1962.

Heimert, Alan. *Religion and the American Mind.* Cambridge, Mass.: Harvard University Press, 1966.

Joyce, Lester Douglas. *Church and Clergy in the American Revolution: A Study in Group Behavior.* New York: Exposition Press, 1966.

Morgan, Edmund S., ed. *Puritan Political Ideas: 1558–1794.* New York: The Bobbs-Merrill Company, 1965.

Wood, Gordon S. *The Creation of the American Republic 1776–1787.* Chapel Hill: The University of North Carolina Press, 1969.

6

The Theater and Drama

CALHOUN WINTON

*[Pamphlets and sermons were not the only forms used to argue the patriots'
and Loyalists' cases. Drama and theater were used as well. Since it requires
a cultural context with special characteristics, the theater was slow in establishing itself in America. In New England it was regarded as corrupting, and
in other areas population patterns and the lack of urban centers delayed its
development. During the revolutionary years theater and original American
drama grew substantially in popularity, despite (and to some extent because
of) the war.]*

Of all the literary arts that of the theater—with its need for a suitable stage and
properties, a group of actors, and an audience—would seem to be the most
fragile in an age employed to quote Freneau, "in edging steel." Most especially would this be true, or so one would think, of the American colonies,
because the theater is by its very nature city- or town-oriented and the colonies
were still predominantly rural in 1776. In terms of financial support, furthermore, the theater had experienced a number of lean years as well as a few
fat ones in the English-speaking colonies before the Revolution, and the
American stage would only just have been on the way to reasonable health if
there had been no Lexington or Concord.

And yet the interesting fact remains that, with every influence against them,
the theater and dramatic literature retained a place in the imagination of many
and occupied some of the time of a few during the war. Nathan Hale echoed
Addison's Cato on the scaffold, Gentleman Johnny Burgoyne's farce *The
Blockade* was acted in occupied Boston, and Hugh Henry Brackenridge wrote
a play about the Battle of Bunker Hill for production by his students at
Somerset Academy in Maryland. A sprinkling of plays and dramatic sketches
was written, some others were produced. On occasion, the dramatic medium
was used as a forum for debate on the questions of the hour. The drama did

not die. By the 1780s and with the war behind them, at least two young men, William Dunlap and Royall Tyler, buoyed up by successful runs of *The Father* and *The Contrast*, could think seriously of careers as dramatic authors, Americans writing for American audiences.

I

The American stage had preceded the creation of original dramatic literature. Although there had been and would continue to be a residue of hostility toward the theater in many places and among different segments of American society, by the early 1760s support was forthcoming for theatrical seasons in New York, in Baltimore, in Philadelphia and Annapolis, in Williamsburg and Charleston, and in the British West Indies. Touring companies, notably that of David Douglass, were finding audiences for the staples of the London repertory theaters, audiences which felt they were reclaiming or renewing their own literary heritage. Years later one of Douglass's actors recalled lines from the prologue written for the opening of the first play in their first season, at Williamsburg:

> To this New World, from famed Brittania's shore,
> Through boist'rous seas where foaming billows roar,
> The Muse, who Britons charm'd for many an age
> Now sends her servants forth to tread your stage.[1]

The Muse is making restitution, as it were, for having overlooked the colonies. Significantly for the future of the American theater, an enthusiastic patron of those early seasons in Williamsburg was the young Tidewater planter, George Washington. All his life Washington was an intense stage buff. If a theater was open he would go, taking a party when he could, attending alone if he must. When he lent his immense prestige to the cause of drama after the Revolution it was a gesture of incalculable value.

The company with which Douglass toured in the 1760s and early 1770s was apparently a competent professional group, drawn largely from the London and Dublin stage. Their repertory as they traveled up and down the coast was the repertory of those stages, insofar as it could be adapted to their small company, and certainly the audiences were willing to pay stiff prices for the privilege of seeing Susannah Centlivre's *The Busybody* or George Farquhar's *The Recruiting Officer*. Washington spent five pounds and twelve shillings on tickets in one month of the 1772 Williamsburg season. The Anglican rector of

---

1. William Dunlap, *History of the American Theatre* (London: Richard Bentley, 1833), p. 17.

Annapolis, Jonathan Boucher, pronounced his favorable judgment flatly: "The Merit of Mr. Douglass's Company is, notoriously, in the Opinion of every Man of Sense in *America*, whose Opportunities give him a Title to judge—*take them for all in all*—superior to that of any Company in *England*, except those of the Metropolis."

Knowing very well, however, that "the drama's laws the drama's patrons give," Douglass and his group became adept at taking on the protective coloration of their environment, in 1763 adopting as their name "the American Company of Comedians." This was a compliment to the colonists, who were beginning to think and speak of themselves as Americans, and also an echo for the knowing of the title of London's Drury Lane actors, the Royal Company of Comedians. In 1767 Douglass provided for the professional debut in Philadelphia of young Samuel Greville, a stagestruck Princetonian who later recovered and returned to practice medicine in his hometown of Charleston, South Carolina. He was the first native-born professional actor. In that same year the resourceful company arranged for a performance in honor of Chief Attakullakulla (Little Carpenter) and his fellow Cherokee leaders at the John Street theater in New York. These genuine native Americans, on their way from Carolina to Albany to negotiate a treaty with the Iroquois, were regaled with the company's version of *Richard III*. Heading for home the following April the braves requested another evening at the theater, offering to perform a war dance on stage as recompense. This was somewhat alarming even for Douglass, relations between the races being what they were, but after warning his audience not "to forget the proper Decorum so essential to all public Assemblies" the event went off without a hitch.

Indians had provided the inspiration for a literary curiosity by one of the most bizarre characters thrown up by the turbulence of the frontier wars. Robert Rogers's play *Ponteach* (that is, Pontiac) was allegedly drawn from his experiences in the so-called conspiracy led by that chief. Historians nowadays view with the utmost skepticism the historicity of Rogers's account of his dealings with Pontiac, as he set it forth in *A Concise Account of North America* (1765) published the year before the play. The *Concise Account* was of course influential on Francis Parkman's portrait of the Indian leader in *The Conspiracy of Pontiac*. Certainly Rogers derived little or nothing from history in *Ponteach* (1766) beyond the name of the central character, but it is an interesting dramatic piece nonetheless, charged with considerable vehemence. Its genre is that of the eighteenth-century Roman play: Dryden's *All for Love*, Nathaniel Lee's *Lucius Junius Brutus*, Addison's *Cato*. Within those terms it is not at all a contemptible work. Pontiac, to use the familiar spelling, is possessed of the Roman virtues as the eighteenth century saw them: magnanimity, generosity, love of country and of liberty. He is encompassed by chicanery and treachery on every side, but of the three groups of peoples involved, the British, the French, and the Indians, certainly the Indians come off best. The British and French are exploiters, neither pure nor simple, whereas the Indians are, when they are not quarreling among themselves, defending their land and families.

In a sort of ascending order of villainy are the English hunters Honnyman and Orsbourn, who at least are good hunters; McDole and Murphey, traders who use rum as bait in cozening the Indians; Colonel Cockum and his subordinate Captain Frisk, leaders of His Britannic Majesty's garrison, who agree that dead Indians are good Indians; and the infamous British envoys from the king to the Indians, Sharp, Gripe, and Catchum, who are engaged in defrauding everyone, including their own government. The French are represented by a priest, lecherous and disingenuous, a standard property in Enlightenment anticlericalism, but Pontiac observes that though the French are bad they deal honestly whereas the British

> Are false, deceitful, knavish, insolent;
> Nay think us conquered, and our Country theirs,
> Without a Purchase, or ev'n asking for it.
>
> (p. 33[2])

At the Indians' council Pontiac ends a stirring speech with

> Rouse, then, ye Sons of antient Heroes, rouse,
> Put on your Arms, and let us act a Part
> Worthy the Sons of such renowned Chiefs.
>
> (p. 57)

It will be observed that Pontiac habitually speaks in stately English blank verse. The Indian warriors end the conclave with a war song in tetrameter couplets to the tune of "Over the Hills and Far Away." The conspiracy begins promisingly but fails when one of Pontiac's sons betrays the cause and his allies withdraw. In the closing scene Pontiac vows to "wait a Respite from this Storm of Woe;" "*Ponteach* I am, shall be *Ponteach* still."

The play was never produced and the script found its way into print at the author's expense. It is odd that Rogers, born in New Hampshire, should have been disappointed at his neglect by the ministry in London. The play is, after all, directed at British policy in America and, although the heroes are Indians, their intransigence in the defense of homeland and liberties against British exploitation could easily be applied by the colonists to their own cause, as they were so fond of doing with Addison's *Cato*. Indeed, one wonders if Rogers did not intend this application.

Another play of the 1760s which, like that of Rogers, made no impact in the

---

2. Quotations are from [Robert Rogers], *Ponteach: or the Savages of America* (London: J. Millam, 1766).

theater but which has some historical significance is Thomas Godfrey's *The Prince of Parthia*. Godfrey had been a pupil of Provost William Smith at the College of Philadelphia and the friend there of both Francis Hopkinson, later the poet-composer, and Benjamin West, the painter. In all probability Godfrey saw the Douglass company during one of their seasons in Philadelphia; they played a benefit for the Charity School of the college in 1754. Some time before his death in 1763 Godfrey completed his tragedy, which was published in 1765 along with a selection of his juvenile poems. On April 24, 1767, after appropriate advertising in the local newspapers, Douglass and his troupe presented *The Prince of Parthia* to a Philadelphia audience, which did not request a second performance.

In fact, aside from its importance as a historical monument, *The Prince of Parthia* has little to recommend it. It is a romantic tragedy, descended from Dryden's *Aureng Zebe* and the French romances of the seventeenth century, with descriptive passages in attempted imitation of Shakespeare. The principal characters include a conniving stepmother; a tender heroine beloved by a villainous prince; a heroic prince; an autocratic king; and a captive general who, it turns out, is the long-lost father of the tender heroine. All of these invoke the deities (''ye powers,'' ''ye gods,'' ''ye heavens'') with quite remarkable frequency. The plot moves languidly toward a final scene in which the king's youngest son, almost the only principal left alive, muses on the dismal fate of monarchs: ''Nor can the shining honours which they wear, / Purchase one joy, or save them from one care.'' Perhaps this could be read as a veiled admonition to George III; otherwise the play has nothing whatever to do with the people and events of Godfrey's time, or of any other for that matter.

The most interesting aspect of *The Prince of Parthia's* production was that Douglass bothered to go through with it. He was picking his way, conciliating local public opinion where and as he could. These were troubled times, of course, and in addition to the attacks on the theater from religious zealots there was the growing problem of treading a path among the political factions. In New York during the spring of 1769 Douglass with fine impartiality presented Susannah Centlivre's *The Busybody* with an afterpiece of *The Brave Irishman* for the Sons of Saint Patrick, and Richard Steele's *The Tender Husband* for the Masons. In April *Othello* was staged, starring Major James Moncrief of the British garrison in the title role. But if Douglass and his group were politic they did not lack sand. When the Reverend George Whitefield denounced them from his Philadelphia pulpit in 1770, Douglass threatened to stage Samuel Foote's satire on Methodism, *The Minor*, in retaliation. After the Boston Massacre in that same year Douglass got up a new production of *Julius Caesar* and the significance of the ''Noble Struggles for liberty of those renowned Romans'' was not lost on American audiences.

In 1768 and 1769 the Douglass company had along with their other problems competition from a troupe calling itself the Virginia Company, playing in Virginia and Maryland. This group had been formed by William Verling, who had acted with the American Company, and included others formerly in the employ of Douglass, especially Henrietta Osborne. Her specialty was breeches parts, that is, men's roles, but not even the beautiful Mrs. Osborne as Sir Harry Wildair in Farquhar's *The Constant Couple* could save the Virginia Company from financial ruin.

In the summer of 1770 Douglass's troupe returned to Williamsburg, to the delight of George Washington, who saw *The Beggar's Opera* and four other productions in two weeks. Douglass drove his company hard: during the spring and summer of 1771 they played in Fredericksburg, Virginia—with Washington in the audience of course—then Dumfries, Alexandria, and, in Maryland, Piscataway, Port Tobacco, and Upper Marlboro on their way to Annapolis for the opening of a new theater there. Douglass imported new scenery from London, and enthusiasm among the Marylanders ran high. Nancy Hallam's Imogen in *Cymbeline* stirred "Paladour" to poetry in the October 10, 1771, issue of the *Maryland Gazette*: Shakespeare, he feels, is gazing benevolently on the American Company:

> Methinks I see his smiling Shade,
> And hear him thus Proclaim,
> "In Western Worlds, to this fair Maid,
> "I trust my spreading Fame."

Charles Willson Peale, then working in Annapolis, painted Nancy Hallam in costume; the portrait is now at Colonial Williamsburg.

Through the years Douglass and his company had made their increasingly popular way not only by effective public relations and by reading the moods of their colonial audiences, but also by sound professional acting and interesting repertory. Douglass was in continuing touch with London for scenery, players, and plays. In the fall of 1771, for example, the company, back in Williamsburg, played the American premiere of Richard Cumberland's *The West Indian*, which had opened to great acclaim in London only the preceding January. It was a natural choice for reasons beyond its popularity; its hero Belcour, the American, is portrayed sympathetically: "Wild . . . as the manner of his country is, but . . . not unprincipled." At the end of the play his long-lost father pronounces Belcour as having a "heart beaming with benevolence . . . ." The symbolism of the reunion of English father and American son is obvious enough. To underline their mission of reconciliation the company opened the season in Annapolis on September 1, 1771, with a new prologue which hailed "blest Concord."

> Whilst Patriots plead, without one private View,

And glorious Liberty alone pursue!
So shall the Mother Isles with Joy approve,
And aid their Offspring with parental Love![3]

Although political tempers were rising, the American Company were received
almost everywhere they went with affection: they were making a place for
themselves in the society. Perhaps they would in time even crack the walls of
Puritan New England. But that would require some doing. Josiah Quincy
expressed in his journal the simultaneous attraction and repulsion he—and
many other Americans—felt for the stage. On his way home to Boston from
South Carolina in 1773 he stopped in New York and saw the Douglass troupe
playing at the John Street Theater. Quincy wrote: "I was . . . much gratified
upon the whole, and I believe if I had staid in town a month I should go to the
theatre every acting night. But as a citizen and friend to the morals and
happiness of society, I should strive hard against the admission, and much
more the establishment of a play-house of any state of which I was a
member."

During the 1773 season in Philadelphia the Company staged a full-scale
production of George Cockings's *The Conquest of Canada, or the Siege of
Quebec*. Douglass is said to have been urged by local citizens to present this
play, which had been published in London in 1766 and reissued in Philadelphia in 1772. Dramatically it is a nonstarter, without a shred of conflict
beyond the obvious Montcalm-Wolfe conflict. Cockings manufactures a
mother, Sophronia, and a fiancee, Sophia, for Wolfe, who lament his departure for the wars in the opening scenes and his death in the closing. No man
alive ever spoke such turgid rhetoric as Wolfe and Montcalm have fathered on
them. The point, however, is patriotic: Cockings, as he writes in the preface, is
attempting to "display, in the different scenes, a representation of real and
genuine facts . . . amply worthy of being registered in the annals of fame, as
rival actions of those patriotic deeds of the . . . ancient Greeks and Romans."
Douglass presumably glanced at the feeble script and decided that *The Conquest* must be done as spectacle or not at all. The stage, he advertised, "will
be much crowded with the Artillery, Boats, &c. necessary for the representation of the piece; and with the Men from both Corps, whose assistance the
Commanding Officers are glad enough to indulge us with."

As one would imagine, for this glorification of British soldiers and sailors.
How the audiences reacted to the ideology it is impossible to say. In the last
scene Sophia, having set her mourning heart to rest, turns to the audience and
asks: "Who wou'd not fight the treaty-breaking Gaul! / When George, and
liberty, and martial honour call!" It seems possible, though it cannot be
proved, that the decision of the Continental Congress a year later to close all

3. *The Maryland Gazette*, September 3, 1772, p. [2].

theaters may have owed something to memories in Philadelphia of Cockings's propaganda play.

There appeared, however, to be little or no hostility to the company when they moved to New York for the spring season of 1773. George Washington saw them play when he was in town, and when in June one of the original members of the cast died, she was buried in the cemetery of Trinity Church. Catherine Maria Chark Harman was a link with the theatrical past indeed: granddaughter of Colley Cibber, her recollections went back to the London stage of Henry Fielding's day, and through her grandfather, to the era when Congreve and Farquhar were young playwrights. A local newspaper called her "a just actress. . . . In private life, she was sensible, humane and benevolent. . . . Her obsequies were on Saturday night attended by a very genteel procession. . . ." The professional theater had indeed come a long way in America, but it would not go much further for a while.

When the company opened the Charleston season of 1773–74, in the new theater there, with new costumes, they were enthusiastically received. Yet there were undertones of discontent. A presentment to the grand jury complained of the theater as an unnecessary expenditure and of the drama as "a Means of promoting the frequent Robberies that are committed and of Vice and Obscenity." The presentment was not approved; the officers of the South Carolina militia attended a performance of *The Recruiting Officer* to show their support for the troupe and the season closed in May 1774 to general applause.

The mainpiece of the very last night, May 19, 1774, was *King John*. Colonists were more concerned about the actions of one of King John's successors, but the troupe, having completed the most successful year in the history of the American stage, was ebullient. Douglass disbanded his group, with plans to meet again in New York for a bigger and better season yet. They were in rehearsal when the Continental Congress resolved, on October 20, 1774, to "encourage frugality, economy, and industry . . . and [to] discountenance and discourage, every species of extravagance and dissipation, especially all horse racing, and all kinds of gaming, cock fighting, exhibitions of shews, plays, and other expensive diversions and entertainments." When Douglass was informed of this he packed up most of his troupe and set sail for Jamaica. Professional theater was dead in the continental colonies for the duration of the war.

II

Amateurs were not idle, however. A number of individual writers grasped the notion that plays were potential instruments of propaganda, whether they were actually performed or only read or declaimed. An early example had been the anonymous *The Paxton Boys*, printed in Philadelphia in 1764, which depicts the Paxton Boys, a protorevolutionary group of artisans, in unflattering colors as feckless Presbyterian conspirators. Hugh Henry Brackenridge, then teaching at Somerset Academy in Maryland, reacted to the news of Bunker Hill by writing a play on the subject, which was published by Robert Bell of Philadelphia (1776). It was, Brackenridge tells us in the dedication to Richard Stockton, "first drawn up for an Exercise in Oratory, to a number of young Gentlemen in a southern Academy, but being now Published, may serve these same Purposes, in other AMERICAN Seminaries." *The Battle of Bunkers-Hill* is indeed an oratorical piece but it possesses interest as an early example of the Glorious Fourth school of American patriotic oratory which would dominate pulpit and platform for many decades. The verse is eighteenth-century Miltonic blank verse, but the content is 100 percent American patriotic rhetoric. Warren calls on his troops to face the invaders:

> Our noble ancestors,
> Out-brav'd the tempests, of the hoary deep,
> And on these hills, uncultivate, and wild,
> Sought an asylum, from despotic sway;
> A short asylum, for that envious power,
> With persecution dire, still follows us.
>
> (p. 23[4])

The British leaders, on the other hand, are unstinting in their admiration of the Americans' valor, General Gage relating their heroic service at Quebec and Louisburg. Warren is mortally wounded and goes, he says, to join the shades of those foes of tyrants, "to mingle with the dead, / Great Brutus, Hampden, Sidney, and the rest." At the end the British survey their Pyrrhic victory. Lord Pigot pronounces the colonists unbeatable:

> Not the united forces of the world,
> Could master them, and the proud rage subdue
> Of these AMERICANS.
>
> (p. 34)

Brackenridge, whose literary ambitions never deserted him, went on to write and publish in 1777 another drama of the Revolution, this one entitled *The Death of General Montgomery*. Although the author asserts in the dedication that he wishes to have it "considered only as a school piece," he calls attention to his strict maintenance of the unities of time, place, and action, and declares it intended for "the private entertainment of Gentlemen of taste . . . but by no means for the exhibition of the stage." Like its predecessor, *The Death* is

---

4. Quotations are from [Hugh Henry Brackenridge], *The Battle of Bunkers-Hill* (Philadelphia: Robert Bell, 1776).

oratorical instead of dramatic and is interesting for Brackenridge's rhetorical
strategy rather than for characterization or plot. The pivotal character is the
dead General Wolfe: Montgomery and the other Continentals assembled before
Quebec recall the contributions of colonial militia to Wolfe's victory and
Montgomery calls on the shade of Wolfe to remember this "unnatural strife/
Where a rude mother doth her children stab." Wolfe is thus associated with
the Americans. His ghost appears after Montgomery's death and confirms
where Wolfe's sympathies lie:

> For from your death, shall spring the mighty thought
> Of separation, from the step-dame rule
> Of moon-struck Britain.
>
> (p. 38)

In the final scenes the British general Carleton displays Montgomery's body
from the walls, reviles the American prisoners, and hands three of them over
to Indians for torture. The captive American general Morgan closes the play
with a prediction that on the Day of Judgment, "Pointing to him [Carleton],
the foul and ugly Ghosts / Of Hell, shall say, 'That was an Englishman.'"
Brackenridge is thus using his play, as Thomas Paine was using his pamphlets, to associate the Continentals with the side of justice and Providence, to
shore up the cause of separation from Britain, and to bring over to the American side the wavering Tory.

Two closet dramas published in 1776 presented opposing views of that
year's events. The anonymous *The Battle of Brooklyn* shows Washington
confessing in a soliloquy that the war is his fault, that he is driven by ambition
to "entail a war upon my fellow-subjects of America." In *The Fall of British
Tyranny*, perhaps by John Leacock, it is the British leader Lord Bute (as
"Lord Paramount") who accepts blame for the war, it being the result of his
desire to "rise superior to all superlatives . . . ." Neither play is memorable
for language or action. A third version of those events, however, deserves
consideration as the best play written about the American Revolution. Although never produced and not published until after his death, Robert Munford's *The Patriots* is a bittersweet comedy about American life during the
war years, as he saw it. Munford had earned his right to be censorious by
active service in both the Seven Years' War and the Revolution. He had
earlier written a satiric comedy about electoral practices in colonial Virginia
entitled *The Candidates*. *The Patriots* spares neither canting Whig nor canting
Tory. Trueman and Meanwell, two gentlemen of Virginia, are accused of
Toryism by the local revolutionary committee on the grounds that they have
been seen having dinner with certain local men of Scottish descent. The Scots
are similarly accused on the basis of being natives of Scotland, a charge they
are unable to deny. Meanwell scornfully confronts the committee's accusa-

tions: "The cause of my country appears as dear to me as to those who most passionately declaim on the subject . . . but I hope my zeal against tyranny will not be shewn by bawling against it, but by serving my country against her enemies. . . ." Farquhar is Munford's dramatic master but the setting and themes—xenophobia, superpatriotism, cliquishness—are native American. The play merits production during the bicentennial years.

In and around Boston a continuing literary-political skirmish involving the use of dramatic pieces for political propaganda took place. At the center of the commotion was the redoubtable Mercy Otis Warren, one of the most remarkable women of her era. Her first play, *The Adulateur* (1773), subtitled *A Tragedy, As it is now acted in Upper Servia*, is an eighteenth-century Roman play, of the same genre as Rogers's *Ponteach*; there is even an apposite quotation from *Cato* on the title page. The central figure is Brutus, leader of the patriots in Upper Servia, a country now under the domination of Rapatio and his henchmen, Bagshot, "Aga of the Janizaries"; Meagre, Rapatio's brother; Dupe, the secretary of state; and others. In spite of the names, this is not a farce. The soldiers of the rulers are engaged in persecuting and even murdering the natives, escaping punishment for their misdeeds by official connivance. It is Brutus to whom his countrymen turn for counsel. At first he is inclined to advise caution but the repeated outrages of Rapatio's followers lead him to change his mind. In a somewhat ambiguous final speech he leaves the country in the hands of his young patriot friend Marcus, with a prediction:

> And may these monsters find their glories fade,
> Crush'd in the ruins they themselves had made,
> While thou my country, shall again revive,
> Shake off misfortune, and thro' ages live.[5]

The dilemma of the patriot leader Brutus is presented with considerable insight, perhaps deriving from the similar dilemma of Warren's brother, James Otis. The parallels between the situation in Upper Servia and that in Massachusetts were obvious enough (Rapatio and Governor Hutchinson, assaults on the citizenry and the Boston Massacre, and so on).

Presenting the Tory side of the argument with effectiveness in letters to the Boston newspapers and finally in a closet drama or dialogue was Jonathan Sewall, like Mercy Warren the descendant of an old New England family. His *A Cure for the Spleen. or Amusement for a Winter's Evening; Being the Substance of a Conversation on the Times, over a Friendly Tankard and Pipe* (1775) reveals a group of Americans discussing the issues of the day. Sharp, the parson, argues the Tory case for constitutional government, while Puff, a delegate to the Continental Congress, presents the Whig side. Sharp easily has

5. Mercy Otis Warren, *The Adulateur* (Boston: New Printing Office, 1773), p. 32.

the better of the discussion, converting Trim the barber to Toryism in the process. As John J. Teunissen has observed, the gravamen of Sewall's case is that the Whigs are "false prophets who counsel misgovernment and that actually the colonists are the most blessed of mankind."

Mercy Warren emphatically disagreed. During 1773 she had published parts of a new play, *The Defeat*, using two numbers of the *Boston Gazette* to carry excerpts. Governor Hutchinson returns as Rapatio, and Sewall as Crito, "a Scribbler," is depicted as a venal timeserver. By the time her next play, *The Group*, appeared in print (1775) Governor Hutchinson had departed the colonies forever. The group of the title are those Tories who are still around executing his purposes: Lord Chief Justice Hazelrod, Judge Meagre, Ben Trumps, Crusty Crowbar, "the whole supported by a mighty army and navy, from blunderland, for the laudible purpose of enslaving its best friends." Crusty Crowbar speaks for the group when he says that Rapatio "has betray'd his country / And we're the wretched tools by him mark'd out / To seal its ruins—." The common people are represented as united against the wretched rulers; Bostonians have even forsworn tea-drinking, Collateralis asserts, in one of literature's most high-flown allusions to the Boston Tea Party. Bostonians will not

> pay the hunters of the Nabob shores
> Their high demand for India's pois'nous weed,
> Long since a sacrifice to *Thetis* made.[6]

A lame effort dramatically, the play was sufficiently topical: editions were printed and sold in New York and Philadelphia as well as Boston.

When the mighty army Warren referred to arrived from "blunderland" in 1775 it included a number of stagestruck officers—none more so than General John Burgoyne. Still enjoying acclaim for his successful London musical, *Maid of the Oaks*, Burgoyne set about enlivening the Boston scene and striking a blow for the Tories at the same time. Live drama came to Boston, where it had been forbidden by statute since 1750. In September "a Society of Ladies and Gentlemen" performed the Voltaire-Hill *Tragedy of Zara* in Faneuil Hall, with a prologue by Burgoyne. Some time that winter Burgoyne's farce *The Boston Blockade* was staged. Although the bulk of the script is lost, words of the final song have been preserved which perhaps give some impression of the flavor. The character Doodle addresses his verse to

> Ye tarbarrell'd Lawgivers, yankified Prigs,
> Who are Tyrants in Custom, yet call yourselves Whigs;
> In return for the Favours you've lavished on me,
> May I see you all hang'd upon *Liberty Tree*.

6. [Mercy Otis Warren], *The Group* (Boston: Edes and Gill, 1775), p. 12.

Mean Time take Example, decease from Attack,
You're as weak under Arms as I'm weak in my Back,
In War and in Love we alike are betray'd,
And alike are the Laughter of BOSTON BLOCKADE.[7]

The Boston Gazette, then being printed in Watertown, got wind of the play
before it was produced and on the first of January predicted that *"before that
time* [of its production] *the poor wretches will be presented with a* Tragedy,
called the Bombardment of Boston.'' In fact the colonials chose the night of
a performance, January 8, to conduct a raid on houses occupied by the British
outside Boston. This was the occasion for the well-known anecdote, first
recounted in the *Gazette,* that the arrival in the theater of the messenger
reporting the attack was thought by the audience to be part of the farce, "but
soon convinced that the actor meant to represent a solemn *reality,* the whole
assembly left the house in Confusion, and scampered off with great precipita-
tion.''

The military situation was becoming steadily worse for the British, as the
anecdote betokened. After their hasty evacuation of the city in April 1776,
the penultimate blow in the Whig-Tory controversy was struck with the publication of the anonymous colonial farce, *The Blockheads.* This play, often
attributed to Mercy Otis Warren on dubious evidence, alludes to Burgoyne's
farce in its title, and in the final scene describing the evacuation one British
soldier comments that *"Burgoyne* could not have contriv'd a *prettier satyr"* on
the British than their pell-mell withdrawal. There is some notably effective
dialogue, particularly that between the wavering Tory farmer Simple and his
wife, but little dramatic movement. As has been noted, the author presents a
contrast of the effete, city-dwelling British and their American Tory hangers-
on, and the sturdy, virile American farmers. It was a contrast which Royall
Tyler was to develop more skillfully after the war for the professional stage.

Warren's *The Motley Assembly* (1779) continues the controversy by attacking Tories for planning an assembly—a ball—and Whigs for associating with
them. "Blush B[oston]! blush!—Thy honest sons bewail, / That dance and
song o'er patriot zeal prevail.''

Associated with the Boston controversy dramas, *The Blockheads; or, Fortunate Contractor* (published 1782) is actually set in New York, but the title
may be derived from the earlier play of the same name. Because it is a
musical comedy, or more precisely a ballad opera with masque scenes, John
Teunissen has argued with some plausibility that Burgoyne himself may have
been the author. Both ballad opera and masque recognize the conclusion of
the war. The confused diplomatic maneuverings in 1782 probably account for

7. From a microprint copy of a broadside (Evans no. 15195) in the Massachusetts Historical
Society advertising "A Vaudevil" (n.p., n.d.).

the opacity of the plot, although the general intent of the masque sequence is clear enough. It is a warning to America—personified as Americana—not to drift into the hands of the French and thus lose her liberty—Liberta, also personified. The ballad opera scenes concern the efforts of Deception, the French doctor, to induce Van Braken Peace (Holland, presumably) to exchange his English spectacles for French blindfold. The New York barber Shaver (that is, Trimmer, in the sense of the Halifax character who takes either side), having thrown away all his wigs (paronomasia for Whigs) now finds himself friendless. In the final scene, with the American Congress in an enchanted sleep, Americana implores

> Dear Albion come, my love to prove
> These galling fetters (proofs of love)
> From Gallic faith these friends I find,
> They bind these hands, but not my mind. [8]

Whatever the difficulties of interpretation, and they are considerable, the spirit in which the play is composed is clearly friendly toward America. It was a pleasing note on which to end a bitter war.

In fact the theater had provided on many occasions throughout the war, in London and in America, a solace, an "escape" if one will. Theater people have detested the term *escape*, and yet over the ages audiences have continued to come to the theater, as Aristotle recognized, for precisely that. When British troops occupied Philadelphia in 1777 they reopened the theater in Southwark, where the American Company had played *Hamlet* and *The West Indian* four years earlier. Major John Andre, a gifted painter, was the principal set designer. Farquhar's plays were popular—Farquhar himself had of course worn a red coat—and the British officers and Philadelphia Tories also presented *Henry IV*, part 1, with its warning to rebels. Out in Valley Forge, as soon as the snows were gone, the colonials formed their own theatrical troupe, with General Washington's approval. By May 1778 they were presenting Addison's *Cato* to large audiences, which included the commanding general, and, one soldier reported, had *The Recruiting Officer* in rehearsal, thus proving Farquhar common military property. A Continental foot soldier recorded in his diary the morning after the performance, "my head achd very badly this morning occasioned by my last nights frolic."

The British evacuated Philadelphia in the summer of 1778, moving army headquarters to New York. There Loyalists had protected the theater on John Street and with the backing of theatergoers among the army it had been reopened the previous winter, with Fielding's *Tom Thumb* as the first production. Determined to keep a stiff upper lip, the author of the prologue for the

---

8. *The Blockheads; or, Fortunate Contractor* (London: G. Kearsley, 1782), p. 39.

opening of Home's *Douglas* in January 1778 reminded the audience of their duty:

> Though scowling faction's interested band
> At home asperse us, and with envious hand
> Our well earn'd laurels tear, the public weal
> Bids us not murmur, whatso'er we feel.[9]

Major James Moncrief of the Royal Engineers revived his lead in *Othello*, which he had played with the American Company, an excellent orchestra was recruited from the various regimental bands, Major Andre painted the scenery, and all in all the John Street theater gave good value for money received. Or so at least thought young William Dunlap, whatever his views on the politics of occupation.

Back in Philadelphia theatergoers were less fortunate. Some American officers reopened the Southwark theater when they recaptured the city. Rising in righteous indignation, as congresses will do, the Continental Congress resolved that any person holding office under the United States who "shall act, promote, encourage or attend . . . plays" should be dismissed. Invited by Lafayette to accompany him to a play, the president of the Congress, Henry Laurens, sent his regrets to the astonished French officer. In March 1779 the Pennsylvania legislature passed a statute forbidding the building of playhouses or stages and acting in them "any part of a play whatsoever."

III

With the war over and the soldier-actors on both sides returned home, it at first appeared that the foes of the drama had triumphed. Loyalist refugees in East Florida, it is true, produced plays to keep up their flagging spirits, doing such old favorites as as the Voltaire-Hill *Zara*, Home's *Douglas*, and Congreve's *The Mourning Bride*. In the new states veterans from Douglass's old American Company began reassembling and found that though they had many enemies still they also had some friends, including the most influential man in the country, George Washington. In 1784 Lewis Hallam, one of the original troupe, gathered a company in Philadelphia and reopened the Southwark theater, where he presented "Lectures" to interested persons, including Washington, on such topics as a "*serious* examination of Shakespear's morality." Like the players in England during the Interregnum, Hallam's

---

9. Dunlap, *History of the American Theatre*, p. 98.

company was staying just within the letter of the law by presenting dramatic performances labeled something else.

In New York the atmosphere was more receptive to actors and plays, and Hallam moved his band there in the fall of 1785, opening with Hall Hartson's harmless *The Countess of Salisbury*. During the season Hallam acted Hamlet and many of the old standbys were revived: *Cato* of course, and, in the American premiere performance, Sheridan's *The School for Scandal*. Theaters were reopened for amateur theatricals in Charleston and Baltimore; up and down the coast south of New England the new country was reclaiming its dramatic heritage. In April 1787 an American made an important addition to that heritage.

Royall Tyler's *The Contrast* continues to surprise readers who come upon it for the first time, just as the play, announced in New York newspapers as having been written by "a Citizen of the United States," surprised and delighted New York audiences. This is no warmed-over classical turkey but a perky comedy, as American as Yankee Doodle, which is in fact sung by the New Englander Jonathan in the third act. The play's ancestor is of course the English comedy of manners. Jonathan even attends a performance of *The School for Scandal*, thinking he is looking "right into the next neighbour's house." As the title indicates, a contrast is presented between the stalwart Colonel Henry Manly and the frenchified and anglified fop, Dimple. Even Manly, however, is not above criticism. He rejoices "that I have humbly imitated our illustrious WASHINGTON, in having exposed my health and life in the service of my country, without reaping any other reward than the glory of conquering...." "Well said heroics," his sister Charlotte remarks dryly, commenting that the belles of New York will take him to be "a player run mad, with your head filled with old scraps of tragedy...."

The play is a contrast between the old and the new, between American and foreign customs and manners, between the country and the city. But it is also a celebration of national unity. One should remember that the Constitutional Convention was gathering while Tyler wrote his play, and that the union which Washington envisioned was anything but a certainty. Manly has just returned from helping to put down Shays's Rebellion, imitating in fiction what his creator Royall Tyler had done in fact. American diversity appeared on the way to destroying American unity. In presenting his various characters—Jonathan the New England rustic, Van Rough the patroon, Charlotte the city belle, and so on—Tyler underlines that diversity but argues in effect for a unity of national purpose. America, Dimple points out, has her faults. "Yes, Sir," Manly replies; "and we, her children, should blush for them in private, and endeavour, as individuals, to reform them." After the various obstacles to true love are in due course removed, Manly and his Maria are united with her father Van Rough's blessing, Manly having learned, he says at the curtain, that "probity, virtue, honour, though they should not have received the polish of Europe, will secure to an honest American the good graces of his fair countrywoman, and, I hope, the applause of THE PUBLIC."

Applause resounded for Tyler's play, in New York, in Baltimore, and—after the legislature repealed the ban on theaters—in Philadelphia. Tyler's metier, however, was the law rather than the stage. Although he wrote other plays and saw at least one of them produced, he was not to be a force in the new theater. That his contemporary William Dunlap assuredly was. Encouraged by Tyler's success Dunlap began writing for the stage and in 1789, after a false start or two, had the satisfaction of seeing Hallam's Old American Company produce his new comedy, *The Father, or American Shandyism*, for enthusiastic audiences. That same year Washington attended the premiere of Dunlap's comic sketch, *Darby's Return*, laughed heartily at its humor, and received the acclamations of the crowded theater, the "genuine effusions," as the *Gazette of the United States* put it, "of the hearts of FREEMEN." Dunlap's long career in the American professional theater was launched.

Certainly those who valued the theater and drama had reason to express this gratitude to Washington. When Tyler's *The Contrast* appeared in print in 1790, at the head of the list of subscribers was "The President of the United States." It was in a sense Washington's final gesture in support of American drama, an affirmation for all to see that the American theater had survived the turmoil of almost two decades and was now, like the young republic itself, ready to develop.

SUGGESTIONS FOR FURTHER READING

Editions

There are no satisfactory modern editions of any of the plays referred to. All American imprints, however, are available in the American Antiquarian Society Readex Microprint microcard series, with the exception of Mercy Otis Warren's *The Defeat*. Excerpts from this play were printed in the *Boston Gazette* for May 24 and July 19, 1773, copies of which are to be found in the Boston Public Library. *Ponteach* and *The Blockheads; or, Fortunate Contractor* are reproduced on microcard from the London original printings in the Readex Microprint series, *Three Centuries of Drama*, edited by Henry W. Wells.

Scholarship and Criticism

Baine, Rodney M. *Robert Munford: America's First Comic Dramatist*. Athens: University of Georgia Press, 1967.

Ford, Paul Leicester. *Washington and the Theatre*. New York: The Dunlap Society, 1899. Reprinted, New York: Benjamin Blom, 1967.

Mates, Julian. "The Dramatic Anchor: Research Opportunities in the American Drama Before 1800." *Early American Literature* 5 (Winter 1970–71): 76–79.

Pollock, Thomas Clark. *The Philadelphia Theatre in the Eighteenth Century*. Philadelphia: University of Pennsylvania Press, 1933. Reprinted New York: Greenwood Press, 1968.

Quinn, Arthur Hobson. *A History of the American Drama from the Beginning to the Civil War*. 2d ed. New York: Appleton-Century-Crofts, 1943.

Rankin, Hugh F. *The Theater in Colonial America*. Chapel Hill: University of North Carolina Press, 1965.

Tanselle, G. Thomas. *Royall Tyler*. Cambridge, Mass.: Harvard University Press, 1967.

Teunissen, John J. "Blockheadism and the Propaganda Plays of the American Revolution." *Early American Literature* 7 (Fall 1972): 148–62.

7

Benjamin Franklin

MARY E. RUCKER

[*Literary talents, great and small, were put to use during the revolutionary years; no really great ones were used, alas, in the creation of drama. One can imagine the many-talented Benjamin Franklin producing plays with amusing dramatic dialogue, for what he produced in the dialogue between himself and the gout is delightful. The leading writer of the revolutionary years, Franklin as printer, inventor, and statesman accomplished so much that it is easy to disregard his great literary imagination. Combining a brilliant comic sense with an accomplished style, Franklin created probably the most enduring literary works occasioned by the Revolution.*]

By the time he wrote the last sections of his *Autobiography* in 1789 and 1790, Benjamin Franklin was, as Carl Van Doren has noted, "a harmonious human multitude." He had been, in varying degrees of commitment and competence, a printer, philologist, musician, demographer, economist, inventor, scientist, educator, politician, soldier, and man of letters. A recipient of the Royal Society's Copley Medal, he was also a member of the society and of the Royal Academy of Paris. Harvard, Yale, and William and Mary awarded him honorary M.A. degrees, the University of St. Andrews an honorary LL.D., and Oxford an honorary D.C.L. During his lifetime Franklin became an international hero whose role in the Revolution, John Adams surmised, made him a hero of legendary proportions: "The History of our Revolution will be one continued Lye from one end to the other. The essence of the whole will be *that Dr. Franklins electrical Rod, smote the Earth and out sprung General Washington. That Franklin electrified him with his rod—and thence forward these two conducted all the Policy, Negotiations, Legislatures and War.*" Adams's jealous exaggeration cannot obscure the fact that as a private citizen, colonial

This essay is dedicated to the memory of Joe Lee Davis.

agent, and minister plenipotentiary to the court of Louis XVI, Benjamin Franklin did indeed help to forge the United States of America.

I

Later critics have concurred in David Hume's judgment of Franklin as America's "first great man of letters," some of them dating the birth of our literature from the publication of the Dogood and Busy-Body essays that imitated while domesticating the Addisonian essay. Franklin's comments on the art of writing place him squarely in the neoclassical tradition, with its emphasis upon correctness, perspicuity, and order, and his compositions, even his personal and familiar letters, attest his devotion to such techniques as balance, antithesis, and parallelism. With the probable exception of the bagatelles and the familiar letters written in France, his *belles-lettres* were never an end but rather a means. For Franklin also embraced the neoclassical ideal of instruction: "I shall venture to lay it down as a Maxim," he wrote, *"That no Piece can properly be called good, and well written, which is void of any Tendency to benefit the Reader, either by improving his Virtue or his Knowledge."* He may have said too that good writing is that which serves a cause, for he used his pen to further his civic and political endeavors. The satires for which he donned a variety of masks reflect not only the influence of Swift but also the chameleonlike adaptability that Franklin exploited from the beginning of his public career. This adaptability, which was of enormous importance to his official negotiations in England and France, is revealed in the content and artistry of the *Autobiography,* which was soon as popular as his earlier *Poor Richard's Almanac.*

With part I of the *Autobiography,* written at Twyford in 1771 as an ostensible letter to his son, Franklin willy-nilly achieved a masterpiece, selecting and arranging episodes so that they appeal to those values and emotions attached to what we regard as the archetypal American experience. Posing as the prosperous father with leisure to relive his life through recollection and thereby instruct future generations in the ways to success, he renders a candid and intimate account of his Boston youth, of his brief formal and longer informal education, and of the beginnings of his career as a printer. Typically, as a young man he first asserts his freedom—from the older brother to whom he was apprenticed, from his father, and from the Boston Assembly whom his proclivity to satire and libel and his unorthodox religious beliefs offended— and leaves home to begin anew in New York with only his trade and self-sufficiency. Although he is "near 300 Miles from home, a Boy of but 17, without the least Recommendation to or Knowledge of any Person in the

Place, and with very little Money in my Pocket,'' and although his attempt to establish a career is later complicated by the perils of his journey from New York to Philadelphia and by the usual threats of the city, his success is a foregone conclusion.

To dramatize the contrast between his not-too-promising childhood and his later achievements, Franklin artfully elaborates his entry into the city, playing upon his physical dirtiness, poverty, innocence, and aloneness and underplaying both the anticipated arrival of his trunk and the affluence that allows him to give away food and money. The emotionally charged image of the tired, hungry, and poorly clad country boy who does not know how to purchase bread and who wanders through the streets eating a puffy roll prefigures, paradoxically, a rise to riches. Because of his industry and integrity Franklin attracts the attention of leading citizens, and he shrewdly displays the manners and qualities of a worthy laborer in order to secure the opportunities immediately provided him.

Part 2, written at Passy in 1784, centers on the well-known "Project of arriving at moral Perfection." As he earlier acknowledged his moral shortcomings, or "errata," Franklin here amusedly acknowledges his failure to attain the moral perfection that he believed necessary to man's earthly felicity. Assuming the mask of the sage moral philosopher, he instructs his posterity in the religious and social validity of his thirteen virtues and, at the same time, intimates that the youth who sought to conquer all the evils into which custom, inclination, and other people could lead him was indeed naive and arrogant: "As I knew, or thought I knew, what was right and wrong, I did not see why I might not *always* do the one and avoid the other. But I soon found I had undertaken a Task of more Difficulty than I had imagined. While my *Attention was taken up* in guarding against one Fault, I was often surpriz'd by another. Habit took the Advantage of Inattention. Inclination was sometimes too strong for Reason.'' To master habit and inclination, he adopted a methodical scheme: the ordered virtues, the chart for self-examination, and the like. Ironically, examination served only to reveal a surprising plethora of faults whose corrigibility was not to be realized easily. The effort to be orderly, Franklin confesses, was so frustratingly difficult that he was willing to rationalize his lack of order into a virtue: "'something that pretended to be Reason was every now and then suggesting to me, that such extream Nicety as I exacted of my self might be a kind of Foppery in Morals, which if it were known would make me ridiculous; that a perfect Character might be attended with the Inconvenience of being envied and hated; and that a benevolent Man should allow a few Faults in himself, to keep his Friends in Countenance.'' Rationalizing that humility was opposed to his inclination, he sought to achieve merely the appearance of humility, the reality of which he doubts that one can attain: "In reality there is perhaps no one of our natural Passions so hard to subdue as *Pride*. Disguise it, struggle with it, beat it down, stifle it, mortify it as much as one pleases, it is still alive, and will every now and then peep out and show itself. . . . For even if I could conceive that I had compleatly overcome it, I should probably by [be] proud of my Humility.'' Despite his failures, Franklin attributed his health, fortune, fame, and good nature to his moral scheme, which he considered using, along with his religious creed, as the bases of his proposed worldwide party for virtue, the Society of the Free and Easy.

In parts 3 and 4, written at Philadelphia in 1789–90, Franklin overtly moralizes upon his civic projects and political career from 1731 to 1757. This didacticism was perhaps prompted by Abel James's and Benjamin Vaughan's emphasis upon the instructive value of Franklin's life. Vaughan, who had read part 1, encouraged Franklin to complete his memoirs because they would be both ''a sort of key to life'' and an ''efficacious advertisement'' insofar as Franklin's life was ''connected with the detail of the manners and situations of *a rising* people.'' While these parts, in which Franklin poses as the successful citizen, demonstrate the status to be attained by a self-educated, industrious, and frugal American with the freedom to move in a fluid society, they fail to be more than an account of relatively isolated events that allow Franklin to offer instruction on the method of conducting public projects, forming partnerships, stowing cargo, teaching language, and the like. Unfortunately, he did not treat his role in the Revolution.

II

His involvement in the events leading to the Revolution began with his participation in the 1750s disputes between the Pennsylvania Assembly and the proprietary government. The governors' denial of the rights of the Assembly tested Franklin's belief in the prevalent notion underlying the Revolution: a populace may exercise its right to rebellion once government ceases to ensure the general welfare. From the beginning of the crises until 1774, Franklin directed his ministry to the realization of his dominion view of empire, which would secure charter rights and the political autonomy of the colonies and thereby preserve the union. He had asserted colonial autonomy as early as his *Observations Concerning the Increase of Mankind* (1751) and *The Interest of Great Britain Considered* (the ''Canada Pamphet'' of 1760), both of which advocate territorial expansion and home manufacture in order to allow expansion of the empire. Because the colonies were basically agrarian, and because he believed that their differences in government, religion, and customs precluded their uniting for independence of England, he viewed neither expansion nor home manufacture as a necessary threat to the dominion status of the colonies. Nevertheless, he struck a rebellious note: ''When I say such an union is impossible, I mean without the most grievous tyranny and oppression. People who have property in a country which they may lose, and privileges which they may endanger; are generally dispos'd to be quiet; and even to bear much, rather than hazard all. While the government is mild and just, while important civil and religious rights are secure, such subjects will be dutiful and obedient. The waves do not rise, but when the winds blow.''

When the winds that began to blow during the 1750s reached tornado proportions during the 1760s, Franklin argued that Parliament's usurped control should be limited to mercantile affairs that benefited the empire rather than England alone. Although he tended to avoid the question of rights issuing from the Glorious Revolution, his radical interpretation of charter rights, and hence of Parliament's relation to the colonies, is revealed in his marginal response to a passage in Allan Ramsay's *Thoughts on the Origin and Nature of Government* (1769):

> When an American says he has a Right to all the Privileges of a British Subject, he does not call himself a British Subject, he is an American Subject of the King; the Charters say they shall be entitled to all the Privileges of Englishmen as if *they had been* born *within* the Realm. But they were and are *without* the Realm, therefore not British Subjects; and tho' within the King's Dominions, because they voluntarily agreed to be his Subjects when they took his Charters, and have created those Dominions for him, yet they are not within the Dominion of Parliament which has no Authority but *within the Realm.* (*Papers*, 16: 316[1])

Despite his sometimes acknowledging the king rather than Parliament as the legislator of the colonies, Franklin consistently held that neither king nor Parliament could legislate unilaterally. Realistically recognizing both the dependence of the colonies on Britain for military protection and, given the mercantile relation, the need to regulate trade, he unwillingly accepted Parliament's trade regulations even though such legislation curtailed colonial legislative autonomy. And he accepted crown demand for support of its wars, which were the wars of the empire. But beyond military and commercial ties, he recognized only bonds of loyalty and affection, which he judged of ultimate importance.

Franklin was serving as agent for Pennsylvania when he became involved in the Stamp Act crisis. In light of his vigorous expression of American

---

1. In quoting Franklin's work, I have given priority to the Leonard Labaree et al. edition of *The Papers of Benjamin Franklin* and of *The Autobiography of Benjamin Franklin*. References to works that have not yet appeared in the *Papers* are to the Albert Henry Smyth edition of *The Writings of Benjamin Franklin*.

concerns in works such as the *Observations* and in his well-known letters to Governor Shirley, his initial capitulation to the act is surprising. In these letters he responded to a proposed union of royal governors and commissioners who would be empowered to draw upon the British treasury for money due from colonies for defense. Funds thus borrowed were to be repaid through a tax levied by Parliament. Franklin, protesting both the tax and what he believed to be the exclusion of assemblies from selecting the commissioners, contended that "where heavy burthens are to be laid on them, it has been found useful to make it, as much as possible, their own act; for they bear better when they have, or think they have some share in the direction; and when any public measures are generally grievous or even distasteful to the people, the wheels of Government must move more heavily." Although the Stamp Act entailed the kind of royal intervention to which he objected, Franklin offered the ministers an alternative to the act and eventually proposed a collector. Writing to Charles Thompson, he maintained that Parliament had used the act as a means to assert American dependence and suggested the futility of protest: "We might as well have hinder'd the Suns setting. That we could not do. But since 'tis down . . . and it may be long before it rises again, Let us make as good a Night of it as we can. We may still Light Candles. Frugality and Industry will go a great way towards indemnifying us. Idleness and Pride Tax with a heavier Hand then Kings and Parliaments; If we can get rid of the former we may easily bear the Latter." He obviously miscalculated colonial reaction and was forced to seek repeal.

Franklin's most notable immediate efforts were the publication of the letters to Shirley and his appearance before the House of Commons, which was debating repeal of the Stamp Act. His marginal notes on a copy of the published *Examination of Doctor Benjamin Franklin* hint that many of his supporters' questions were designed to elicit affirmation of the self-sufficiency of the colonies, the extent of opposition to the act, the impracticality of distributing stamps, and, of course, the feasibility, in terms of trade and union, of repeal. When his examiners raised the question of rights, Franklin realized the tenuity of the distinction between internal and external taxation upon which he relied to reconcile the British policy of mercantilism and colonial autonomy. Granting that assemblies in obeying parliamentary acts levying duties to regulate trade had virtually given crown officers the right to tax the unrepresented colonies, Franklin nevertheless asserted that the charters could be interpreted in a manner that would deny Parliament the right to levy both internal and external duties. By March 13, 1768, he himself was no longer able to make the distinction, for, as he confided to his son, "no middle doctrine can be well maintained, I mean not clearly with intelligible arguments. Something might be made of either of the extremes; that Parliament has a power to make *all laws* for us, or that it has a power to make *no laws* for us; and I think the arguments for the latter more numerous and weighty than those for the former." During debate in the Commons, however, he had very casually ceded Parliament the right to tax the colonies, believing that "the reconciliation of right" was of little importance if the right were not exercised. The Commons repealed the Stamp Act on February 22, 1766, and his supporters, tending to ignore the financial disaster resulting from the boycott of British goods, gave Franklin credit for the victory. The publication of the *Examination* established his reputation, which had been threatened by his being a crown officer and by his initial capitulation, as a staunch advocate of American rights.

Like other Americans who became patriots, Franklin moved slowly toward advocacy of independence, preferring to defend colonial rights without forfeiting union. Two events of 1767, however, led him closer to a revolutionary stand. Parliament's declaration of its right "to make laws and statutes of sufficient force and validity to bind the colonies and people of America, subjects of the Crown of Great Britain, in all cases whatsoever" and the issuance of the Townshend Duty Act voided the terms upon which he sought to preserve the union. Franklin now encouraged Americans to adopt a policy of nonimportation. But he also urged loyalty to the king regardless of parliamentary infringement on colonial rights, which he believed could be adequately asserted through resolution and petition. Other events of the early 1770s confirmed his growing sense of the futility of reconciliation. His role in the complicated "Hutchinson letters" affair inadvertently increased the gulf between England and America. Judging the letters to be treasonous, Franklin sent them to Boston so that the Assembly could know that the coercive measures of Lord Hillsborough were due to colonial officers. Although Franklin hoped that the letters would serve as a means of reconciliation, Solicitor General Wedderburn cleverly and illegally used the incident to abuse Franklin before the Privy Council, to deprive him of his crown office, and to destroy his official effectiveness as American representative in London. Yet even after the Boston Tea Party he sought reconciliation, urging that Boston pay for the tea. The king's declaration of the legislative supremacy of Parliament, however, assured Franklin that George III had forfeited the loyalty of his American subjects. As an overt revolutionary, he now wrote to Thomas Cushing suggesting that the colonies withhold aid from the king as a means of attaining redress: "perhaps it would be best and fairest for the Colonies . . . to engage firmly with each other, that they will never grant Aids to the Crown in any General War, till those Rights are recogniz'd by the King and both Houses of Parliament." Such a united declaration would, he surmised, perhaps "bring the Dispute to a Crisis." While Franklin negotiated unofficially with Pitt, Howe, and Dartmouth until he left England in 1775, he had come to question the virtue of union with England, and the outbreaks at

Lexington and Concord confirmed his disaffection. The old system of empire, the "large and beautiful porcelain vase" that he had sought to preserve, was broken beyond repair.

III

As early as the 1720s, when he sedulously aped the *Spectator*, Franklin gave vent to his proclivity to satire—directed to social conduct and to political issues. He later evidenced his skill in Swiftian irony and hoax in "The Speech of Polly Baker," "A Witch Trial at Mount Holly," and a caustic essay on the exportation of felons. Given his conception of the value of the press which such essays attest, Franklin naturally buttressed his official negotiations with political satire. From 1764 to 1775 he appropriated British periodicals— primarily *The London Chronicle; or, Universal Evening Post*, the *Public Advertiser*, and the *Public Ledger*—as a forum from which to wage a propaganda war, explaining the American cause, defending American rights and customs, pointing out the futility of coercion, deprecating violence, and pleading for the preservation of the empire either through a return to requisitioning finances or through colonial representation in Parliament. His vehicles were varied: anecdote, colloquy, query, fable, parody, fictitious controversy, hoax, and tall tale, among others. Although no single piece of his propaganda was as effective as, say, Paine's *Common Sense,* his numerous contributions won support among those in England who were potentially sympathetic toward the colonies, and the reprinting of this journalism in American periodicals reinforced emerging separatist attitudes. His journalism was effectively ancillary to the formal petitions of various assemblies, the protests of British merchants, the nonimportation agreements, and the riots. He defined his aim in his comment on two of his most enduring satires, "Rules by Which a Great Empire may be Reduced to a Small One" (1773) and "An Edict by the King of Prussia" (1773): "Such papers may seem to have a tendency to increase our divisions; but I intend a contrary effect, and hope by comprising in little room, and setting in a strong light the grievances of the colonies, more attention will be paid to them by our administration, and that when their unreasonableness is generally seen, some of them will be removed to the restoration of harmony between us." In these satires, which respond most immediately to the several acts regulating colonial trade and to the subsidiary measures aimed to enforce the Townshend Duty Act, Franklin mines the foundations of Anglo-American relations.

He built his "Rules" upon an ironic inversion of the assumption that imperial rulers ideally desire to increase or at least to preserve the vastness of their empires. Donning the mask of "a modern simpleton," Franklin proffers "all ministers who have the management of extensive dominions" the "science" of diminishing them so that they may have time to gratify their desire to fiddle. His science, which satirically apes King George's unjust colonial policy, calls for a tyrannical exercise of power and involves faulty governance, a denial of constitutional liberties, and military mismanagement. Relying upon a comparison between a cake and an empire, the "modern simpleton" first offers a ground rule that will ensure the possibility of separation between the mother country and her dominions: a distinction between domestic and foreign subjects, the latter to be more severely governed than the former and by officers in whose selection they have not participated. The specific rules to be followed, once this distinction is made, center on the destruction of the colonists' good will. Although they make use of emotionally charged words such as *suppress, treason, oppression,* and *arbitrary,* the rules themselves are, on the whole, relatively objective statements given an ironic twist through the simpleton's comments on their advantages. The comments lead the reader to question the persona's feigned unawareness and his charitable attitude toward the ministers whom he purports to assist. For the end of his science is, clearly, to damn them.

Franklin's simpleton advises ministers to foster schism through withholding the rewards that colonists expect as a result of their contribution to the military and commercial power of the mother country, through treating with them as if they were on the brink of revolution, and through imposing upon them insolent, rapacious, and incompetent officers who will assure them of the king's disregard of justice and his lack of interest in their welfare. Anticipating colonial objection, he instructs ministers to delay hearing petitions and eventually to rule in favor of oppressive royal officers. The latter gesture will be particularly advantageous: "This will have an admirable effect every way. The trouble of future complaints will be prevented, and Governors and Judges will be encouraged to farther acts of oppression and injustice; and thence the people may become more disaffected, and at length desperate."

In his treatment of the various taxes and the often bizarre ways in which they were to be collected, Franklin almost loses control of his passions. His staunch commitment to and defense of colonial rights preclude his maintaining the distance necessary to sustain the pose of a modern simpleton willing to abet the ministers in their monstrous quest. His persona advises Parliament not to accept freely tendered money but rather to extort it, to tax the unrepresented colonies regardless of mercantile regulations and of their ability to pay. This arbitrary tax may be made more odious, and hence become a means to effect colonial disaffection, if Parliament asserts an unlimited power to tax: "This will probably weaken every idea of *security in their property*, and convince them, that under such a government they *have nothing they can call*

their own; which can scarce fail of producing the *happiest consequences!*"
The sense of play characteristic of this passage turns to savagery when
Franklin, after noting the advantage of complex and obscure trade regulations
and of dealing with violations of those regulations through admiralty courts
and other judiciary systems that deny the right of habeas corpus and the right
to trial by a jury of peers, refers to the Declaratory Act:

> And, lest the people should think you cannot possibly go any farther, pass
> another solemn declaratory act, "that King, Lords, Commons had, hath, and
> of right ought to have, full power and authority to make statutes of sufficient
> force and validity to bind the unrepresented provinces IN ALL CASES WHAT-
> SOEVER." This will include *spiritual* with temporal, and, taken together,
> must operate wonderfully to your purpose; by convincing them, that they are
> at present under a power something like that spoken of in the scriptures,
> which can not only *kill their bodies*, but *damn their souls* to all eternity, by
> compelling them, if it pleases, *to worship the Devil.* (*Writings*, 6: 132)

This passage exhibits not only the simpleton's superiority to the ministers
but also Franklin's outrage.

Franklin regains control during his treatment of customs officers, the mis-
application of revenue, the dissolution of assemblies, and Parliament's failure
to believe that the colonists had just cause for complaint. He seems to delight
in pointing out England's military faux pas. After indicating the feasibility of
usurping colonial forts and arms and of quartering troops, not on the frontier
where they are needed but rather in cities where the inhabitants may protect
them, the simpleton concludes his counsel with a rule that will allow ministers
virtually to give away their dominions. They are advised to grant to their
general absolute and unconstitutional power, to provide him with sufficient
troops, and to watch the results: "who knows but . . . he may take it into his
head to set up for himself? If he should, and you have carefully practised these
few *excellent rules* of mine, take my word for it, all the provinces will
immediately join him; and you will that day (if you have not done it sooner)
get rid of the trouble of governing them, and all the *plagues* attending their
commerce and connection from henceforth and for ever."

Franklin was particularly pleased by the impact of "An Edict by the King of
Prussia" upon several of his friends. He wrote to his son that on the day that
the satire appeared in print, he was breakfasting with several other guests at
Lord Le Despencer's home. Soon Paul Whitehead, who was in another room
reading newspapers,

> came running in to us, out of breath, with the paper in his hand. Here! says
> he, here's news for ye! *Here's the King of Prussia, claiming a right to this
> kingdom!* All stared, and I as much as anybody; and he went on to read it.
> When he had read two or three paragraphs, a gentleman present said, *Damn
> his impudence, I dare say, we shall hear by next post that he is upon his*

march with one hundred thousand men to back this. Whitehead, who is very shrewd, soon after began to smoke it, and looking in my face said, *I'll be hanged if this is not some of your American jokes upon us.* (*Writings*, 6: 146)

Franklin noted with satisfaction Lord Mansfield's declaring the satire "*very* ABLE *and very* ARTFUL indeed" and Lord Le Despencer's preserving it in his collection. Readers were "*taken in*" not only by the skill with which Franklin mocks the form and tone of the traditional edict but also by the format of the satire. Henry Woodfall participated in this hoax insofar as he conspicuously placed it as the lead item of the *Public Advertiser* under the following caption: "The SUBJECT of the following Article of FOREIGN INTELLIGENCE being exceedingly EXTRAORDINARY, is the Reason of its being separated from the usual Articles of *Foreign News.*" The hoax attacks three assumptions: that descendants of the first settlers were automatically subjects of the king; that the health of the colonies was due to Britain's financial support; that her participation in North American wars was for the sole benefit of the colonies. The major targets, however, are those trade regulations that denied American rights.

Frederick's edict is framed within introductory and concluding statements of a resident of Danzig who, pretending ignorance of the nature of the bond between Prussia and England as well as that between England and America, transmits to London the edict that may explain why the English so passively accept Prussian restrictions upon their trade with Danzig. The reason is, as Frederick explains in his preamble, that the English are descendants of the ancient Teutons: "Whereas it is well known to all the world, that the first German settlements made in the Island of Britain, were by colonies of people, subject to our renowned ducal ancestors, and drawn from their dominions, under the conduct of Hengist, Horsa, Hella, Uff, Cerdicus, Ida, and others; and that the said colonies have flourished under the protection of our august house for ages past; have never been emancipated therefrom; and yet have hitherto yielded little profit to the same." These farfetched ties between the modern English and the ancient Teutons and the claim that England's prosperity is due in part to Prussian military support satirize English conceptions of the status of the American colonies. (Since the Stamp Act crisis especially Franklin had held that the charters did not bind the descendants of the original settlers, that those descendants are voluntarily subjects of the king.) Frederick bases his right to tax and in other ways oppress his English subjects upon these specious claims. Making use of the "leisure" issuing from the recently established peace, he seeks financial ease for his domestic subjects through regulating British trade so severely that he denies the natural and constitutional rights of his foreign subjects. His obvious favoritism clearly belies his use of *dominions*, mocks his and his ministers' "certain knowledge," and recalls England's consistent exploitation of the American colonies for the benefit of England alone.

Because the Navigation, Iron, Woollen, Hat, and Treason acts were in themselves woefully absurd, to effect his satire Franklin had only to paraphrase or quote directly certain passages of those acts. Yet he frequently drives his point through sharp interpolations, condensations, and exaggerations that constitute his overt judgments. For instance, the relevant passage of the Navigation Act, 12 Chas. II, c. 18 (reinforced by 4 Geo. III, c. 15) reads:

> that for every ship or vessel, which . . . shall set sail out of or from England, Ireland, Wales or town of Berwick upon Tweed, for any English plantation in America, Asia, or Africa, sufficient bond shall be given with one surety to the chief officers of the custom-house of such port or place from whence the said ship shall set sail . . . ; that in case the said ship or vessel shall load any of the said commodities at any of the said English plantations, that the same commodities shall be by the said ship brought to some port of England, Ireland, Wales, or to the port or town of Berwick upon Tweed, and shall there unload and put on shore the same, the danger of the seas only excepted; (2) and for all ships coming from any other port or place to any of the aforesaid plantations . . . that such ship or vessel shall carry all the aforesaid goods that shall be laden on board in the said ship to some other of his Majesty's English plantations, or to England, Ireland, Wales, or town of Berwick upon Tweed.

To exaggerate the ludicrousness of this stipulation, Franklin wittily omits the qualifying circumstance and alternative ports at which duties may be paid: "We do hereby ordain, that all ships or vessels bound from Great Britain to any other part of the world, or from any other part of the world to Great Britain, shall in their respective voyages touch at our port of Konigsberg, there to be unladen, searched, and charged with the said duties."

The Iron Act of 1750, 23 Geo. II, c. 29, restricted colonial manufacture for the benefit of Great Britain. Franklin responds to the injustice of this restriction through Frederick's specious edict, which overtly denies the natural rights of his British subjects. Referring to Prussian introduction of the manufacture of iron into England and thereby claiming for his domestic subjects an exclusive right to that manufacture, Frederick suggests that the English erred in "presuming that they had a natural right to make the best use they could of the natural productions of their country for their own benefit." Because British manufacture of iron and steel products threatens a "diminution of the said manufacture in our ancient dominion," he prohibits foreign manufacture (the regulation is a very slightly altered quotation from the Iron Act): "We do therefore hereby farther ordain, that . . . no mill or other engine for slitting or rolling of iron, or any plating-forge to work with a tilt-hammer, or any furnace for making steel, shall be erected or continued in the said island of Great Britain." To reinforce the injustice and absurdity of the proviso, Franklin offers an ironic interpolation: "We are nevertheless graciously pleased to permit the inhabitants of the said island to transport their iron into Prussia, there to be manufactured, and to them returned; they paying our Prussian subjects for the workmanship, with all the costs of commission, freight, and risk, coming and returning.'' The Woollen Act of 1699 (10 and 11 William III, c. 10) and the Hat Act of 1732 (5 Geo. II, c. 22) receive similar treatment, for they too denied colonial rights for the sake of British profit. The Woollen Act prohibited foreign and intercolonial shipping not only of wool and woolen products but also of products containing wool. Franklin's rage against this restriction surfaces when Frederick confesses that although he cannot indulgently allow the transportation of wool to Prussia for manufacture, he will graciously permit his "loving subjects . . . (if they think proper) to use all their wool as manure for the improvement of their lands.''

The fifth article echoes the 1751 "Exporting of Felons to the Colonies" in which Franklin satirized England's defense of 7 Geo. I, c. 11, an elaboration of 13 and 14 Chas. II, c. 12. When England judged colonial laws designed to discourage England's exportation of indentured felons to be "against the Public Utility, as they tend to prevent the IMPROVEMENT and WELL PEOPLING of the colonies,'' he urged the colonists to transport rattlesnakes to England as an expression of gratitude for her parental concern. The edict attacks this statute through a highly charged paraphrase: "Being willing farther to favour our said colonies in Britain, we do hereby also ordain and command, that all the *thieves*, highway and street robbers, housebreakers, forgerers, murderers, s——d——tes, and villains of every denomination, who have forfeited their lives to the law in Prussia; but whom we, in our great clemency, do not think fit here to hang, shall be emptied out of our gaols into the said island of Great Britain, for the better peopling of that country.''

The last section of the edict states the penalty for opposition to the articles and alludes to the Treason Act, which required the transportation of colonials to England for trial. Confident that his foreign subjects will find his provisos both reasonable and just because they are modeled upon English laws, Frederick decrees that any opposition will be judged treasonous and that all suspects "shall be transported in fetters from Britain to Prussia, there to be tried and executed according to the Prussian law.''

This concluding paragraph weakens the ironic mode that Franklin has sustained successfully up to this point. The preamble and the articles are effectively satiric because of Frederick's blindness to their moral and political implications. His drawing the direct parallel between his regulations and English regulations of American and Irish commerce must, however, be predicated upon a consciousness of their injustice—just as his offering a penalty for their violation anticipates protest. A similar shift from blindness to awareness characterizes the framework of the edict. The correspondent first claims that he had not understood England's passiveness in regard to Prussian restrictions

upon her trade with Danzig. But he infers from the edict that England submits
to the restrictions because of her sense of duty and equity. The value of the
discrepancy between the correspondent's discernment of equity and the overt
inequities of the edict is negated in the final paragraph of the essay. Not
content to let his satire operate dramatically, Franklin there portrays the
erstwhile naive correspondent as appalled by Frederick's stating that his regulations are based upon those by which England has governed Ireland and
America. To be appalled is obviously to be aware of the gross injustices, and
the correspondent directly and passionately judges British ministerial policy.
He writes that although some residents of Danzig accept the edict as a *jeu
d'esprit* while others believe it is genuine, they are all distressed by the
reference to British law, finding it "impossible to believe, that a people
distinguished for their love of liberty, a nation so wise, so liberal in its
sentiments, so just and equitable towards its neighbours, should, from mean
and injudicious views of petty immediate profit, treat its own children in a
manner so arbitrary and tyrannical!" The dismay is Franklin's.

I V

Franklin was sixty-nine years old when he returned to Philadelphia and in July
1775 unsuccessfully proposed to the Second Continental Congress his Articles
of Confederation and Perpetual Union for the United Colonies of North
America whereby the colonists would assert their right to declare war, to enter
alliances, and to regulate trade and other domestic affairs. He suggested that
once the articles were ratified and the union thus established, it was to continue until England agreed to the terms of reconciliation, repealed all acts
restraining American commerce, made reparation for acts of violence, and
withdrew British troops. Despite the strategic hint that Britain may have met
these demands and reestablished ties, Franklin had become a confirmed revo-
lutionist who now worked to procure artillery and foreign alliance, to establish
an intercolonial postal system and uniform paper currency, and to regulate
colonial trade.

When in December 1776 he arrived in France as one of the commissioners
to seek a treaty of alliance and commerce, he could capitalize on his international reputation as a scientist and as the author of *Poor Richard*. For the
French he was a symbol of all the values implicit in the doctrines of the
physiocrats, and he was quite willing to play the expected role—dressing as
the unspoiled backwoodsman and consciously displaying unaffected manners
in the court of Paris. Noting that Franklin's reputation there was more far-
reaching and his character more esteemed than those of Voltaire, Newton,

Leibnitz, and Frederick, John Adams declared that "his name was familiar to government and people, to kings, courtiers, nobility, clergy, and philosophers, as well as plebians, to such a degree that there was scarcely a peasant or a citizen, a *valet de chambre,* coachman or footman, a lady's chambermaid or a scullion in a kitchen, who was not familiar with it, and who did not consider him as a friend to human kind. When they spoke of him, they seemed to think he was to restore the golden age." Franklin could also capitalize on the military weakness of France. Comte de Vergennes, eager to rectify the imbalance between French and English power, welcomed the opportunity to sever ties between England and America, for he believed that colonial independence and subsequent free trade would hamper England's maritime power. Hence the reason for France's offering the colonies secret aid prior to the opening of official negotiations. When the American commissioners arrived in France, Vergennes was ready not only to grant aid but also to intervene militaristically—once the colonists had proved their strength and determination. Immediately after Burgoyne's surrender at Saratoga, the king of France entered a treaty of alliance with America.

In June 1781 Congress appointed Franklin, John Jay, Henry Laurens, and Thomas Jefferson to assist John Adams in negotiating treaties of peace and commerce with England. As sole commissioner in France as late as March 1782 Franklin began preliminaries with Richard Oswald and defined what he judged necessary and advisable terms. He advised that Britain acknowledge her error in distressing the colonies, offer indemnification and free trade, and cede all of Canada. His necessary terms were, essentially, those officially agreed upon as preliminary articles: absolute independence, the settlement of boundaries, the limitation of Canadian boundaries as defined prior to the Quebec Act, and fishing rights on the banks of Newfoundland.

In addition to treating with France and England, Franklin was engaged in shipping supplies to America, assisting vessels in French waters, commissioning privateers, adjudicating prizes, exchanging prisoners of war, recommending officers for the American military, attending salons, and writing bagatelles, familiar letters, and political satires, notably "The Sale of the Hessians" (1777) and the "Supplement to the Boston Independent Chronicle" (1782). These satires focus on the brutality of the war and, again, on the greed and corruption of the British government.

"The Sale of the Hessians" responds to Washington's capture of nearly a thousand Hessians at Trenton and, through the tension between the greed of the fictitious Count de Schaumberg, who is supplying England with mercenaries, and his espousals of humaneness and glory, protests England's use of these mercenaries. Perhaps because its form is that of the personal letter, in which Franklin excelled, he here impressively controls his point of view. Although his letter to Hohendorf, the man Franklin creates commander of the

Hessian troops in America, ostensibly addresses military matters, Schaumberg engages in inadvertent self-revelation and deliberate self-concealment. During the process of writing, he attains an insight into his callous disregard of human life and his inordinate greed and is compelled to conceal or to justify these negative attributes. To the extent that he offers Hohendorf a persuasive justification falsely based upon time-honored values, Schaumberg ironically affirms his callousness.

He is a man of the world with whom the commander has been out of touch for nearly two months because Schaumberg was in Naples when Hohendorf's letter, to which Schaumberg now responds, arrived in Rome. Attempting to assume his official role although preoccupied with Italian opera, Schaumberg begins his reply with an expression of the ''unspeakable pleasure'' that he derives from the performance of his troops at Trenton: their ''courage'' resulted in the deaths of 1,605 of the 1,950 Hessians fighting for the British. Hohendorf too is praised for his sending an exact list of the dead to the Hessian minister at London and hence securing all of the florins due the count. He next reminds Hohendorf of the importance of obeying instructions. Because the British have objected to the inclusion of wounded soldiers in lists of the dead, Hohendorf must, as he was ordered, not attempt ''by human succor to recall the life of the unfortunates whose days could not be lengthened but by the loss of a leg or an arm. That would be making them a pernicious present, and I am sure they would rather die than live in a condition no longer fit for my service.'' Apparently sensing the implications of this instruction, he justifies, or at least qualifies, the order so that it will seem less inhumane: ''I do not mean by this that you should assassinate them; we should be humane, my dear Baron, but you may insinuate to the surgeons with entire propriety that a crippled man is a reproach to their profession, and that there is no wiser course than to let every one of them die when he ceases to be fit to fight.''

Just as he deviously appeals to the pride of the surgeons, so he appeals to the honor and glory once associated with war in order to secure the quick mortality of the new recruits he plans to send to America: ''Remember glory before all things. Glory is true wealth. There is nothing degrades the soldier like the love of money.'' Thus concealing from himself his unsoldierly lust for money, and convinced that he is indeed desirous of the glory accruing from heroic death in battle, Schaumberg imagines himself experiencing a joy similar to that of Leonidas at Thermopylæ: ''Do you remember that of the 300 Lacedæmonians who defended the defile of Thermopylæ, not one returned? How happy should I be could I say the same of my brave Hessians!'' Again the count evidences an insight into the awful reality of that for which he yearns and, significantly, into the import of his not fighting with the troops. But his contending, in justification, that he is not committed to the British cause is finally a condemnation of his behavior, and his pleading the need to be in Europe to receive pay and to send recruits attests his devotion to the profit motive. Hence he looks forward to the higher prices that young boys will bring because of the scarcity of adults. Hence too his sanctioning Hohendorf's sending Dr. Crumerus, who successfully treated soldiers suffering dysentery, back to Europe: "Don't bother with a man who is subject to looseness of the bowels. That disease makes bad soldiers.... Better that they burst in their barracks than fly in a battle, and tarnish the glory of our arms. Besides, you know that they pay me as killed for all who die from disease, and I don't get a farthing for runaways."

No longer attempting to justify or to conceal his inhumanity, Schaumberg openly confesses that his trip to Italy has proved costly and "makes it desirable that there should be a great mortality" among his soldiers. Therefore, the commander is to promise a promotion to all Hessians who will "expose themselves" and to "exhort them to seek glory in the midst of dangers." The climatic irony of the letter results from the antithesis of the count's total disregard of the value of human life ("let it be your principal object to prolong the war and avoid a decisive engagement on either side, for I have made arrangements for a grand Italian opera, and I do not wish to be obliged to give it up") and his easy prayer that God have Hohendorf "in his holy and gracious keeping."

Franklin wrote to Charles Dumas that the first edition of the "Supplement," a hoax printed on his press at Passy, "places in a striking light, the English barbarities in America, particularly those committed by the savages at their instigation. The FORM may perhaps not be genuine, but the *substance* is truth; the number of our people of all kinds and ages, murdered and scalped by them being known to exceed that of the invoice." Because he intended to shame the British, he exploited the sentimentality inherent in his gruesome details. The various voices of the work, however, are controlled, and the control serves only to heighten the emotional content of the satire.

The structure of the work is complex: it purports to be an extract from a letter of a British captain, Gerrish, which frames a letter of James Craufurd, a British soldier, to Governor Haldimand of Canada. Craufurd's letter, in turn, contains one from Chief Conejogatchie beseeching the governor to petition King George for Indian succor. In addition to these three points of view, a fourth is provided by a journalist who refers to an earlier edition of the *Chronicle* and, in a passage dated one week after the publication of Gerrish's letter, comments on the disposition of the booty now in possession of the New England militia and of which Gerrish provides an inventory. This structure allows Franklin to consider either directly or indirectly the British, Indian, Canadian, and American responses to the brutalities treated.

Gerrish states that although the Americans were first delighted to capture the packages that the Senecas had directed to Haldimand, who was to transmit them to England, they were horrified by the scalps contained in eight of the packages. Withholding further reaction until his concluding paragraph, Gerrish next introduces Craufurd's letter, which is primarily a mercilessly objective inventory of approximately seven hundred and fifty "cured, dried, hooped, and painted" scalps. As he must be if the reader is to experience the intended shame and outrage, Craufurd is not at all cognizant of the probable emotional impact even upon Haldimand and George III of the Indians' murdering innocent farmers, children, women, and fetuses. The following account typifies his persistent objectivity: "No. 4. Containing 102 of Farmers, mixed of the several Marks above; only 18 marked with a little yellow Flame, to denote their being of Prisoners burnt alive, after being scalped, their Nails pulled out by the Roots, and other Torments." With the same apparently subhuman aloofness he speaks of mothers' scalps marked with red tadpoles to indicate the grief of relatives, of older women's scalps that have "no Mark, but the short Club or *Casse-tête*, to shew they were knocked down dead, or had their Brains beat out," and of "a Box of Birch Bark, containing 29 little Infants' Scalps of various Sizes; small white Hoops; white Ground; no Tears; and only a little black Knife in the Middle, to shew they were ript out of their Mothers' Bellies."

Conejogatchie's speech, which portrays the Indians as victims of the war, indicates that Franklin intended to condemn not Indian savagery as such but rather British exploitation of that savagery. Desirous of proving Indian allegiance, the chief beseeches "Father" Haldimand "to send these Scalps over the Water to the great King, that he may regard them and be refreshed; and that he may see our faithfulness in destroying his Enemies, and be convinced that his Presents have not been made to ungrateful people." As he makes clear, their plight is pathetic: they have been driven from their homes; they suffer exploitation from English traders who now exact inflated prices; they suffer from a scarcity of game. Confronting ruin, Conejogatchie asks not only for land but also for more immediate necessities such as blankets and shirts rather than the arms that England customarily provides.

Craufurd's coldness and moral blindness and Conejogatchie's innocent pathos stand in contrast to the controlled outrage that Gerrish exhibits in his concluding paragraph and that of the journalist who comments on the proposed disposition of the scalps. Gerrish writes that the American troops preferred not to bury the scalps but rather to hang them in St. James's Park so "that the Sight of them might perhaps strike Muley Ishmael (as he called [the King]) with some Compunction of Conscience." But, the reporter explains, the furious Bostonians who viewed them chose to direct individual packages of scalps to the king, the queen, both houses of Parliament, and the bishops. Franklin thus indicts church and state.

The second edition of the "Supplement" offers a letter from privateer John Paul Jones to Sir Joseph York, British ambassador to Holland. Although his letter details the causes of the Revolution, it is, like "The Sale of the Hessians," primarily a personal letter in which Jones defends his role in the war. Its most salient features are his forceful moral indignation and the seemingly unimpeachable logic with which he first clears himself of Sir Joseph's charge that he is a pirate and then justifies the Revolution according to Whig principles. Jones coolly offers the first part of his two-pronged definition— "A pirate is defined to be *hostis humani generis*"—and easily demonstrates that while he is an enemy to England alone, she is not only an enemy to and at war with one-quarter of the world but is also "in a fair way of being at war with the rest." Because a pirate makes war for rapine and because England has sought to appropriate the colonists' property "without our consent, in violation of our rights, and by an armed force," she is waging a piratical war. Having thus proved that the British themselves are pirates, Jones demonstrates that the war is an expression of the nation's rapacious daemon: "Your common people in their ale-houses sing the twenty-four songs of Robin Hood, and applaud his deer-stealing and his robberies on the highway: those, who have just learning enough to read, are delighted with your histories of the pirates and of the buccaniers; and even your scholars in the universities study Quintus Curtius, and are taught to admire Alexander for what they call 'his conquests in the Indies.'" To gratify this spirit, England provoked a war with her colonies and justified the plunder of American property through a parliamentary act that legalized theft and thus "repealed the law of God."

To counter the argument that Americans forfeited their property when they refused to pay the taxes that Parliament had levied, and thereby to justify colonial rebellion, Jones refers to compact, to the right to property, and to the Whig principles of the Glorious Revolution. First reminding Sir Joseph of the foundation of Hampden's lawsuit against Charles I—"'what an English king has no right to demand, an English subject has a right to refuse'"—and of a principle of Sir Joseph's father—"if subjects might in some cases forfeit their property, kings also might forfeit their title, and all claim to the allegiance of their subjects"—he lists the specific acts by which George III has forfeited the allegiance of his American subjects. The enumeration of these injustices and barbarities, not surprisingly, destroys the predominantly logical approach that Jones has taken toward his essentially emotion-laden subject. From this point to the end of his letter, he becomes more and more frantic. He judges the king's tyrannical treatment of his domestic and foreign subjects to be the worst treatment inflicted by any other tyrant "since the beginning of the world," and to defend his position, he compares George III and Nero, "one of the worst and blackest" of tyrants. On the whole, Jones regards Nero more favorably than he regards George, who with his Parliaments has proved worse than public calamities, for "plagues, pestilences, and famines are of this world, and arise from the nature of things; but voluntary malice, mischief, and murder, are from hell; and this King will, therefore, stand foremost in the list of diabolical, bloody, and execrable tyrants. His base-bought parliaments too, who sell him their souls, and extort from the people the money with which they aid his destructive purposes, as they share his guilt, will share his infamy."

V

Before retiring from public office in October 1788, Franklin served as president of the Supreme Executive Council of Pennsylvania for three terms and as a delegate to the Constitutional Convention. Although none of the issues that he championed at the convention—a unicameral legislature, plural executive, and nonsalaried officials—was adopted, he had participated in each of the crucial events that gave rise to the republic, which he described in "Information to Those Who Would Remove to America" (1782?) and "The Internal State of America" (1786). The contradiction between the economic and social status that Franklin had attained by the 1780s and the vision of America offered in these essays does not deny their validity as statements of a general trend and of the value that he attached to a democratic and agrarian society. In both works, he praised the country as a land of "happy Mediocrity" that fostered virtue:

> Whoever has travelled thro' the various Parts of Europe, and observed how small is the Proportion of People in Affluence or easy Circumstances there, compar'd with those in Poverty and Misery; the few rich and haughty Landlords, the multitude of poor, abject, and rack'd Tenants, and the half-paid and half-starv'd ragged Labourers; and views here the happy Mediocrity, that so generally prevails throughout these States, where the Cultivator works for himself, and supports his Family in decent Plenty, will, methinks, see Reason to bless Divine Providence for the evident and great Difference in our Favour, and be convinc'd, that no Nation that is known to us enjoys a greater Share of human Felicity. (*Writings*, 10: 120)

The nation's religious, social, economic, and political situation constituted a postlapsarian Eden, and the personal letters that Franklin wrote from 1785 until his death in 1790 reveal his satisfaction with the republic for which he labored more than a quarter of a century. The large body of literature through which he supported his political endeavors makes him a founder of American literature as well as of the United States of America.

SUGGESTIONS FOR FURTHER READING

Editions

The Autobiography of Benjamin Franklin. Edited by Leonard W. Labaree et al. New
    Haven, Conn.: Yale University Press, 1964.
Benjamin Franklin's Letters to the Press, 1758–1775. Edited by Verner W. Crane.
    Chapel Hill: University of North Carolina Press, 1950.
The Papers of Benjamin Franklin. Edited by Leonard W. Labaree et al. 18 vols. to
    date. New Haven, Conn.: Yale University Press, 1959—.
The Writings of Benjamin Franklin. Edited by Albert Henry Smyth. 10 vols. New
    York: Macmillan, 1905–7.

Scholarship and Criticism

Aldridge, Alfred Owen. Franklin and His French Contemporaries. New York: New
    York University Press, 1957.
Amacher, Richard E. Benjamin Franklin. New York: Twayne, 1962.
Becker, Carl L. Benjamin Franklin: A biographical sketch. Ithaca, N.Y.: Cornell
    University Press, 1946.
Cohen, I. Bernard. Benjamin Franklin: His Contribution to the American Tradition.
    New York: Bobbs-Merrill, 1953.
Crane, Verner W. Benjamin Franklin and a Rising People. Boston: Little, Brown,
    1954.
Granger, Bruce Ingham. Benjamin Franklin: An American Man of Letters. Ithaca,
    N.Y.: Cornell University Press, 1964.
Lemay, J. A. Leo. "Franklin and the Autobiography: An Essay on Recent
    Scholarship." Eighteenth-Century Studies 1 (1967–68): 185–211.
Miles, Richard D. "The American Image of Benjamin Franklin," American Quarterly
    9 (1957) : 117–43.
Stourzh, Gerald. Benjamin Franklin and American Foreign Policy. Chicago: The
    University of Chicago Press, 1954.
Van Doren, Carl. Benjamin Franklin. New York: Viking, 1938.

8

Philip Freneau and Francis Hopkinson

WILLIAM D. ANDREWS

[*The Philadelphia of Benjamin Franklin produced other important men of letters during the Revolution, including the poet Francis Hopkinson. His career and that of another poet of the middle colonies, Philip Freneau, provide a good deal of insight into the problems of the man of letters in late-eighteenth-century America. The writings of both men are also closely related to the great events of their day. Freneau's activities won him the title "Poet of the American Revolution."*]

Several decades before the Revolution, the cultural center of the American colonies shifted south from Boston to Philadelphia, which by the time of the war was in both its size and the quality of its intellectual life second in the British empire only to London itself. The great political events of the last third of the eighteenth century which occurred in the middle colonies—meetings of the Continental Congresses, signing of the Declaration of Independence, drafting of the Constitution—symbolized not merely the triumph of American nationalism but also the maturation of the colonies of New York, New Jersey, and Pennsylvania. The life of the mind as it was lived in New England in the seventeenth century and after influenced ideological developments that culminated in the Revolution, but the middle colonies and the South provided organizers and penmen who planned goals and strategy and popularized them, through writing, among other colonials. The importance of the middle colonies in the Revolution is of course partly due to mere geography: central location made Philadelphia the logical seat of the Continental Congresses and the Constitutional Convention. More significant than geography, though, was the cultural life of the middle colonies which nurtured the men and women and the ideas which encouraged separation from England and the establishment of a new nation.

127

Philosophy and art—both of which played key roles in the making of the Revolution—enjoyed hospitable receptions in New York, New Jersey, and Pennsylvania. Although hardly alien in either New England or the South, they were especially cultivated by residents of the middle colonies, where an atmosphere of openness and tolerance endorsed the pursuit of thought and art and encouraged their growth and communication through literature. The instruments of literary and intellectual development were widely available in the middle colonies in the form of lending libraries (like Franklin's Library Company, founded in 1731 in Philadelphia); colleges (King's, now Columbia, founded in New York in 1754; the College of New Jersey, now Princeton, in 1746; the College of Philadelphia, now the University of Pennsylvania, in 1751); publishers of newspapers, magazines, and books; and philosophical and literary societies (like the Junto and American Philosophical Society in Philadelphia), which brought together persons of like interests for the purpose of sharing ideas and supporting one another's work. Such institutions are themselves insufficient to explain the growth of cultural life in the middle colonies, but their presence—and the presence of theaters, private libraries, collections of scientific instruments, studios of painters, and so forth—reflects the commitment of residents of the area to the life of the mind. Active and successful in trade and agriculture, residents of the middle colonies had ready access to the instruments of culture and the desire and capacity to make profitable use of them.

The flourishing of culture in New York, New Jersey, and Pennsylvania in the middle decades of the eighteenth century serves as necessary background to an understanding of two important writers of the American Revolution, Francis Hopkinson (1737–91) and Philip Freneau (1752–1832). Sons of the middle colonies (Hopkinson was a native of Philadelphia and lived for a time in New Jersey; a New Yorker by birth, Freneau was reared and educated in New Jersey and wrote and published in those colonies and in Pennsylvania), both were nourished by the active intellectual life of the area and represented the best of its educational and literary traditions. One cannot conclude that either man owed his talents and intentions solely to his place of birth, but in their literary and political interests and accomplishments both writers reflected the high level of cultural life characteristic of the middle colonies and essential to a recognition of the role those colonies played in the Revolution. Different in many respects, Hopkinson and Freneau shared a commitment to the Revolution and to the new nation it established, and both served the cause of patriotism with the literary skills that had been stimulated and trained through the education and experience the middle colonies provided them. They became loyal Americans in part because they were in the beginning sons of the middle colonies and grateful recipients of its culture.

I

Francis Hopkinson enjoyed an early and long acquaintance with the active intellectual life of his native Philadelphia. His father, Thomas Hopkinson, a lawyer, who first appeared in Philadelphia in 1731, served as secretary of Franklin's Library Company and as the first president of his American Philosophical Society. He died in 1751, the year his son Francis, born in 1737, matriculated as a member of the first class of the Academy of Philadelphia, an institution also created through Franklin's efforts and modeled upon his practical philosophy for the education of youth. The Academy was later extended to include a college, and Hopkinson was in its first graduating class in 1757. While at the Academy and College of Philadelphia, Hopkinson came under the influence of the Reverend William Smith, a Scot appointed first provost of the school after Franklin had read approvingly his writings on education, published in New York while Smith lived there as a tutor immediately after coming to the colonies. Smith served the young college with considerable skill and inspired many of its students to follow careers in art and literature. (Benjamin West, the Pennsylvania painter who became president of the Royal Academy in London, owed his success to Smith's early encouragement and support.) Smith gathered at the college a group of erstwhile poets and playwrights called the Swains of the Schuylkill (for the river bordering Philadelphia on the west); among the Swains were Hopkinson, Jacob Duché (later Hopkinson's brother-in-law and a famous Anglican minister and writer of *belles lettres*), Nathaniel Evans (minister and poet), and Thomas Godfrey (author of the early play *The Prince of Parthia*).

Following his graduation in 1757, Hopkinson continued to court the muses, both of poetry and music, to whom Provost Smith had introduced him. He also undertook the study of law under Benjamin Chew, attorney-general of Pennsylvania. Admitted to the bar in 1761, Hopkinson later obtained the position of collector of customs for the port of Salem, New Jersey (a task performed from Philadelphia, with the help of a deputy in Salem), and operated a store in Philadelphia. Although he remained happily active in the affairs of the Library Company and Christ Church, Hopkinson apparently was dissatisfied with his career and resolved to travel to England in search of a higher political appointment in the colonies. In 1766 he left for a year in England, living some of the time with Benjamin West and visiting with his relatives by marriage, Lord North and the Bishop of Worcester, from whom he anticipated some important position. Nothing concrete came of his sojourn abroad— Hopkinson's intentions were vague in the first place—so he returned to Philadelphia and in 1768 married the affluent Ann Borden of Bordentown,

New Jersey. Hopkinson finally received an appointment in 1772 as collector of customs at New Castle, Delaware, a position that brought him sufficient income, in combination with his wife's money, to afford him leisure to pursue his interests in literature and music. He published *A Collection of Psalm Tunes* in 1763 and remained active in song-writing and playing as well as in versifying. Around 1773 or 1774 he moved to Bordentown, became active in politics, and through the good offices of his father-in-law and his friend William Franklin, governor of New Jersey and illegitimate son of Benjamin Franklin, obtained profitable but undemanding political appointments.

As a delegate from New Jersey, Hopkinson attended the Second Continental Congress in Philadelphia in June of 1776 and voted for and signed the Declaration of Independence. During the Revolution he served as chairman of the Congress's Navy Board, as treasurer of loans, and as judge of admiralty. In these positions he contributed directly to the revolutionary cause, and as the designer of the new flag for the United States Hopkinson made the most symbolic gift of his many talents to his new country. After the war he remained active in politics, serving as judge of admiralty for Pennsylvania and later as a federal judge. A member of the Constitutional Convention, he used his literary talents in support of ratification and the Federalist philosophy. Hopkinson devoted his later years to music and science as well as literature and politics; he produced innovations in the candlestick and harpsichord, corresponded with Jefferson, Franklin, and others on scientific matters, and continued to write and perform music. He died in 1791, celebrated and loved by his many famous friends and the citizens of the new nation who appreciated his service in the revolutionary cause.

The details of Hopkinson's long and busy life yield few clues to explain his commitment to the Revolution. A member of the Anglican establishment in Philadelphia, he was influenced in other respects by such men as William Smith, whose attitude toward the Revolution was at best lukewarm, and enjoyed the close friendship of his brother-in-law Jacob Duché, who fled the colonies rather than support the Revolution. Through marriage, moreover, he was related to several of the most powerful Englishmen of his day. So well connected and established in Anglo-American society, holding political appointments from the crown, and having such a material as well as cultural stake in the continuation of British rule, Hopkinson had little to gain from independence—and a good deal to lose. Yet without apparent hesitation and soul-searching of the sort that even such acclaimed patriots as Franklin occasionally suffered, Hopkinson endorsed the American cause and served it vigorously, both in political positions and through his writing. Affected most, probably, by a strong sense of place and rootedness—he was devoted to the Philadelphia area and the friends and institutions he enjoyed there—Hopkinson cast his lot with a cause whose outcome he was hardly sure of.

Chief among his contributions to the Revolution were his writings—ballads and satires in verse and prose. In a letter to Franklin of October 22, 1778, Hopkinson remarked that "I have not Abilities to assist our righteous Cause by personal Prowess & Force of Arms, but I have done it all the Service I could with my Pen—throwing in my mite at Times in Prose & Verse, serious & satirical Essays &ca." His literary and musical talents served Hopkinson especially well in the writing of ballads like his famous "The Battle of the Kegs" (1778), an eighty-eight line poem based on a real incident of war. The Navy Board commissioned Asa Bushnell to invent floating mines in the form of kegs of gunpowder which were sent down the Delaware River in January of 1778 to sink British ships in the Philadelphia harbor; but because the ships were drawn to the docks to avoid ice floats, the kegs missed their mark and exploded harmlessly in the river. Hopkinson exploited the humor of this failure in "The Battle of the Kegs," turning it against the British reaction rather than the colonists' miscalculations. The ballad depicts the chaotic and fearful response of the British:

> The solider flew, the sailor too,
>   And scar'd almost to death, sir,
> Wore out their shoes, to spread the news,
>   And ran till out of breath, sir.
>
> . . . .
>
> Some fire cried, which some denied,
>   But said the earth had quaked;
> And girls and boys, with hideous noise,
>   Ran thro' the streets half naked.
>
> Sir William he, snug as a flea,
>   Lay all this time a snoring,
> Nor dream'd of harm as he lay warm,
>   In bed with Mrs. L———g.[1]

Misperceiving the nature of the attack, the British rallied to defend Philadelphia against what turned out to be an empty threat. Their feeling of success in this mission drew Hopkinson's best satire:

> An hundred men with each a pen,
>   Or more upon my word, sir,

---

1. Except where otherwise noted, quotations from Hopkinson's works are from *The Miscellaneous Essays and Occasional Writings of Francis Hopkinson;* poetry appears in the third volume. Since just prior to his death Hopkinson revised much of his work for this edition, it is worthwhile to compare revised versions with original texts as they appeared in book and periodical form.

> It is most true would be too few,
>   Their valor to record, sir.
>
> Such feats did they perform that day,
>   Against these wick'd kegs, sir,
> That years to come, if they get home,
>   They'll make their boasts and brags, sir.

Satirical treatment of British pomposity in thinking they had repelled the attack gave "The Ballad of the Kegs" its contemporary fame. It was set to music and song by colonial soldiers and reprinted in newspapers and as a broadside.

"A Camp Ballad" (1778), another of Hopkinson's popular verses also sung by soldiers, took a more serious attitude toward the war, depicting the bold actions of colonists to overcome the loss of freedom threatened by England:

> MAKE room, oh! ye kingdoms in hist'ry renowned
> Whose arms have in battle with glory been crown'd,
> Make room for America, another great nation,
> Arises to claim in your council a station.
>
> Her sons fought for freedom, and by their own brav'ry
> Have rescued themselves from the shackles of slav'ry.
> America's free, and tho' Britain abhor'd it,
> Yet fame a new volume prepares to record it.

The sentiments in these ballads, conventionally patriotic, probably explain less well their contemporary popularity than do the clever phrasing and Hopkinson's musical gift, which fashioned memorable songs to rouse and entertain the embattled colonists. His ballads had a contemporary use and fame in excess of their inherent literary merit, but they retain their interest to historians as reflections of American popular attitudes during the Revolution.

The most pleasing and probably most effective of Hopkinson's writings on the Revolution, a work that deserves extended consideration, is his transparent political allegory, *A Pretty Story Written in the Year of our Lord 2774, by Peter Grievous, Esq; A.B.C.D.E.* Published in Philadelphia on September 5, 1774, during the meeting of the First Continental Congress, *A Pretty Story* attracted sufficient attention to warrant a second edition the same year in Philadelphia and an additional reprinting in Williamsburg; it was issued in 1857 as a plea for unity in a nation heading toward civil war, under the title by which it is sometimes known, *The Old Farm and the New Farm. A Pretty Story* is a tale of "a certain Nobleman, who had long possessed a very valuable Farm, and had a great Number of Children and Grandchildren." The reader quickly discovers that the Nobleman is the allegorical representation of the king of England. His wife, "sole Mistress of the Purse Strings," represents Parliament. His children, who settle the New Farm, an "immense Tract of wild uncultivated Country at a vast Distance from his Mansion House," are the American colonists. Despite the rights guaranteed them in the Great Paper (Magna Carta) and their deep love of their father the Nobleman, the settlers are subjected to harrassment and financial control by the father's Steward (Lord North), who "had debauched his [the Nobleman's] Wife, and by that Means gained an entire Ascendency over her." Loving appeals to their father bring no relief to the settlers as the Steward and wife continue their campaign to control the New Farm and use its wealth for their own ends. The Steward's motives in this endeavor include his lust for power, but he is principally governed by simple hatred: "Now the Steward continued to hate the new Settlers with exceeding great Hatred, and determined to renew his Attack upon their Peace and Happiness." Such a view of the Steward conformed to the prevalent colonial attitude toward Lord North, but Hopkinson's depiction of him as a nearly satanic figure is especially striking since North was Hopkinson's relative by marriage.

Reprisals against the settlers of the New Farm continue, despite their protests. A particularly vexing tax on *"Water Gruel"* (tea) leads to confrontation with one of the settlers, Jack (Massachusetts), who destroys the commodity in his port rather than pay the hated tax. Because of his disobedience the gate to Jack's home is padlocked (the Boston Port Bill), and an Overseer (General Gage) is sent to enforce the laws of the Old Farm as interpreted by the Steward. Jack's brothers rally to his cause but are prohibited by the Overseer from meeting to express their grievances and solidarity with Jack. *A Pretty Story* ends inconclusively after the description of the Overseer's prohibition of assembly: "These harsh and unconstitutional Proceedings irritated *Jack* and the other Inhabitants of the new Farm to such a Degree that * * * * * * *." *"Caetera defunt,"* "the rest is lacking," are the last words of the piece, an indication of Hopkinson's belief that his allegorical depiction of the events of the 1760s and 1770s would lead to action, probably dramatic action, by the Continental Congress just then meeting to consider such matters as the Boston Port Bill and General Gage's suppression of dissent.

No one in Hopkinson's day could miss the meaning of *A Pretty Story*; its allegory was, by design, bald. More than that, the piece addressed familiar political events in a literary form equally familiar to Hopkinson's contemporaries. Modeled in part upon John Arbuthnot's *The History of John Bull* (1712), a popular British political allegory, *A Pretty Story* derives also from Hopkinson's familiarity with the satires of such other British writers as Joseph Addison, Richard Steele, and Jonathan Swift. Well versed in the conventions of satire and allegory practiced by his transatlantic counsins, Hopkinson, like so many American writers of his day and after, added to British forms the urgency of American experience, thus creating a work which resembles contemporary British writing on the surface—in its dependence on form and style—but at core addresses the American situation unmistakably and powerfully. *A Pretty Story* thus deserves to be remembered not only for its significance as a literary document of the Revolution but also because it shares with so much later, and better, American literature a critical distinguishing characteristic: the use, and modification, of English conventions to fit the special requirements of the American experience.

The allegory also reveals much about Hopkinson's view of the Revolution. Blame for British mistreatment of the colonies was directed squarely at Lord North, the real-life steward whose "exceeding great Hatred" toward the prosperous and happy settlers of the New World motivated British actions. Hopkinson absolved George III, pictured in *A Pretty Story* as a dear but ineffectual old father, and laid the failure of Parliament to check North's rule on its having been "debauched" by the minister. Greed and lust for power on the part of the ministry, resulting in unjustifiable hatred of the colonists, appeared to Hopkinson as the explanation for British conduct. To him the whole sad affair boiled down to politics and the pettiness of those who practiced it at the highest levels of the imperial government. Abstract questions of liberty and slavery which moved such other revolutionary writers as Freneau played no part in Hopkinson's view of the cause of the revolt as it is revealed in *A Pretty Story*. To Hopkinson the Revolution was the result of power-hungry politicians acting for their own purposes. At them he aimed his satire, the literary weapon British writers of the eighteenth century honed so finely for their attacks on ministers and bishops, poetasters and pretenders. Hopkinson's effective use of satire, couched in allegory, reflected his fundamental belief that the Revolution was the reaction of men against men, of wronged colonists against their transgressors, and not the result of cosmic forces or the reflection of national destiny.

Hopkinson's distinguished friend Dr. Benjamin Rush observed "that the various causes which contributed to the establishment of the independence and federal government of the United States, will not be *fully traced*, unless much is ascribed to the irresistible influence of the *ridicule* which [Hopkinson] poured forth . . . upon the enemies of those great political events." *Ridicule* describes precisely Hopkinson's contribution to the polemics of the Revolution. His writings were never bitter; good-natured himself, prone to humor and wit, Hopkinson turned these qualities against the enemies of *causes* he supported—he seldom had personal enemies. Behind the Revolution he perceived only the failings of particular individuals, British ministers like Lord North, and not the corruption of a whole nation or the movement of destiny. Decency, which Hopkinson had in abundance, required action, defense of principles and property when they were threatened. But Hopkinson's writing, though pointed and vigorous, never partook of invective and never lost its essentially humorous quality. In the justness and good nature of his revolutionary writings Hopkinson probably represented faithfully the sentiments of the majority of his fellow patriots. Certainly in his love of place, his commitment to the cause of independence, and his willingness to employ art to support politics he shares much with later Americans, writers and others, who lived in a society made possible by the revolution Hopkinson lent his literary talent to advance.

II

In a book he owned, beside a mention of "The Ballad of the Kegs," Philip Freneau identified the author of the piece as "Francis Fiddlesticks." What appears a touch of gentle humor of the sort Hopkinson himself practiced masks only imperfectly the antagonism Freneau felt for his older contemporary and fellow literary soldier of the Revolution. Both were natives of the middle colonies, educated there and active in the cultural life of the area, and both were also patriot writers. The similarities end there. Where Hopkinson was rational and witty, Freneau was fiery, full of invective and bitterness, both against persons and causes. Hopkinson's view of the Revolution was pragmatic, Freneau's (as we shall see) mythic. Hopkinson was an eminently urban man, at home in cities, while Freneau longed for the rural life his best writings celebrate. Hopkinson, despite his support of the Revolution, was Anglican and a member of the establishment; Freneau, of Dissenting stock, was a rebel by nature, enemy of the status quo, champion of unpopular causes. Most important, Hopkinson viewed literature as a hobby, a fit pursuit for a cultured man whose interests included science, painting, and music as well; Freneau dedicated himself to art and considered himself principally a writer, a claim justified by his accomplishments and maintained by even the least sympathetic of his later critics.

Philip Freneau was born near New York City in 1752, the son of a French Huguenot father, a wine importer who emigrated to America in the mid-1740s, and a mother of Scottish ancestry. A smallpox epidemic in New York in the year of the poet's birth dictated a removal to Mount Pleasant, New Jersey, in Monmouth County, where Freneau was reared at "Locust Grove," the house his father built on his in-laws' property. A pious man, the father encouraged his son toward the ministry, a fact of value in understanding Freneau's lifelong, if unorthodox, interest in religion. Freneau's father died in 1767, with his business in uncertain straits. Despite family financial problems Freneau entered the College of New Jersey (now Princeton) in 1768, following his father's wishes that he attend the school then the center of Presbyterian strength in the middle colonies. Exposed there to the classics and to British literature, Freneau was attracted to a career in writing, a choice encouraged by his classmates and good friends James Madison and Hugh Henry Brackenridge, themselves political and literary figures of high stature in later years. After graduation in 1771, Freneau tried his hand at schoolteaching on Long Island; thirteen days of the routine persuaded him that it was unsuitable, and he returned to Princeton for six months of informal graduate residence.

Freneau's vocational life was divided between marine commerce (he captained many ships on voyages along the American coast and to the West Indies) and journalism. After his marriage in 1790 he edited the New York *Daily Advertiser*; he also edited two politically oriented papers in Philadelphia, *The Freeman's Journal* (1781–84) and the *National Gazette* (1791–93); and after he left active politics he edited his own *Jersey Chronicle* (1795–96) and the New York literary periodical, *The Time-Piece* (1797–98). Temperamentally incapable of resisting a quarrel, Freneau devoted (his critics say wasted) much of his newspaper career to acrimonious debates. As editor of *The Freeman's Journal* he supported not only the Revolution but also the Constitutionalist party in Pennsylvania politics, which opposed the Republican Society, whose members included Franklin and Hopkinson. Venomous attacks were traded between the two sides, and the rancor of *The Freeman's Journal* became widely known and drew sharp criticism from Hopkinson and others. Hopkinson attacked Freneau's paper in "The Rise of the *Freeman's Journal*," published in the *Pennsylvania Packet* on April 2, 1782. A parody of the witch scene in *Macbeth*, Hopkinson's piece began with the speeches of the scribblers who founded the paper:

> Seeds of Discord will we sow,
> Seeds that never fail to grow.
> Dire Dissension, Envy, Hate
> Shall not cease to propagate.
>
> Num'rous shall their Offspring be
> Scorpion tongu'd—Hell's Progeny,
> Fair is foul & foul is fair,
> Haste, th' infernal Ink prepare!

Justified or not, such attacks on Freneau's journalistic endeavors were common, particularly when his devotion to political causes outran his taste for art and resulted in vicious and bitter satire—which was not infrequent.

No doubt Freneau's most celebrated newspaper war occurred during his tenure as editor of the *National Gazette*, an Antifederalist paper which he founded in Philadelphia in 1791 with the encouragement of Thomas Jefferson and James Madison. The *National Gazette* was designed to compete with the

Gazette of the United States, a Federalist organ edited by John Fenno. During his editorship of the *National Gazette* Freneau held a post as translating clerk in Jefferson's State Department, a situation which led to charges that Freneau was being subsidized by the federal government his paper attacked. The controversy stimulated by this apparent conflict of interests was compounded by Freneau's virulent attack on Federalist causes and his open support of the French Revolution. Freneau easily managed to infuriate the federal establishment, drawing from President Washington the famous epithet, "That rascal Freneau!" Jefferson supported him fully, remarking to Washington that "his paper has saved our Constitution which was galloping fast into monarchy." Whatever the merits of the case, Freneau's editorship of the *National Gazette* was a typically stormy period in his life, the kind of public activity he relished but could tolerate only in limited doses. He abandoned the failing paper in 1793 and returned, as he did so often following such unsatisfying public exposure, to Mount Pleasant. His financial condition, never strong, deteriorated sharply during his later years, despite further newspaper work in New Jersey and New York; as an old man he was forced to work on the public roads in Monmouth County to pay his taxes. He died in December of 1832, lost in a blizzard as he tried to find his way home at night.

During his chaotic and largely unsuccessful career as sea captain and editor Freneau wrote a large quantity of poetry which was collected in five editions during his lifetime (1786, 1788, 1795, 1809, 1815). A collection of his extensive prose writings and numerous separate printings of his poems, all in addition to his newspaper verse, also appeared during his lifetime. In 1822 Freneau proposed another edition of his poetry, which never appeared; his chief motive was to reprint his revolutionary writings, which he thought would be most attractive to a modern audience that had probably forgotten his literary service to the founding of the nation:

> The writings of that Memorable period of Seventy-Six, and the seven Revo-
> lutionary Years [he wrote] will ever, it may be presumed, be particularly
> interesting to the American readers of the present day, and to the generations
> that are to succeed, more especially when they accompany, and have refer-
> ence to the historical Events of those times, which now seem to bid fair in no
> small degree to influence the future destinies as well as Moral and political
> character of mankind at large.[2]

Freneau's desire, at age seventy, to recapture his fame as Poet of the American Revolution provides sad and touching testament to both his own self-
image as patriotic writer and the shortness of popular memory.

Despite the decline of his fame in his last years, and the current view of him
as chiefly a poet of nature and a precursor of romanticism in American

2. Quoted by Lewis Leary, *That Rascal Freneau: A Study in Literary Failure,* p. 350.

literature, Freneau's claim to the title Poet of the American Revolution is amply justified by both the extent and nature of the poems he wrote in support of the American cause. His verse was widely known in the colonies, reproduced in newspapers to rouse and delight the civilian population, and reportedly sung by soldiers and sailors in battle. Although he spent two critical years of the Revolution (1776–78) in the West Indies, engaged in shipping, Freneau was active in nonliterary ways, joining the New Jersey militia in 1778, for example. Still, like Hopkinson, Freneau's principal contribution to the Revolution derived from his skill as satirist and polemicist. His characteristically scorching occasional pieces on officers, battles, and political events spare nothing in the praise of patriots and the damnation of British foes. In "A Political Litany" (1775), for example, Freneau described two British leaders, North and George III, in typically acid terms:

> . . . the caitiff, lord *North,* who would bind us in chains,
> . . . a royal king Log, with his tooth-full of brains,
> Who dreams, and is certain (when taking a nap)
> He has conquered our lands, as they lay on his map.[3]

The British general Cornwallis Freneau depicted as "The *plundering servant of a bankrupt king,*" a "reptile," and a monstrosity: "Nature in him disgrac'd the form divine; / Nature mistook, she meant him for a—swine." Invective against the British was matched in Freneau's writing with wholehearted praise of the Americans, including especially General Washington (the later target of Freneau's Antifederalist attacks), whom he described in 1783 as "the *Hero* of our land," redeemer of "our western reign," and virtuous patriot-soldier upon whose military skill, wisdom, and moderation would depend the future of the new nation ("Occasioned by General Washington's Arrival in Philadelphia"). Satanic Britons and Adamic colonials played nearly allegorical roles in Freneau's verse, acting out the battle of evil and good against the backdrop of the War for Independence. Like any effective polemicist, Freneau reduced the complexities of the political situation to simplistic choices between right and wrong and then called for vigorous action to support the American cause: "So just, so virtuous is your cause, I say, / Hell must prevail, if Britain gains the day" ("To the Americans," 1775).

The best known and most vitriolic of Freneau's revolutionary poems is "The British Prison Ship," written in 1780 (published in 1781) following Freneau's incarceration for six weeks on prison ships in New York harbor. Lewis Leary called the piece a "hymn of hate," and Freneau's biographers

3. For convenience, all of Freneau's poems are quoted from Harry Hayden Clark's edition of the *Poems of Freneau,* but since this work is neither complete nor textually precise, the reader should see the other editions cited in the "Suggestions for Further Reading" as well as original book and periodical publication of the poems.

often ascribe his intense hatred of the British and willingness to use his literary talents against them to the experience which gave rise to the poem. Hatred and strong language were hardly absent from Freneau's work before 1780, but it is true that his apparently horrible prison experience did fan his hatred to even greater heights. "The British Prison Ship" comprises three cantos of verse, the first narrating Freneau's capture by the British while sailing on the ship *Aurora* out of Philadelphia, the second describing the horrors of the prison ship he was condemned to, and the third describing the hospital prison ship he was eventually transferred to for treatment of disorders contracted on the first ship. Freneau's hatred of the British animates the whole; they are a "host of fiends," "brutes," "slaves," and "the tribe I hate." "Heat, sickness, famine, death, and stagnant air" abound on their prison ship, causing suffering beyond the poet's capacity, or will, to describe:

> BUT such a train of endless woes abound,
> So many mischiefs in these hulks are found,
> That on them all a poem to prolong
> Would swell too high the horrors of my song—
> Hunger and thirst to work our woe combine,
> And mouldy bread, and flesh of rotten swine,
> The mangled carcase, and the batter'd brain,
> The doctor's poison, and the captain's cane,
> The soldier's musquet, and the steward's debt,
> The evening shackle, and the noon-day threat.

For the Britons and their king he had only contempt and hatred:

> The years approach that shall to ruin bring
> Your lords, your chiefs, your miscreant of a king
> Whose murderous acts shall stamp his name accurs'd,
> And his last triumphs more than damn the first.

Transfer to the hospital ship brought no relief because of a Hessian doctor who "kill'd at least as many as he cur'd." The horror of his treatment at the hands of the British and their Hessian minions motivated Freneau's passionate plea to his fellow rebels: "AMERICANS! a just resentment shew, / And glut revenge on this detested foe."

Freneau's experience on the prison and hospital ships, at least by his own account, warranted this display of outrage and call for revenge. As an intensely felt personal piece, effective as propaganda, "The British Prison Ship" is impressive for its credible depiction of British cruelty and its justification of the American cause; the unmistakable hatred at the center of the poem is made persuasive through Freneau's use of vivid, concrete details descriptive of his British captors and their methods. Whatever the merits of the claim that the prison ship experience proved a turning point in Freneau's attitude toward the British, it is still true that his description of that experience in the poem contributed to the developing view held by the colonists of the British as cruel oppressors.

It need hardly be remarked that Freneau's literary treatment of revolutionary subjects differed markedly from Francis Hopkinson's uniformly light and good-humored satires and polemics. Explanation for this difference lies partly, perhaps, in Freneau's treatment by the British; a deeper source may be discovered in several of Freneau's earlier poems, predating his imprisonment. What distinguishes Freneau from Hopkinson in their attitudes toward the Revolution is the presence in Freneau's writings of a mythic conception of American destiny which served consistently as a motivating force. Although often written in response to specific individuals and situations, and nearly always bitter and vituperative, Freneau's verse was animated by a conception of America's future glory that appears only occasionally in Hopkinson's writings (as in his College of Philadelphia commencement *Exercise* of 1761) and seldom with Freneau's depth of passion. This view of America was set forth clearly in *A Poem on the Rising Glory of America*, a commencement ode written by Freneau and delivered by Hugh Henry Brackenridge at Princeton in 1771 and published the next year in Philadelphia. A blank verse dialogue in sixteen speeches among three speakers, the poem celebrates America's future glory as an inevitable consequence of the westward movement of civilization and the unique benefits bestowed by nature on the New World. It begins with description and celebration of Columbus's discovery (''a theme / More new, more noble, and more flush of fame / Than all that went before''), proceeds to an inquiry into the origins of American Indians and a sketch of their suffering at the hands of the Spanish (an implicit parallel to later British mistreatment of white settlers), and concludes with a prediction of American greatness culminating in the millennium. Commerce and science are seen as handmaidens of the civilizing movement which brings culture irresistibly westward from the Old to the New World, and agriculture and ''the rustic reign'' are portrayed as the ideal state of society to be achieved in America. The benefits conferred by commerce, science, and agriculture are threatened in the poem by British tyranny, the cause of ''angry tumults'' destructive of the promise of the new land. Against the view of an American nation unjustly spoiled by British mismanagement Freneau poses a mythic vision of national destiny which will prevail in spite of political and military impositions from the Old World. American glory cannot be checked:

> A new Jerusalem, sent down from heaven,
> Shall grace our happy earth,—perhaps this land,
> Whose ample bosom shall receive, though late,
> Myriads of saints, with their immortal king,
> To live and reign on earth a thousand years,

Thence called *Millennium*. Paradise anew
Shall flourish, by no second Adam lost,
No dangerous tree with deadly fruit shall grow,
No tempting serpent to allure the soul
From native innocence.—A *Canaan* here,
Another *Canaan* shall excel the old
And from a fairer Pisgah's top be seen.

Freneau's depiction of the Adamic promise of the New World, consistent in American history from Puritan settlement through the twentieth century, assumed political significance in *A Poem on the Rising Glory of America* as a prediction of the happy consequences destined to follow independence. Predating the Declaration by over four years, the poem is prophetic rather than descriptive, and the prophecy remained at the center of Freneau's thought about the Revolution and its consequences. This vision of a divinely appointed American nation, heir to the best of Western tradition and the site of the millennium, animated Freneau's writing before and after the Revolution and persisted as an explicit theme in American literature for generations (present in the work of such disparate writers as Thoreau and Whitman in the nineteenth century and Fitzgerald in the twentieth).

Freneau's mythic conception of American destiny informed a group of important poems produced in the several years following *A Poem on the Rising Glory of America*. "The American Village" (1772) describes New World uniqueness through contrast with Oliver Goldsmith's image of the dying British village in *The Deserted Village* (1770). Fecund nature, sympathetic to Americans who husband it as farmers, explains the difference between the prosperous American village and its moribund counterpart in the mother country; the American nation—economically, politically, and morally rooted in agriculture—is seen in the poem as escaping the fate of decadent European nations (Carthage and Rome as well as England) whose pursuit of "dread commerce" made them prey to "the monster LUXURY" which topples even the proudest of empires. Its reliance on nature, expressed in the national occupation of agriculture, and its unique geographic position in the West guaranteed America favorable treatment at the hands of destiny; the decline which overtook nations of the Old World could not challenge American hegemony: "But if AMERICA, by this decay, / The world itself must fall as well as she." The fall of America would signal not the rise of another, more westward empire, but the end of the world, the millennium. Such confidence in America's special position reflects what appears to modern readers an unduly optimistic, even naive, perception of reality, but Freneau, who derived his thought from preromantic tendencies current throughout Western civilization in the late eighteenth century, cannot be dismissed as a fuzzy dreamer out of touch with reality. Although he looked forward to the reign of peace and liberty in the pastoral paradise of the New World, the poet understood how easily corruption and decay may occur. His treatment of American Indians in "The American Village" reflects this understanding; highly sympathetic to their claims on the land, Freneau shows them as victims of European greed, cheated of their natural inheritance by the lust for wealth characteristic of the early explorers and settlers. In "Discovery" (also written in 1772), he addressed this issue directly, considering the problems inherent in discovery of western lands and the transfer of civilization from east to west. "Avarice," dogmatic religion, and "Vain pride" led Europeans to rape the New World:

> Slaves to their passions, man's imperious race,
> Born for contention, find no resting place,
> And the vain mind, bewildered and perplext,
> Makes this world wretched to enjoy the next.
> Tired of the scenes that Nature made their own,
> They rove to conquer what remains unknown.

The impulse toward discovery, viewed by Freneau as a worthy trait in its own right, brought cruelty and misery to the original inhabitants of the New World precisely because the explorers were products of decadent European culture: "What are the arts that rise on Europe's plan / But arts destructive to the bliss of man?"

Freneau's most moving artistic consideration of this unpleasant fact is "The Pictures of Columbus" (written in 1774), a series of eighteen verse sketches of Columbus at various stages in his career. In an overall narrative structure, heightened throughout with effective uses of dramatic conventions, "The Pictures of Columbus" traces the discoverer's growing realization that his inspired act of discovery can lead only to enslavement and suffering for the unspoiled natives subjected to forced "civilizing" at the hands of greedy Europeans. Columbus sees "Sweet sylvan scenes of innocence and ease" contaminated by "hard laws to crush fair freedom" and "gloomy jails to shut up wretched men"—characteristic products of European nations. His hope that "we may fortune find without a crime" is unfulfilled, and his own career ends in shameful imprisonment. Optimistic about the opportunities to keep America pure as an asylum for those who flee European corruption and as a new Eden from which sin was barred, Freneau nonetheless recognized that the very discovery of America was motived by base impulses and carried out with cruel disregard for the rights of its original inhabitants. Later American writers—Joel Barlow in *The Columbiad* (1807) and Robert Frost in "America is Hard to See" (1951)—followed Freneau in this perception, using Columbus's ironic career as the basis for exploration of the missed opportunities and failed dreams of American life. That Freneau gave sensitive and effective expression to the issue on several occasions in the four year before the Declaration of Independence testifies to the intensity of his vision of American destiny

—a vision predictive of future glory yet qualified by the awareness of man's capacity to debase his own high ideals.

The strength of Freneau's vision of American destiny—apparent also in writers like Joel Barlow and Timothy Dwight—and its presence as an informing motif in his revolutionary writings distinguish him from Francis Hopkinson and account for his fame as an early American poet. At a time when self-conscious nationalism, political and literary, abounded, Freneau retained a central position as a prophet of America's future. The pastoral image at the center of Freneau's conception of America motivated the later poetry upon which his literary reputation today rests, as reflected in such respected poems as "The Wild Honey Suckle," "To a Caty-Did," and "The Indian Burying Ground." The basis of these and other "poems of romantic fancy" (as Harry Hayden Clark calls them) is identical to that which informed his writings on America in the years when its future was the subject of political debate and military activity. The consistency in his poetic career—founded on a unifying vision of pastoral America and its rising glory—sets Freneau apart from Hopkinson as a literary contributor to the Revolution; a more prolific and more serious writer than the gentleman satirist from Philadelphia, Philip Freneau, like Hopkinson, lent his pen to the patriot cause, but the intensity of his vision and his competence as a literary craftsman gave to Freneau's revolutionary writings a wider significance in the American literary tradition. Hopkinson used his skills on behalf of the American cause. Freneau helped to form that cause, to define its meaning beyond immediate political and military events, and to meld his personal vision of America with ancient myths in the creation of a national image which outlived both the poet and the cause of independence he served.

SUGGESTIONS FOR FURTHER READING

Editions

Comical Spirit of Seventy-Six: The Humor of Francis Hopkinson. Edited by P. M. Zall. San Marino, Calif.: The Huntington Library, 1976.

The Last Poems of Philip Freneau. Edited by Lewis Leary. New Brunswick, N.J.: Rutgers University Press, 1945. Reprinted, Westport, Conn.: Greenwood Press, 1970.

The Miscellaneous Essays and Occasional Writings of Francis Hopkinson. 3 vols. Philadelphia: Dobson, 1792.

Poems of Freneau. Edited by Harry Hayden Clark. New York: Harcourt, Brace, 1929. Reprinted, New York: Hafner, 1960.

The Prose Works of Philip Freneau. Edited by Philip M. Marsh. New Brunswick, N.J.: Scarecrow Press, 1955.

Scholarship and Criticism

Adkins, Nelson F. *Philip Freneau and the Cosmic Enigma: The Religious and Philosophical Speculations of an American Poet.* New York: New York University Press, 1949.

Hastings, George Everett. *The Life and Works of Francis Hopkinson.* Chicago: University of Chicago Press, 1926. Reprinted, New York: Russell & Russell, 1968.

Kyle, Carol A. "That Poet Freneau: A Study of the Imagistic Success of *The Pictures of Columbus." Early American Literature* 9 (1974): 62–70.

Leary, Lewis. *That Rascal Freneau: A Study in Literary Failure.* New Brunswick, N.J.: Rutgers University Press, 1941. Reprinted, New York: Octagon, 1964, 1971.

———. "Philip Freneau." In *Major Writers of Early American Literature,* edited by Everett Emerson, pp. 245–71. Madison: University of Wisconsin Press, 1972.

9

Thomas Jefferson

THOMAS PHILBRICK

[*The city of Philadelphia was the cultural center of America in the late eighteenth century. Just to the south, the sister colonies of Maryland and Virginia were enjoying what has been called an "intellectual golden age," with interest in the arts, religion, and politics very widespread. The greatest of the many great men to emerge from this milieu was probably Thomas Jefferson. Like Franklin, Jefferson is too complex a figure to be treated adequately here. His career, of course, extends well beyond the period we are examining. But during his first forty-five years, Jefferson made significant contributions to both the American Revolution and American literature.*]

In 1776 Thomas Jefferson learned from Benjamin Franklin the motto that he was to adopt as his own: "Rebellion to tyrants is obedience to God." It was to serve him as more than a slogan. Beneath the dazzling variety of Jefferson's interests and the versatility of his pursuits, beneath all the contradictions of his experiments in policy, runs the current of the conviction that the overthrow of arbitrary external restraints upon mankind is the essential religious act, the act that enables the human species to fulfill its divinely ordained nature and thus to complete the scheme of creation. In Jefferson's mind the American Revolution outgrew its specific causes and purposes and took shape as the critical event in a long process of liberation that, beginning with the example of Bacon, Locke, and Newton and ending in the future triumph of political justice and intellectual freedom throughout the Western world, was at last to bring the lives of men into harmony with the self-regulating order and beneficence of nature. In 1821, at the age of seventy-seven, he reaffirmed that vision of the on-going revolution:

As yet we are but in the first chapter of it's history. The appeal to the rights of man, which had been made in the U S. was taken up by France, first of

145

the European nations. From her the spirit has spread over those of the South. The tyrants of the North have allied indeed against it, but it is irresistible. Their opposition will only multiply it's millions of human victims; their own satellites will catch it, and the condition of man thro' the civilized world will be finally and greatly ameliorated. This is a wonderful instance of great events from small causes. So inscrutable is the arrangement of causes & consequences in this world that a two-penny duty on tea, unjustly imposed in a sequestered part of it, changes the condition of all it's inhabitants. (1: 156[1])

Undismayed by Napoleon's perversion of the revolutionary cause or by the systematic repressions of the Holy Alliance, Jefferson could hold fast to the belief that the little sphere of debate and resistance that he had entered in 1769 as a newly elected member of the Virginia House of Burgesses was in fact the source of a change that would sweep and redeem the world.

I

The essential education of Thomas Jefferson was in the teachings of the British Enlightenment, and it began in 1760 when, at the age of seventeen, he entered the College of William and Mary. His childhood had been spent within the virtually self-contained world of the inland plantation, for a time far up the James River at Tuckahoe and then still farther west at Shadwell in the newly formed county of Albemarle, of which his father was a founder and the leading citizen. A newcomer to the plantation aristocracy of Virginia, the self-educated Peter Jefferson had won a reputation as a surveyor, had married into the extensive and influential Randolph family, and, by skillful specula-tion in western lands, had acquired large holdings in Albemarle, among them the future site of Monticello. On his death in 1757 he left an estate of some seven thousand acres, sixty slaves, and forty volumes of books.

Apparently Jefferson's first contact with anyone having pretensions to scholarship came in the next year when he was placed under the tutelage of William Maury, an Anglican clergyman who kept school in a log house in Albemarle. There Jefferson and his four classmates received a thorough grounding in the classics and a less welcome exposure to Maury's humorless orthodoxy. Nothing at Maury's school or in Jefferson's other childhood ex-periences had yet given him access to those new views of man and nature that Locke, Newton, and their followers had promulgated and that were shaping

1. Unless otherwise noted, quotations from Jefferson's writings prior to 1791 are from Julian P. Boyd's edition of *The Papers of Thomas Jefferson*. Quotations from the later works are from Paul Leicester Ford's edition of *The Works of Thomas Jefferson*.

the age of revolution in which his manhood was to be lived. Nor were there other influences in that childhood which challenged the settled values and received opinions of the plantation aristocracy. It is true that the society of Albemarle was simpler and more open than that of the Tidewater counties, but it was hardly a frontier community. New though it was, it was firmly planted on the foundation stones of family connection, public office, and the rigid requirements of a tobacco economy. As yet there had been nothing in Jefferson's experience like the young Washington's encounter with continental wilderness or the young Franklin's encounter with London, nothing that could open up the prospect of a new and wider sphere of action and achievement.

Williamsburg gave Jefferson his first glimpse of such a sphere. The one layman on the tiny faculty of William and Mary was the professor of mathematics, a Scotsman named William Small. Small, in effect, was the faculty. During the twenty-five months of Jefferson's residence at the college, Small instructed him not only in mathematics but in natural philosophy, natural history, logic, ethics, rhetoric, and *belles-lettres*. Valuing the young man's intelligence and hunger for ideas, Small befriended him and introduced him to his own little intellectual circle. From Small's conversation, Jefferson recalled in old age, "I got my first views of the expansion of science, and of the system of things in which we are placed"; his association with Small, he thought, "probably fixed the destinies" of his life. Clearly Small, a man with "an enlarged and liberal mind," introduced Jefferson not only to the Newtonian universe and the principles of scientific inquiry but to the application of reason and empirical investigation to the realms of religion and ethics.

The example of an enlarged and liberal mind was amplified and confirmed by the two other figures in the Williamsburg circle to which Small gave Jefferson access. One was Francis Fauquier, then the royal governor of Virginia, who furnished an elegant model of intellect and taste in the man of affairs, for Fauquier was not only an able governor but a fellow of the Royal Society, an accomplished musician, and a reader of the latest French literature and philosophy. The other member of the group that gathered for dinner, conversation, and music at the Governor's Palace was the lawyer George Wythe. His influence was to be the most lasting of all, for upon completing his studies at the college in 1762, Jefferson stayed on in Williamsburg to read law with Wythe for a period of five years.

The most learned lawyer in Virginia, Wythe was also, so Jefferson affirmed, the best classical scholar in the colony and an eager student of mathematics, science, and philosophy. The legal education that he laid out was of the sort that Jefferson himself was later to recommend to young men who sought his guidance, one that approached the law as part of a more general study of history and politics. Devoted, in Jefferson's words, "to liberty, and the natural and equal rights of man," Wythe schooled his pupil in Locke's theories of the social contract and human rights and in the Whig interpretation of British history that traced the origins of English liberties from the ancient Saxon practices described by Tacitus. And as if to give point and immediacy to his readings under Wythe, in 1765 the great debate over the Virginia response to the Stamp Act gripped the House of Burgesses. Standing at the lobby door, the law student listened in astonishment to the oratory of Patrick Henry, who "appeared to me to speak as Homer wrote."

With Jefferson's admission to the bar in 1767 his formal schooling came to an end. That statement, of course, has less meaning in his case than in those of most, for no one was more the lifelong student than he, an omnivorous purchaser and reader of books and a tireless follower of political speculation, scientific investigation, and technological innovation. But perhaps it is safe to suggest that the decisive intellectual influences that shaped the writer of *A Summary View,* the Declaration of Independence, and the *Notes on Virginia* had by this time taken effect. In 1770 he read Montesquieu, and Buffon and Raynal a few years later. But important though the theories of environmental influence advanced by the three French writers are to the strategies and stances of the *Notes on Virginia,* the fundamental outlook of that work, as well as of the great manifestoes that preceded it, stems from the seven years in Williamsburg, those years in which Jefferson discovered and came to possess the world of the British Enlightenment.

II

Seven more years were to elapse before the publication of *A Summary View* in 1774 and Jefferson's emergence on the scene of continental politics as a primary spokesman for the radical opposition to British colonial policy. In those years, the only period of his life in which he practiced his profession of law, he widened his acquaintance throughout the colony and established a reputation for quiet ability. By 1770 the construction at Monticello had advanced to the point that when in that year the family house at Shadwell burned, he could move into an outbuilding on his little mountain. In early 1772 he married the widow Martha Wayles Skelton, thereby eventually doubling his property, and, before the year was out, was presented with his first child. Like his father, Jefferson accepted the public duties that devolved upon him as the leading citizen of Albemarle, among them election in 1769 to the House of Burgesses.

When he took his seat in May of that year, he found himself in the midst of a rare and to him most welcome commotion in the political affairs of the colony. The House, agitated by the controversy over the Townshend duties, went so far in its opposition to the royal authority and in its support of rebellious Massachusetts that the governor dissolved the body. Meeting on their own initiative in the Raleigh Tavern, the burgesses defied the governor and formed an association against the importation of taxed articles from Great Britain. Jefferson signed the agreement and returned to his county, where, like the others who had supported the association, he was triumphantly reelected. But the excitement was short-lived. Frustrated in his efforts to engage the legislature in the reform of the laws of the colony, he soon lost interest in the politics of Williamsburg, for, as he was to recall, "nothing liberal could expect success" in the climate of dull conservatism that the colonial structure promoted.

In the spring of 1773, however, events in New England once again roused Virginia from its torpor. Alarmed by the British response to the burning of the *Gaspee*, Jefferson joined with the small radical group in the House of Burgesses to draw up a resolution establishing a standing committee of correspondence to coordinate resistance throughout the colonies. Although the governor dissolved the House as soon as it passed the resolution, the mood of the burgesses was still more defiant when they reassembled in the following spring. To protest Parliament's passage of the Boston Port Bill, Jefferson conceived the stratagem of appointing a day of general fasting and prayer in commemoration of the suffering of Boston. When the motion was passed, the governor once more dissolved the House, and once again the burgesses assembled in the Raleigh Tavern, this time to form another nonimportation association, to propose to the other colonies the annual convening of a congress, and to affirm that an attack upon one colony should be regarded as an attack upon all. The effect of the fast day on June 1, 1774, was, Jefferson remembered, "like a shock of electricity, arousing every man, and placing him erect and solidly on his center," and delegates, himself among them, were promptly elected to appoint the Virginia representatives to the First Continental Congress. When the convention assembled in August, he was prevented by illness from attending, but he nonetheless submitted to the convention a draft of proposed instructions for the Virginia delegation to the forthcoming Congress. Although the proposal was considered too bold by the convention and was not adopted, its supporters had the draft printed in Williamsburg as a pamphlet entitled *A Summary View of the Rights of British America*. Reprinted in Philadelphia before the end of the year and carried to England, where it was published in two editions, Jefferson's defense of colonial rights won a hearing nearly as wide as it might have received had it been adopted, and it was quickly recognized as a major contribution to the growing literature of controversy on the issue.

A Summary View is indeed bold both in substance and tone. Addressed to the king, it advances a radical redefinition of the relation of the colonies to

Great Britain, specifies a long list of past and present violations of that relation by Parliament and the royal authority, and ends by summoning the king to cleanse his house of would-be tyrants, assume his proper function of chief magistrate of all the empire, and let "not the name of George be a blot in the page of history." Jefferson's closing reference to the verdict of history is no mere rhetorical gesture, for the idea of the past, shaped by his readings under Wythe's direction, plays a more prominent part in *A Summary View* than in any other of his major writings. The first of the three major sections of the pamphlet founds the claims of the American colonies upon the right, "which nature has given to all men, of departing from the country in which chance, not choice has placed them, of going in quest of new habitations, and of there establishing new societies, under such laws and regulations as to them shall seem most likely to promote public happiness." Acting on that right, the ancient Saxons had "left their native wilds and woods in the North of Europe" and established the society from which modern Great Britain derives. The same right of expatriation defines the true state of the American colonies, for "America was conquered, and her settlements made and firmly established, at the expence of individuals, and not of the British public. Their own blood was spilt in acquiring lands for their settlement, their own fortunes expended in making that settlement effectual. For themselves they fought, for themselves they conquered, and for themselves they have right to hold." History thus demonstrates that the colonists are related to the people of Great Britain only by their voluntary submission "to the same common sovereign" and that the colonial legislatures are parallel to Parliament, not subordinate to it.

History also adds weight to the charge of tyranny that Jefferson lodges against the British government in the second section of *A Summary View*. The oppressive measures of that government have long threatened the rights that the colonists have inherited from their Saxon ancestors and that are enshrined in the English constitution. The abuse of power has been intensified in the present reign to a degree that indicates the operation of a sinister policy: "Single acts of tyranny may be ascribed to the accidental opinion of a day; but a series of oppressions, begun at a distinguished period, and pursued unalterably thro' every change of ministers, too plainly prove a deliberate, systematical plan of reducing us to slavery." The author of that plan, Jefferson implies, is George himself, who has revealed his hand by the actions that he has taken on his own initiative to reinforce the effect of Parliament's usurpations of colonial rights. It is the king who has frustrated the efforts of American legislatures to prohibit the slave trade; who has dissolved those legislatures at his will; who has disrupted the free-holding system of land tenure in the colonies by introducing the feudal principles that belonged to the alien Normans, and not to the Saxons; and who has stationed armed forces in the colonies without their consent. When Jefferson concludes by exhorting the king to heed the verdict of history, he is, then, once more associating the colonial cause with the values and traditions affirmed by the Whig interpretation of British history. King George should align himself with the monarchs who, over the years, have upheld the rights that Englishmen derive from their Saxon forebears and not with those who, like the Norman conquerors or the Stuarts, sought to introduce tyrannical innovations.

But the main function of the appeal to history is to support Jefferson's denial of the authority of Parliament over the colonies. He was not the first to put forth the radical proposition that the king constitutes the only tie between the colonies and England. Richard Bland and Benjamin Franklin had advanced it in the preceding decade, and, perhaps more significantly, George Wythe was, according to Jefferson's own testimony, one of the very few who from the moment when the question of the relation of the colonies to the mother country first arose "hung our connection with Great Britain on its true hook, that of a common king." The proposition was nonetheless a daring one, for it abandoned the traditional Whig reliance on Parliament as the defender of English liberties and made the fate of the colonies depend on the frailest of reeds, the royal capacity for common sense, self-restraint, and fairness. Paradoxically, it would seem, Jefferson's effort to associate his argument with a distinctively British tradition of civil liberties thus has the effect of severing the argument from the most central assumptions of that tradition.

There is no evidence that the inconsistency troubled Jefferson. Indeed, the attentive reader of *A Summary View* is forced to question the firmness of Jefferson's belief in the authority of history. On one level, the pamphlet surely does attempt to define the present by reference to the precedents of the past, but on another level, one that becomes visible in its most emphatic passages, the appeal is made not to the experience of the past and to the sanctity of a national inheritance but to the intrinsic nature of man and to the rights that belong to that nature. On this level, Saxon society is significant not as the historic source of distinctively English rights but as a mythic representation of the contractual basis of all societies. The rights that were embodied in the practices and institutions of the Saxon golden age derive their validity not from the fact that they were Saxon rights but from the fact that they are natural rights, the possession of men of whatever nation, of whatever era. Thus the right of expatriation is "a right, which nature has given to all men," and the exercise of free trade is "possessed by the American colonists as of natural right." Jefferson begins *A Summary View* by attributing a double origin to the rights of British North America: they are "those rights which god and the laws have given equally and independently to all." The rights that are conferred by God rather than by the laws belong to this unhistorical argument, the argument that controls the conclusion of the pamphlet. The grievances of the colonists have been "laid before his majesty with that freedom of language and sentiment which becomes a free people, claiming their rights as derived from the laws of nature, and not as the gift of their chief magistrate." And they are a free people not because they fall under the protection of the British constitution but because the "god who gave us life, gave us liberty at the same time."

If the appeal to history ends by tying the welfare of British North America to the good will of George III, the appeal to natural rights ends by indicating a way of cutting that knot if need be. Let Great Britain take warning: "It is neither our wish nor our interest to separate from her. We are willing on our part to sacrifice every thing which reason can ask to the restoration of that tranquillity for which all must wish." But if wish and interest should alter and if the demands of Britain should exceed the limits of reason, separation itself would clearly become a proper exercise of the natural rights of a free people.

A Summary View failed to win endorsement as the official expression of the colonial position. It failed to change the hearts and minds of the shapers of British policy, only furnishing them another example of colonial intransigence and impudence. But in respect to the development of Jefferson's own thought and to his future revolutionary role, the pamphlet was of crucial significance. In it he is in mid-passage, moving from the historical and constitutional understanding of the controversy with England that his long study of the common law had enforced and toward the position he would take two years later when in the Declaration of Independence he would ground his argument unequivocally on the natural rights of man and thereby associate the American cause not with the Saxon past but with the revolutionary aspirations that were soon to ignite the Western world. *A Summary View,* moreover, furnishes unmistakable evidence of Jefferson's growing sense of an American national identity. Hitherto his concerns had been exclusively Virginian. Only once, on a brief excursion in 1766 to Philadelphia and New York, had he crossed the boundaries of the province that he regarded as his "country." In *A Summary View* he writes for the first time not as a citizen of Albemarle or of Virginia but as an American. The audience that he addresses is characterized by the circumstance that it is not American, that it does not belong to the continental community of experience and interest for which he speaks. The voice of the pamphlet is that of the "four millions in the states of America," a voice which expresses the confident determination of a free people who can speak to kings without servility or abashment: "Let those flatter, who fear: it is not an American art."

Less compact and consistently elevated than the Declaration of Independence, *A Summary View* nonetheless marks the emergence of a public style that, at its best, indeed seems to be the expression of a whole people or even, at times, of their Creator. The cadenced inevitability of its phrasing, the generality of its reference, and the simple nobility of its tone make it the perfect language of pronouncement. It has the power to generate aphorisms that, if they have nothing of the wit and familiarity of Franklin's maxims, seem fit to be chiseled in marble: "kings are the servants, not the proprietors of the people. . . . The great principles of right and wrong are legible to every reader. . . . The whole art of government consists in the art of being honest." These are among the truths that the conclusion of *A Summary View* hurls in quick succession at the head of poor King George, and their force depends not on the charm of personality but on the solemnity of impersonality. The achievement of such a style established Jefferson's reputation as an author of public papers. More than any other single document from his hand, *A Summary View*, with its "peculiar felicity of expression," as John Adams called it, was the credential which was to earn him the assignment of drafting the Declaration of Independence.

III

As a consequence of the intensifying quarrel between the royal governor and the elected officials of Virginia, the courts of the province had ceased to function by the end of 1774. Jefferson was now required to abandon his law practice and was free to devote himself to the political concerns that hitherto had only intermittently claimed his attention. In March 1775, a month before fighting broke out at Lexington and Concord, he attended a provincial convention at Richmond as a delegate from Albemarle, heard Patrick Henry make his demand for liberty or death, and was elected an alternate member of the Virginia delegation to Congress. Taking a seat in that body in June, he quickly formed a friendship with the influential John Adams and won the respect of his colleagues as a shrewd and diligent committeeman. In August he was elected a regular member of the Virginia delegation and returned to Philadelphia when Congress reconvened in the fall. In response to the king's proclamation of a state of open rebellion in the colonies, Congress in December adopted the position of *A Summary View* by affirming the sovereignty of the king but denying the authority of Parliament over the colonies.

Between early January and early May of 1776, while Jefferson was in Virginia, the tide of events made even that position untenable. Thomas Paine's *Common Sense*, with its vigorous call for independence, appeared in mid-January and deeply impressed its American audience, including Thomas Jefferson, who read the pamphlet that winter at Monticello. Although the British evacuated Boston in March, it was apparent that there would be no quick end to hostilities, for the Canadian expedition was failing, and Clinton was threatening to carry the war into the South. Negotiations were underway to secure military supplies from England's ancient enemies, France and Spain, an act that would seem to make the drift toward independence irreversible. On April 12 North Carolina instructed its delegation in Congress to vote for independence, and Virginia gave similar instructions to its delegates in May.

When Jefferson returned to Philadelphia in the middle of that month, it was with some reluctance. Virginia seemed about to form a new government, "a work," he wrote to Thomas Nelson, "of the most interesting nature and such as every individual would wish to have his voice in." Enmeshed in the business of Congress, he nevertheless found time to draft a constitution for Virginia in the hectic weeks of late May and early June. Jefferson's draft, an embodiment of advanced republican principles, arrived too late to receive full consideration, but its preamble, a lengthy indictment of George III, was incorporated in the more conventional document that had already been approved. Meanwhile, on June 7 the Virginia delegation in Congress moved a resolution·declaring the independence of the colonies from Great Britain. Although Congress decided to postpone a decision on the resolution until July 1 in order to give South Carolina and the middle colonies time to rally popular support for independence, a committee consisting of Jefferson, Franklin, John Adams, Robert Livingstone, and Roger Sherman was appointed to prepare a formal declaration. The committee assigned Jefferson the task of drafting the document. Upon its completion, he showed the draft first to Adams, then to Franklin, and finally to the committee as a whole, incorporating the alterations, most of them minor, that were suggested in this process of review. On June 28 the draft was reported to Congress and tabled.

Debate on the Virginia resolution began on July 1. Those who wished to delay until popular feeling forced Congress to act, until assurances of support came from Europe, or until the military fortunes of the colonies showed a better face were overcome by the arguments that the king had already dissolved the bond of allegiance by proclaiming the colonies to be out of his protection, that a formal declaration of independence was necessary to secure European aid, and that the military campaign might soon take a turn for the worse. When a vote was taken on the next day, twelve of the colonies supported the motion for independence; New York, whose delegates were forbidden by their instructions to vote on the issue, abstained. On that same day and on July 3 and 4 Congress, sitting as a committee of the whole, considered Jefferson's draft, striking from it, much to his distress, its censure of the people of England and its denunciation of the king's encouragement of black slavery. Late on the fourth the Declaration as amended was adopted and signed, so Jefferson recalled, by every voting member present except John

Dickinson. An engrossed parchment copy was prepared and signed, this time by the New York delegates as well as the others, on August 2.

Unlike *A Summary View*, then, the Declaration of Independence is in certain respects a committee document, the compromise of many minds. Several of the revisions by Congress drastically changed the stance and structure of Jefferson's draft. Thus the insertion of the pious references to "the Supreme Judge of the world" and "the protection of divine providence" in the concluding sentences dulls the edge of his revolutionary assertion of the right and capacity of a free people to govern and defend themselves. And to Jefferson, whose draft of a constitution for Virginia had guaranteed religious freedom and put an end to state support of the Anglican church, those phrases must have seemed to come perilously close to associating a belief in God with the fundamental principles of the new nation. Still more damaging was the deletion of the denunciations of the king for countenancing the slave trade and of the British people for supporting their government in its oppression of their American brethren.

The passage on slavery supplies the climax of the second of the three major sections of the Declaration as Jefferson drafted it, the long litany of the king's offenses against reason and justice in the prosecution of his design to impose a tyranny upon the colonies. The list begins rather mildly in the draft, as it does in the final version, with the charge that "he has refused his assent to laws the most wholesome and necessary for the public good," proceeds through increasingly serious violations of the principles of law and proper governance, and builds toward still more violent instances of the abuse of royal power: "he has plundered our seas, ravaged our coasts, burnt our towns & destroyed the lives of our people"; he has introduced foreign mercenaries to prey upon us, forced our impressed seamen to kill their compatriots, bribed the Indians to butcher us, incited domestic insurrection among us, and finally, to cap this catalog of atrocity, comes the passage that Congress—in deference to the feelings of South Carolina, Georgia, and Jefferson suspected, the northern slavetraders—struck from the draft:

> he has waged cruel war against human nature itself, violating it's most sacred rights of life & liberty in the persons of a distant people who never offended him, captivating & carrying them into slavery in another hemisphere, or to incur miserable death in their transportation thither. this piratical warfare, the opprobrium of *infidel* powers, is the warfare of the CHRISTIAN king of Great Britain. determined to keep open a market where MEN should be bought & sold, he has prostituted his negative for suppressing every legislative attempt to prohibit or to restrain this execrable commerce: and that this assemblage of horrors might want no fact of distinguished die, he is now exciting those very people to rise in arms among us, and to purchase that liberty of which *he*

has deprived them, by murdering the people upon whom *he* also obtruded them; thus paying off former crimes committed against the *liberties* of one people, with crimes which he urges them to commit against the *lives* of another. (1: 426)

The passage begins with a deliberate echo of the opening of the Declaration itself, all the more apparent in Jefferson's original phrasing: "We hold these truths to be sacred & undeniable; that all men are created equal & independant, that from that equal creation they derive rights inherent & inalienable, among which are the preservation of life, & liberty, & the pursuit of happiness." Black slavery constitutes a radical denial of human nature; it is an atrocity still more horrible, as the violence of the diction that Jefferson employs in the deleted passage reminds us, than the most bloody means by which the British have attempted to subdue the colonies. As Edwin Gittleman has recently demonstrated, moreover, the reference to black slavery completes the mythic substructure of the Declaration, an implicit narrative that associates the plight of the colonies under British rule and their attainment of independence with the patiently endured sufferings of an enslaved people at the hands of a cruel king and their subsequent exodus to a land beyond his reach. In the crescendo of the deleted passage, the literal enslavement of the blacks brings that submerged narrative to the surface and drives home its claim on the imagination.

The second of the two major deletions by Congress deprived Jefferson's draft of still another important effect. Nearly all that Congress retained of the original passage in which Jefferson turns an accusing eye on the people of Great Britain is a severe abridgment of its first sentence, a stiffly formal and abstract statement of the fact that the British people have rebuffed American appeals for relief from the oppressions of the Parliament that they have elected. But the draft goes on to make a far more grievous complaint:

> at this very time too they are permitting their chief magistrate to send over not only soldiers of our common blood, but Scotch & foreign mercenaries to invade & deluge us in blood. these facts have given the last stab to agonizing affection, and manly spirit bids us to renounce for ever these unfeeling brethren. we must endeavor to forget our former love for them, and to hold them as we hold the rest of mankind, enemies in war, in peace friends. we might have been a free & a great people together; but a communication of grandeur & of freedom it seems is below their dignity. be it so, since they will have it: the road to glory & happiness is open to us too; we will climb it in a separate state, and acquiesce in the necessity which pronounces our everlasting Adieu! (1: 427)

Coming as it does between the end of the outraged denunciation of King George and the stately firmness of the actual declaration of American independence in the last two sentences of the document, this passage works a complex tonal transition. In it the accents of shocked horror give way to an appeal to sentiment and sensibility that in turn modulates to regret and brave determination. An entire sequence of emotional experience is encapsulated in the passage, a sequence that makes the resolute dignity of the final sentences seem less loftily grand than they do in the version that Congress approved, and far more human and necessary.

But the passage was stricken in complaisance to what Jefferson called "the pusillanimous idea that we had friends in England worth keeping terms with." As much as the revisions altered the meaning of the draft, they nevertheless served its governing intention. Nearly fifty years after its composition, Jefferson described that intention in a letter to Henry Lee:

> This was the object of the Declaration of Independence. Not to find out new principles, or new arguments, never before thought of, not merely to say things which had never been said before; but to place before mankind the common sense of the subject, in terms so plain and firm as to command their assent, and to justify ourselves in the independent stand we are compelled to take. Neither aiming at originality of principle or sentiment, nor yet copied from any particular and previous writing, it was intended to be an expression of the American mind, and to give that expression the proper tone and spirit called for by the occasion. (12: 409)

To achieve an authentic expression of the American mind in 1776 it was necessary to suppress those passages in which Jefferson's own most intense feelings obtruded—the deep sense of the atrocity of slavery that was to torment him in one way or another throughout his lifetime, and the equally deep if less lasting sense of betrayal which arose from his recognition that, despite the concentration of the Declaration on the guilt of the king, the responsibility for England's policy toward the colonies lay less with her limited monarch than with her electorate and the ministries that it sustained in office.

At the same time that the revisions of the Declaration made it a more representative expression of American opinion, they made it in certain respects a more characteristically Jeffersonian document. By limiting its emotional range and amplification, they enhanced its cleanly logical structure. Wilbur Samuel Howell has shown the remarkable degree to which the tripartite design of the Declaration adheres both generally and in detail to the standards of "scientific" or mathematical proof as they are set forth in William Duncan's *Elements of Logick* (1748), the text in which William Small, who had once been Duncan's student at Aberdeen, apparently schooled the young Jefferson. But one need not have an acquaintance with Duncan's *Logick* to recognize the controlling syllogistic form of the Declaration by which the opening section furnishes the major premise in the people's right to overthrow a destructive government, the second section with its evidence of the destruction worked by British rule in America supplies the minor premise, and the third section states the conclusion by declaring the independence of the colonies. For all the emotional power of the deleted passages, they complicate the simple linearity of the logical argument. The passage on black slavery unavoidably reminds its reader that the oppressed colonists are themselves implicated in oppression, while the passage on the English people diffuses the focus on the king as an arbitrary and uncontrollable tyrant, the enemy and not the agent of the people. Both passages give access to truths that are not encompassed by the controlling syllogism and thereby tend to subvert the assertion on which the entire Declaration rests, that the action which it proclaims is the result of the reasonable decision of rational men.

The amended version of the draft thus sustains far more consistently than the draft the elegant simplicity and cool assurance that are the hallmarks of the felicitous style admired by Jefferson's contemporaries. If the tone is not confined to the gentlemanly detachment that Carl Becker assigns it, neither does it rise to the fervor of a "war-song," as Moses Coit Tyler would have it. In both substance and style, the Declaration is not a summons to violence but to reason and dignity. The stately rhythms of the phrasing, the latinate nobility of the diction, and the whole inexorable march of the logic are in keeping with the high seriousness of the occasion and the purpose, and they give the Declaration that extraordinary durability which has enabled it to withstand generations of abuse at the sweating hands of Fourth of July orators. Repetition may not have made Jefferson's great truths any more self-evident than they ever were, but it has not succeeded in reducing them to banality. Still, it is one thing to affirm the equal creation and unalienable rights of all men, and another to specify black slavery as the most hideous contradiction of those truths. One wonders whether the Declaration as Jefferson originally wrote it might have been not only a less agreeable document to live with than the version that has come down to us, but a more efficacious one.

Nevertheless, what remained of Jefferson's draft was sufficient to found the new nation on the most revolutionary of ideals. The Declaration is, of course, the most fundamental of the national documents, for it precedes, permits, and finally limits the Constitution. By its assertion of the Lockean doctrines of natural rights and the consent of the governed as the only basis of legitimate rule, it reduces any particular form of American government, whether that of the Articles of Confederation or that of the Constitution of 1789, to the status of serving as its own instrumentality. When such a government ceases to uphold the values set forth in the Declaration, it loses its legitimacy, and the people are empowered to institute a new government that will indeed seek to secure life, liberty, and the pursuit of happiness. It thus establishes the existence of the American people as an independent society squarely on those

most central of all Jeffersonian principles, the sanctity of human nature and
the justifiability of any change that will permit man to fulfill that nature. And
in doing so, the Declaration not only enunciated the moral standards by which
American national life would thenceforth be judged, but it took its place as the
first of the great manifestoes of human rights to be issued in the age of
revolution that was opened to the world in 1776 and that is with us still.

In 1776, however, little of the significance of the Declaration was apparent
to Jefferson and those around him. For them the national existence was only a
distant possibility, threatened by every report from the battlefield, every inventory of supplies, and every accounting of public funds. They looked for
support not to the spread of revolutionary opinion in Europe but to the ancient
monarchical rivalry of France and Spain with England. For them the act of
separation rather than the document that declared it was the crucial matter at
hand. Although the Declaration met with wide approval in America, it was
not in itself a catalyst of opinion or action. Nor did its authorship propel
Jefferson into celebrity. The first public reference to his composition of the
Declaration appeared in a Boston newspaper in 1784, a full eight years after
the event.

I V

For the present, Jefferson's strongest concerns were not for the hypothetical
nation that might come into being but with the establishment of a government
in Virginia that would embody the ideals of the Declaration. The Declaration
itself, in keeping with the language of the original Virginia resolution, proclaims the colonies to be "Free and Independent States," not a single American nation. Although the Articles of Confederation were presented to Congress at the same time as the Declaration, they were not finally ratified until
1781. Jefferson, who took no part in drafting the Articles, shared the belief of
most Americans that the critical task of creating republican forms of government was to be accomplished in the individual states. Resigning from Congress and declining appointment as commissioner to France along with
Franklin and Silas Deane, he left Philadelphia and took his seat in the Virginia
House of Delegates, the successor to the colonial House of Burgesses.

For the next two-and-a-half years, Jefferson devoted himself to the reformation of the government and laws of Virginia. Both as an individual delegate
and as a committee member, he sought to achieve by legislative action the
abolition of privilege toward which his proposed constitution had aimed. In
quick succession he introduced bills for remodeling the defunct judiciary
system of the state, for abolishing entail and primogeniture, for disestablish-

ing the Anglican church, for preventing the further importation of slaves, for liberalizing and rationalizing the criminal code, and for establishing a system of public education throughout the state. Taken up piecemeal and meeting a variety of fates at the hands of the legislature, Jefferson's proposals never were adopted as the coherent system of reform that they in fact constituted.

Despite the frustrations of legislative rejection and delay, this was one of the happiest periods of Jefferson's life. In his public office, he was absorbed in the exciting attempt to embody republican theory in the codes and institutions of his own land and people. At Monticello, where he lived when his duties did not require his presence at Williamsburg, the work of construction and improvement went steadily forward. Another daughter was born, the second of his two children who were to survive to maturity. In January 1779 the embarrassingly large British army that had surrendered at Saratoga took up quarters in Albemarle, near enough to Monticello to afford Jefferson the pleasant company of its English and Hessian officers.

Such a life was a long way from Valley Forge, from the massacres at Wyoming and Cherry Valley, or, indeed, from any direct encounter with the confusion and suffering of war. But in June 1779 Jefferson was elected to the governorship of Virginia, and at last war overtook him. Late in the previous year, the British had shifted their operations to the South and spread the conflict through Georgia and into the Carolinas. In December 1780 Benedict Arnold, recently recruited by the British as a brigadier general, led an invasion up the James River and sacked Richmond, the new capital of the state. For Jefferson, then in his second annual term as governor, the situation was desperate. Crippled by the inadequate executive powers conferred upon him by the Virginia constitution of 1776, harried by competing calls for men and equipment to support the war in the Carolinas and to defend Virginia herself from attack, and alarmed by the near exhaustion of public resources and funds, he worked with frantic effort to keep his leaky ship of state afloat. In May 1781 the British party on the James succeeded in joining forces with Cornwallis, who had led his army into Virginia from North Carolina, and effective government in the state collapsed. The legislature and Jefferson with it withdrew to Charlottesville in disarray. His term as governor expired on June 2, and he retired from the office, even though the legislature, which lacked a quorum until May 28, had not chosen his successor. On June 4 a force of British dragoons under Tarleton entered Albemarle, scattering the legislators and nearly capturing Jefferson at Monticello. A week later the House of Delegates, reconvening still farther to the west in Staunton, voted to initiate an inquiry into Jefferson's conduct of the executive.

To add injury to insult, he suffered a severe fall from his horse at Poplar Forest, the estate at which he and his family had taken refuge from the British invaders, and was house-bound for six weeks. Nursing his humiliation through the summer and autumn, he could take no part in the celebration of the American triumph at Yorktown in October. And yet there is no more compelling evidence of his essential psychic strength than the fact that in these very months and amid these mighty inducements to self-pity and silence, he took up the task, first during the confinement at Poplar Forest and then at Monticello, of writing what was to form the basis of his one book, *Notes on the State of Virginia.*

That task had been given him in late 1780 when he received a list of inquiries concerning the natural, social, political, and economic features of his state from the Marquis de Barbé-Marbois, secretary of the French legation to the United States. Marbois, who had sent his questionnaire to several states and was seeking the sort of routine information that would be useful to the French bureaucracy in dealing with an unfamiliar nation, must have been surprised by the more than routine interest that Jefferson immediately took in the project. Welcoming the opportunity to organize his own scattered notes and eager to gather new information, he wrote to Marbois in March 1781 that he was looking forward to the end of his term as governor "when it shall certainly be one of my first undertakings" to answer the queries. In December, the month in which his conduct as governor was at last vindicated by the House of Delegates, he was ready to send his answers, imperfect though he felt them to be, to Marbois.

Over the next few years, the manuscript of those answers became for Jefferson a literary Monticello, a thing to be expanded and corrected by tireless tinkering. He began soliciting his circle of correspondents, from George Rogers Clark to John Sullivan, for information that might help him to improve the manuscript, particularly the section of it that sought to refute Buffon's contention that animals degenerated in the New World. It was among the first interests to which he returned when he revived from the crushing shock of his wife's death in September 1782, and it accompanied him to Congress when Virginia once again elected him as her delegate in 1783. By early 1784 the manuscript, now nearly thrice the size of the original reply to Marbois, had grown too bulky for circulation among his correspondents, and he made plans to print a few copies for private distribution. Failing to find an American printer who would do the job for a reasonable sum, he took the manuscript with him when he sailed for France in July as the newly appointed minister plenipotentiary. Finally, after the manuscript had been subjected to one more revision, it was printed in Paris on May 10, 1785, in a private edition of two hundred copies. Jefferson presented copies to many of his acquaintances, from his old mentor George Wythe to his new scientific antagonist Buffon, each time cautioning the recipient against letting the book fall into the hands of the public. Concerned that his strictures against slavery and the Virginia constitution might prove offensive and counter-productive,

Jefferson did his best to protect the privacy of his book, but the threat of pirated editions forced him to authorize publication of a French translation in 1787 and to arrange in the same year with the London publisher John Stockdale for an English edition, one that would carry for the first time the name of the author on the title page. Still the tinkering kept on; over the next decades Jefferson added to and deleted from his copy of the Stockdale edition, not abandoning the idea of a new edition until 1814.

But the changes made after the first edition are peripheral. The views and visions of *Notes on Virginia* belong to the Jefferson of 1781–85, the period in which a viable republican society in the New World was less an achievement to be recorded than a possiblity to be nourished. The result is a book that alternates between statistical description and moral exhortation, between sunny affirmation and anxious apprehension. The audience that it addresses is sometimes foreign, one that must be told that Virginia is organized by counties, and sometimes native, one that must be urged to replace its defective constitution and emancipate its slaves. The scope of the book alternately expands to embrace the entire United States and contracts to its ostensible subject, as if Jefferson were still unsure whether the phrase *my country* should have its old Virginian application or its new national one. His vision of the future is still clouded by the disasters of 1781, his confidence in the success of the new republic still qualified by the lonely uniqueness of the experiment.

Perhaps because of this uncertainty, Jefferson too readily retained the formal structure that Marbois's queries supplied him. Although he expanded their number from twenty-two to twenty-three and rearranged their order, he remained committed to an organization that by its rigid compartmentalization and topical specificity was far better adapted to Marbois's purpose, the acquisition of useful information, than to Jefferson's, the contemplation of American possibilities. Thus the sequence of the queries, neatly systematic though the movement from the terrain and its resources to the population and its society may be, is often out of phase with the direction and emphases of the discourse. Some queries are dismissed as soon as they are stated or given only a perfunctory response. Others trigger replies that balloon into speculations and arguments which, viewed from the perspective of the formal structure, are sharply digressive. The modest title that Jefferson gave his book is accurate. It is an assemblage of notes, and the reader must find the points of focus and the lines of relationship without benefit of the customary logical and rhetorical guides.

If there is a single proposition from which the accumulation of data, conjectures, and contentions rays out, it is the suggestion, buried in the answer to query 22 on public finances, that the success of the American experiment depends upon its ability to direct "the whole generative force of nature" toward filling the country "with people and with happiness," to found a society that draws its strength from its cooperation with natural process and from its obedience to natural law. That proposition underlies Jefferson's extraordinary emphasis on bigness and abundance in his accounts of the American landscape and its productions, for he must first establish the fact, called in question by Europeans like Buffon and Raynal, that nature in the New World is indeed at least as potent in its generative force as in the Old and can be relied upon as the basis of a sturdy and happy society. Here Jefferson is at his most confident, ticking off the dimensions of a Virginia that is "one-third larger than the islands of Great Britain and Ireland" and is traversed by rivers that run for more than a thousand miles. The celebrated descriptions of the passage of the Potomac through the Blue Ridge and of the Natural Bridge, a portion of his own property, contribute to the argument, for both of them in their transitions from the rhetoric of sublimity to the rhetoric of beauty picture the operation of gigantic natural forces which, terrific though they may be, have formed a world that welcomes man and yields a final impression of calm or delight.

In his account of the plants and animals of the New World, Jefferson takes to the offensive, burying Buffon beneath tables that demonstrate the larger size and greater variety of American species by comparison to those of Europe. But the most devastating evidence is furnished by the discovery of the bones of the mammoth in America, that "largest of all terrestrial beings." Whether or not the mammoth still inhabits the continental interior, clear proof that he once roamed the banks of the Ohio "should have sufficed to have rescued the earth it inhabited, and the atmosphere it breathed, from the imputation of impotence in the conception and nourishment of animal life on a large scale: to have stifled, in its birth, the opinion of a writer, the most learned too of all others in the science of animal history, that . . . nature is less active, less energetic on one side of the globe than she is on the other." To be rescued, too, from the imputation of impotence is the American Indian, to whom Buffon had assigned feeble sexual organs as well as a deficiency in courage, energy, and feeling. Not as a romantic primitivist but as the defender of all creatures, from mice to mammoths, who have lived in the American habitat, Jefferson celebrates the full human dignity and capacity of the Indian, attributing his departures from European norms to nurture rather than nature. As for the most outrageous of the slanders against nature in the New World, Raynal's assertion that the blight extends to the Europeans who have settled there, Jefferson can only point to the genius of Washington, Franklin, and Rittenhouse, wonder whether France is doing proportionately as well, and note that England is "passing to that awful dissolution whose issue is not given human foresight to scan."

The human society that is to draw its strength and integrity from the generative force so irrefutably manifested by American nature must devise laws and institutions and shape a way of life that are in accord with natural law. The political structure of that society must ensure the natural rights of man by putting an end to slavery, abolishing privilege, extending the suffrage, establishing religious freedom, and in general enacting the legislative program and legal reforms for which Jefferson had long labored and which he summarizes in the *Notes on Virginia*. Its economy must be based not on commerce or on manufacturing but on agriculture, for those "who labour in the earth are the chosen people of God, if ever he had a chosen people, whose breasts he has made his peculiar deposit for substantial and genuine virtue." The Virginia and the America of the future are to be Jeffersonian versions of the pastoral idyll—stable, virtuous, and in full harmony with nature. The only change to be admitted is extension: there will be more farmers, more land brought under cultivation, and hence more happiness.

Any state of equilibrium is precarious, and none more so than American society as Jefferson envisages it. The most urgent passages of the *Notes on Virginia* are those in which he warns against the pressures and tendencies that jeopardize the stability of that society by disturbing its delicate balance. Government must be contrived to diffuse and limit power and to forestall the threat of dictatorship that in the crisis of 1781 nearly laid the people "prostrate at the feet of one man!" Manufacturing must be sharply curbed, for "the natural progress and consequence of the arts" is to corrupt a population by weaning it from the soil and crowding it in great cities whose mobs "add just so much to the support of pure government, as sores do to the strength of the human body." Commerce, too, is a source of infection, involving the national interest in the wars of Europe; if our habits permitted it, "it might be better for us to abandon the ocean altogether." Immigration presents still another danger, for those who have not been bred in "natural right and natural reason," as native Americans have been, will infuse into the national policy their own alien spirit, "warp and bias its direction, and render it a heterogeneous, incoherent, distracted mass."

But the direst threat to the poise and peace of American society comes from its own peculiar institution of slavery. Jefferson's denunciation of slavery in the answer to query 18 is the most powerful single passage in his book. He begins by pointing out how slavery corrupts both master and slave, encouraging the one to tyranny and indolence and instilling in the other an unnatural hatred of his native land, for "if a slave can have a country in this world, it must be any other in preference to that in which he is born to live and labour for another." But the pernicious effects extend beyond master and slave and endanger the entire national existence:

> And can the liberties of a nation be thought secure when we have removed their only firm basis, a conviction in the minds of the people that these liberties are of the gift of God? That they are not to be violated but with his

wrath? Indeed I tremble for my country when I reflect that God is just: that his justice cannot sleep for ever: that considering numbers, nature and natural means only, a revolution of the wheel of fortune, an exchange of situations, is among possible events: that it may become probable by supernatural interference! The Almighty has no attribute which can take side with us in such a contest. (p. 163[2])

Jefferson's vision of the intervention of a wrathful God, so strangely at odds with his usual conception of historical process, is a measure of the intensity of his conviction that slavery itself constitutes a monstrous disruption of the order of nature.

By contrast, the ugliest passage in the *Notes on Virginia* comes in the answer to query 14, where Jefferson justifies his recommendation that the blacks, once emancipated, should be removed "to such place as the circumstances of the time should render most proper" and there supported until they become self-sufficient. Such a policy, rather than the incorporation of the freedmen into American society, is necessary for a superabundance of reasons: "Deep rooted prejudices entertained by the whites; ten thousand recollections, by the blacks, of the injuries they have sustained; new provocations; the real distinctions which nature has made; and many other circumstances, will divide us into parties, and produce convulsions which will probably never end but in the extermination of the one or the other race.—To these objections, which are political, may be added others, which are physical and moral." And at this point Jefferson launches upon an inquiry into the relative merits of whites and blacks, an inquiry that finds the blacks inferior in physical beauty, forethought, sensibility, reason, and imagination. Even the poems of a Phillis Wheatley "are below the dignity of criticism." The Roman slave, Jefferson concludes, "when made free, might mix with, without staining the blood of his master." But the American black is different: "When freed, he is to be removed beyond the reach of mixture."

Perhaps, as most commentators on this passage urge, one should attribute Jefferson's remarks to his unavoidable participation in the prejudices of his age and place and leave them at that. And yet one must wonder why a man who so frequently triumphed over the dogmas and superstitions of his culture should acquiesce in these. More specifically, one wonders why he felt compelled on this occasion to pursue an inquiry which he found, as he at several points and with apparent sincerity reminds us, to be both ungrateful and uncertain. Perhaps the necessities of his larger argument supply the clue. Just as the need to refute Buffon and to affirm the salubrity of the New World as a human environment inspires his tribute to Indian vigor and virtue, so the need to ensure the fragile harmony of his new republic requires him to insist upon the removal of this most threatening source of discord, the accumulated mass

2. Quotations from *Notes on the State of Virginia* are from William Peden's edition.

of black resentment, and to reinforce that "political" point, as he calls it, with an uneasy excursion in the guise of a "lover of natural history" through the racial fantasies of the white imagination.

The mood to which the *Notes on Virginia* returns, here as elsewhere, is one of anxiety. The reader is again and again told that the great goods toward which the Revolution has reached must be caught and fixed now while the liberal and humane spirit is still upon America and before she falls victim to the tyranny and corruption that the example of Europe would suggest are the inevitable lot of all civilizations: "the spirit of the times may alter, will alter. Our rulers will become corrupt, our people careless. . . . From the conclusion of this war we shall be going down hill." The legislators of Virginia, like all who are entrusted with the task of securing the goals of the Revolution, must act swiftly, for the "time to guard against corruption and tyranny, is before they shall have gotten hold on us. It is better to keep the wolf out of the fold, than to trust to drawing his teeth and talons after he shall have entered." In the *Notes on Virginia* Jefferson assumes the role of the American shepherd, and as such, his delight in his flock and his fields is shadowed by his fear of the wolf.

V

The five years which Jefferson spent abroad engendered significant changes in his outlook. Sent to Paris initially in 1784 to join Adams and Franklin in negotiating treaties of amity and commerce between the new nation and the governments of the Old World, he soon was given the more permanent post of minister to France, in which he served until late 1789 when he was appointed secretary of state in Washington's first administration. The years of residence in France removed him in space as well as time from the humiliation of his last months as governor of Virginia and from the devastating sense of loss that he had experienced at the death of his wife. Accompanied by his elder daughter, he soon established an elegant household in Paris, renewed his friendship with John Adams, then on diplomatic duty in London, and steeped himself in the art, science, and politics of France in these final years of the old regime. His efforts to win a place for American products in the world market, to manage the European funding of the national debt, and to secure the release of American seamen held captive by the Barbary states often put great demands on his attention, but in the intervals there was time for him to play Franklin's old part as the representative of American enlightenment in the liberal and intellectual circles of Paris, time for tours of southern France and the Low Countries, time even for his bittersweet adventure with the lovely Maria Cosway.

The residence in France gave him distance, too, from the dismaying uncertainties and contentions of his own country in the aftermath of the Revolution. From France the picture looked considerably brighter and more composed. The ardent Americanism of Lafayette and his liberal friends made it impossible to doubt the international significance of the establishment of republican government in the New World, and the survival and growth of the United States year by year through all the vicissitudes of the 1780s made those republican forms seem more elastic and tough than they had before, especially when viewed from the troubled scene of European politics. The residence in France and the official responsibilities it involved, moreover, sharpened Jefferson's national consciousness. No longer did America seem Virginia writ large. Now he was required both to acknowledge the diversity that distinguished the Albemarle planter from the Nantucket whaleman and to identify the common interests and values that bound them in one nation.

This recovery of confidence and enlargement of vision are everywhere evident in Jefferson's letters of the period. Of the some nineteen thousand letters that he is estimated to have written in his lifetime, those that he wrote in Europe constitute the richest vein of literary interest. Coming to them from the formality and watchful reticence of his previous American correspondence, the reader is surprised to find in the European letters an extended revelation of Jefferson's personality in its full complexity and responsiveness. At no other time in his life was he involved in a network of correspondence of greater range or intricacy. He had left behind him in America political allies and protégés like Madison and Monroe, sources of news of the latest developments in Congress or the Virginia legislature and recipients of his counsel. He had joined an international exchange of artistic, scientific, and political intelligence, a circle that embraced such various figures as Francis Hopkinson, Richard Price, and Thomas Paine. He had accumulated a small army of distressed widows and distraught wives, of hopeful young men and bankrupt older ones, who sought his advice and aid. And he had discovered the sheer pleasure of writing, of trading gossip and jokes with Abigail Adams or of making literary love to Mrs. Cosway.

Whatever the occasion, the central theme around which most of the letters revolve is America—her people, principles, interests, and destiny. Europe, for all the fascination of her high culture and graceful manners, served to clarify the value of America and the society that she had achieved. To Monroe, who was contemplating a European tour, Jefferson could give the benefit of his own experience: "The pleasure of the trip will be less than you expect but the utility greater. It will make you adore your own country, it's soil, it's climate, it's equality, liberty, laws, people and manners. My God! How little do my countrymen know what precious blessings they are in possession of, and which no other people on earth enjoy. I confess I had no idea of it myself." Although, as he told another correspondent, he could gaze "whole hours at the Maison quarée, like a lover at his mistress," or affirm that the sun of Provence would bring the dead to life, he agreed with the learned who hold that America is a new creation, "not for their reasons, but because it is made on an improved plan. Europe is a first idea, a crude production, before the maker knew his trade, or had made up his mind what he wanted."

If the continuance of slavery and the growing appetite for luxury in America were to be deplored, Jefferson nevertheless was sure that the American system was sound at heart, and he could not share the alarm of his American correspondents over turmoils like Shays's Rebellion. "The commotions which have taken place in America," he wrote to Ezra Stiles in late 1786, "as far as they are yet known to me, offer nothing threatening. They are proof that the people have liberty enough, and I would not wish them less than they have. If the happiness of the mass of the people can be secured at the expence of a little tempest now and then, or even of a little blood, it will be a precious purchase." Repeating that assurance to other correspondents in letter after letter, Jefferson found nearly a year later the metaphorical phrasing by which it has been remembered: "The tree of liberty must be refreshed from time to time with the blood of patriots and tyrants. It is it's natural manure."

Republican government no longer seemed to him a structure to be framed in constitutions and statutes as a defense against the wolf of tyranny and corruption but a loose and pliant system that derived its strength from the good sense and good will of an informed people. Indeed, he told Edward Carrington in 1787, "were it left to me to decide whether we should have a government without newspapers, or newspapers without a government, I should not hesitate a moment to prefer the latter." From Madison he learned of the progress of the Constitutional Convention, but he felt nothing of his friend's urgent interest in strengthening the American government. The Articles of Confederation had served well enough, and, he confided to John Adams, "all the good of this new constitution might have been couched in three or four new articles to be added to the good, old, and venerable fabrick, which should have been preserved even as a religious relique." By the end of 1787 he was ready to accept the document, though its failure to limit the presidency to a single term worried him, and he insisted that its enlargement of the powers of the national government be accompanied by a bill of rights.

Jefferson's letters of the succeeding months show an increasingly favorable response to the Constitution. Paine had argued in its favor, and *The Federalist* struck him as "the best commentary on the principles of government which ever was written," rectifying his own views "in several points." But for him the notable achievement was not the new frame of government itself but the process by which it had come into being and won acceptance. In July 1788, amid the increasingly clamorous calls for change in France, he pointed out to Edward Rutledge that America "can surely boast of having set the world a beautiful example of a government reformed by reason alone without bloodshed.'' Not constitutions but the capacity to change them, by reason if possible or by bloodshed if necessary, was the essential thing if in truth, as he told Madison in 1789, ''the earth belongs to the living.''

Delaying his departure for the United States in order to witness and applaud the stunning progress of revolution in the streets of Paris in the summer of 1789, Jefferson at last landed in Virginia in November. The five years of absence made him uneasy about his relation to the new government, and he resisted the pressure of Washington and Madison to accept appointment as secretary of state. But by February 1790, when he responded to the welcoming address by the citizens of Albemarle, he was ready to endorse the Constitution publicly and to indicate his willingness to serve under it. To the constituency which had first elected him to office in 1769 he declared his now confident belief in the spread of ''the happy influence of reason and liberty over the face of the earth.'' If, as it soon seemed to him, his associates in the new government—Washington, Adams, and Hamilton—did not share that faith, he for one would persevere in it.

SUGGESTIONS FOR FURTHER READING

Editions

Notes on the State of Virginia. Edited by William Peden. Chapel Hill: University of North Carolina Press, 1955.
The Papers of Thomas Jefferson. Edited by Julian P. Boyd. 19 vols. to date. Princeton, N.J.: Princeton University Press, 1950–74.
The Works of Thomas Jefferson. Edited by Paul Leicester Ford. 12 vols. New York: Putnam's, 1904–5.

Scholarship and Criticism

Becker, Carl. *The Declaration of Independence: A Study in the History of Political Ideas.* New York: Harcourt, Brace, 1922.
Boorstin, Daniel J. *The Lost World of Thomas Jefferson.* New York: Holt, 1948.
Gittleman, Edwin. ''Jefferson's 'Slave Narrative': The Declaration of Independence as a Literary Text.'' *Early American Literature* 8 (1974): 239–56.
Howell, Wilbur Samuel. ''The Declaration of Independence and Eighteenth-Century Logic.'' *William and Mary Quarterly,* 3d ser., 18 (1961): 463–84.
Malone, Dumas, *Jefferson and His Time.* 5 vols. to date. Boston: Little, Brown, 1948–74.
Peterson, Merrill D. *Thomas Jefferson and the New Nation: A Biography.* New York: Oxford University Press, 1970.
Tyler, Moses Coit. *The Literary History of the American Revolution, 1763–1783.* 2 vols. New York: Putnam's, 1897.

10

African-American Writers

BERNARD W. BELL

[*As Jefferson originally penned it, the Declaration of Independence included a strong statement of grievance against the British king for having "waged cruel war against human nature itself." Though the passage attacking slavery was deleted from the Declaration, the work remains, as Edwin Gittleman has shown, a slave narrative, for Jefferson conceived of Americans as living the lives of slaves under British tyranny. While he hated slavery in every form, Jefferson did not see the black victims of absolute slavery as fully human. If the enlightened Jefferson was not able to embrace the principle of equality, other Americans were even more racist in their sentiments. Nevertheless there developed in revolutionary America some notable black writers, who are now beginning to receive their due.*]

Because of the distinctive history and acculturation of Africans in the English colonies during the revolutionary period, their literary gifts are most meaningful assessed when viewed in the context of the tension between African-American attitudes toward integration and separatism on the one hand and the oral and literate cultural heritages on the other. Most modern historians accept the fact that American slaves were the descendants of peoples with a history and culture. Since culture is basically the symbolic and material resources developed in the process of interaction between the individual, his society, and his environment, it is neither acquired nor lost overnight, whether as the result of conditions imposed by the slave system or by the urban ghettoes. That the African slave's way of life did change radically with his introduction to a new environment and social system goes without saying. But the change was seldom rapid, never uniform, and generally accretive and syncretic rather than a sloughing off of Old World values and survival techniques with the adoption of New World values.

Too many students of American character and culture overlook the fact that the first blacks did not arrive in the colonies with a group identity as "neegars" but with specific African identities. The majority were Ibo, Ewe, Biafada, Bakongo, Wolof, Bambara, Ibibio, Serer, and Arada. Unlike the first white immigrants, they were the only involuntary servants brought to seventeenth-century Virginia in chains and systematically deprived of their Old World cultural heritage and social systems in order to transform them into better slaves. This development was the result of the interaction between slavery and racism, for the increasing demand for cheap labor led to political acts and a social ideology that severely restricted the rights of blacks. Prior to the end of the seventeenth-century free blacks in Virginia could acquire property, vote, and even intermarry with whites. But with the growth of slavery the black codes of the eighteenth century reduced them to a quasifree lower caste. Christian principles prevented neither southerners nor northerners from arrogating to themselves supreme power over other human beings, yet in practice Africans in the non-slave-based economies of the North fared better than their southern brothers. Many colonial slaves and free blacks in New England, for example, were taught to read and write in order to make them better Christians and more efficient porters, clerks, and messengers. It is also important to remember that the names of such eighteenth-century organizations as the African Society (1787), the New York African Free School (1787), the African Mason Lodge (1787), and the African Methodist Episcopal Church (1794) established the first formal self-conscious group identity of free blacks as African.

While Egyptian, Ethiopian, and Arabic script were known in parts of Africa for centuries, eighteenth-century Africa was basically an oral culture. As Olaudah Equiano, the European-African abolitionist, tells us in his classic slave narrative, the spoken word, music, and dance were at the center of a communal, profoundly religious way of life. In contrast, industrialized Europe and England had moved beyond the oral stage and medieval thinking to a reverence for print and man. The literary tradition and its attendant values, especially reading and writing, were cherished as the exclusive heritage of civilized man. Until the twentieth century these two modes of perceiving, organizing, and communicating experience were believed by Europeans to be related to different stages of development of the mind. But as Claude Lévi Strauss notes, these alternative approaches are actually "two strategic levels at which nature is accessible to scientific enquiry: one roughly adapted to that of perception and imagination: the other at a remove from it . . . one very close to, and the other at a remove from sensible intuition." Each has its own advantages. While a literate orientation heralds the advancement of technology and abstract learning, an oral orientation reinforces the primacy of events and disciplined yet improvisational acts of a group nature. One culture conceives of man as the measure of all things; the other conceives of him as a deeply religious being, living in harmony with a mystical, organic universe.

By 1764 the institution of slavery had been established in the colonies for more than a hundred years, and by 1789 the compulsion of whites to remake blacks into harmless, civilized Christians was a matter of record. As Vernon Loggins observes, Cotton Mather's *Rules for the Societies of Negroes,* written in 1693, was typical of the general attitude of the Puritan and Anglican divines, whose interest in Christianizing blacks was to make them more honest, useful servants. Freedom in the form of manumission or a privileged status was the reward for those considered acceptably acculturated. The deprivation of educational, economic, and political opportunities for the majority of blacks, however, made cultural assimilation the prize of precious few. In addition, the process of adopting the dominant, racist Anglo-Saxon cultural pattern of the revolutionary period resulted in the ethnic double-consciousness that W. E. B. Du Bois eloquently described in *The Souls of Black Folk:* (1903) "it is a peculiar sensation, this double-consciousness, this sense of always looking at one's self through the eyes of others, of measuring one's soul by the tape of a world that looks on in amused contempt and pity. One ever feels his twoness,—an American, a Negro; two souls, two thoughts, two unreconciled strivings; two warring ideals in one dark body, whose dogged strength alone keeps it from being torn asunder." African-Americans were both people of African descent and nonpeople to the majority of whites; they were part of the society yet alienated from it; they were among the first colonists to build the nation, but the nation has yet to grant them first-class citizenship. African-Americans were therefore destined to function on two levels of reality, and their attitudes toward integration and separatism were largely determined by the degree of alienation from or faith in the principles of the dominant white Anglo-Saxon Protestant society.

Integration may be defined as the dual processes of cultural and social assimilation. While cultural assimilation during the revolutionary era involved essentially learning the English language, the Bible, the classics, the popular English and neoclassical writers, and colonial behavior patterns, social assimilation meant full participation in the organizations and institutions of the emerging nation. Fear for their physical and psychological security led white colonists to redefine Africans as a distinctive group of subhumans who ought to be culturally but not socially assimilated, especially in southern colonies where their numbers were a cause of alarm. This was particularly true of Virginia where there were only 300 blacks in the mid-seventeenth century but 120,156 blacks and 173,316 whites by the mid-eighteenth. Consequently, in 1662 the colony imposed a fine for interracial fornication; in 1691 it banned interracial marriages; and in 1723 it deprived free blacks of the right to vote. In seventeenth-century New England, where the black population was never more than 20,000, blacks were excluded from the militia; nevertheless, from the French and Indian wars to the Battle of Bunker Hill slaves and free blacks alike took up arms in the struggle for American independence.

Although confrontations with British soldiers like that of Crispus Attucks, the fugitive slave and New England seaman who was among the five colonists killed in the Boston Massacre, may be interpreted as integrationist acts of patriotism, the early petitions of slaves for permission to purchase their freedom and to return to Africa have the ring of separatism. In truth, however, the major loyalty of colonial blacks was not so much to a place or a people as it was to the principle of freedom, the principle the white colonists themselves expressed in terms of the natural rights of man as they laid the philosophical foundation for their separation from England. At least three petitions from New England slaves in 1773 sounded a similar note. The first was in January to Governor Hutchinson and the general court from "many slaves, living in the Town of Boston, and other Towns in the Province . . . who have had every Day of their Lives imbittered with this most intollerable Reflection, That, let their Behavior be what it will, nor their Children to all Generations, shall ever be able to do, or to possess and enjoy any Thing, no not even *Life itself,* but in a Manner as the *Beasts that perish.* We have no Property! We have no Wives! No Children! We have no City! No Country . . . ." The second, a letter addressed to delegates to the House of Representatives by four slaves—Peter Bestes, Sambo Freeman, Felix Holbrook, and Chester Joie—"in behalf of our fellow slaves in this province and by order of their Committee," came in April. After expressing "a high degree of satisfaction" with the legislative efforts of the colony "to free themselves from slavery," the letter boldly asserts: "We expect great things from men who have made such a noble stand against the designs of their *fellow-men* to enslave them" and goes on to request "one day in a week to work for themselves, to enable them to earn money to purchase the residue of their time . . . ." Seeing no relief from degrading prejudice and discrimination in America, they were willing to submit to the law "until we leave the province . . . as soon as we can from our joynt labours procure money to transport ourselves to some part of the coast of Africa, where we propose a settlement." The third petition addressed to Governor Hutchinson arrived in June and echoes the sentiments of James Otis's 1764 protest in the *Rights of the British Colonies:* "Your Petitioners apprehend they have in common with other men a natural right to be free and without molestation to injoy such property as they may acquire by their industry, or by any other means not detrimental to their fellow men . . . ." None of these petitioners was granted relief by the courts, the legislature, or the governor.

Perhaps the most historically revealing petition for freedom was dated May 25, 1774—less than a week before the British blockaded the Port of Boston in retaliation for the Boston Tea Party of December 1773—and addressed to Governor Thomas Gage and the General Court of Massachusetts by "a Grate Number of Blacks of the Province . . . held in a state of Slavery within the bowels of a free and Christian Country.'' This moving document, which speaks volumes about the priority given by blacks to the forging of personal identities on the basis of their common condition and the evolving consciousness of a people in transition from an oral to a literate culture, reads:

> That your Petitioners apprehind we have in common with all other men a natural right to our freedoms without Being depriv'd of them by our fellow men we are a freeborn Pepel and have never forfeited this Blessing by aney compact or agreement whatever. But we were unjustly dragged by the cruel hand of power from our dearest frinds and sum of us stolen from the bosoms of our tender Parents and from a Populous Pleasant and plentiful country and Brought hither to be made slaves for Life in a Christian land . . . .How can the master be said to Beare my Borden when he Beares me down whith the Have chanes of Slavery and operson. . . . Nither can we reap an equal benefet from the laws of the Land which doth not justifi but condemns Slavery or if there had bin aney Law to hold us in Bondage we are Humbely of the Opinion ther never was aney to inslave our children for life when Born in a free Countrey. We therefore Bage your Excellency and Honours will give this its deer weight and consideration and that you will accordingly cause an act of the legislative to be pessed that we may obtain our Natural right our freedoms and our children be set at lebety at the yeare of twenty one . . . .[1]

As in the past, the legislature voted to let the question ''subside''—did they find the petition unintelligible? unacceptable? inexpedient? —but subside it did not.

Despite the scores of antislavery petitions by blacks—some in the eloquent prose of the period, others acceptable, all intelligible—Quakers, and other groups, the Founding Fathers chose political expediency over principle when they deleted all reference to slavery from the final draft of the Declaration of Independence. According to Jefferson, the condemnation of slavery was deleted in deference to the economic interests of Georgia and South Carolina, who argued for the continuation of the slave trade. To compound this fracture between principle and practice, between the emerging national belief in the inalienable rights of man and colonial laws, between the antislavery, industrial North and the proslavery, agrarian South, the Constitutional Convention of 1787 gave explicit sanction to slavery by providing that representation in Congress and taxes were to be determined by the numbers of free persons in each state ''and excluding Indians not taxed, three fifths of all other persons.'' In addition, the slave trade was extended for twenty years and fugitive slaves were to be surrendered to their owners. If it is true that the fathers of the Constitution were dedicated to the principle of freedom, it is no less true, as

---

1. Herbert Aptheker, ed., *A Documentary History of the Negro People in the United States,* pp. 7–9.

John Hope Franklin points out in *From Slavery to Freedom,* that they were even more dedicated to the ethnocentric, socioeconomic proposition that "government should rest upon the dominion of property."

Although the antislavery movement was set back by the Three-fifths Compromise of the ruling class and its political repudiation of the natural rights of blacks, many African-Americans felt that the preamble to the Declaration of Independence still held out the promise of "Life, Liberty and the pursuit of Happiness" for them as well as whites. For them the Revolutionary War had been a struggle more for personal freedom than for political independence. And at the end of the war, hundreds of the 5,000 blacks who fought for the patriots were freed by the states even though some masters contested the promises of manumission. By 1790 there were nearly 4,000,000 whites and slightly more than 750,000 blacks in the United States. In the southern states there were 641,691 slaves and 32,048 free blacks. The mid-Atlantic states had approximately 36,000 slaves and 14,000 free blacks. In contrast, New England had only 3,700 slaves in a black population of more than 13,000. While Vermont and Massachusetts reported no slaves at all, Connecticut had 2,600. The only city able to boast no slaves was Boston. Her 761 blacks were free.

By virtue of his unique situation as a slave or quasifree person in a society that was growing painfully aware of its paradoxical role as the oppressed and the oppressor, the African-American writer's struggle for independence provides a classic metaphor for the psychological and political schism of the new nation. Even more than the slave petitions for freedom, the writings of two African-Americans and a European-African reveal how individual processes of cultural and social assimilation in a basically hostile white Anglo-Saxon literate society fostered the twoness of early black identity. For Jupiter Hammon, Phillis Wheatley, and Olaudah Equiano, the necessity of functioning on two planes of reality was a challenge that each met in terms of his own unique situation and gifts.

I

In the case of Jupiter Hammon, we see the influence of the Bible and slavery in shaping an otherworldly view of liberty and equality that distorted his social vision. What little is known about his life is found in scraps of information in letters and in the poetry and prose itself. Born a slave on October 17, 1711, Hammon was owned by the Lloyds, a merchant family of Long Island. A dutiful, intelligent servant, he was apparently encouraged in his efforts to read and write by Henry Lloyd, his first master, for in one of his discourses he refers to the English divines, Burkitt and Beveridge, whose works were in

Lloyd's library. In 1733 he purchased a Bible from his master for seven shillings and six pence, an indication of the depth of his religious commitment, his thriftiness, and the nature of his master's benevolence. Since he was well-read in the Bible and considered an exemplary slave, and since there were black and Indian churches on Long Island and in Connecticut during this era, it is highly possible that Hammon was a slave exhorter. In 1760 he became the first black American to publish a poem in the colonies. Apparently this distinction and the prestige it brought his owner contributed to the poet not being freed upon the elder Lloyd's death in 1763. Instead, he was inherited by Joseph, one of four sons. After Joseph's death during the Revolutionary War, the family retainer was passed on to John Lloyd, Jr., a grandson. With the British takeover of Long Island, the patriotic Lloyd family took their talented, faithful servant with them to Hartford, Connecticut, where he is believed to have died a slave around 1800, even though slavery was abolished in the state in 1784 and the Revolutionary War ended in 1783.

Hammon's first broadside poem was titled *An Evening Thought. Salvation by Christ, with Penetential Cries: Composed by Jupiter Hammon, a Negro belonging to Mr. Lloyd of Queen's Village, on Long Island, the 25th of December, 1760.* Lacking the originality, ironic tension, graphic imagery, and call and response pattern of black American spirituals, the poem reveals Hammon's personal resignation to slavery and the inspiration of the Psalms and Methodist hymnals:

> Lord, hear our penetential Cry:
> Salvation from above;
> It is the Lord that doth supply,
> With his redeeming Love.[2]

The repetition of "Salvation" in twenty-three of the poem's eighty-eight lines does not significantly elevate the prosaic quality of the verse. The next broadside was *An Address to Miss Phillis Wheatly, Ethiopian Poetess, in Boston, who came from Africa at eight years of age, and soon became acquainted with the gospel of Jesus Christ.* Published in Hartford on August 4, 1778, this twenty-one stanza poem celebrates the salvation of his more famous and youthful contemporary from "heathen" Africa:

> Thou hast left the heathen shore;
> Through mercy of the Lord,
> Among the heathen live no more,
> Come magnify thy God.

. . . .

2. Quotations are from Oscar Wegelin's edition of *Jupiter Hammon, American Negro Poet.*

> Thou, Phillis, when thou hunger hast,
>   Or pantest for thy God,
> Jesus Christ is thy relief
>   Thou hast the holy word.

As usual, the poet reminds his reader that ultimate freedom and joy is not earthly but heavenly:

> While thousands muse with earthly toys,
>   And rage about the street,
> Dear Phillis, seek for heaven's joys,
>   Where we do hope to meet.

Contrary to the poet's view, Phillis Wheatley was more capable of coping with and giving poetic form to the two planes of reality than he. A third poem, *An Essay on the Ten Virgins,* was printed in 1779 and advertised in the *Connecticut Courant* on December 14, 1779, but no copy has been preserved. Hammon's unimaginative use of the meter, rhyme, diction, and stanzaic pattern of the Methodist hymnal combined with the negative image of Africa and conciliatory tone of these early poems reveal the poet's limitations and the costly sociopsychological price he paid for the mere semblance of cultural assimilation.

As his first published sermon indicates, Hammon was under fire from his black brothers and sisters for his otherworldly view of freedom. *A Winter Piece: Being a Serious Exhortation with a Call to the Unconverted: and a Short Contemplation on the Death of Jesus Christ,* published in Hartford in 1782, attempts to explain his ostensible betrayal of his people's struggle for freedom in this life:

> My dear Brethren, as it hath been reported that I had petitioned to the court of Hartford against freedom, I now solemnly declare that I never have said, nor done any thing, neither directly nor indirectly, to promote or to prevent freedom; but my answer hath always been I am a stranger here and I do not care to be concerned or to meddle with public affairs, and by this declaration I hope my friends will be satisfied, and all prejudice removed, Let us all strive to be united together in love, and to become new creatures. (p. 174[3])

The lessons of the Bible and slavery had taught him that for body and soul, black and white, individual and nation, freedom was God's alone to grant:

> Come my dear fellow servants and brothers, Africans by nation, we are all invited to come, Acts x, 34. Then Peter opened his mouth and said, of a truth I perceive that God is no respecter of persons, verse 35. But in every nation he that feareth him is accepted of him. My Brethren, many of us are seeking

---

3. Unless otherwise noted, quotations from Hammon's prose are from Sidney Kaplan's *The Black Presence in the Era of the American Revolution.*

a temporal freedom, and I wish you may obtain it; remember that all power
in heaven and earth belongs to God; if we are slaves it is by the permission of
God, if we are free it must be by the power of the most high God. Stand still
and see the salvation of God, cannot that same power that divided the waters
from the waters for the children of Israel to pass through, make way for your
freedom. (p. 175)

Hammon's reference to himself and his people as "Africans by nation"
reflects his awareness of the duality of his identity, a duality he unfortunately
sought to transcend rather than synthesize through religiosity. Appended to
the sermon is the seventeen quatrain "Poem for Children with Thoughts of
Death" as further testimony to the poet's piety.

The sermon and poem believed to have been written soon after *A Winter
Piece* contain references to "the Present War." In *An Evening's Improvement. Shewing the Necessity of beholding the Lamb of God* . . . Hammon is
true to his apolitical, religious philosophy of life:

And now my brethren, I am to remind you of a most melancholy scene of
Providence; it hath pleased the most high God, in his wise providence, to
permit a cruel and unnatural war to be commenced. . . . Have we not great
cause to think this is the just deserving of our sins . . . . Here we see that we
ought to pray, that God may hasten the time when the people shall beat their
swords into a ploughshares and their spears into pruning-hooks, and nations
shall learn war no more. (pp. 175–76)

And in the second half of "A Dialogue Intitled the Kind Master and the
Dutiful Servant," the two-page poem concluding the sermon, the poet stands
above the battle praying for peace:

Servant

Dear Master, now it is a time,
    A time for great distress;
We'll follow after things divine,
    And pray for happiness.

Master

Then will the happy day appear,
    That virtue shall increase;
Lay up the sword and drop the spear,
    And Nations seek for peace.

Banal, bloodless, unoriginal, and nonracial, these lines on Christian virtue tell
us as much about the theology whites imposed on colonial blacks as they do
about Hammon's warped sense of identity and poetry.

The most decisive evidence of the poet-preacher's exploitation by those
who found his religious convictions a model for African-American character
and behavior is found in Hammon's final discourse, *An Address to the Ne-*

groes of the State of New York. Dedicated to the African Society of New York
in 1786, the *Address* was published two years after slavery was outlawed in
the state and a year before it became the eleventh state to ratify the Constitution. Since Hammon was seventy-six at the time, he sincerely intended this
discourse to be the "last . . . dying advice, of an old man." With an uncommon if not unnatural faith in God and white people, whose sinful habits, he
believed, did not in God's eyes and his own condone the slaves', Hammon
preaches against the sins of disobedience, stealing, lying, swearing, and idleness. Consciousness of the irony of his people's oppression by those who had
waged a costly and bloody war to end their own oppression is expressed but
quickly suppressed by personal resignation to slavery and otherworldliness:

> Now I acknowledge that liberty is a great thing, and worth seeking for, if
> we can get it honestly, and by our good conduct prevail on our masters to set
> us free. Though for my own part I do not wish to be free: yet I should be
> glad, if others, especially the young negroes were to be free, for many of us
> who are grown up slaves, and have always had masters to take care of us,
> should hardly know how to take care of ourselves; and it may be more for our
> own comfort to remain as we are. That liberty is a great thing we may know
> from our own feelings, and we may likewise judge so from the conduct of
> the white people, in the late war. How much money has been spent, and how
> many lives have been lost to defend their liberty. I must say that I have hoped
> that God would open their eyes, when they were so much engaged for
> liberty, to think of the state of the poor blacks and to pity us . . . . But this,
> my dear brethren, is by no means, the greatest thing we have to be concerned
> about. Getting our liberty in this world is nothing to having the liberty of the
> children of God.[4]

Jupiter Hammon's importance as a poet is essentially historical and sociologi-
cal, for his blind faith in the benevolence of whites and the kingdom of heaven
is a vivid illustration of the ambiguous political role of too many early
African-American integrationist writers and preachers whose double-
consciousness was both a blessing and a curse in the struggle of blacks for
independence.

II

In contrast to Jupiter Hammon, several eighteenth-century black ministers
asserted their right to be free of prejudice and to run their own affairs by
breaking off from the established white churches and organizing their own

4. William H. Robinson, Jr., ed., *Early Black American Prose*, p. 42.

separate institutions. Although the dates and themes of their miscellaneous writings do not fall within the scope of this book, their struggle for freedom of worship paradoxically has much in common with one of the ultimate goals of the Revolution. David George, a slave, started the first black Baptist church among the slaves in the colonies in Silver Bluff, South Carolina, between 1773 and 1775. In 1788 Andrew Bryan, another slave exhorter whose master encouraged his preaching because he believed it had a salutary influence on other slaves, established the First African Baptist Church in Savannah, Georgia. But the most celebrated black church fathers are ex-slaves Richard Allen and Absalom Jones. Dragged from their knees while praying in St. George's Methodist Episcopal Church of Philadelphia, these two ministers and the other blacks attending service "all went out of the church in a body, and they were no more plagued with us in the church." In Reverend Allen's words, "we were determined to seek out for ourselves, the Lord being our helper." Thus in 1794 Allen founded the Bethel African Methodist Episcopal Church and fought for many years to protect his church and congregation from the hostility of white Methodist preachers and trustees. During the same year Jones, who had earlier accepted an Episcopalian pastorate, dedicated the St. Thomas African Episcopal Church of Philadelphia. Less assertive but no less pious nor significant is Phillis Wheatley.

As the first slave and second woman writer in America to publish a book of poems, Phillis Wheatley's literary achievement was considered an extraordinary development on both sides of the Atlantic. To many of her contemporaries her poetry was indisputable evidence of the mental equality of blacks. But Moses Coit Tyler's observation in *The Literary History of the American Revolution* (1897) that "her career belongs rather to the domain of anthropology, or of hagiology, than to that of poetry—whether American or African" is more useful as an example of the tenacity of eighteenth-century prejudices and the limitations of nineteenth-century American scholarship than as a just assessment of the literary gifts of "Afric's muse," as she calls herself in "Hymn to Humanity." Like Jefferson, Tyler believed her poetry "below the dignity of criticism." But as Julian Mason, Jr., rightly observes in the authoritative edition of the poet's complete works: "Her poems are certainly as good or better than those of most of the poets usually included and afforded fair treatment in a discussion of American poetry before 1800, and this same evaluation holds true when she is compared with most of the minor English poets of the eighteenth century who wrote in the neoclassical tradition."

A frail, precocious African child of seven, Phillis Wheatley was brought to Boston on a slave ship from Senegambia, the territory known in modern Africa as Senegal and Gambia, in 1761. She was purchased by John Wheatley, a prosperous tailor and owner of several household slaves, as a special servant for his wife, Suzanna Wheatley. The Wheatleys were dedicated to missionary work among Indians and blacks; their home was a well-known meeting place for Boston's cultured society. Once Mrs. Wheatley and her daughter Mary discovered Phillis Wheatley's quickness of mind, their humanitarian impulse to provide her with the proper cultivation was irresistible. In a letter to her London publisher in 1772, Mr. Wheatley wrote: "Without any assistance from School Education, and by only what she was taught in the Family, she, in sixteen Months Time from her Arrival, attained the English Language. to which she was an utter stranger before, to such a Degree, as to read any, the most difficult parts of the Sacred Writings, to the great Astonishment of all who heard her." Thanks mainly to Mary Wheatley's teaching, as Benjamin Brawley points out in *The Negro in Literature and Art,* Wheatley soon learned "a little astronomy, some ancient and modern geography, a little ancient history, a fair knowledge of the Bible, and a thoroughly appreciative acquaintance with the most important Latin classics, especially the works of Virgil and Ovid." She took pride in Terence's African heritage, became proficient in grammar, and favored Pope's translations of Homer among the English classics. Mrs. Wheatley's favorite, the young poet was not allowed to associate with the other domestics nor do hard work. Her memory of Africa was vague, and her only recollection of her mother was that she poured out water before the rising sun. Gradually her frail health and literary genius earned her privileged treatment as a companion to her mistress and an adopted member of the family. "I was treated by her more like her child then her servant," Wheatley wrote in 1774 to her African friend, Obour Tanner; "no opportunity was left unimproved of giving me the best of advice; but in terms how tender! how engaging!"

Eager to write, "she learnt in so short a Time, that in the Year 1765, she wrote a Letter to the Rev. Mr. Occum, the Indian Minister," who later published a hymnal for his people. In 1767, when she was only only fourteen, Wheatley wrote her first poem, "To the University of Cambridge, in New England," in blank verse. Bearing witness to the success of Mrs. Wheatley's missionary efforts, the first stanza of the original manuscript reads:

> While an intrinsic ardor bids me write
> The muse doth promise to assist my pen.
> 'Twas but e'en now I left my native shore
> The sable Land of error's darkest night.
> There, sacred Nine! for you no place was found.
> Parent of mercy, 'twas thy Powerful hand
> Brought me in safety from the dark abode.[5]

With the restrained moral fervor of a young New England convert, she admonishes the Harvard students:

5. Quotations from Phillis Wheatley are from Julian D. Mason, Jr.'s, edition of *The Poems of Phillis Wheatley.*

> Let hateful vice so baneful to the Soul,
> Be still avoided with becoming care;
> Suppress the sable monster in its growth,
> Ye blooming plants of human race, divine
> An Ethiop tells you, tis your greatest foe
> Its transient sweetness turns to endless pain,
> And bring eternal ruin on the Soul.

Six years later in the first edition of her work, she significantly revised the poem, compressing it from thirty-two to thirty lines, and changing "The sable Land of error's darkest night" to "The land of errors, and *Egyptian* gloom" and "the sable monster" to "the deadly serpent." Unlike Jupiter Hammon, maturity, success, and travel brought increasing artistic and ethnic pride to the young black woman who became a kind of poet laureate for what was then the literary capital of America.

Between 1768 and 1769 the young poet wrote at least three more poems. The first, "To the King's Most Excellent Majesty. 1768," praises King George III for his last favor to the colonies, the repeal of the Stamp Act, and wishes him God's blessings so that he may give further evidence to "his subjects" of his concern for peace and freedom. The second, "On the Death of the Rev. Dr. Sewell, 1769," was the first of several occasional poems celebrating or lamenting the birth or death of Boston's elite. The Reverend Doctor Joseph Sewall (son of Chief Justice Samuel Sewall, who was both presiding judge at the Salem witch trials and the author of the first New England antislavery tract) was pastor for fifty-six years at Boston's famous old South Church where Wheatley became the first of her race to be baptized in 1771. The third poem, "On Being Brought from Africa to America," is the earliest effort of the fifteen-year-old poet to come to grips with the dual nature of her identity. Her shortest poem, it reads:

> 'Twas mercy brought me from my *Pagan* land,
> Taught my benighted soul to understand
> That there's a God, that there's a *Saviour* too:
> Once I redemption neither sought nor knew.
> Some view our sable race with scornful eye,
> "Their colour is a diabolic die."
> Remember, *Christians, Negroes,* black as *Cain,*
> May be refin'd, and join th' angelic train.

As in the original poem to the Harvard students, the poet accepts the social prejudices and religious mythology of the revolutionary period and considers herself fortunate to have been redeemed by Christ and "refin'd" by the Wheatleys. At the same time, the closing couplet boldly and ingeniously reminds Christians who look on her people with "scornful eye" that it is their duty to cultivate the moral and intellectual capacities of "Negroes" so that they, too, may enjoy spiritual if not social equality. Circulated among the Wheatleys and their friends, these poems soon won a local reputation for the young poet. "The Wheatleys had adopted her," writes J. Saunders Redding in *To Make A Poet Black,* (1939) "but she had adopted their terrific New England conscience."

From her first appearance in print with the elegy *An Elegaic Poem, on George Whitfield* (1770) to the London publication of her first edition of *Poems on Various Subjects, Religious and Moral* in 1773, Wheatley became the object of curiosity and admiration. Her poems and her person were used as evidence in the debate over the intellectual equality of blacks. Reprinted in Boston, Newport, New York, Philadelphia, and England, the elegiac broadside, addressed primarily to the Countess of Huntingdon, philanthropist and Whitefield's patron, immediately extended the poet's reputation. The lines "Great Countess, we Americans revere / Thy name, and mingle in thy grief sincere" allude to the Countess of Huntingdon's philanthropic work and the poet's sense of identity as an American. But her silence about the Boston Massacre, especially the death of the fugitive slave Crispus Attucks, which occurred a few blocks from the Wheatley house in the same year as Whitefield's death, is curious. The circumstances of her privileged position in the Wheatley household seem to have vitiated the poet's sense of ethnic and national identity.

In Boston Wheatley was frequently invited to the homes of people in Mrs. Wheatley's social and missionary circle, where she was regarded with "peculiar interest and esteem." Her trip to England with Nathaniel Wheatley in May 1773, we now know from the recent discovery of new letters by the poet, was not merely for reasons of health but also for an introduction to British missionary circles during a politically volatile time. For in April Parliament had passed the Tea Act and sparked yet another chain of events destined to culminate in the Revolution. Against this backdrop, Wheatley's new admirer and patron, Selina, Countess of Huntingdon, to whom the poet's first edition was dedicated, introduced her to British society, where her exceptional talent and tact as a conversationalist apparently steered her clear of political subjects and won her praise and presents, including a copy of the 1770 Glasgow folio edition of *Paradise Lost* from the lord mayor of London. Mrs. Wheatley's illness and request for her prevented the poet from accepting an invitation to stay in England for presentation at the court of George III. In October Wheatley, little improved in health but much in reputation, was back in Boston. Before she left London, however, she participated in arrangements for the publication of her first volume of poetry.

The first edition of *Poems on Various Subjects, Religious and Moral* contains Wheatley's best poetry. Critics have noted the influence of English writers on her poetry, especially the debt to Milton for "An Hymn to the

Morning'' and "An Hymn to the Evening,'' to Gray for the Whitefield elegy, and to Addison and Watts for "Ode to Neptune" and "Hymn to Humanity." But the greatest influence on the volume of thirty-nine poems was religion and neoclassicism. Her Christian convictions and the influence of the Bible are most clearly seen in the inventive use of biblical narrative in "Goliath of Gath," one of her longest poems, and "Isaiah lxiii. 1–8." In the tradition of New England colonial writers, she freely embellishes the biblical account of David and Goliath—a convention that became even more distinctively employed in the African-American tradition. She casts the poems, however, in the neoclassical mode of iambic pentameter couplets, invocation to the muse, elevated language, classical allusions, and panoramic scope. Here— particularly in her precision of meter, use of heroic couplet, and stilted diction—her models were Alexander Pope and the Latin writers themselves. The mixture of Christian and classical references in *Poems on Various Subjects* impressed some of her contemporaries with her genius and acculturation. Others were more fascinated by her youth, sex, race, or class.

Wheatley was certainly aware of the twoness of her identity and reception. Her pride in and exploitation of her African identity is apparent in the reference to Terence in "To Maecenas" and in her self-image in several poems as "Ethiop," "Afric's muse," and "vent'rous Afric." The degree to which she is also conscious of the larger society's Manichean image of Africa and her descendants is obvious in "On Being Brought from Africa to America," "To the University of Cambridge, in New England," and "To the Right Honourable William, Earl of Dartmouth, His Majesty's Principal Secretary of State for North America, etc." In the last poem, written in 1772 upon the Earl of Dartmouth's appointment, with the hope of encouraging him to use his new power to support the colonies' struggle for freedom, we see the skillful manner in which the nineteen-year-old poet gives poetic form to her double vision:

> Should you, my lord, while you peruse my song
> Wonder from whence my love of *Freedom* sprung,
> Whence flow these wishes for the common good,
> By feeling hearts alone best understood,
> I, young in life, by seeming cruel fate
> Was snatch'd from *Afric's* fancy'd happy seat:
> What pangs excruciating must molest,
> What sorrows labour in my parent's breast?
> Steel'd was that soul and by no misery mov'd
> That from a father seiz'd his babe belov'd:
> Such, such my case. And can I then but pray
> Others may never feel tyrannic sway?

Wheatley, as these lines indicate, was more conscious of her African heritage and sophisticated in her craftsmanship than Jupiter Hammon, but her religious indoctrination and unique status in the Wheatley family dictated against the expression of more positive, unequivocal sentiments about her African past.

The poet's visit to England was the high point in her brief career and a test of her piety. In London she was received as a "most surprising genius," but a very important friend of the American missionary movement, John Thornton, believed such praise a worldly snare and cautioned her against pride in her intellectual gifts. Thornton, merchant, philanthropist, and Calvinistic Anglican, and the Countess of Huntingdon, who as the patron of John Marrant, another colonial black writer, persuaded him in 1785 to go to Nova Scotia as a missionary, supported Eleazer Wheelock's Indian Charity School in New Hampsire. Both philanthropists, we learn from a recent critic, kept in close contact with the Wheatleys, who "disbursed the funds Thornton donated to Indian missionary work, posted him on its progress, and sent their son to him for improvement." Thornton was particularly interested in hearing about the progress of Wheelock's famous pupil, the Monhegan Indian preacher Samson Occom. It was to Occom, of course, that eleven-year-old Phillis wrote her first letter. Occom and Thornton both considered the young poet a potential missionary and encouraged her to become "a Female Preacher to her kindred." But in writing to Thornton in 1774 she respectfully declined this role, considering it "too hazardous" and herself "not sufficiently Eligible." Moreover, she did not want to leave her "British & American Friends" and confessed that she was no longer an African but an African-American: "how like a Barbarian should I look to the Natives; I can promise that my tongue shall be quiet for a strong reason indeed being an utter stranger to the Language of Anamaboe . . ." In this manner the poet tactfully responded to Thornton's view that "silent wonder and adoration of the wisdom and goodness of God" more becomes faith than does the ability to "talk excellently of divine things, even so as to raise the admiration of others." In the same letter the poet informs Thornton of Mr. Wheatley's "generous behaviour in granting me my freedom . . . about 3 months before the death of my dear mistress & at her desire, as well as his own humanity . . . ."

Mrs. Wheatley's death on March 3, 1774, and Wheatley's personal hardships over the next decade were to test her faith even more. Writing to her friend Obour Tanner on March 21, she expresses the depth of the loss of her best friend: "I have lately met with a great trial in the death of my mistress; let us imagine the loss of a parent, sister or brother, the tenderness of all were united in her." Despite this loss, the poet continues to invoke her muse for occasional poems such as the 1775 encomium "To His Excellency General Washington." Washington was so pleased by the poem that he invited Wheatley to visit him at Cambridge, an invitation she gladly accepted in 1776. In that poem, *Liberty and Peace,* and "On the Capture of General Lee," the poet coined the term *Columbia* to refer to America. With the death of Mr.

Wheatley on March 12, 1778, the family household broke up, and the next month Wheatley married John Peters. Legend has it that her husband was a respectable but excessively proud black man who tried his hand as a baker, grocer, doctor, and lawyer without much success. The marriage resulted in estrangement from her former white friends and a life of poverty. Yet on October 30, 1779, the *Evening Post and General Advertiser* outlined her "Proposals" for publishing by subscription a new volume of "Poems & Letters on various subjects, dedicated to the Right Hon. Benjamin Franklin Esq: One of the Ambassadors of the United States at the Court of France." Since the treaty ending the war was not signed until 1783, she was unable to secure enough subscribers and the book was not published. Misfortunes began to multiply. Her husband was jailed for debt; two of her children died between 1783 and 1784; and she was reduced to working in a cheap lodging house. On December 5, 1784, Phillis Peters died and was buried with her third child, who had died soon after his mother. Her husband disappeared with the unpublished manuscript of her second book. Two years later her first and only book was republished in America.

A vivid example of cultural and ethnic divisions during the revolutionary era is the manner in which Wheatley's genius and poetic talents were praised in the beginning by General Washington in 1776 and dismissed at the end by Thomas Jefferson in 1784. In different degrees and under different circumstances, both Washington and Jefferson were Virginia slaveholders who believed that slavery ought to be abolished by law; that blacks were inferior to whites; and that blacks and whites should be separated. Of the two, however, Jefferson seems to have held the stronger convictions. In response to the letter and poem sent to him by the poet, Washington wrote to "Miss Phillis":

> I thank you most sincerely for your polite notice of me in the elegant lines you enclosed; and however undeserving I may be of such encomium and panegyric, the style and manner exhibit a striking proof of your poetical talents; in honor of which, and as a tribute justly due you, I would have published the poem, had I not been apprehensive that, while I only meant to give the world this new instance of your genius, I might have incurred the imputation of vanity. This, and nothing else, determined me not to give it a place in the public prints.
>
> If you ever come to Cambridge, or near head-quarters, I shall be happy to see a person so favored by the Muses, and to who nature has been so liberal and beneficient in her dispensations.[6]

The sincerity of these sentiments take on a different color in the light of a letter written a few weeks earlier to his former secretary in which Washington

6. George Washington, *Writings*, ed. John C. Fitzpatrick, 39 vols. (Washington, D.C.: U.S. Government Printing Office, 1931–44) 4: 360–61.

says: "I recollect nothing else worth giving you the trouble of, unless you can be amused by reading a letter and poem addressed to me by Miss Phillis Wheatley." In contrast to Washington's amused benevolence, Jefferson's "suspicion" that "the blacks are inferior to the whites in the endowments both of body and mind" sounds more like a conviction when we read the following remarks in *Notes on Virginia*:

> Misery is often the parent of the most affecting touches in poetry. Among the blacks is misery enough, God knows, but no poetry. Love is the peculiar oestrum of the poet. Their love is ardent, but it kindles the senses only, not the imagination. Religion, indeed, has produced a Phillis Whately; but it could not produce a poet. The compositions published under her name are below the dignity of criticism. The heroes of the Dunciad are to her, as Hercules to the author of that poem.[7]

No African-American writer during the revolutionary period was more integrated in her society than Wheatley, yet when she was not the object of paternalistic indulgence from admirers, she was the object of intellectual derision for detractors. In either case, the genius and piety that inform her double-consciousness and love of liberty commanded the attention of the age and the ages to follow.

III

Five years after Phillis Wheatley's death, Olaudah Equiano published in London *The Interesting Narrative of the Life of Olaudah Equiano, or Gustavus Vassa, the African* and became the new celebrated black writer of the period. While Wheatley's memories of Africa were vague and essentially religious, those of Equiano are unquestionably the earliest, most detailed description of the nature of bondage and freedom in Africa, the Caribbean, and colonial America from a black perspective. The *Narrative* is the first major slave narrative, a genre that became popular during the abolition movement of the nineteenth century and remains a literary testament to the will of an oppressed people to be free. Completed in 1788, it was first published in America in 1791 and by 1794 had gone into its eighth edition in London.

Neither a black American nor a black Englishmen, Equiano was born in 1745, spent his early childhood in Benin, now a part of southern Nigeria, and his mature years in antislavery work in England. But, as Arna Bontemps notes, his slavery in Virginia and years in the service of a Philadelphia Quaker merchant, who saw to his education and put him to work on small trading

---

7. Thomas Jefferson, *Notes on the State of Virginia*, ed. William Peden (Chapel Hill: University of North Carolina Press, 1955), p. 140.

vessels in the Caribbean, were the years that shaped his consciousness and provided the frame of reference for his *Narrative*. In addition, bibliophiles and students of American cultural history generally consider Equiano's *Narrative* the most influential of the eighteenth-century black autobiographies. Two others are Briton Hammon's fourteen-page *A Narrative of the Uncommon Sufferings and Surprising Deliverance of Briton Hammon, a Negro Man*, published in Boston in 1760, and John Marrant's more popular *A Narrative of the Lord's Wonderful Dealings with J. Marrant . . . Taken Down from His Own Relation*, published in London in 1785.

Living in the fertile province of "Essaka," some distance from the capital of Benin and the sea, Equiano "had never heard of white men or Europeans, nor of the sea; and our subjection to the king of Benin was little more than nominal, for every transaction of the government . . . was conducted by the chief of elders." His father was an elder who with other "chief men, decided disputes and punished crimes." In most cases, the trial was short and "the law of retaliation prevailed."

The youngest and favorite of seven children, Equiano lived for his first eleven years in a collective, agrarian, religious society whose basic modes of expression were oral. "We are almost a nation of dancers, musicians and poets," he says. "Thus every great event such as a triumphant return from battle or other cause of public rejoicing is celebrated in public dances, which are accompanied with songs and music suited to the occasion." To improve the blessing of an uncommonly rich and fruitful land, agriculture was his people's chief industry; "and everyone, even the children and women are engaged in it. . . . Everyone contributes something to the common stock; and, as we are unacquainted with idleness, we have no beggars." As for religion, Equiano—revealing his European acculturation by assuming a third person voice—writes:

> the natives believe that there is one Creator of all things, and that he lives in the sun, and is girted round with a belt; that he may never eat or drink, but, according to some, he smokes a pipe, which is our own favorite luxury. They believe he governs events, especially our deaths or captivity; but, as for the doctrine of eternity, I do not remember to have ever heard of it; some, however, believe in the transmigration of souls in a certain degree. Those spirits which were not transmigrated, such as their dear friends or relations, they believe always attend them, and guard them from the bad spirits of their foes. For this reason they always, before eating as I have observed, put some small portion of the meat, and pour some of their drink, on the ground for them; and they often make oblations of the blood of beasts or fowls at their graves. (pp. 12–13[8])

8. Quotations are from Arna Bontemps's edition of Equiano's *Narrative* in *Great Slave Narratives*.

In contrast to Phillis Wheatley, Christianity altered but by no means destroyed Equiano's respect for the holistic culture and tribal religion of his people and their reverence for priests, magicians, and wise men.

Despite obvious differences in color and culture between Europeans and Africans, Equiano does not accept the absurd correlations between the color of one's skin and the content of one's mind that characterizes Thomas Jefferson's *Notes on Virginia*. "Are there not causes enough to which the apparent inferiority of an African may be ascribed," Equiano observes, "without limiting the goodness of God, and supposing he forebore to stamp understanding on certainly his own image, because 'carved in ebony.' Might it not naturally be ascribed to their situation. . . . Does not slavery itself depress the mind, and extinguish all its fire and every noble sentiment. . . . Let the polished and haughty European recollect that his ancestors were once, like the Africans, uncivilized, and even barbarous. Did Nature make *them* inferior to their sons? and should *they too* have been made slaves?" In short, inferiority to an acculturated yet proud African writer of the eighteenth century was not an innate, racial constant for nonwhites but the result of different historical and social circumstances.

Regarding slavery in Africa, he confesses that sometimes his nation sold slaves to traders, "but they were only prisoners of war, or such among us as had been convicted of kidnapping, or adultery, and some other crimes which we esteemed heinous." Although his nation and family kept slaves, the difference between the system of slavery in Africa and the New World was crucial:

> With us, they do no more work than other members of the community, even their master; their food, clothing, and lodging were nearly the same as theirs (except that they were not permitted to eat with those who were free-born); and there was scarce any other difference between them, than a superior degree of importance which the head of a family possesses in our state, and that authority which, as such, he exercises over every part of his household. Some of these slaves have even slaves under them as their own property, and for their own use. (p. 12)

When he was eleven, Olaudah Equiano and his sister were kidnapped by native traders, and during his manhood he saw first-hand the difference in slavery in Africa, America, and the Caribbean.

After the wonder of seeing the sea for the first time and the mysterious movement of slave ships as well as the terrors of the middle passage and the dread that "we should be eaten by these ugly men," the narrator was sold to a Virginia planter. He received his most indelible impression of the treatment of slaves in Virginia when he was called to his master's house to fan him and saw a black woman cooking with an iron muzzle locked on her head so that she could neither speak, eat, nor drink. Equiano was sold after ''some time'' to the captain of a merchant ship and lieutenant in the royal navy, who renamed him Gustavus Vassa and took him to England. In two or three years he not only spoke English and felt ''quite easy with these new country-men, but relished their society and manners. I no longer looked upon them as spirits, but as men superior to us; and therefore I had the stronger desire to resemble them, to imbibe their spirit, and imitate their manners.'' The next step in adopting his new culture was to persuade his mistress in 1759 to have him baptized. He did not become ''a first-rate Christian'' and missionary, however, until much later after he had searched in vain for the key to salvation among the Quakers, the Roman Catholics, the Jews, and the Turks. He ultimately found the key in Methodism and sought unsuccessfully to be ordained for missionary work ''among his countrymen'' in Africa.

In 1763 he was sold to Robert King, a Quaker merchant in the West Indies. While working on his master's boats, Equiano witnessed the general practice of white men brutally raping female slaves, including ''females not ten years old.'' He also observed how the system of absentee landlords left many island estates in the hands of managerial incompetents and human butchers. As in America, the Caribbean had its instruments of torture. ''The iron muzzle, thumb-screws, &c., are so well known as not to need a description, and were sometimes applied for the slightest faults.'' The inhumanity of slavery made him ''determined to make every exertion to obtain my freedom and to return to Old England.''

In 1766 while the colonists were stiffening their resistance to the Stamp Act, Equiano finally accumulated enough money by trading goods to buy his freedom from King but agreed to continue working for him as a free ''able-bodied sailor at thirty-six shillings per month.'' In this capacity he made several trips to America and experienced the precarious existence of a free black in the colonies. In Savannah, Georgia, for instance, he was severely beaten one night and left for dead by white men. The next morning he was carted off to jail. A similar fate occurred to a free black carpenter he knew, ''who, for asking a gentleman that he worked for for the money he had earned, was put into gaol; and afterwards this oppressed man was sent from Georgia, with false accusations, of an intention to set the gentleman's house on fire, and run away with his slaves.'' On another occasion only his intelligence, facility in English, and independent spirit prevented his kidnapping by ''white ruffians.'' As a free, acculturated black (he became a hairdresser, played the French horn, and went to night school), Equiano was a restless man who continued to respond to the call of the sea and different cultures: Madeira, Jamaica, Barbados, Smyrna, Genoa, Portugal, Spain, Honduras, and Nicaragua. In the 1780s he became London's most celebrated black abolitionist, culminating his fight against oppression with the first publication of the *Narrative* in 1789, the same year that George Washington was inaugurated first president of the United States. Until his death on April 31, 1797, Olaudah Equiano's vision of himself and the world was that of a European-African Christian convert.

I V

In the beginning of *A History of American Literature* (1878), Moses Coit Tyler writes: "The American people, starting into life in the early part of the seventeenth century, have been busy ever since in recording their intellectual history in laws, manners, institutions, in battles with man and beast and nature, in highways, excavations, edifices, in pictures, in statues, in written words. It is in written words that this people, from the very beginning, have made the most confidential and explicit record of their minds." In contrast, as descendants of Africa and bearers of the legacy of an oral tradition, black petitioners for freedom, Jupiter Hammon, Phillis Wheatley, and Olaudah Equiano were more attuned to the power of the spoken word and the wonder of man as a child of God. Confronted by the paradox of their situation as slaves in a largely white Anglo-Saxon Protestant society that had waged a war to realize its belief in the equality and inalienable rights of man, colonial African-American writers, with the exception of Hammon, were more interested in struggling for physical and spiritual freedom than political and economic independence. Their introduction to the written word was primarily to make them better servants, yet they used their acquired knowledge of reading and writing to solicit the good will of the larger white society. Since it was the Bible that served as the principal tool of cultural assimilation and the Protestant church that allowed partial social assimilation, the most striking quality of the writings of African-Americans between 1764 and 1789 is their Christian piety, faith in the philosophy of natural rights as expressed in the Declaration of Independence, and dual vision of the writers themselves as African-Americans.

In the colonial African-American writer's efforts to resolve his double-consciousness and attain recognition of his freedom and human rights, he did not, as many black writers of the 1960s sought to do, voluntarily seek to reject either aspect of his identity. In the words of Du Bois, "he would not Africanize America, for America has too much to teach the world and Africa. He would not bleach his Negro soul in a flood of white Americanism, for he knows that Negro blood has a message for the world." He wanted simply "to make it possible for a man to be both a Negro and an American, without being cursed and spit upon by his fellows, without having the doors of Opportunity closed roughly in his face." Of early white American writings, Tyler says:

"Literature as a fine art, literature as the voice and the ministress of aesthetic delight, they had perhaps little regard for; but literature as an instrument of humane and immediate utility, they honored, and at this wrought with all the earnestness that was born in their blood." No less is true of the writings of early black Americans.

SUGGESTIONS FOR FURTHER READING

Editions

A Documentary History of the Negro People in the United States. Edited by Herbert Aptheker. New York: The Citadel Press, 1951.

Early Black American Prose. Edited by William H. Robinson, Jr. Dubuque, Iowa: William C. Brown, 1971.

"Four New Letters by Phillis Wheatley." Edited by Kenneth Silverman. *Early American Literature* 8 (1974): 257–71.

The Interesting Narrative of the Life of Olaudah Equiano, or Gustavus Vassa, Written by Himself. In *Great Slave Narratives,* edited by Arna Bontemps. Boston: Beacon Press, 1969.

Jupiter Hammon, American Negro Poet: Selections from his writings and a bibliography. Edited by Oscar Wegelin. New York: Heartman, 1915.

The Poems of Phillis Wheatley. Edited by Julian D. Mason, Jr. Chapel Hill: University of North Carolina Press, 1966. [Authoritative edition, with comprehensive but condescending introduction.]

Scholarship and Criticism

Brawley, Benjamin. *The Negro in Literature and Art in the United States.* 3d ed. New York: Duffield and Company, 1929.

Davis, Arthur P. "Personal Elements in the Poetry of Phillis Wheatley." *Phylon* 14 (1953): 191–98.

Kaplan, Sidney. *The Black Presence in the Era of the American Revolution 1770–1800.* Greenwich, Conn.: New York Graphic Society Ltd., 1973. [Excellent visual and biographical chronicle.]

Loggins, Vernon. *The Negro Author: His Development in America to 1900.* New York: Columbia University Press, 1931. Reprinted, Port Washington, N.Y.: Kennikat Press, 1964.

Nichols, Charles H. *Many Thousand Gone: The Ex-Slaves' Account of Their Bondage and Freedom.* Leiden: E. J. Brill, 1963. Reprinted, Bloomington: Indiana University Press, 1969.

Richmond, Merle A. *Bid the Vassal Soar: Interpretive Essays on the Poetry of Phillis Wheatley and George Moses Horton.* Washington, D.C.: Howard University Press, 1974.

11

Three Travelers
Carver, Bartram, and Woolman

PATRICIA M. MEDEIROS

[*Despite the dreadful fact of slavery, America was for many people the land of opportunity, and a prime reason that opportunity existed was the great continent stretching out behind the seacoast settlements. During the revolutionary years the movement westward continued. It was in the year 1769 that Daniel Boone set out for Kentucky from North Carolina to become the first American "western" hero. His story became known as early as 1784, when it was set forth in John Filson's* The Discovery, Settlement, and present State of Kentucke. *Americans came to know of the land that was to become theirs through two books of substantial literary merit, William Bartram's accounts of Florida and Jonathan Carver's of the upper Midwest. And another traveler, one who stayed closer to home, offered a striking view of an America cursed by slavery.*]

At a time when travel was difficult at best, and often hazardous as well, travelers' accounts of their journeys served both to entertain and to inform their readers. Before the first settlers arrived in America, accounts of the New World were popular reading in England and Europe; after the first settlements were established, accounts of inland explorations were devoured on both sides of the Atlantic. At the time of the Revolution these travel accounts provided the bulk of the little information most Americans had about the extent and nature of the largely unknown American continent, and the substantial body of such works gives historians a rich source of material for their study of the period.

Travel writers played an important role in history, for often their books persuaded adventurers and settlers to enter otherwise unknown regions. English settlers crossed the Atlantic, and Americans pushed westward from their coastal settlements, on the strength of such reports. Writers who described their travels in settled areas also helped to forge a sense of national identity by making distant places familiar, so that readers could see that they shared some important traits, and had common interests, with their countrymen hundreds of miles away.

Other travelers journeyed through unsettled areas, and their books describing remote and strange landscapes were widely read and enjoyed. Indeed, William Bartram's *Travels* was one of the earliest American books to receive widespread acclaim for its literary quality. In the hands of such skillful writers as Bartram and Jonathan Carver, travel accounts became more than mere descriptions and approached the status of literary classics. In addition they appealed to a sense of pride of ownership and a sense of collective responsibility for the proper use of the land. While they did not explicitly call for a revolution or the formation of an American nation, these works contained the seeds of nationalism: an understanding of and a pride in the physical aspects of the continent, including the Indians, and a call for collective action to develop the land for the benefit of its inhabitants and consequently to protect it from outside exploiters. More and more the inhabitants came to identify themselves as Americans, and the exploiters—whether English or French—as outsiders.

Of the travel books of the revolutionary years, three in particular provide us with a picture of the country as it was before urbanization changed it profoundly. In his *Travels* William Bartram describes Florida, a semitropical area foreign to the experience of his contemporary reader; in his *Travels* Jonathan Carver shows us the Midwest, equally strange to his reader; and John Woolman's *Journal* gives us a picture of New Jersey. The last is the least exotic; indeed, for the most part the landscape is assumed to be so ordinary, so common to the reader's experience, that Woolman is able to ignore it and to use his travels in a way totally different from the way Bartram and Carver used theirs.

For all their historical interest, these three travel books are also, in a very real sense, literary, for they are in no way diaries or artless recitals of events. Each author consciously and artistically distilled and shaped his materials— the experiences of his travels—into a form that served his own purpose, and thus to read any of these books as purely a historical document, or as merely a travel book, is to do it a gross injustice.

Carver, Bartram, and Woolman each produced a book that has attained the status of an American classic. Each is a complex literary production that lends itself to examination from many diverse points of view, and each is deserving of appreciation for its own very real literary merits. Yet, different as they are, these works have two very important aspects in common: each author constructed his book upon the framework of his travels, and each used his book in a conscious effort to help the reader understand the nature of the American continent. The journey provides an external framework that can be imposed upon the chaos of facts and impressions of the vast continent and gives the writer a convenient structure within which to organize his work of making the chaos coherent. And in each case, the coherence reflects the author's outlook on the world.

These three writers are representative of three very different ways of looking at the world: Carver is almost completely materialistic, Bartram exhibits an early romanticism, and Woolman has a spiritual outlook. Each of these three disparate and often conflicting viewpoints was widely accepted in the eighteenth century, and an understanding of the premises of each can help us to understand more deeply the complex moral, intellectual, and political climate that provided the context for the American Revolution. Though these three men were confronted by the same object, the American continent, each saw in it something different, his perception colored by his beliefs and his expectations. In spite of the great differences among them, however, these writers are united by their common view of America as both the symbol of an ideal and the context for its realization.

I

Because his purpose in writing is readily apparent, Jonathan Carver clearly illustrates the function of the author, not as a mere recorder of events, but as a shaper and manipulator of his materials. Simply stated, his goal was economic: he wanted to encourage settlement in the Great Lakes area, and he succeeded to a great extent, for his work gave impetus to the vast and rapid westward migration that took place from the end of the Revolution through the 1830s. For almost a century before Carver explored the upper Mississippi valley between 1766 and 1768, the French knew and exploited the area; but for obvious reasons they were not eager to share their knowledge with their English enemies. Thus Carver's description of the region in his *Travels through the Interior Parts of North America in the Years 1766, 1767, and 1768* (first published in 1778) was new and exciting information to most of his readers, and it captured imaginations in England and Europe as well as in the new United States. Within a few years some thirty editions of the book were published, including translations into French, German, Dutch, and Greek. Internationally, it was probably the best-known and most admired work of eighteenth-century American literature, not only because of its subject matter, but also because of its real literary merit.

The facts about Carver's life are not known with any certainty; twentieth-century biographers have concluded, however, that he was born in Weymouth, Massachusetts, in 1710 and was raised in Canterbury, Connecticut, where his father was a highly respected member of the community. Presumably, therefore, the boy was given such educational advantages as the community offered. Around 1750 Carver purchased an ensigncy in the Connecticut regiment, and in his book he describes his participation in the massacre at Fort William Henry in 1757. After the French and Indian War ended in 1763, Carver returned to his wife and children in Montague, Massachusetts; soon, however, he left again to explore some of the western territory newly granted to Britain. As a subordinate to Robert Rogers, the sometime commandant of Detroit celebrated by Kenneth Roberts in *Northwest Passage,* he traveled west to the Mississippi, then up that river to the Falls of St. Anthony. He spent the winter of 1766–67 at a Sioux village on the Minnesota River, and in the spring proceeded farther up the Mississippi and skirted the shores of Lake Superior to the Grand Portage. He had hoped to continue westward, but the supplies Rogers promised him were not forthcoming, and so he returned via the north shore of Lake Superior to the fort at Michillimackinac, between Lake Huron and Lake Michigan. He tried to publish his *Travels,* an account of his journey, in Boston shortly after he returned home in 1768, but he had no success, and the next year he sailed to England to try for publication there. Despite the success of the book when it was finally published in 1778, he died in desperate poverty in London in 1780.

There has been a great deal of discussion and controversy about the sources of Carver's material, particularly since he was erroneously assumed to be an ignorant shoemaker, and since it is well known that much of his book was taken from other published sources, in particular the writings of the French explorers Hennepin, LaHontan, and Charlevoix and *The History of the American Indians* (1775) by James Adair of Charleston. While the question of his sources is of historical interest, from a literary point of view the central issue is the use Carver made of his material. In order to achieve his purpose, to convince his readers to settle the area that is now Michigan, Wisconsin, and Minnesota, Carver felt it was imperative first to win the reader's trust. He did this by inundating him with facts, and the source of those facts is of secondary importance. Whether they were gleaned from reading or from firsthand experience, the sheer weight and volume of the facts convince us of the author's veracity and knowledge—two vital traits in a man who is trying to persuade people to leave their homes and strike out for the unknown.

Probably the most impressive example of Carver's method is to be found in his treatment of the Indians, which takes up more than half the book. He includes chapters on their origins, their physical attributes and clothing, their manners and intelligence, their method of computing time, their forms of government, their feasts, their dances, their hunting practices, their manner of making both war and peace, their games (including an interesting description of the original version of lacrosse), their marriage ceremonies and customs, their religious beliefs, their diseases and medical knowledge, and their manner of burying the dead. He also includes a basic vocabulary of the "Chippeway" and "Naudowessie" (Sioux) languages. All of this mass of material is presented with the sole purpose of making the Indian familiar and therefore less frightening; and certainly to the would-be settler contemplating life in the Midwest, Indians would be the single most fearsome aspect of the area.

The encyclopedic nature of the book determines its style and structure. Because he is conscious of presenting facts and drawing conclusions about them, Carver does not even pretend that his book is a diary, the recording of spontaneous events as they occur. The book is a finished narrative, written after the fact, and he never pretends otherwise. With distance in time and space from the events described, the author attains at least the appearance of objectivity, which is of course most appropriate for his purpose.

In the introduction Carver apologizes for the plainness of his style, "as it is the production of a person unused, from opposite avocations, to literary pursuits." He begs the reader not to "examine it with too critical an eye," affirming that his main concern is with the content of the book: "his attention has been more employed on giving a just description of a country that promises, in some future period, to be an inexhaustible source of riches to that people who shall be so fortunate as to possess it, than on the stile or composition; and more careful to render his language intelligible and explicit, than smooth and florid." His apology is not necessary, however, since the plain style is precisely appropriate to his purpose of setting forth facts and establishing a credible narrator; a more "smooth and florid" style would, by its very literariness, detract from his credibility as a forthright, knowledgeable man of action; in other words, it would render his narrator less trustworthy. Therefore we may conclude that, far from being artless, his plain style is a conscious and effective artistic choice.

One of the ways in which Carver asserts his own veracity is by discrediting previous explorers, particularly the French. He comments that their maps are very bad, whether "through design, or for want of a just knowledge of the country, I cannot say." He goes on to play upon the rivalry between Britain and France, criticizing the French for not knowing how to take advantage of the potential of the land; by extension, it becomes almost a patriotic duty of the American to make better use of the abundant resources.

The theme of nature's bounty, which is a common one in American travel literature from as early as Captain John Smith, and particularly in that dealing with virgin territory, is very much present here. Carver lists a dizzying number of natural resources, all available in undreamed-of amounts. He claims to have seen "many . . . small islands . . . covered with copper ore.

They appeared like beds of copperas, of which many tuns lay in a small space.'' He repeats a story that the Indians ''who inhabit those parts that lie to the west of the Shining Mountains, have gold so plenty among them that they make their most common utensils of it.'' Along with copper and gold, of course, there are many other minerals; but like most other travel writers, Carver is chiefly interested in the plants and animals of the region, and in the last section of his book he presents a long list of them with descriptions and accounts of their abundance. He describes trees of all kinds, many of them useful sources of building materials; there are wild rice, maize, herbs, and roots everywhere for use as food; and there are a great number of fruit trees, all full of excellent fruit, and ''all the spontaneous productions of nature.'' There are innumerable kinds of birds, fish, and animals in this land as well. Describing trout fishing at Lake Michillimackinac, Carver declares, ''we frequently caught two at a time of forty pounds weight each; but the common size is from ten to twenty pounds.'' Presumably the trading center that Carver hopes will be established in the interior will be based on the fur trade, and he takes the opportunity to describe the ''great numbers of excellent furs'' to be found everywhere in the region.

In his introduction Carver predicts that ''as the seat of Empire from time immemorial has been gradually progressive towards the West, there is no doubt but that at some future period, mighty kingdoms will emerge from these wildernesses, and stately palaces and solemn temples, with gilded spires reaching the skies, supplant the Indian huts, whose only decorations are the barbarous trophies of their vanquished enemies.'' In the appendix with which he concludes the book he draws together the themes of the bounty of nature in the wilderness, the obligation of the Anglo-Americans to surpass the French in the utilization of the available natural resources, and his own veracity in his account of the territory, into a splendid vision of future prosperity:

> The countries that lie between the great lakes and River Mississippi, and from thence southward to West Florida, although in the midst of a large continent, and at a great distance from the sea, are so situated, that a communication between them and other realms might conveniently be opened; by which means those empires or colonies that may hereafter be founded or planted therein, will be rendered commercial ones. The great River Mississippi, which runs through the whole of them, will enable their inhabitants to establish an intercourse with foreign climes, equally as well as the Euphrates, the Nile, the Danube, or the Wolga do those people which dwell on their banks, and who have no other convenience for exporting the produce of their own country, or for importing those of others, than boats and vessels of light burden: notwithstanding which they have become powerful and opulent states.
>
> The Mississippi, as I have before observed, runs from north to south, and passes through the most fertile and temperate part of North America, exclud-

ing only the extremities of it, which verge both on the torrid and frigid zones.
Thus favourably situated, when once its banks are covered with inhabitants,
they need not long be at a loss for means to establish an extensive and
profitable commerce. They will find the country towards the south almost
spontaneously producing silk, cotton, indico, and tobacco; and the more
northern parts, wine, oil, beef, tallow, skins, buffalo-wool, and furs; with
lead, copper, iron, coals, lumber, corn, rice, and fruits, besides earth and
barks for dying. (pp. 527–28[1])

In Carver's vision the western territory is divided into colonies and settled by
Americans, who, unlike the French, have the knowledge, skill, and industri-
ousness to turn the land to a profit by farming, cultivating, and mining as well
as trading. To communicate this vision of the boundless prosperity possible in
the interior of America, and to stimulate his readers to make that vision a
reality, are his purposes in writing the book. He is obviously propagandizing,
although he is usually able to avoid heavy-handedness in his promise of a
glorious future. His detached point of view and scientific, fact-minded narrator, although they make the book less exciting to read, enable him to
achieve enough distance from his material to give the appearance, at least, of
objectivity, and such objectivity lends credence to his optimistic vision of the
future. In fact he deserves much of the credit—or blame—for the settlement
of what was then called the Northwest.

II

Carver consciously attempted to describe an unknown land in such a way as to
remove its mystery, and hence its fearsomeness; in his *Travels* William Bartram uses quite a different sort of descriptive process. Between 1773 and 1777
Bartram traveled through Georgia and Florida, a semitropical land very foreign to his English and American readers. Unlike Carver, however, Bartram
does not attempt to minimize the strangeness of the area; instead, he tries very
hard to describe and appreciate the land as it is, because he conceives of wild
nature as the manifestation of God on earth. Because of his religious perception, Bartram demonstrates a reverence for nature that contrasts vividly with
Carver's commercial, exploitative outlook.

Born in 1739, the son of John Bartram, the well-known botanist and one of
the founders of the American Philosophical Society, William Bartram grew
up near Philadelphia, where he enjoyed the advantages of the urban atmosphere and the special opportunities offered to the son of a man whose friends

---

1. Quotations from Jonathan Carver's *Travels* are from the 1781 London edition.

included Benjamin Franklin, Cadwallader Colden, Peter Collinson, and Peter Kalm. John Bartram took his son along on several of his botanical expeditions, including a nine-month journey into Georgia and Florida in 1765–66. Seven years later William Bartram returned to the same area under the patronage of Dr. John Fothergill, ostensibly to collect samples and seeds of plants that might be hardy enough to survive the English winter, for unusual botanical specimens were in vogue and wealthy Englishmen could be expected to pay generously for such curiosities.

Bartram's account of his travels, however, makes it clear that Dr. Fothergill's requirements were at best a pretext. Bartram's interest lay not in English gardens, but in the American continent, and in the end the journey served his purposes much more than his patron's. Bartram did prepare a report to Fothergill, a factual record of his travels that was published finally in 1943. But the most significant product of Bartram's five-year journey was his literary description of it. Apparently completed by the mid-1780s, his volume of *Travels through North and South Carolina, Georgia, East and West Florida* was published first in Philadelphia in 1791, and it quickly went through two London editions (1792 and 1794) and one in Dublin in 1793. Its popularity indicates both his artistry and the appeal of his descriptions to early English and European romantics. It is well known that Bartram's work provided a wealth of material that was used by such writers as Wordsworth, Coleridge, and Chateaubriand in their descriptions of the New World; but what is even more important is that this book represents one of the first artistic interpretations of the American continent.

For Bartram the exotic landscape is not a background, but the subject of a treatment that falls into the traditional three-part pastoral pattern of withdrawal from society, encounter with wild nature, and return. During his encounter Bartram sees both gentleness and destructiveness, both the sweetness and the terror of raw nature. His powerful artistic imagination and his strong religious belief enable him to reconcile the seeming contradictions into a complex but harmonious unity. For him it is vitally important to understand and to appreciate the nature of the land itself because the physical surroundings are central to an understanding of America as a physical, a political, and a spiritual entity.

Bartram combined the qualities of an artist, a scientist, and a religious philosopher, and this combination—virtually inconceivable in the twentieth century, though not unusual in the eighteenth—gives the book its unique quality. Bartram states his purpose thus: "Whilst I, continually impelled by a restless spirit of curiosity, in pursuit of new productions of nature, my chief happiness consisted in tracing and admiring the infinite power, majesty and perfection of the great Almighty Creator, and in the contemplation, that through divine aid and permission, I might be instrumental in discovering, and introducing into my native country, some original productions of nature, which might become useful to society.'' In this declaration we can see quite clearly the combination of motives that impelled Bartram: the scientist's "restless spirit of curiosity" and the practical goal of finding "useful" "productions of nature," combined with the religious impulse to worship the Creator of these "productions." Throughout the book, Bartram maintains the dual aim of "tracing and admiring" God's working in nature.

The picture of the world that emerges from the *Travels* is clearly the product of Bartram's combination of motives. It is a world bursting with life, full of movement. The senses are assailed from all sides: sounds and smells as well as sights and textures crowd in on one, as in this typical passage:

> How harmonious and sweetly murmur the purling rills and fleeting brooks, roving along the shadowy vales, passing through dark, subterranean caverns, or dashing over steep rocky precipices, their cold humid banks condensing the volatile vapours, which fall and coalesce in crystalline drops, on the leaves and elastic twigs of the aromatic shrubs and incarnate flowers. In these cool, sequestered, rocky vales, we behold the following celebrated beauties of the hills, i.e. fragrant Calycanthus, blushing Rhododendron ferruginium, delicate Philadelphius inodorus, which displays the white wavy mantle, with the sky robed Delphinium, perfumed Convalaria and fiery Azalea, flaming on the ascending hills or wavy surface of the gliding brooks. The epithet fiery, I annex to this most celebrated species of Azalea, as being expressive of the appearance of it in flower, which are in general of the colour of the finest red lead, orange and bright gold, as well as yellow and cream colour; these various splendid colours are not only in separate plants, but frequently all the varieties and shades are seen in separate branches on the same plant, and the clusters of the blossoms cover the shrubs in such incredible profusion on the hill sides, that suddenly opening to view from dark shades, we are alarmed with the apprehension of the hills being set on fire. (pp. 204–5[2])

The effect of Bartram's descriptions is not one of voluptuous lushness, for he rarely allows his artistic self to gain control over the scientific and religious selves; in the passage quoted above the "admiring" Bartram revels in a sensuous appreciation of the scene, while the "tracing" Bartram catalogues the flowers and discourses on the varieties of azaleas. Bartram's combination of purposes is reflected also in his style, in which scientific precision and poetic extravagance are joined, sometimes with absurd results, in what Carlyle characterized as "a wondrous kind of floundering eloquence." Despite his reliance on stylistic devices typical of English neoclassical poetry, and despite his vision of the orderliness and harmony of the universe, Bartram consistently displays a genuine sensitivity to and sympathy with nature, and it is this appreciation that makes him closer in spirit to the romantics than to his neoclassical contemporaries.

2. Quotations from William Bartram's *Travels* are from the Francis Harper edition.

One of the most striking of Bartram's themes, not surprisingly, is the abundance of natural goods to be found in America. Again and again he describes in almost fanciful terms the incredible bounty of God in nature. For example, he describes a brief rest on the banks of the Tanase River: "[I] advanced into the strawberry plains to regale on the fragrant, delicious fruit, welcomed by communities of the splendid meleagris, the capricious roebuck, and all the free and happy tribes, which possess and inhabit those prolific fields, who appeared to invite, and joined with me in the participation of the bountiful repast presented to us from the lap of nature."

There are hundreds of such descriptions in the *Travels,* all designed to demonstrate God's bounty. Of course, the plenty of nature is not meant to be admired merely, but to be used as well, and the use of natural resources, whether for food or for other purposes, is another important theme. In discussing the "crocodile alligator," or garr, for example, he comments that "the Indians make use of their sharp teeth to scratch or bleed themselves with, and their pointed scales to arm their arrows." He suggests taming chicken snakes, saying that they "would be useful to man if tamed and properly tutored, being great devourers of rats"; and he mentions that the so-called wax tree "is in high estimation with the inhabitants for the production of wax for candles, for which purpose it answers equally well with beeswax, or preferably, as it is harder and more lasting in burning."

Bartram realizes that the land has a use, and he does not feel that it is wrong to utilize the land for human purposes; but unlike Carver he sets a moral limitation: at the point where the use of the land is the result of greed, and where it unnecessarily destroys a beautiful object, Bartram judges it to be immoral. His sense of morality with regard to the land itself is central to Bartram's thinking, and much of his book is devoted to the demonstration of the divine order and harmony in nature and the possibilities for man either to shatter that harmony by his greed or to enter into it, as the Indian does, by fitting his life into the rhythms of nature.

Perhaps the clearest illustration of the difference between Carver and Bartram is to be seen in the treatment each gives to the Indian. Carver regarded the Indian as the most frightening aspect of nature to be found on the continent, and he devoted much of his effort to making the Indian a less terrifying creature to the prospective settler. Bartram, on the other hand, did not see the Indian as a creature to be understood and conquered by the white man in his drive to subdue nature; rather, his was a unified vision that saw Indians and whites and plants and animals as separate members of the same whole, a morally ordered, God-created universe. His ideal vision of America is founded on this concept, and it is here that he draws an implicit distinction between English and American: the Englishman plunders and destroys the land, but the American has a chance to begin anew, in an untouched wilderness, and to learn to live in harmony with nature.

For all his meticulous detail of description, in his writing the Indian becomes a symbol of man living in such harmony, and he relates an incident that
illustrates the extent to which civilized man has divorced himself from the
ability to live peaceably with the other creatures in the world: "our people
roused a litter of young wolves, to which giving chase, we soon caught one of
them, it being entangled in high grass; one of our people caught it by the hind
legs, and another beat out its brains with the but of his gun—barbarous
sport!" An Indian would take the wolf cub and train it to guard his herd of
horses; the brutality that derives enjoyment from beating out the brains of a
terrified baby animal is the white man's brutality. Bartram's hope is that
Americans can suppress that brutality and express a reverence for nonhuman
life that is more characteristic of the Indian than of the Englishman.

Bartram clearly conceives of the Indian as the "noble savage": "Can it be
denied," he asks, "but that the moral principle, which directs the savage to
virtuous and praiseworthy actions, is natural or innate?" In his portraits the
Indian is always very human, responsive to kindness and to mistreatment. In
fact, Bartram makes it a point to contrast the Indian with the supposedly more
civilized white man, insisting that while the Indians share the same motives
for making war with other men, he "cannot find, upon the strictest inquiry,
that their bloody contests at this day are marked with deeper stains of inhumanity or savage cruelty, than what may be observed amongst the most
civilized nations."

His treatment of the Indian is characteristic of his entire outlook, with its
simultaneous emphases on the scientific, religious, and esthetic perception of
raw nature. This multiple perception gives the book its artisitic unity, drawing
together the wide variety of episodes and descriptions into a unified vision of a
utopia based on fact. Bartram is describing a beautiful continent, obviously
God's universe, but he has a clear sense that civilization is at odds with
nature, that the white man can be brutal and destructive. In his concept of a
morally ordered universe, Bartram is able to find parallels and lessons in
nature to guide man to a better future, but it is obvious that the better future
depends on man's ability to recognize his own proper place in the natural
order of which, in Bartram's hands, the American continent becomes a potent
symbol.

III

Like William Bartram, John Woolman demonstrates a religious outlook on
the world; yet Woolman avoids Bartram's romantic leanings, the result of his
focus on the beauty of nature as almost an end in itself. Woolman's religious
perception is much narrower in focus, concentrated on man rather than on his

surroundings. Like Bartram, Woolman was a Quaker. He was born at Ran-
cocas, New Jersey, not far from Philadelphia, in 1720. At the age of twenty-
one Woolman left the family farm for Mount Holly, about five miles away,
where he was hired to manage a store. Later he set up his own store and began
to prosper, but the prospect of commercial success disturbed him, for he
believed so strongly in moderation that he was unable to justify either the
great amount of time he put into his business or the unnecessarily large return
from it; therefore, in order to return to a plainer style of life, he curtailed his
business and supplemented his income as needed by working as a surveyor,
drawing up wills and deeds, teaching, and cultivating his orchard.

Of the three writers considered here, Woolman was the one who most
nearly touched the subject of revolution, for he is the only one who really
discussed daily living. Moreover, Woolman's Quaker philosophy made his
thinking political; he advocated rebellion by counseling Friends to resist government demands for tax revenue and men for the war with France.

In the eighteenth century it was common for Quakers with an especially
strong sense of vocation to travel to other meetings to preach, and the recommendation of one's own meeting facilitated this missionary work. Woolman
received a certificate from his meeting and set out on his first journey in 1743,
when he was twenty-three years old; he continued to make such journeys
throughout his life, becoming one of the best-known of the hundreds of such
itinerant ministers. Woolman was about thirty-six years old when he began
writing his *Journal*, and he continued to work at it intermittently, revising and
adding new material from time to time, until shortly before he died in England
in 1772. After further editing by a committee appointed by the Quaker Meeting for Sufferings in Philadelphia, it was first published in 1774 and has gone
through many subsequent editions. Although it is based on Woolman's life
and travels, the *Journal* is in no sense a diary, and it makes no pretense of
being one. It was carefully composed and revised to serve, not as a record of
the life and experiences of John Woolman, but as an example of the Christian
progress of a soul, and as such it is simultaneously intimate and impersonal,
for Woolman the author manages to achieve a remarkable degree of detachment in recounting the experiences of Woolman the character.

Woolman enumerates the travels of nearly thirty years, from his home in
rural New Jersey south to the Carolinas, north to Cape Cod, and westward
into the wilderness; yet the reader who hopes to find in his journal a description of eighteenth-century America will be disappointed. Woolman showed
no interest in describing the external details of the areas he visited. One reason
for this difference between Woolman's book and Bartram's and Carver's, of
course, could be that the latter were describing lands that were completely
unknown to their readers, while Woolman was traveling for the most part
through settled territory. There is a more fundamental reason for the dif-

ference, however: Bartram and Carver both traveled and then wrote about their experiences, but Woolman traveled with his essential experience already present in him. For Woolman the travels merely provided a context for the essence of his work, which is a spiritual autobiography squarely within the Quaker tradition. What he saw on his journeys was not the subject of his writing; rather, what he saw provided him with evidence that reinforced his inner vision.

It is not surprising that in Bartram and Woolman, both Quakers, we see a similar view of wild nature as a manifestation of God. Both men opposed the exploitation of nature's gifts and held as their ideal a more moderate use, an adaptation to existing rhythms and patterns. Woolman, however, avoids Bartram's focus on nature as an end in itself; his focus is always on man, his soul, and his strivings for improvement. For Woolman improvement means progress toward the obliteration of the ego, the suppression of selfish desires that block the working of God's will through man.

A good illustration of Woolman's point of view can be found in the well-known boyhood incident:

> Another thing remarkable in my childhood was that once, going to a neighbour's house, I saw on the way a robin sitting on her nest; and as I came near she went off, but having young ones, flew about and with many cries expressed her concern for them. I stood and threw stones at her, till one striking her, she fell down dead. At first I was pleased with the exploit, but after a few minutes was seized with horror, as having in a sportive way killed an innocent creature while she was careful for her young. I beheld her lying dead and thought those young ones for which whe was so careful must now perish for want of their dam to nourish them; and after some painful considerations on the subject, I climbed up the tree, took all the young birds and killed them, supposing that better than to leave them to pine away and die miserably, and believed in this case that Scripture proverb was fulfilled, "The tender mercies of the wicked are cruel" [Prov. 12:10]. I then went on my errand, but for some hours could think of little else but the cruelties I had committed, and was much troubled.
>
> Thus he whose tender mercies are over all his works hath placed a principle in the human mind which incites to exercise goodness toward every living creature; and this being singly attended to, people become tenderhearted and sympathizing, but being frequently and totally rejected, the mind shuts itself up in a contrary disposition. (pp. 24–25[3])

The focus is not on the birds, but on the boy, and Woolman turns the incident into a sermon to illustrate the thesis that man's impulses are destructive, at odds with God's will, and that he must work to suppress his tendency

---

3. Quotations from John Woolman are from Phillips P. Moulton's edition of *The Journal and Major Essays of John Woolman*.

to evil. Woolman does not merely state the precept, however; his whole *Journal* is an illustration of the process, a record of the suppression of his own ego to enable God to use him as an instrument of His will. Because Woolman believed that slavery was contrary to God's will, he organized the *Journal* with slavery as its central subject, treating three aspects of it: why slavery was wrong, how he knew it was wrong, and what he himself did about it. Obviously, such a subject could easily become the vehicle for the worst kind of self-righteous boasting; that it is not is a tribute both to Woolman's genuine humility and to his artistic craftsmanship.

The question of what is wrong with slavery is dealt with lucidly, as Woolman eloquently declares that slaves are oppressed without their consent, to their own detriment and that of their oppressors: "These are a people by whose labour the other inhabitants are in a great measure supported, and many of them in the luxuries of life. These are a people who have made no agreement to serve us and who have not forfeited their liberty that we know of. These are souls for whom Christ died, and for our conduct toward them we must answer before that Almighty Being who is no respecter of persons."

Whether he was speaking of slaves or of Indians, Woolman clung to his basic conviction that all humans are equally human, equally the children of God. He did not think of Indians as Bartram and Carver did, as a part of the landscape; to him they were primarily human beings, and he declared: "I believed some of them were measurably acquainted with that divine power which subjects the rough and froward will of the creature." He preaches that a Christian must obey God by giving "no just cause of offense to the Gentiles, who do not profess Christianity, whether the blacks from Africa or the native inhabitants of this country." Of course Woolman could scarcely claim to believe that all Indians were gentle creatures, particularly in view of the bloody uprisings in western Pennsylvania that began in 1755: indeed, he himself describes tortures and horrors they committed. Nevertheless, he held up the Wyalusing Indians as an example of the possibility that, given the proper guidance, Indians could become peaceable, gentle Christians.

In answer to the question of how he knew the oppression of nonwhite people was wrong, Woolman would simply reply that, after the clamor of his own ego was stilled, God spoke to him. In a sense, his recounting of his youthful failings and weaknesses in the early chapters is Woolman's way of "presenting his credentials": he shows that he has been through the purifying process of the suppression of his own selfish will, so that when he speaks it is truly in God's words.

Finally, the subject of what he did about his convictions is treated in the bulk of the *Journal*, as Woolman recounts his journeys to other meetings and his conversations on the subject of abolition. Throughout his life, Woolman's major social concern was with slavery, and he spoke strongly against it wherever he went. As a young man he was often employed to write wills; he refused to do so when slaves were to be given as property. On his travels he noted: "As it is common for Friends on a journey to have entertainment free cost, a difficulty arose in my mind with respect to saving my own money by kindness received which to me appeared to be the gain of oppression." As a result of his scruples, he insisted on paying the slaves for their services to him. This, of course, would ordinarily be taken as a gross insult to his host, but it is a tribute to Woolman's gentle, tactful nature that he was able to act on his principles without offending his hosts. Woolman's entire book is based on the premise that it is possible for man to achieve purity: the *Journal* depicts his own progress toward the suppression of his ego, and it is clear that he believed that America offered the best social context for spiritual progress.

While traveling in England in 1772 he was appalled at the materialism of the English: "So great is the hurry in the spirit of this world that in aiming to do business quick and to gain wealth the creation at this day doth loudly groan!" In America, however, he saw the chance to begin afresh, and the causes he espoused—abolition of slavery, humane treatment of the Indians, economic equality, pacifism—were practical steps in the achievement of utopia. He was a true radical in his belief that Christian love could replace material prosperity as the national goal of a viable society.

John Woolman's vision, in strong contrast to Jonathan Carver's materialism, was spiritual. He saw America in terms of people, a landscape brought to life and given meaning by man. He shows us a string of Quaker meetings stretching from Cape Cod to the Carolinas and gradually moving westward. His dream was the union of these separate meetings into a single Christian community, unified by a common goal of individual and collective morality. His book, like Carver's, was an instrument of his purpose, an attempt to convince people individually of the immorality of treating men unequally; ultimately, his hope was that individually moral men would unite to form a collectively moral, truly Christian nation, based on justice and equality for all men. For Woolman, the abolition of slavery was a practical step toward the realization of his ideal, and thus his book can be likened to Carver's in that both are attempts to persuade the reader to begin acting to achieve the author's end.

I V

Woolman, Bartram, and Carver represent three distinct ways of looking at America, and the reader would be justified in seeing more differences than similarities among them. In spite of the very real differences, however, the three share the conception of America as the embodiment of the possibility of a new and better way of life. For Carver the better life meant economic prosperity, and America offered an abundance of resources to be exploited and turned to profit. Woolman's ideal was the polar opposite, the suppression of the selfish, acquisitive instincts in the effort to achieve spiritual purity, but Woolman was like Carver in envisioning America as possibly the only place in the world where his ideal had a chance of being realized. Ironically, the same abundance of natural goods that inspired Carver to visions of economic empire inspired Woolman to a vision of a world where everyday living would be so easy that men could turn their attention away from daily survival and toward spiritual progress.

Bartram saw in America a third possibility, no less utopian: a land where man could finally learn to live not by exploiting nature as Carver would have him do, and not by ignoring or trying to transcend his own physical nature, as Woolman would advocate, but in harmony with his surroundings, accepting his animal and his spiritual nature, not as warring factions but as complementary aspects of a complex creature.

No matter what the content of the dream, however, each man saw in America the one landscape where he could believe that his dream could become a reality: an unspoiled place where man could fulfill his destiny with the minimum of external restraints, where man could in the deepest sense be himself and become himself, where he could have the best chance of reaching his aspirations, material and spiritual.

SUGGESTIONS FOR FURTHER READING

Editions

Bartram, William. *Travels in Georgia and Florida, 1773–1774: A Report to Dr. John Fothergill.* Edited by Francis Harper. Philadelphia: American Philosophical Society, 1944.
Carver, Jonathan. *Travels through the Interior Parts of North America in the Years 1766, 1767, and 1768.* 3d ed. London: C. Dilly, 1781.
The Journal and Major Essays of John Woolman. Edited by Phillips P. Moulton. New York: Oxford University Press, 1971.
The Travels of William Bartram. Edited by Francis Harper. New Haven, Conn.: Yale University Press, 1958.

Scholarship and Criticism

Abel, Darrel. *American Literature.* Vol. 1. Woodbury, N.Y.: Barron's Educational Series, 1963.

Arner, Robert D. "Pastoral Patterns in William Bartram's *Travels*." *Tennessee Studies in Literature* 18 (1973): 133–45.

Bourne, Edward G. "The Travels of Jonathan Carver." *American Historical Review* 11 (1906): 287–302.

Fridley, Russell W. "The Writings of Jonathan Carver." *Minnesota History* 34 (1954): 154–59.

Gummere, Richard M. "William Bartram, a Classical Scientist." *Classical Journal* 50 (1955): 167–70.

Lee, John Thomas. "A Bibliography of Carver's Travels." *Proceedings of the State Historical Society of Wisconsin at Its Fifty-Seventh Annual Meeting* (1910): 143–83.

Shea, Daniel B. *Spiritual Autobiography in Early America*. Princeton, N.J.: Princeton University Press, 1968.

12

Hector St. John de Crèvecoeur

A. W. PLUMSTEAD

[*Probably the most striking and penetrating view of America was that provided by an immigrant from France. One who knows other lands is often able to capture the special quality of a place, and so it was with St. John de Crèvecoeur, whose attractive but troubled* Letters from an American Farmer *is a classic worthy to stand beside the* Autobiography *of Benjamin Franklin.*]

Born in France, resident of England and adopter of her tongue, surveyor-merchant-farmer-author in America, Hector St. John de Crèvecoeur is today one of the most admired literary men of his epoch. *Letters from an American Farmer* captures the excitement of freedom in the New World, but also the tensions encountered in a community which would fight for its freedom. Many students of literature in America read the frequently anthologized chapter 3, "What is an American?," with its idyllic descriptions of the American Dream. More recently attention has been given the whole book, including the dark ambiguities which temper the idealism of its romantic vision. My purposes here are to attempt a summary of Crèvecoeur's English writings, to characterize his contribution to the development of a literary voice in his day, to speculate on how he wrote his book (and the difficulties of editing his manuscripts), and to assess his place in the writing of our early national period.

I

Michel-Guillaume-Jean de Crèvecoeur was born January 31, 1735, in Caen, Normandy, and attended the Jesuit Collège du Mont. When nineteen, he was

Portions of this essay first appeared in *The Massachusetts Review* 17, no. 2 (Summer 1976): 286–301.

sent to England. A year later, now conversant in English, he emigrated to Canada and joined the French militia as a geographer and cartographer. There he gained a second lieutenant's commission, was wounded on the plains of Abraham in the battle for Quebec, and hospitalized. Under mysterious circumstances of what appears to be some disgrace, he resigned his commission in October 1759 and the following month arrived in New York City. Adopting a new name, J. Hector St. John, he became a surveyor and merchant, making several prolonged exploring expeditions inland to Indian country, to Vermont, Ohio, and the Great Lakes.

In 1769 he married Mehetable Tippet of Westchester, and at the end of the year, now a naturalized citizen of New York, he purchased 120 acres of unworked land in Orange County (about three miles east of Chester, New York, on what is now Route 94). He called his farm "Pine Hill." He had about six years to clear the land, build his house and barns, raise a family (a girl and two boys), and discover what it is to be an American farmer—to be free to enjoy a life he could create himself—about six years until the American Revolution. By the time he purchased the farm he had already sketched some observations made on his travels; now he would take time from his farm duties to draw up further sketches of his new life and surroundings.

Early in 1779 St. John was granted permission to leave Pine Hill. He worked his way along the Hudson to British lines and New York City, where he arrived with his six-year-old son, Ally, and a trunk full of manuscripts. In spite of his attempts to exaggerate his sufferings at the hands of the patriots, he was imprisoned by the British in New York for three months as a suspicious character. Released on bond, he retrieved his son from a family on Long Island in late summer 1780, and sailed for Britain. In May 1781 he contracted with the London publishing firm of Davies and Davis to bring out *Letters from an American Farmer*. Then, with Ally, he went on to France, arriving in August. *Letters* was published in London early in 1782.

II

Letters from an American Farmer is a collection of sketches (though called letters), ostensibly written for one person, an English friend, Mr. F. B., but actually designed for a wide reading audience in Europe. The letter writer is James, a simple (or "vulgar," meaning unlearned or unpretentious) American farmer. At times James apologizes for the presumptuousness of an American rustic's assuming that he could command the attention of learned Europeans with his chatter about bees, whaling, snowstorms, clearing the land, and other sketches of pioneer life. This posture is a ruse, deliberately fabricated by

Crèvecoeur, who was an educated man. But the author wields a light hand; the apologetic tone of the introduction is soon dropped. The strategy here is irony; the more the American farmer talks, the more Crèvecoeur intends to lure European common readers into becoming enamored of his farmer and the life he describes—to the point where some of them will want to embark on the next boat for America.

The book is dedicated to, and apologizes for its rusticity to, members of the upper class. But it is really written for, and identifies with, the lower classes, the downtrodden of the world. While acknowledging on the one hand that elegant readers must find this American farmer rather quaint, the sketches call to the oppressed of Europe to leave their oppressors behind and come to the New World to a better life. *Letters* is a very class-conscious book. It manipulates its deference to European high culture around the edges of its central, radical message—that America makes metamorphosis possible; *new* men and women in a New World thrive because they are removed from the Old World "prejudiced . . . by . . . ancient manners and customs." In *Common Sense* and *The Rights of Man*, Paine lashed out at European superstition through invective, confrontation, and mockery; Crèvecoeur bows politely, observes the formalities of addressing his superiors, then gently proceeds to say the same things.

Letters might be summarized as having four parts that are both chronological and thematic. First Crèvecoeur presents the happy valley, the age-old dream of a pure, idyllic life in a sequestered vale. This is James's farm, its gentle geography of meadowland, adjacent woods, cattle, hogs, birds, bees, fertility of land, loving children, industrious happy wife, friendly neighbors, cheer, parties, and songs on social occasions, freedom to own, raise, and sell without hindrances other than natural causes. (Crèvecoeur locates the farm in Pennsylvania, not New York; perhaps he saw the former as a more likely symbolic place for the Quaker values he admired and for his European readers' association of Pennsylvania with freedom.) A second group of letters dealing with Nantucket and Martha's Vineyard complement the farm scenes by showing that there are other happy places in America. At first glance, Nantucket would seem calculated for poverty and marginal subsistence, with its barren sands; but the same joy of freedom which allows the American farmer success has worked its wonders on these shores in their fishing trade. Here too is a happy people, modestly prosperous, a joy to observe in all their work and play. The point is that the new man does not necessarily need fertile soil; he needs freedom, a geographical and political climate that will encourage him to develop his "natural genius." In another sketch, James tells of his travels to South Carolina. Here the scene is more ambiguous in his eyes; a harsher slavery than the northerners' benevolent treatment of blacks, and the warm climate, which tends to breed laziness and useless elegance, detract from scenes of successful, lush plantations and a happy people. There are more distinct class lines here between haves and have-nots, rulers and oppressed, than in the homogeneous harmony of society painted by James in the earlier sketches. Man's inhumanity to man is shockingly demonstrated here in the description of the punishment of a slave, dying in agony in a cage. Finally, the book closes with "distress"; the happy valley is invaded by enemies; there is a revolution; sleep is disturbed, guns and fire come in the night, a responsible family man must retreat with his loved ones from this chaos and attempt to recapture the peace and joy of former days in an Indian village.

The dominant tones of the first two-thirds of the book are joy, pride, wonder. The early sketches combine to form the image of a utopia. "Here we have in some measure regained the ancient dignity of our species," James writes; "we have no princes for whom we toil, starve, and bleed; we are the most perfect society now existing in the world." American farms are intended by providence as asylums to the oppressed of the world. There is much hard work, and the farmer will not become rich, but he can attain "an easy subsistence" and "live free and independent under the mildest government, in a healthy climate, in a land of charity and benevolence." America is the harbinger of a "reformation" which the world sadly cries for—to relieve mankind from "shameful shackles."

At the heart of this utopia is a pastoral vision, a matter of both place and climate, of principles or consciousness informing a way of life. Both geographically and psychologically, this ideal place lies between two extremes—town and wilderness, urban elegance and savagery, high culture and ignorance. In his fine introduction to *Letters,* Albert E. Stone, Jr., links Crèvecoeur with Thoreau and romanticism. Yet there is a great deal of the eighteenth century in *Letters*; for all its parallels with Thoreau's classic, it is not a *Walden*-type pastoral. Crèvecoeur distrusts hunters; Thoreau emulates the wild, desires a dialectic within himself between the hunter and scholar. Crèvecoeur's ideal farm is "well-regulated," not wild; a wilderness "converted" into a garden. Gentle meadows are superior to "hideous wildernesses" and "howling swamps" (Thoreau loved bogs and swamps); "rural song," gentle and domestic, replaces wild yells, hisses, and screeches; harmony replaces discord. Hunting is good as avocation, bad as vocation. The chase renders man "ferocious, gloomy, and unsocial." Crèvecoeur attributes much of his metamorphosis as a new man to the good feeling he gets from being able to own his farm in fee simple. "As soon as men cease to remain at home and begin to lead an erratic life," they degenerate. For Thoreau, home was where his hat was; he loved to "saunter," and he saw his inner, essential life as a circle of excursions. Thoreau had an Indian sense of ownership—not the Anglo-Saxon's pride of deed but custodianship. The land was not his. Crèvecoeur's American farm is a microcosmic society; man is a social animal who "cannot live in solitude" but needs community. Thoreau needed community too, but to rub up against so as to test himself and then flee, as in a dialectic.

Central to the value system in the happy valley-farm is simplicity. Complexity, sophisticated argumentation, logical peccadilloes, elaborate laws or theorems—these are the bane of Crèvecoeur's farmer. "Simple objects of contemplation suffice me," says James; "simple cultivation of the earth purifies." The American farmer is free of "contention between parties" and political jousting for power and control. The farmer exercises order, regulation, and harmony, with nature, among his animals, with his family and neighbors. A work ethic is a strong theme in *Letters*. Work is a virtue; affluence, laziness, administration of work through slaves are vices. Virtues in the happy valley are "temperance, the calm of passions, frugality, and continual exercise," moderation, sobriety, benevolence.

Letters respects law, order, regulation, and social harmony, but these come from the individual farmer's administration of his own farm-society. Local and central governments figure little, other than in having established gentle laws which respect virtue, punish vice, and otherwise allow the farmer to buy, sell, and regulate his affairs. With Jefferson's adage that the best government is that which governs least, Crèvecoeur would agree. *Letters* is sprinkled with gratitude for prerevolutionary American "silken bands of mild government," one which "demands but little for its protection" of the immigrant. The farmers' lands are free of soldiers with bayonets requiring subservience to a central power; taxes are low and protective. This good, mild government should "wink" at the irregularities of barbarous frontier life, knowing that a certain amount of roistering must needs precede the flow of sober, settling farmers. Above all, the happy valley is peaceful and quiet; there is no war.

Crèvecoeur's ideal social, political and psychic world, then, might be summarized by the word *repose*. It is a static world. For all its persuasive writing about being American, *Letters* lacks a major element in traditional Americanism—the doctrine of progress. The farmer-narrator frequently takes joy in the thought that he has been able to secure and stabilize a farm on which he has brought up his children according to certain simple, basic virtues, and that he can hand down this farm to them so that they in turn can bring up their children the same way, on the same farm, unto many generations. "I have never possessed or wished to possess anything more than what could be earned or produced by the united industry of my family. I wanted nothing more than to live at home independent and tranquil and to teach my children how to provide the means of a future ample subsistence, founded on labour, like that of their father."

In the final sketch, "Distresses of a Frontier Man," the American Revolution bursts into the American farmer's meadowland, bringing chaos and agony. Those patriots who fired the first shots at Concord and Lexington were mostly farmers; James's position, however, is apolitical; he keeps aloof from the reasons for the Revolution, he refrains from the specifics of names and issues as he does throughout the book, supplying ink lines in places where the name of a person or locale is unimportant to the general nature of the scene or issue. The simple farmer hero of repose suddenly finds himself unable to be neutral any longer. He must declare himself, loyal or patriot, Tory or Whig, and this he cannot or will not do. Crèvecoeur keeps the sketch of the Revolution personal and views it from within. Theory has never interested James. All that he has gloried in as a new man in the New World is now shattered; peace is replaced by guns in the night; political controversy which had hitherto left him alone comes knocking at his door; "calmness which is necessary to delineate our thoughts" is replaced by urgent confrontation; "sleep is disturbed," danger is come.

> Once happiness was our portion; now it is gone from us. . . . I am a lover of peace; what must I do? . . . Books tell me so much that they inform me of nothing. Sophistry, the bane of freemen, launches forth in all her deceiving attire! After all, most men reason from passions; and shall such an ignorant individual as I am decide and say this side is right, that side is wrong? . . . Alas, how should I unravel an argument in which Reason herself has given way to brutality and bloodshed! . . . Great Source of wisdom! Inspire me with light sufficient to guide my benighted steps out of this intricate maze! (pp. 194, 197, 198[1])

For many writers discussed in the present volume, the American Revolution was an inevitable, necessary birth pang in securing freedom for a new nation, a necessary fight to rid Americans of the very kinds of tyranny Crèvecoeur castigates in his book. Strange irony. In *Letters*, the Revolution is ambiguous, terrifying, the end of an era, the casting out of a family from a pastoral eden into the wilderness, to an Indian village where they may be able to regain something of the good life. The happy farm is threatened by fire; joy has become distress.

III

The box of manuscripts which Crèvecoeur so carefully guarded through British lines, inspection by authorities in New York, incarceration, a sea voyage, up to his arrival in London, contained some thirty-two separate

---

1. Quotations are taken from Albert E. Stone, Jr.'s, edition of *Letters from an American Farmer and Sketches of Eighteenth-Century America*.

sketches. Written in America between approximately 1765 and 1779, these manuscripts were composed as separate pieces, some true to their insights and descriptions of the moment, others drawn from memory and other sources, oral and written, but each composed without regard to the others in matters of consistency of narrative, tone, or subject matter. They appear to have been intended from the outset for publication, for several address a "you"; in the case of the "Susquehanna" sketch, omitted from *Letters*, the person addressed is an Englishman: "The warm patriots of N.E. gave it the name of Wilkesbury [Wilkes-Barre] in honor of the then potent popular Lord Mayor of London. Strange it may appear to you that the great stream of applause he enjoy'd with you should have caused his name to be given to a little town founded on the shores of Susquehanna. . . ."

On May 20, 1781, an agreement was drawn up between Crèvecoeur and the English publishers, and on August 2 he arrived in France. The first edition of *Letters* appeared in 1782, followed in 1783 by a second edition with corrections by the author. In 1925 Henri Bourdin, Ralph H. Gabriel, and Stanley T. Williams edited *Sketches of Eighteenth Century America*, containing twelve sketches based on eleven of the manuscripts (one they made into two). In separate journals they published an additional four (one of which, "Susquehanna," was the first two-thirds of the manuscript, the last third of which they published in *Sketches* as "The Wyoming Massacre.") Five other sketches remain unpublished.[2] The relationship of *Letters* to the posthumously published and unpublished sketches in English is obscure and may prove to be one of the most complicated editing challenges of eighteenth-century American literature.

Let me suggest several scenarios:

1. In London Crèvecoeur turned all his manuscripts over to the publisher for consideration; they decided, however, on a one-volume selection. By this time Crèvecoeur was close to leaving (or had left) for France, and the *publisher* selected and arranged the sketches, asking Crèvecoeur for an introduction and title, which he supplied, inventing James the narrator. Henri Bourdin says in *Sketches,* that "the selection of the papers [in *Letters*] seems to have been the work of the English publisher."

2. Same as above, except that the publishers asked *Crèvecoeur* to select and arrange the sketches before he left England (or, for that matter, in France).

3. Once the publishers decided that one volume was all they wished to undertake initially (though, if the book were well received, they might bring

2. They are: "Rock of Lisbon"; "Sketches of Jamaica & Bermudas & Other Subjects"; "The Commissioners"; "Ingratitude Rewarded"; "An Happy Family Disunited by the Spirit of Civil War."

out a second book of the other pieces), Crèvecoeur, faced with the editor's chore of selection and arrangement, decided to go a step further. He polished, revised, worked at seeing his book as a whole, rewrote parts and shuffled scenes to create a new whole that told an unfolding story yet remained true to the insights of his original sketches. This rewriting might have been packed into his few months in England, or completed after he arrived in France.

4. Same as 3, except that Crèvecoeur did not submit all the manuscripts. Either in England or, more likely, earlier (in prison?), he decided to make a book of his material, and he submitted in London a finished manuscript, telling the publisher he had material for a second volume if they should be interested.

Which of these (or other) scenarios comes closest to the truth is, of course, important for several reasons. First is the matter of interpretation. *Letters* has seemed to some readers strangely inconsistent in American tone, with a rift, a disturbing failure in nerve, if not in insight. It extols the American Dream in a classic, often quoted, chapter; it praises the qualities of individual freedom in a language and voice shared by Jefferson. Yet it closes in bewilderment and distress, its vision failing to see the political inevitability of a revolution needed to protect inviolate the very freedoms heralded earlier in the book. Such juxtaposition of tone has perhaps no other precedent in as finely wrought a work written in America before 1800.[3] Part of the answer lies in the psyche of the author, a man of many masks, a man sensitively fearful of disorder and violence. But if Crèvecoeur merely went along with the publisher's choice and arrangement of twelve of his thirty-two submitted pieces, so that *they* chose "Distresses of a Frontier Man," which would titillate British readers without alienating those who thought Britain's policy toward America that of blockheads, then those who feel the book's disjuncture may rest easy. It was not basically Crèvecoeur's vision at all, but merely his acquiescence in getting some of his American sketches published.

More important is the question of the quality and unity of the book compared to the posthumously published and unpublished manuscripts discovered by Bourdin. For Gabriel, Williams, Bourdin, and J. B. Moore in the 1920s, all the sketches were, generically, of a piece. Some went into *Letters*, most of the rest were now available in *Sketches*. Their commentary treats the mass as a unit, and in their view some of the new pieces are superior to those in *Letters*. "The new book of letters," says Moore, referring to *Sketches*, "was undoubtedly completed at the same time as the old book of letters"; he believes these new materials call for a "rehabilitation or reconstruction of Crèvecoeur," who was too "untrustworthy" in *Letters*.

3. John Brooks Moore writes, "Possibly this posture of frantic cowardice represents an artistic effort to portray the feverish thoughts which frequently raced through the brains of the bewildered settlers. Perhaps the whole book has more fiction in it than meets the first perusal" ("The Rehabilitation of Crèvecoeur," *Sewanee Review* 35 [1927]: 221).

For Stone, and Thomas Philbrick, however, *Letters* is not a collection of miscellanies but "a work of the imagination" with "a degree of structural unity," and polarities which anticipate Melville. Thomas Philbrick devotes an impressive chapter in *St. John de Crèvecoeur* to the book's "submerged plot" and "the myth which underlies the narrative." Now if Crèvecoeur merely acquiesced in a book put together by his publishers, the arguments for his mythic response to America drop with a thud into the limbo of embarrassing misfires. Or, to protect the validity of such a reading, we must hand over "the submerged plot" to the instincts of one or more persons in the publishing house. (Discretion prevents me from suggesting that it was some underling who dreamed of going to America to live with the Indians.) Further, Philbrick takes issue with the Gabriel, Williams, Bourdin, and Moore group's praise of some of the newly discovered sketches over those in *Letters*; he finds *Sketches* "a non-book," "drafts, not yet subjected to the revision that surely would have preceded publication"; he thus further emphasizes his contention that Crèvecoeur must have revised the material he chose for *Letters*.

There is one further consideration that asks for the clarification which the unraveling of the manuscript mystery would provide. The 1925 editors claim that Crèvecoeur chose deliberately to suppress those manuscripts which showed that he was a Tory sympathizer. If, as they claim, the publisher probably selected the manuscripts for *Letters*, I find the suppression thesis unconvincing. If Crèvecoeur was so busy with his new duties in New York that he could not find time to assemble a second volume, this can hardly be called suppression. If, on the other hand, Crèvecoeur *did* put the *Letters* together, then the suppression thesis appears more creditable.

Before attempting an answer to these questions, we must return to the contents of the box, to those pieces not included in *Letters* and, even, to those not included in *Sketches*. Internal evidence is important in the case; let us look at the material left out of *Letters* for clues to help us determine who controlled, and for what reasons, what was put in, and also to help us toward an interpretation of this early classic of our literature.

I V

The first five of *Sketches of Eighteenth-Century America* are observations on snowstorms, ants, manners, home-made implements, and liberty of worship. Similar in mode to the farm, Nantucket, and Charlestown sections of *Letters*, they are essentially descriptive, intended for an English reader curious about life in America. The last seven pieces, all scenes of the American revolution, form a continuous unit of common themes and tone. "The English and the

French Before the Revolution'' is an attempt at historical interpretation (the French and English would get along very well together if not stirred into opposing parties by higher authorities, kings, colonels, Congress); "The Man of Sorrows," "The Wyoming Massacre" (Wyoming, Pennsylvania, not the present state), "History of Mrs. B.," and "The Frontier Woman" are scenes of suffering, episodes showing settlements and single families under attack. "The American Belisarius" (perhaps the best of the seven) is a little biography, a sketch of the life of a good frontier man who converts the wilderness into a prosperous colony, only to fall victim to his Whig brothers' jealousy and the "rage of party and the madness of the times." Like a wild animal, he is hunted in the woods by the militia. In the final section, "Landscapes" (a closet drama in six scenes), a hypocritical deacon and his fashion-conscious wife conspire to help ruin a Tory squire and a widow in the name of People, Congress, and Liberty.

In *Sketches* Crèvecoeur is an acknowledged painter of the pathetic scene in melodramatic stereotypes. His revolutionary scenes depict suffering of innocents under the stress of war, subjects "for a painter who delights to represent mournful events":

> What a spectacle this would have exhibited to the eyes of humanity: hundreds of women and children, now widows and orphans, in the most humble attitude, with pale, dejected countenances, sitting on the few bundles they had brought with them, keeping their little unconscious children as close to them as possible, hiding by a mechanical instinct the babies of their breasts.... What a scene an eminent painter might have copied from that striking exhibition if it had been a place where a painter could have calmly sat with the palette in his hands! (p. 359)

Crèvecoeur wants to arouse his reader to the inhumanity of human suffering, not engage him in the rightness or wrongness of political and intellectual reasons; he speaks to the heart rather than the head. Thus his language is heightened emotionally, his scenes painted to stir passion. The sketches are melodramatic, their tensions and dramatic highlights overpluses of grief, agony, despair; his language is heavy with sentiment, his narrator's commentary rises to bursts of astonishment and indignation.

> I can easily imagine or conceive the feelings of a soldier burying the bodies of his companions, but neither my imagination nor my heart permits me to think of the peculiar anguish and keen feelings which must have seized that of a father, that of a mother avidly seeking among the crowd of slain for the disfigured corpse of a beloved son, the throbbing anguish of a wife—I cannot proceed. (p. 361)

> She was suckling two children, whilst at the same time she was rocking the third in a cradle. At the sight of me who was painted and dressed like an

Indian, she suddenly arose and came towards the door: ''I know your er-
rand,'' she said. ''Begin with these little innocents that they may not lan-
guish and die with hunger when I am gone. Dispatch me as you have
dispatched my poor aged father and my husband last April. I am tired of
life.'' So saying, with her right hand she boldly pulled the handkerchief from
her breast . . . . (p. 377)

The seven revolutionary sketches share common plots, heroes, and
heroines, and a consistent narrator's view. The central plot is a turn from
peace and modest prosperity on the frontier to attack, loss of home, property,
loved ones, near or actual death, imprisonment, escape. Settlements are
ruined; families broken up, children watch as their father is hanged. In *Letters*
the archetypal American story of rags to riches occupies center stage, closing
with a threat, but at least a hope of regaining a good life with the Indians.
Sketches completes the turning around of the myth—from riches to rags, the
metamorphosis of health and harmony to loss and alienation. Hope is gone;
the loss is final. Although ''the man of sorrows'' is saved from death, he has
been hanged, and the scars of terror and fears of further molestation are
shattering. Belisarius, released from prison on bail, returns a ruined man ''to
live in that small part of his own house which is allotted him . . . and to
contemplate in gloomy despair the overthrow of his wife's reason'' (a Faulk-
nerian plot!). Crèvecoeur's women are stereotypes of domestic enterprise but
frailty under stress; they faint rather than endure sights of loved ones harmed,
and in two cases do not recover sanity. Yet in the mouths of Mrs. B. and Mrs.
Marston (''Fifth Landscape''), Crèvecoeur makes some of his most powerful
speeches against the injustice of the Revolution.

Crèvecoeur makes clear who are the heroic subjects of his brush—''heroes
in low disguises'' Emerson would later call them. ''I am now tired of the
company of generals, rulers, imperial delegates, modern governors. . . . I
choose now to converse with those vulgar hands to whom the drudgery of
ploughing and scattering the good seed has been committed, seed from which
that great harvest is to spring forth, ripening fast for the sole use of the great
state reapers.'' These are the common rural people, who will not pretend to be
Whig in order to save their necks, hard-working, apolitical. Their ideals are
''tranquillity of mind,'' ''peace and repose,'' and they shun religious and
political zeal as well as cynicism. In short, they are versions of the central
Crèvecoeur hero delineated in the first person in *Letters*, seen now in the third
person.

A theme touched on in *Letters* now becomes central: the virtuous common
people of the earth suffer most in revolutions. Caught in the middle of a
bloody war they do not fully understand, they are targets of king and Congress
alike; there is no escape for them from suffering and destruction, no side to
join without surrendering their integrity as simple folk. The securities in the

world of these people fall apart: "the son is armed against the father, the brother against the brother [as in 'Belisarius'], family against family [as in 'Landscapes' and 'Mrs. B.'].'' Slander and psychic alienation are worse than loss of property: "I could, methinks, harden myself to the dangers, to the noise, to the perturbations of war; but contumely unmerited—contumely, to an honest mind, is daggers to one's soul," says Mrs. B. Crèvecoeur's only full-blown portraits of American patriots (or Whigs) are the Deacon and his family in "Landscapes." They are hypocrites, taking advantage of the American cause to swell their coffers and local power. Elsewhere in *Sketches* Crèvecoeur suggests that many farmer patriots are really confused people acting out of fear of retaliation. There is not even a potential hero of the rebel cause here.

Sketches, then, rounds out a view of the Revolution introduced in *Letters*. Although *Sketches* denounces the Revolution in a more positive tone than *Letters*, the central posture is still "astonishment." How could so much achievement be undone so quickly? "The collective industry of twelve years could not well be supposed, in so great an extent, to require in its destruction less than twelve days. . . . My astonishment is boundless when I recollect in a short retrospect the beginning and progressive increase of this unnatural revolt." Crèvecoeur is more the polemicist in *Sketches* than in *Letters*, and his acknowledged aim is to correct the glamorous view that Europeans will have of the patriots' cause and uphill battles. Convinced that lurking beneath the attractive mantle of liberty are avarice and hypocrisy, he sets out to expose these evils, to correct the popular image. Ecclestone sums it up in "Fourth Landscape":

> The brave, the warlike Americans will be blazoned out as the examples of the world, as the veteran sons of the most rational liberty. Whereas we know how it is: how this country has been trepanned and insensibly led from one error to another, conducted by the glare of false-deceiving meteors. . . .
>
> The people can never believe what they have never felt. I am very sure 'tis not the weight nor the galling of the yoke which has hurried them on in this sorrowful career. 'Tis a multitude of motives adapted to the locality of provinces, which they have artfully reunited into one grand motive. The whole has been gilded by deception, and now forms a singular phantom, to which it is sacrilegious not to pay proper adoration. (pp. 422–23)

One final note deserves consideration. In many of the revolutionary sketches, the heroes and heroines reenact patterns experienced by Crèvecoeur himself: attack from both sides, refusal to join the military of one or the other, escape, imprisonment, and return to a ruined home and dead or scattered loved ones. The stereotypes of his art should not overshadow the fact that he was not composing from hearsay alone or writing fictional stories and dramas.

He wrote about what he had personally experienced; he wrote "sketches." The revolutionary *Sketches* constitutes in addition an apologia for his own actions, a defense of his political ambiguity, his retreat to Europe and abandonment of his family.

Eight of the manuscripts discovered by Bourdin were not included in *Sketches*; one was only partially printed there, the rest of it in the *Yale Review*. I am baffled as to why three and a half were selected for separate publication. Judged by literary merits they seem to me no poorer than those included, and "Susquehanna" is much superior. The Yale University Press may have imposed a maximum page restraint.

"The Grotto" is a short sketch in which the narrator discovers that some missing neighbors are hiding out in a cave from patriot harrassment; their grotto contains a disguised entrance and has books. The narrator spends a pleasant evening there, tucked away in a wilderness sanctuary. (The amenities of this cave, something like Pope's grotto, contrast with the horror of the cave in Charles Brockden Brown's *Edgar Huntley*, published approximately twenty years after this sketch was written. "The Grotto" will interest those interested in attitudes toward the wilderness in early American literature.) "Susquehanna" is a travel sketch of two journeys. It describes the narrator's route and invites his reader to trace his journey on a map. The narrator describes the soil, timber, flora, and fauna and the little outpost settlements he encounters, from a one-family dwelling to larger groups. They are happy, industrious, self-sufficient, noble pioneer stock; their settlements are utopian. This sketch is one of Crèvecoeur's finest, and it is a great misfortune that readers have been denied the opportunity to read the piece entire, for if one places "The Wyoming Massacre" of *Sketches* after the end of the *Yale Review* "Susquehanna," where it belongs (there is no break or suggestion of a break in the Bourdin typescript), one has a mini-*Letters*. A beautiful wilderness and a happy pioneer people are invaded by revolutionaries, killed and burned by Indians and whites.[4]

"Hospitals" is a subdued sketch, a sentimental lament over the horror of war as seen from the perspective of mutilated soldiers in hastily erected field hospitals. The poorly administered Protestant hospitals are contrasted with the more humane Catholic ones of Quebec and Quaker hospitals. "Sketch of a contrast Between the Spanish and English Colonies" is a more elaborate discussion—approaching propaganda—of a theme frequently touched on

---

4. I am indebted to Everett Emerson for pointing out to me a bound, two-volume set of the carbons of Henri Bourdin's typescript of the manuscripts in the Smith College Library. I have not been able to consult the holograph manuscripts in France, though final answers to some of the questions I raise in this essay will depend, in part, on a careful study of those documents.

elsewhere: the advantages of the freedom and simplicity of Protestant worship, especially Quaker, in stimulating ardor in trade and good manners and work habits. The Catholic churches and worship in South America as Crèvecoeur imagines them hinder initiative by oppression and by draining the people's meager wealth. South American Catholicism encourages laziness and discourages trade, in contrast to the American religious attitude, especially in Pennsylvania, where toleration encourages "all ranks of people . . . to trade, to sow, to till and to embellish and replenish this great continent which wants nothing but time and hands to become the great 5th Monarchy which will change the present political system of the world."

One of the five unpublished sketches, "Rock of Lisbon," is unique, for of twenty-three pages in the Bourdin typescript, nineteen sketch geographical scenes and cultural observations made from a convent high on a mountain outside Lisbon. The sketch opens with the narrator sweeping his eye around dense forests and along the Hudson from a high point in the Adirondacks. He makes some interesting comments on the sublime and the picturesque, moves into a discussion of how lofty thoughts about nature and men come at such times of elevated panorama, then recalls his impressions of viewing Europe from the great rock of Lisbon. The sketch does not return to America except obliquely, by suggestion, for at its conclusion the narrator has gone down to a resort town in the Spanish lowlands and is oppressed by the poor laboring classes who are taxed and robbed of their productivity by church and state.

"Sketches of Jamaica & Bermudas & other Subjects" is an uneven piece, beginning and ending as a letter addressed to someone in Philadelphia urging him to visit the writer. The piece is divided between descriptions of the islands of Jamaica and Bermuda, where the writer has been sent as an agent for his father's American business, and the story of his return to America, his father's death, his problems in dealing with the estate, and his resolution to be an honest man no longer. The cheating he finds in those he must deal with in settling the estate persuades him to adopt the same methods in defense. The Jamaica scene contains Crèvecoeur's typical reservations about hot climates producing lazy people and his outrage at "the severity exercised ag't the Negroes." An "Englishborn Lady" with whom the narrator resides used to be "thrown into Fits" over the sounds of the whip when she first came to the island; now she is a hardened persecutor, whipping her black in the morning; "the length of the Poor wretch's Punishment depended on his ability in keeping his 2 thumbs Immoveably fixed on the Edge of a table which stood in the Middle of the Room, while she was exerting her strength by the Laceration of her blows to make him displace them."

"The Commissioners" is a revolutionary sketch, written after 1773 and akin to those published under "Landscapes" in *Sketches*. A committee requires an oath of three "neutral" citizens, including a Quaker, and Crèvecoeur provides a crisp dialogue between each one and the committee. The dialogue, or debate, keeps the scene dramatic, as in a courtroom, and there is relatively little of Crèvecoeur's usual mix of sentiment and polemic. I find here the first notes of passive resistance that I have encountered in American writing other than that of Quakers. (Did Crèvecoeur consider himself in spirit a Quaker? Certainly, he is their apologist.)

"Ingratitude Rewarded," also a revolutionary sketch, begins with the lament that the writer finds it hard to remain objective and write "some real sketches of our times . . . drawn with a probity and fidelity which excludes all party and rancour"; rather, "My anger gets the better of my wit . . . . I have no method, for I am a free man; when my heart is more than commonly oppressed, I fly to my table, I scribble, and by imparting you some of my keenest sorrows, I feel somewhat relieved." There follows a story of ingratitude, of a young boy adopted by a patron, educated, and after the patron's death, placed in the law profession by the influence of the patron's widow. As revolutionary zeal grows, the patron's son, married and owner of a rich estate, is hounded by patriots to the point where he flees to the woods (the central Crèvecoeur archetype), later followed by his wife; eventually they leave the country. The bounty is rich: "A fine house, rich furniture, ample wardrobe, negroes, horses, etc. etc., these were the first fruits of confiscation in this province." Meanwhile, the young lawyer becomes a patriot, active in the "pamphletic war"; without intervention he watches the breakup of his patron's son's estate. Crèvecoeur appeals to the reader's sense of ingratitude; how can the eternal verities of kindness, respect, and gratitude be so immobilized by revolution?

"An Happy Family Disunited by the Spirit of Civil War" is in my view second in quality only to "Distresses of a Frontier Man" of all the revolutionary sketches. It begins by describing the death of an old pioneer who had lived through the happy days of early settlement, "that happy ignorance" of an age of peace and simplicity. Now, the patriarch's sons have split in allegiance, two to the "left" and two to the "right," and before his death the old man tries to bring them together. The aged pioneer is symbolic, the sketch a parable, the history a simplified typology. He is symbolic of the country, grown through the youth of its frontier innocence and prosperity into its first old age only to find that in handing down the fruits of the colony to the sons, there is discord where unity should prevail, war in a land of peace. The old man's lament recalls Bradford in the closing pages of his history, as he sees the sons of Plymouth moving off into new places and attitudes. The patriarch's death symbolizes the death of the good days for Crèvecoeur; the future is uncertain. Here again, the single sketch covers the pattern of *Letters*; a once prosperous and cooperative people, represented here by one (probably fictional) family, comes to division and a "last dismal scene."

V

Having briefly reviewed all the known English writings which did not appear in *Letters*, we return to the crucial period in Crèvecoeur's life as a writer, to the time, whether before or during his stay in London, when he decided to turn some of his sketches into a book. D. H. Lawrence, Stone, and Philbrick seem to me too persuasive on the book's thematic and artistic unities to assign *Letters* to the choice and arrangement of the publishers, as Bourdin suggests, or to see the book as merely an anthology or gathering of separate pieces. Internal evidence suggests what it is hoped a careful study of the manuscripts will someday sustain, that Crèvecoeur himself selected, arranged, and revised those sketches that seemed to him most meaningful in his backwards glance at life in America. As he considered all the pieces, he saw there were at least three tones: joy at being free in the New World; bewilderment and amazement at how recent patriotic zeal seemed incongruous with an earlier, simple life; and outright indignation and satirical sneer at those who would abrogate the virtues of kindness, filial love, and gratitude in the name of patriotism.

That his book would not end with a Tory denunciation of the Revolution is clear, for he left out the most stinging of his revolutionary sketches from a partisan point of view. The only one he chose carried the tones of bewilderment and confusion. As he reflected on his past and the masks he had worn, from French soldier to English-American traveler, merchant, surveyor, and farmer, distrusted by Tories and patriots alike, threatened by Yankee torches and imprisoned by British chains, now facing a British audience but wishing to retain his French connections, he decided to distance himself far to the rear of his book and invented James, the simple farmer, in an introduction undoubtedly written after his decision to turn the sketches into a book about frontier America. He revised his chosen sketches, adding phrases such as "my simple intellect" in places to identify his narrator. Safely away from torch and chain, looking back on his life in America as he re-read his sketches, he saw that his life had indeed been a mythic and marvellous journey, a European's fantasy of the possibilities of selfhood come true. He would not now gainsay those sketches on freedom and the joy of self-fulfillment in building a free farm and family. And yet he was a man of sorrows; his darker view of his last months in America had to have a place in the book, too.

Reading over all his sketches, he must have seen that two recent ones, "Susquehanna" and "An Happy Family Disunited by the Spirit of Civil War" told the whole epic story, each in miniature, from harmony to discord, prosperity to alienation and abandonment. They were paradigms of his own experience. These gave him the idea—the structure and action—for his proposed work. "Susquehanna" was rich in the sketcher's details of perception:

forests, flowers, animals, harvesting of trees and wheat, tools, canoes for water travel, single cabins on cleared land, and stockaded communities. Such detail about how life was lived in the New World must certainly play a role in his book, appealing to an audience eager to know about life in America. Yet "An Happy Family" gave him the other view; rich in suggestiveness, reaching out into parable and archetypal vision, here was a story almost biblical in its New World setting, a lament over the loss of paradise, focused in one frontiersman as head of his family, a "patriarch" fallen victim to "the corroding poyson of these fatal times." Could Hector in selecting and rewriting his materials build in that larger vision, that his single story would encompass the life of his adopted country, that his voice and farm and experiences might somehow like those of the old man assume the story of the country and the nature of man in the new world, both so full of promise, both, now, seeming to founder? He would try.

V I

For the next three years Crèvecoeur tried to secure the inheritance of his family's French estate for his American children, ostensibly his reason for leaving Pine Hill in the first place. It may seem a lame excuse to retreat from the war, especially since Crèvecoeur would appear to have abrogated his responsibility as husband and father in taking only one child with him. Yet the Revolution seemed a sufficient threat that Pine Hill might be desecrated or legally taken from him (the latter did not happen). *Letters* is evidence enough in its many references to the great joy and value of handing down the farmer's lifetime of work to his children to show that Crèvecoeur considered bequeathal among his highest ideals.

France was never to be a permanent retreat for Crèvecoeur; he wanted to return to America and his family as soon as possible. He received help from Madame d'Houdetot who encouraged him to undertake the French version of the *Letters* and was a friend of Benjamin Franklin's, and from Marquis de Turgot; and, after a lucky incident in which Crèvecoeur befriended five American seamen who had landed in France after escaping a British prison, they promised to work for his return to America and for his family's protection. He was appointed consul to New York, New Jersey, and Connecticut in June 1783. Arriving in New York in November, he was greeted with sad, biting news—the fiery destruction of Pine Hill in the war and the death of his wife. The children Fanny and Louis had been taken in by a Boston benefactor, Gustave Fellowes. The following year Crèvecoeur was reunited with them.

The consul took up his duties with gusto, but the pain of his loss contributed to spells of illness, requiring a year's furlough in France in 1785. Five years later he returned to France to retire, but revolutions still plagued his life. The Reign of Terror chased his son Ally to Hamburg and Louis back to the United States. Crèvecoeur tried to return to America but was not allowed. Poverty-stricken, he completed a new book on America, *Voyage dans la Haute Pensylvanie et dans l'état de New-York,* which was published in Paris in 1801. He lived out his final years with his father, who died in 1799, and with his children in periodic visits to them in London, Lesches, Munich. Ally died in 1806; in 1809 Crèvecoeur moved with his daughter and son-in-law to Sarcelles, where he died of a heart ailment in November 1813.

VII

That those moments when the American Dream has found full dramatic expression are central to our understanding of what classical American literature can be hardly needs elucidation from me here. Nick Carroway's wondering how the green world must have looked to the eyes of the Dutch explorers, coming as the climax to a story which has just left Jay Gatz murdered in his swimming pool, is a famous example of such moments. The important point is that this motif is a drama, a tension, wherein a lyric song of discovery is often undercut in some way; the ongoing promise of America remains a dream, as in a fantasy, tangible, finally, only in the imagination. Michel-Guillaume-Jean Hector St. John de Crèvecoeur was, I believe, the first in our literature to find this dramatic voice in an imaginative work of power. Like Thoreau, Twain, and Fitzgerald later, he came to it honestly through his own experience, and he transmuted that experience into an art that recognized both the dream and its elusiveness. As a sketcher of life in America, he ranks with Jefferson and Bartram; as a symbol maker out of raw experience, however, he was unique in his time and a pathfinder for American writers to follow.

SUGGESTIONS FOR FURTHER READING

Editions

Crèvecoeur, St. John de. "Crèvecoeur on the Susquehanna, 1774–1776." Edited by
H. L. Bourdin and S. T. Williams. *Yale Review* 14 (1925): 552–84.
_____. *Eighteenth-Century Travels in Pennsylvania and New York.* Translated and
edited by Percy G. Adams. Lexington: University of Kentucky Press, 1961.
[Selections from the *Voyage,* containing a valuable introductory essay.]

————. "The Grotto: An Unpublished Letter from the American Farmer." Edited by H. L. Bourdin and Stanley Williams. *Nation* 121 (1925): 328–30.

————. "Hospitals (during the Revolution): An Unpublished Essay." Edited by H. L. Bourdin and S. T. Williams. *Philological Quarterly* 5 (1926): 157–65.

————. *Journey into Northern Pennsylvania and the State of New York.* Translated by Clarissa S. Bostelmann. Ann Arbor: University of Michigan Press, 1964. [Translation of Crèvecoeur's *Voyage dans la Haute Pensylvanie et dans l'état de New-York* (1801).]

————. *Letters from an American Farmer and Sketches of Eighteenth-Century America.* Foreword by Albert E. Stone, Jr. New York: New American Library, 1963. [A convenient edition of Crèvecoeur's two English works, with a good introductory essay.]

————. *Lettres d'un Cultivateur Américain.* 2d ed. 3 vols. Paris: Cuchet, 1787. [A thorough reworking of the *Letters,* by Crèvecoeur himself.]

————. "Sketch of a Contrast between the Spanish and English Colonies." Edited by H. L. Bourdin and S. T. Williams. *University of California Chronicle* 28 (1926): 152–63.

Scholarship and Criticism

Lawrence, D. H. *The Symbolic Meaning.* Edited by Armin Arnold. Fontwell: Centaur Press, 1962. [Includes a long essay on Crèvecoeur, better than the famous one in Lawrence's *Studies in Classic American Literature* (1923).]

Nye, Russel B. "Michel-Guillaume St. Jean de Crèvecoeur: *Letters from an American Farmer.*" In *Landmarks of American Writing*, ed. Hennig Cohen, pp. 32–45. New York: Basic Books, 1969.

Philbrick, Thomas. *St. John de Crèvecoeur.* New York: Twayne Publishers, 1970. [An excellent critical and interpretive study.]

Rice, Howard C. *Le Cultivateur Américain: Étude sur l'oeuvre de Saint John de Crèvecoeur.* Paris: Champion, 1932. [A valuable study, especially of the *Lettres.*]

13

The Connecticut Wits

ROBERT D. ARNER

[*Crèvecoeur was an international figure who experienced life on the American frontier as well as in the salons of Paris; he wrote as an American for a European audience. His cosmopolitanism is a far cry from the provincialism of most of the school of poets known as the Connecticut Wits. Though New England had produced a substantial body of literature before the Revolution, and though in the nineteenth century literature was to flourish on its Puritan soil, only the ten or more wits produced a body of imaginative literature there during the revolutionary years. Most of these today seem so conservative, so reactionary, as to be an anachronism. Three wits survive, however, and these three are examined in the next chapter.*]

In September 1786, amid domestic turmoil that included runaway inflation and open rebellion under Daniel Shays in Massachusetts, a delegation of prominent merchants and politicians from five states met at Annapolis, Maryland, to discuss navigation on the Potomac. Recognizing that they confronted larger, more complicated problems, the delegates exceeded their authority and called for a national meeting to restructure the inadequate government of the Articles of Confederation. The official result of this call to reform, as every American knows, was the Philadelphia Convention of May-September, 1787 and the drafting of the United States Constitution. Among the unofficial results was a proliferation of advisory literature, the most famous of which appeared irregularly in twelve installments in the *New-Haven Gazette, and the Connecticut Magazine* from October 26, 1786, to September 13 of the following year. Entitled "American Antiquities," the series offered Americans a picture of their own chaotic times by means of extended passages from a putative ancient epic, *The Anarchiad*, which the authors claimed had recently been excavated in the Ohio Territory. "The prophetic bard," observed the writers of the first number, "seems to have taken for the point of vision one of the lofty mountains of America, and to have caused, by his magic incantation, the years of futurity to pass before him.'' What he saw from that height was appalling—nothing less than the restoration of the empire of ''Chaos and substantial Night'' on the North American continent:

> For, see! proud Faction waves her flaming brand,
> And discord riots o'er the ungrateful land;
> Lo! to the north, a wild, adventurous crew,
> In desperate mobs, the savage state renew;
> Each felon chief his maddening thousands draws,
> And claims bold license from the bond of laws;
> In other States the chosen sires of shame
> Stamp their vile knaveries with a legal name;
> In honor's seat, the sons of meanness swarm,
> And Senates base the work which mobs perform;
> To wealth, to power, the foes of union rise,
> While foes deride you, and while friends despise.[1]

Highly successful as political propaganda in support of a strong central government, *The Anarchiad* is far less satisfactory as poetry. Nevertheless, it is important to American literary history for bringing to national attention a talented if not gifted group of New England writers; for earning them their nickname of the Wicked Wits, the Hartford Wits, or, more lastingly and inclusively, the Connecticut Wits; and for articulating, mostly implicitly to be sure, a poetic for the new nation. That poetic, subscribed to in some measure by all of the Wits, placed primary emphasis upon the ''moral and political nature'' of literature, as Joel Barlow later wrote in his preface to *The Columbiad*, and based both of those, in turn, upon a trinity of patriotism, practicality, and prophecy. Like Walt Whitman later on, the Wits looked toward the future to justify both America and their own poetic enterprises.

As for the writers themselves, at one time or another the group included, among others, Mason Fitch Cogswell, Richard Alsop, Theodore Dwight, Elihu Hubbard Smith, Noah Webster, Lemuel Hopkins, and David Humphreys, along with its most prominent members, John Trumbull, Joel Barlow, and Timothy Dwight (who seems to have had no direct hand in *The Anarchiad*). They were held together, at least initially, by geographical proximity, a Yale degree (Hopkins was awarded an honorary M.A. in 1784), a commitment to Congregationalism, and a faith in the principles of Federalist politics. One of them, Joel Barlow, would later repudiate both Congregationalism and Federalism in favor of deism and a republicanism possibly to the left even of Philip Freneau's, and all would pursue careers outside of literature. The

---

1. *The Anarchiad: A New England Poem* (1786–87), ed. William K. Bottorff, p. 57.

staunch Federalists among them lived to see their politics rejected with the election of Thomas Jefferson, but in defense of their beliefs, which included a strong championing of the American revolutionary cause despite whatever misgivings they may have entertained about democratic rule, they wrote the first significant chapter in postcolonial American literature.

As a group, the Wits have not fared well with successive generations. As early as 1819 William Cullen Bryant objected to their "artificial elevation of style," the "wearisome regularity" of their verses. "The imagination is confined to the chains of a perpetual mannerism," Bryant wrote in his *Essay on American Poetry*, "and condemned to tinkle the same eternal tune with its fetters." Granting the considerable justice of this view, we must nevertheless recognize, however, that it represents a sensibility attuned not to neoclassicism but to Wordsworth's innovations. Subsequent criticism, tied to a notion of an American poetic style derived from the theories of Emerson and the performances of Walt Whitman and his successors, has been even less favorable. What we need to acknowledge is that the "chains" of the couplet to which Bryant and countless others have objected were self-assumed, not merely out of a desire to imitate approved English models but also out of an awareness that the couplet form, whether heroic or hudibrastic, might serve well the Wits' poetic purposes.

Generally speaking, the elevated style of the heroic couplet seems as accurate a reflection of the Wits' consciousness of their own times as Whitman's free verse is of his bustling and expansive age. In its urbanity and sophistication the couplet insists upon America's continuing membership in the Western community of civilized nations, despite the radical break implied by the Declaration of Independence. In its balance it seems a satisfactory restatement of the government of checks and balances devised by the Philadelphia Convention. Its directness and tendency toward epigrammatic concision make it an effective vehicle for a literature concerned with presenting unambiguous advice to an infant country which badly needed direction. In *The Anarchiad*, as also in Barlow's "Advice to a Raven in Russia," it provides an ideal of order amid scenes of overwhelming disorder. It is flexible enough to express both Dwight's conservatism and Barlow's rationally based faith in the progressive equality of all mankind. As for Trumbull's hudibrastics, has it been sufficiently noted that, in *M'Fingal* at least, they carry well the burden of his divided political consciousness, simultaneously mocking aristocratic traditions and signaling their overthrow in poetry no less than in politics while at the same time suggesting the burlesque of society that may result if all standards of control are overthrown and liberty is extended into license? While we may lament that the Wits explored no new poetic territory, then, we should not on these rather anachronistic grounds condemn their poetry out of hand without the trial of a re-reading.

I

Because of the limitations of space, only the three major Wits will be dealt
with here. Of those who collaborated on *The Anarchiad*, only one, John
Trumbull, was nationally known as a poet before 1786. If we are to believe
family tradition, Trumbull (1750–1831) was born for great things in literature.
By the age of four he had memorized all of Isaac Watts's *Horae Lyricae*, tried
his hand at his own verses, and was ready to begin the study of Latin and
Greek. These he had sufficiently mastered by the time he was seven to pass
the entrance requirements to Yale, though his father kept him back for another
six years. At Yale he made the acquaintance of Timothy Dwight and produced
a number of poems, including the inevitable "Prospect of the Future Glory of
America," part of his master's commencement address in 1770. With a
burlesque "Epithalamion" (1769) inspired by the wedding of his tutor,
Stephen Mix Mitchell, to Hannah Grant, he successfully exploited for the first
time the verse form in which he was to produce his best work, the octasyllabic
couplet devised by Samuel Butler for *Hudibras*.

Trumbull's two major poems, *The Progress of Dulness* and *M'Fingal*, were
both initially published in partial versions. The first grew out of Trumbull's
essay series, "The Correspondent," and his efforts to revise the curriculum at
Yale during his first year as tutor, when he and Dwight sought to introduce
modern literature into the program of study. The first part of *Progress,* featur-
ing the adventures of a ministerial student named Tom Brainless, was published in 1772, and parts two and three, the "Life and Character of Dick
Hairbrain" and "The Progress of Coquetry, or the Adventures of Miss Harriet
Simper," appeared in January and September of the next year. Perhaps, as
some have thought, Trumbull was actually acquainted with the fop and the
coquette upon whom he modeled these last two characters, but nevertheless
they do not have the authority of portraits drawn from life. They seem rather
like those early eighteenth-century American portraits, where stylized costume, gesture, and pose carry the message of status and type at the expense of
individualized character study.

Foppery and coquetry, if they ever existed in New England as they are
represented in the poem (only Dick Hairbrain's rusticity carries conviction on
this count), have long since passed out of fashion as primary concerns for
satire. Not so the abuses, misuses, and illusions of a college education which
Trumbull treats in Canto I, easily the best part of the poem. Modern Trumbul-
lians who complain about the present quality of college graduates or of
Ph.D.'s who could not read their own diploma if it were written in Latin may
take either comfort or despair from Tom Brainless, whose

> wit and learning now may
> Be proved by token of diploma,

> Of that diploma, which with speed
> He learns to construe and to read . . . .
>
> (2: 24–25²)

What Trumbull is against, of course, is not the learning of Latin, but the rote memorization of a dead language that, imperfectly acquired at best, is of no practical advantage even to the future minister except to make him proud in the possession of a parchment. Education in New England, apparently, had not changed much between Tom Brainless's school days and Benjamin Franklin's "Dogood No. IV" (1722), but American schools would eventually walk down a much straighter and narrower path of practicality than either Trumbull or Franklin (see also Franklin's "Proposals Relating to the Education of Youth in Pensilvania" of 1749) dreamed of, perhaps to its present dead end.

In the first section of *Progress*, Trumbull frequently manages an ironic compression more reminiscent of the closed couplets of Alexander Pope than of Butler's galloping overruns: "And hear no prayers, and fear no fine," for instance, deliberately confuses even as it separates over a medial caesura the worlds of the spirit and the flesh, at the same time implying through its ironic echo of the Psalmist's "fear no evil," its alliterative stress, and the end positioning of "fine" that this world is more worrisome to the would-be minister than the next; "Sermons to study, and to steal" again employs alliteration to align two very different verbs with a single noun in order to enforce the flat contradiction between the act of stealing and the content of most sermons. To demonstrate the debasement of true learning, what better way than to show classical Latin at the service of sloth and triviality, this time through rhymes which are reticently metaphoric:

> With sleepy eyes and count'nance heavy,
> With much excuse of *non paravi,*
> Much absence, *Tardes* and *egresses,*
> The college-evil on his seizes . . . .
>
> What silly rules in pomp appear!
> What mighty nothings stun the ear!
> *Athroismos, Mesoteleuton,*
> *Symploce* and *Paregmenon!*
> Thus, in such sounds high rumbling, run
> The names of jingle and of pun . . . .
>
> The scholar dress that once array'd him,
> The charm, *Admitto te ad gradum* . . . .
>
> (2: 15, 20, 24)

---

2. Quotations from Trumbull's poems are taken from the 1820 edition of *The Poetical Works of John Trumbull.*

Shortly after the publication of *Progress*, Trumbull's growing involvement in the revolutionary cause turned his attention to matters more pressing than the quality of higher education, and, while in Boston studying law with John Adams, he wrote his "Elegy on the Times" (1774), a serious attack on the Boston Port Bill which opens with an echo of Goldsmith's *Deserted Village* (1770) and, therefore, an implicit reminder that Britain has been guilty of similar inhumanities in the past. On August 7 and 14, 1775, there followed a burlesque poem, "By Thomas Gage . . . A Proclamation," and later that year, at the request of some members of the Continental Congress, the first version of *M'Fingal*. In a letter to the Marquis de Chastellux dated May 20, 1785, Trumbull acknowledged the congressional urgings and added that his original intention had been "to satirize the follies and extravagances of my country-men, as well as of their enemies." Since we know that he had outlined the third canto and composed parts of the forth as early as 1775, there is no strong reason to doubt this *post facto* statement, as some have done, and accuse the poet of compromising an originally democratic work by adding criticism of the "patriotic" rabble in the finished version of 1782. It is, indeed, in part this balanced view which lifts *M'Fingal* far above the level of other diatribes that passed for political satire in the early years of the Republic.

In the first and second cantos of *M'Fingal*, the Tory M'Fingal and the Whig Honorius debate at length the causes that impel to separation. The forum for their debate is the town meeting, backbone of New England democracy, but when the session ends in a shouting match between the two factions, with every blockhead wishing to have his say, Trumbull has already laid the foundation for his criticism of unrestrained liberty. What the Whigs cannot demonstrate by force of logic, they prove by force of arms in Canto 3, in which M'Fingal leads an assault upon a Liberty Pole outside the meeting house. The attack is repulsed, the laborer's spade besting the aristocrat's sword, and M'Fingal is seized, tarred and feathered, paraded through the town on a cart, and eventually returned to the steps of the meeting house. There, his backside glued to the pole and his optics made gloomy by the flowing pitch, he foresees an ultimate Whig victory. In Canto 4, he calls a convocation of Tories in his cellar and elaborates upon his gloomy vision as it was revealed to him in a dream by another high-ranking Tory, one Malcolm, who was almost lynched by a patriotic mob. The meeting is interrupted by Whig rabble, however, from whom M'Fingal flees toward Boston as the poem closes.

As in *Progress*, in this satire Trumbull occasionally calls upon compression and the suggestiveness of syntax to make his ironic equations: "Till all this formidable league rose / Of Indians, British troops, and Negroes. . . ." For the most part, however, he enjoys his greatest degree of success in this poem with historical and literary allusions. Again the example of Pope, and espe-cially of *The Dunciad*, lurks under the Butlerian surface. There is, for instance, some of Pope's metaphorical interplay between the abstract and the concrete in Trumbull's naming—Honorius and Justic Quorum balanced against Abijah White, Malcolm, and a host of other Tories—but it is the real names that work most effectively. In general, Trumbull's rhymes and catalogues of names, often functioning simultaneously as mock heroic devices, work to implicate the Tories and the British in the creation of a world of improbability and poetic dissonance, to draw them into the unusual, the freakish, and away from the order represented by the traditionally strong masculine rhymes of the heroic couplet. The names may also operate in more specific contexts; "consign'd" pairs with "Burgoyned" and "follies" with "Cornwallis" in tightly compressed statements of what were, for Americans at the time, the essential qualities of these two British generals. So, too, the underlying theme of Tory self-interest is well served by an individualized roll call of M'Fingal's heroes as he expects to see them in their future glory:

> Behold! the world shall stare at new setts
> Of home-made Earls in Massachusetts;
> Admire, array'd in ducal tassels,
> Your Ol'vers, Hutchinsons and Vasalls;
> See join'd in ministerial work
> His Grace of Albany, and York.
> What lordships from each carved estate,
> On our New-York Assembly wait!
> What titled Jauncys, Gales and Billops;
> Lord Brush, Lord Wilkins and Lord Philips!
> Aloft a Cardinal's hat is spread
> O'er punster Cooper's reverend head.
> In Vardell, that poetic zealot,
> I view a lawn-bedizen'd Prelate;
> While mitres fall, as 'tis their duty,
> On heads of Chandler and Auchmuty!
>
> (1: 74–75)

Interlayered among these catalogues are numerous literary allusions, most to the Old Testament but some, significantly in context, to the book of Revelation. Persistently if not systematically, the story of Israel's delivery from Egyptian bondage unfolds behind the day's events at the meeting house and elsewhere, reminding us of Trumbull's strong New England heritage and establishing the frame of values within which the satire operates. "Will this vile Pole, devote to freedom," demands M'Fingal scornfully,

> Save like the Jewish pole in Edom;
> Or like the brazen snake of Moses,
> Cure your crackt skulls and batter'd noses?
>
> (1: 88)

Here and in the lines immediately following them in the third canto, Trumbull seems to be at least partly on M'Fingal's side, decrying the patriot's concept of liberty as "But for crimes a patent license, / To break of law th' Egyptian yoke, / And throw the world in common stock." At other moments, however, the Scotsman stands alone, blasphemously elevating Lord North to the divinity of Christ and proclaiming a Second Coming with material rewards for the faithful:

> I see the day, that lots your   [the Whigs'] share
> In utter darkness and despair;
> The day of joy, when North, our Lord,
> His faithful fav'rites shall reward.
> No Tory then shall set before him
> Small wish of 'Squire or Justice Quorum;
> But to his unmistaken eyes
> See lordships, posts and pensions rise.
>
> (1: 74)

The final cantos of *M'Fingal* and undetermined contributions to *The Anarchiad* in 1786 all but mark the end of Trumbull's poetic career. A combination of ill health and increasing judicial responsibilities kept him from an occupation which was at best, perhaps, chiefly a response to his country's needs. A few "Newscarrier's Addresses," another brief essay serial ("The American"), and, it is thought, a substantial body of anonymous political prose which may well never be definitely attributed to him just about tally his productivity after the adoption of the Constitution. Though he achieved considerable proficiency as a political satirist, Trumbull often remarked that he wielded the satirist's pen only reluctantly, because the age demanded it. On the evidence of his "Newscarrier's Address" for New Year's, 1824, we may easily believe this, for even the highly partisan politics of the constitutional crisis, bitter as they often became, do not appear to have scarred him permanently. An ageing man, he could look back on that time of domestic turmoil and good-naturedly reflect:

> Democracy and Federalism
> That caus'd such uproar once, and schism,
> Have stoutly fought their quarrel out,
> Till nought was left to fight about.

II

Unlike his friend Trumbull, Timothy Dwight (1752–1817) did not attain the mellow serenity that often comes with old age. His position as president of

Yale from 1795 on kept him at the forefront of numerous losing battles, as, for instance, the struggle to maintain Congregationalist control of Connecticut politics. To pass from Trumbull's to Dwight's verses is to abandon all light-heartedness, not to say almost all sprightliness of expression, and enter an America created by a strongly Calvinist imagination. In *The Columbiad*, Joel Barlow, who had every personal and political reason not to, praised Dwight as a poet with "Heaven in his eye, and rapture on his tongue," but, alas!, the modern reader, even after making all due allowances for Dwight's other interests, will find precious little that is either heavenly or enraptured here.

As a poet Dwight possessed at least one thing in common with Trumbull, a strongly biblical concept of the American Revolution and the righteousness of the American cause. He sounded those themes in a short patriotic poem, "Columbia," composed in 1777 but unpublished until 1783. It is perhaps Dwight's only completely readable poem, invoking the contrast between Europe as a land of "conquest, and slaughter" and the American ideals of freedom and justice. The most recently settled of the Four Quarters of the earth is also the purest, the seat of the New Jerusalem which shall remove all mankind from the accumulated guilt of history: "Thy reign is the last, and the noblest of time." American triumphs in this world would, Dwight agreed with his Puritan predecessors, prepare the way for Christ's return at the end of historical time.

Dwight's first major work, following a number of additional early poems on the "Rising Glory of America" and other themes, was begun as early as 1771 but was not finished and published until 1785. Entitled *The Conquest of Canäan*, the work saw two major revisions after Dwight had completed his first draft in 1775; in 1777, recently married and installed as a senior tutor at Yale, he added Books 3 and 5, the love story of Irad and Selima, as a gift to his new wife, and shortly thereafter his service as chaplain to the First Connecticut Brigade inspired the addition of numerous encomiums to American revolutionary heroes.

Like the painter Benjamin West, whose work he interrupts the *Conquest* to praise, Dwight was powerfully attracted to the grand historical style, believing that a rehearsal of the heroic past could be counted on to hallow the present. Too often, however, he mistakes bombast for heroic diction, and, unlike West, who broke from the authority of Joshua Reynolds to paint *The Death of Wolfe* (1771) in contemporary costume while preserving classical poses, he simply invests actual historical figures with the borrowed garments of biblical personages. The result is a loosely conceived allegory which portrays George Washington as Joshua, the Revolutionary War as the conquest of Canäan; when biblical story proves an unwieldy vehicle for American history, as frequently happens, Dwight drops the allegory and either returns to his expansions of the biblical narrative or goes off in other, mostly romantic and sentimental directions. There were, as the poet himself retrospectively confessed when he attempted to disavow any allegorical intention whatsoever, certain basic problems with the allegory, not the least of which, in Dwight's own words, was the aburdity of imagining "the *Conquest* of a country a proper event, under which to allegorize the defense of another country." It would be nice to say that Dwight's addiction to the historical style ruined him the way it worked against West, John Singleton Copley, and later, Washington Allston, but that represents only one aspect of a larger failure of Dwight's critical and creative sensibilities.

Still, though we may be tempted to write off Dwight's epic experiment, his Miltonic visions couched in Popean couplets, as merely another instance of the American artist's attraction for European formulae or of the Anglo-American cultural lag (the epic, after all, was dead before Dwight attempted the *Conquest*), that explanation does not seem adequate to account for his intentions. That Dwight chose to employ the epic even though he must have known it was a moribund genre seems to reflect his awareness of the differences between recent American and British history as much as or perhaps more than it indicates a wrong-headed persistence in the attempt to resurrect a dead literary mode. Viewed in one light, the reemergence of the epic in the early Republic—in the works of Barlow, Freneau, and others as well as in Dwight—simply represents a collective anachronism; viewed another way, it suggests the American's consciousness of the distinction between a waxing and a waning empire, his search for a literary model appropriate to the birth of a nation. Backed by a native literary tradition that dates to Johnson's *Wonder-Working Providence* (1654) and Bradford's *Of Plymouth Plantation* (first published in 1856 but familiar centuries earlier to New England historians, who used it as a source), Dwight was attempting to accomplish for· America what Vergil's *Aeneid* accomlished for Augustan Rome, the simultaneous (and somewhat paradoxical) rehearsal of a national past as a means of rescuing it, in the faith in a fresh beginning, from the gloom of history. For Dwight's Puritan predecessors, biblical parallels were designed to elevate the colonial enterprise and to stress historical and mythic continuities as counters to geographical isolation. Near the end of the eighteenth century, when descendants of the Puritans faced an even more traumatic dislocation from the mother country, it is not surprising that they responded quickly by institutionalizing the quest for their own past in the foundation of state and regional historical societies. Such history as could not be discovered would have to be created, and the *Conquest* is Dwight's contribution to that larger national effort.

In the same year that *Conquest* appeared, Dwight gave vent to his conservative, antidemocratic sentiments and to his fear of the spread of infidelity in America in his "Epistle from Dr. Dwight to Col. Humphreys." Following the tradition, already well established in American literature, of identifying Europe as the center of moral corruption, Dwight discourses on the European-educated American who returns to his native land with a head crammed full of infidel notions. "What tho' his mind no thought has e'er perplex'd, / Converse illumin'd, nor observation vex'd," Dwight demands:

> Yet here, in each debate, a judge he shines,
> Of all, that man enlarges, or refines;
> Religion, science, politics, and song;
> A prodigy his parts; an oracle his tongue,
> Hist! hist! ye mere Americans, attend;
> Ope wide your mouths; your knees in homage bend,
> While Curl discloses to the raptur'd view
> What Peter, Paul, and Moses, never knew;
> The light of new-born wisdom sheds abroad,
> And adds a leanto to the word of God.[3]

Here Dwight's next poem, *The Triumph of Infidelity* (1788), lay in embryo. Like *The Anarchiad*, which may have helped to inspire it, the *Triumph* forecasts the restoration of Satan's kingdom in America. The argument is buttressed by an historical overview of infidelism in the past and an account of its rise in America, a rise aided, somewhat surprisingly for the patriotic Dwight, by the success of the Revolution; paradoxically, cutting adrift from Europe meant an increasing dependence upon its ideas. Though the enemies include the Boston minister Charles Chauncy, the attack focuses mainly on European heretics of one cast or another: Priestley, Hume, Voltaire, and others. Besides this general disproportion among Dwight's "villains," the poem is flawed by a perplexing conclusion which sees Satan "proud with triumph" and yet defeated and "enrag'd." Doubtless this confusing close had something to do with Dwight's friend's, Noah Webster's, dismissal of the anonymous work as a "jumble of unmeaning epithets . . ." (*American Magazine*, July 1788).

At the same time that Dwight was discharging his venom against European corruptions of the American dream and the tendency of the mob to embrace every new (especially imported) idea and to elevate every clown to the status of office-holder, he was meditating a counter-image of his homeland. Begun in 1787, *Greenfield Hill*, typically for Dwight, was not completed until many years later, in 1794. Rather loosely unified by what can be seen or summoned into memory from the elevation of Greenfield Hill, the name of Dwight's rural parish in Fairfield, Connecticut, the poem presents in seven sections the poet's vision of what all America might be: peaceful, pastoral, and above all Congregationalist. The styles of the seven sections are altered to reflect the

3. *The Miscellaneous Works of David Humphreys,* ed. William K. Bottorff (Gainesville, Fla.: Scholars' Facsimiles & Reprints, 1968), p. 218.

changing moods of each part, in imitation of William Mason's *Museus*
(1747): "The Prospect" is written in the blank verse of James Thomson's *The
Seasons* (1730): "The Flourishing Village" in response to *The Deserted
Village*; "The Burning of Fairfield," an historical flashback, in octasyllabic
couplets; "The Destruction of the Pequods," a page from Puritan history, in
Spenserian stanzas; "The Clergyman's Advice to the Villagers" in octasyllabics once again; "The Farmer's Advice to the Villagers," reminiscent of
Franklin's proverbial style, again in octasyllabics; and "The Vision" in
heroic couplets. Though the poem rests heavily upon English traditions, as
this synopsis of its styles makes clear, it bears affinities also to some of
Puritan literature, particularly Samuel Sewall's celebration of Plum Island
near the end of *Phaenomena quaedam apocalyptica* (1697).

Deservedly the best known part of *Greenfield Hill* is section two, "The
Flourishing Village." Goldsmith's poem provides Dwight with the opportunity to contrast America with Europe once more, to sing the joys of competence and household harmony in contradistinction to the luxury and the
widowed, solitary figures who sparsely populate Goldsmith's work. How
closely Dwight followed Goldsmith may be surmised from his opening lines,
an apostrophe to "Fair Verna! loveliest village of the west; / Of every joy, and
every charm, possess'd." Yet he departs from his main source in some things,
particularly in his attack upon slavery. Though the black slave sings merrily
and is well provided for, says Dwight, "Lost liberty" remains

> his sole, peculiar ill,
> And fix'd submission to another's will.
> Ill, ah, how great! without that cheering sun,
> The world is chang'd to one wide, frigid zone;
> The mind, a chill'd exotic, cannot grow,
> Nor leaf with vigour, nor with promise blow;
> Pale, sickly, shrunk, it strives in vain to rise,
> Scarce lives, while living, and untimely dies.[4]

In these lines Dwight focuses attention upon the evil that will again divide
the nation long after the breach between Federalist and republican has been
repaired. Yet he is less than honest about the institution of slavery in America,
and like his political opposite Freneau, he displaces criticism of the slave
system to the British West Indies rather than striking at the American South.
Freneau's reticence may have stemmed from his wish to avoid controversy in
an effort to keep the infant country unified; Dwight's comes from a conviction
that emanicaption is already underway in Connecticut and will be accomplished when the slave is ready for it. As Kenneth Silverman has pointed out,
Dwight is not especially concerned with the South, for he has written off that

---

4. *Greenfield Hill: A Poem in Seven Parts*, p. 37.

area of the country long ago. His praises and predictions hold true not for the nation, but only for the society in and around Greenfield Hill. Thus the apparent contradiction between the gloomy tone of the *Triumph* and the hopeful one of *Greenfield Hill* turns out to be no contradiction at all, but the result of Dwight's imaginative diminishing of the boundaries of America. Only Connecticut and a few other select parts of New England fulfill or promise to fulfill the American dream.

Dwight addresses this same notion once again in the posthumously published *Travels; In New-England and New York* (1821–22), in which, to cite Silverman once more, he locates New England's peculiar virtues in the architectural symbol of the white clapboard cottage. A conservative all his days (except where the American Revolution was concerned, and then "radical" only according to a special definition), Dwight ended his literary career by suggesting, in *Travels*, that perhaps America was mistaken to sever political ties with England; Connecticut and England, at any rate, turn out to be almost exact counterparts of each other, at least so far as their conservative temperaments are concerned. But history was against Dwight's politics, and the very year of his death saw the final defeat of Federalism and Congregationalism in Connecticut with the election of Oliver Wolcott to the governorship. It was an appropriate time for Dwight to die.

III

Like Dwight, Joel Barlow (1754–1812) was also attracted to the grand style, though he scored his greatest success when he deliberately deflated that style in *The Hasy Pudding*. The youngest of the major Wits, Barlow was by turns a printer, chaplain, lawyer, political propagandist, successful merchant, and diplomat, an honorary French citizen and the confidante of presidents Jefferson and Madison. That he found time for poetry at all in so kaleidoscopic a career is a tribute both to his energy and, more important, to his overriding conviction that a new nation demanded a new literature to express its ideals, state its moral aspirations, and sinew its commitments to the future. Affectionately dedicating *The Columbiad* to his country in 1807, he put his convictions into words which clearly foreshadow Whitman's prefaces. "This is the moment in America," he wrote, "to give such a direction to poetry, painting and the other fine arts, that true and useful ideas of glory may be implanted in the minds of men here, to take place of the false and destructive ones that have degraded the species in other countries . . . ." On and off throughout his life, Barlow strove mightily to produce the kind of literature of which he spoke, to create an American point of view and an American character. If he did not ultimately succeed, perhaps because his definitions remain too largely in the realm of the abstract, he nevertheless laid the foundation upon which more gifted poets, Whitman in particular, would be able to build more stable and enduring structures.

Barlow's poetic career commenced during his undergraduate days at Yale with a mock epic account of a snowball fight between freshmen and sopho- mores, with some poems strikingly cavalier in intonation and imagery, and with a parody of the book of Chronicles aimed at Yale's president, Naphtali Daggett. With his reputation established locally, he was called upon to com- pose the commencement poem, which he entitled *The Prospect of Peace* and delivered July 23, 1778. In couplets more distinguished for patriotism than poetic quality, he discovered the theme that was to occupy him throughout most of the rest of his literary life. Always more at home poetically in the future or the past than in the present, he turned from the historical moment, the "scenes of Tyrant's fruitless rage," to contemplation of the glorious tomorrow which victory would usher in; in a pattern that would obtain in his other handlings of the same theme of the future, he praised Franklin, Rit- tenhouse, Timothy Dwight, and the memory of Jonathan Edwards less for what they had accomplished than for what their accomplishments presaged for Americans and all mankind. The poem concludes with a vision of the Second Coming and with the "Church elect" sailing "triumphant thro' the yielding skies." Though Barlow would later tone down his millenarian ideas and, as he embraced the cosmopolitan religion of deism, delete the Congregational elect entirely from his thinking, he was never to abandon completely the notion of transhistorical deliverance from the historical patterns of fall and failure. Indeed, as we shall see, his continued attachment to the notion of some sort of Second Coming caused him serious problems in *The Vision of Columbus* (1787) and *The Columbiad*.

Writing the *Prospect*, Barlow also discovered the solar imagery which was to run through nearly all of his important poetry. As originally conceived, the solar image derives chiefly from a multitude of biblical sources and is useful for bringing America's destiny within a framework of Christian history, the progress of Christian empire from East to West; it is a fundamental image for Barlow's Puritan forbears from Bradford on. Like most Americans, Barlow had also taken to heart the numerous predictions about the westward course of secular empire and looked forward to the time when "Earth's blood-stain'd empires, with their Guide the Sun / From orient climes their gradual progress run." Barlow's patriotism remained inseparable from his millennial thinking, but he was gradually to refine the solar image into a symbol of the agrarian American in harmony with the soil and with his fellow man. In an essay "On the Genius and Institutions of Manco Capac," the Peruvian lawgiver he celebrates in Books 2 and 3 of the *Vision* and again in *The Columbiad*, he wrote: "The cultivation of the soil, which in most other countries is considered as one of the lowest employments, was here regarded as a divine act. . . . [T]he people viewed it as a sacred privilege, and considered it as an honour, to imitate and assist the Sun in opening the bosom of the earth and producing vegetation." Even though he might also praise commerce and the useful products of science, the stability represented by this archaic agricultural society was always a prerequisite of his visions of future bliss in a world of trade and technology.

In the years between the *Prospect* and the *Vision*, Barlow turned out another poem of prophecy, *A Poem, Spoken at the Public Commencement at Yale College* (1781), an elegy on Titus Hosmer (1781), whom he would lament again in the *Vision* and *The Columbiad*, a translation of "Sundry Psalms" (in collaboration with Trumbull in 1785), and some conventional "Meditations on Death and the Grave" (1785), as well as contributing to *The Anarchiad*. He had also formed a plan for the *Vision* as early as 1779, and, in the commencement poem of 1781, had begun to poeticize certain ideas he would develop more extensively in the later work. In particular, he experimented with the device of the vision, which in this poem is displayed to the poet himself by the Genius of Learning. Looking forward to the preface to *The Columbiad*, Barlow gives to Learning a prediction about the new American poetry. The American writer, says Learning, will sing

> No more of vengeful chiefs and bickering Gods,
> Where ocean crimsons and Olympus nods,
> Or heavens, convulsing rend the dark profound,
> To chain fierce Titans to the groaning ground,
> But, fir'd by milder themes, and charms refin'd,
> Beam'd from the beauties of the fair one's mind,
> His soul awakes the peace inspiring song,
> And life and happiness the strain prolong.
> To moral beauties bids the world attend,
> And jarring realms in social compact blend;
> Bids laws extend and commerce stretch the wing,
> Far distant shores their barter'd tributes bring;
> He sees the nations join, their bliss increase,
> (Leagu'd in his lays) and sings them into peace.
>   (2: 41[5])

This passage states succinctly the moral purpose Barlow hoped to accomplish in all his poems, most especially in the *Vision* and *The Columbiad*. In many respects, these two poems are quite different affairs, to be sure. Bar-

---

5. Quotations from Barlow's works are taken from the William K. Bottorff and Arthur L. Ford edition of *The Works of Joel Barlow*.

low's change in political philosophy, for instance, transforms Louis XVI of France, to whom the *Vision* had been dedicated in token of his foresight and humanity, into a foolish monarch who has been misled into aiding America by his enlightened court councilors. The poet's religion of reason tones down the piety of the *Vision*, so that in *The Columbiad* "Moral Science" takes over from "blest Religion" the task of instructing the "lively" (as opposed to the earlier "raptured") mind in the Newtonian secrets of universal harmony. Yet for all the differences, the two poems may with some justification be discussed together, for they share themes, identical lines, and, on the negative side, defects. The chief problem in both is that Barlow's notion of history as a progressive manifestation of the Genius of Liberty, a lineal continuum as it were, is repeatedly undercut by a strong counter-theme which presents historical time as cyclical and repetitive rather than progressive. In his view the rise and fall of all past empires have been but the birth throes of American democracy, as America itself ushers in a new age of international cooperation. But his poetic method of indicating that Liberty burned in some breasts even during the darkest ages is to present us with a series of recurrent solar archetypes—Columbus, Manco Capac, Sir Walter Raleigh, George Washington, and the anonymous "sire elect" who presides over the Congress of all nations in Book 10 of *The Columbiad*, among others. The important historical differences among these and other solar figures in both poems easily overmaster whatever imagistic connections Barlow attempts to establish and leave us not with a sense of forward movement but of recurrent types. Moreover, despite Barlow's insistence that the Golden Age of man is a lie perpetuated by despots to keep men from striving to improve their social and political condition, the best he can do by way of earthly felicity is to imagine mankind gathered together at the original site of the Garden of Eden. Here, too, progress would seem to have turned back upon itself to leave the race no better off than when it started, in spite of technological and political advances.

It is easy enough to sympathize with Barlow's poetic and philosophical dilemma. He faced, for one thing, the familiar eighteenth-century paradox of a faith in social progress founded upon an ideal Golden Age, and he was not able, any more than most of his contemporaries were, to extricate himself from the contradiction. For another thing, since the future alone could justify America, Barlow confronted the all-too-insistent pattern of rise and fall which forced itself upon him as he surveyed the history of man since the discovery of the New World. The example of Britain's military defeat by its infant offspring, together with the recent publication of Gibbon's *Decline and Fall* (1776–88) and Volney's *Ruins* (1791) (which Barlow had translated) doubtless helped to impress upon him the vulnerability of the American dream of future greatness to the corrosive power of time. In *The Columbiad*, in fact,

Columbus raises at length this very objection to Hesper's happy visions, but Hesper replies mildly that the Muse of Science, rather than the ancient Muses of Fine Arts, guides modern destiny. A new trinity—the Press, the Magnet, and the Copernican theory—has come into being, and with the aid of knowledge, which once damned mankind to slaughter and warfare, the effects of the Fall may be reversed. But if this silences Columbus, it does not, finally, seem sufficient either for Hesper or for Barlow, and the best both manage to offer as a rescue from the threat of historical time is the eventual reappearance of the "Prince of Peace." This salvation will presumably arrive for all men, but apart from modifying his originally Calvinistic position into a sweepingly Arminian one, Barlow has not really changed the framework of his thinking very much since the early days in Connecticut.

Intensifying Barlow's problems in both vision poems is his failure to develop a strong sense of the present, a moment in time upon which to base an integrated and integrating American identity. Rehearsals of a dark and doomed past give way almost immediately to predictions of a bright and blessed future, and the historical present, which must be fully developed if it is to serve as a point of dislocation from the old patterns, is glanced at only in passing. It is like watching an interminable panorama of the sort so popular in the early Republic (see *The Columbiad*, Book 7, for Barlow's familiarity with this form of popular art, a form which certainly underlies the structure of that book and, perhaps, of the entire vision as well), with Hesper as lecturer, Columbus, Barlow, and ourselves as an audience essentially suspended in time. History, in fact, tends to be mostly spectacle in Barlow's poetry, a source of entertaining and, occasionally, enlightening stories which, however, are not allowed to exert the pressure of the past either on the present or the future. Perhaps what is at work here is the newly created American's discomfort with a past not entirely his own, a willingness—not to say a necessity—to find the meaning of America in tomorrow. In any event, as Whitman, Emerson, and Thoreau (among others) later demonstrate, in order for the conceptual America to become available for artistically valid expression, it had first to be filtered through individual perceptions of the here and now. There is, strictly speaking, no subjective present in any of Barlow's poems except *The Hasty Pudding*; his philosophical strain does not, we might say, blend with a lyrical strain, with a sense of involvement in the world of flux and change, and the result is that his view of history remains at a level of philosophical contradiction.

In this context it is instructive that Barlow's attempts to view contemporary events end either in banality (like the unfinished "The Canal"), or in unintentional political ambivalence (like *The Conspiracy of Kings*, where the common man is both celebrated and seen as the stupid pillar of the power of kings), or in an apocalyptic vision of despair. This last is the case of "Advice to a Raven in Russia," written hastily in 1812 as Barlow pursued the retreating Napoleon through Lithuania and Poland in an effort to begin negotiations which might have averted the War of 1812. There is, appropriately, no solar imagery in this poem, only the dark, frozen wastes of Russia, littered with bodies. The speaker, addressing an extended prosopopeia to a raven which, as an "Imperial Scavenger," is clearly Napoleon's alter ego, surveys a trans-European scene of carnage and predicts still more slaughter yet to come. He urges the nations of the world to unite and "Hurl from his blood-built throne this king of woes," a long way indeed from the phrophecy that unites mankind in "enlighten'd zeal" as *The Columbiad* closes. In that poem Columbus sees all "bloody banners sink in darkness furl'd / And one white flag of peace triumphant walks the world"; in this, Napoleon advances in satanic pride, "Clothed in his thunders, all his flags unfurl'd / Raging and storming o'er the prostrate world." The poet who, just five short years before, had celebrated the inevitable "future progress of society and the civilization of states" ends his poem and his poetic career with a wish for mere "repose." An American Columbus who had rediscovered European history, he was forced to acknowledge mankind's entrapment in the web of guilt and time.

There is, perhaps, no escape from such a world, but there is imaginative release. Most successfully, Barlow achieved that by going back to his own childhood, as many another American writer was subsequently to do, to find in *The Hasty Pudding* (1793) a rich remembrance of things past which, by means of a complex cluster of solar and circular imagery, he links to national agrarian idealism. As in Franklin's *Autobiography* the story of the poet's boyhood becomes suggestive of the nation's past, while the literary style communicates the adult's cosmopolitan awareness of history. With its celebrations of rural New England folkways framed by classical allusions and presented in the stately heroic couplet, the poem represents perhaps our most important surviving literary document of the impact of the lingering colonial mentality, that dependence upon foreign fashions for the forms of expression, in the early Republic. The poem begins with a rejection of European nature, the European historical canvas, and the epic mode in favor of a "softer theme":

> Ye Alps audacious, thro' the Heavens that rise,
> To cramp the day and hide me from the skies;
> Ye Gallic flags, that o'er their heights unfurl'd,
> Bear death to kings, and freedom to the world,
> I sing not you.
>
> (2: 87)

But the new song proves to be equally derived from European sources, beginning with Vergil's *Eclogues* and continuing through Thomson's *The Seasons*.

Even here, in other words, in what is probably the most American poem penned by any member of the Connecticut group, memory is filtered through a series of European literary devices, with a resulting tension between the remembered real, itself qualified by the poet's nostalgic yearning for the treats of youth, and the European ideal—between native regionalism and conventional pastoralism. Barlow's comic stance, which makes *The Hasty Pudding* still enjoyable reading today, permits laughter both at the expense of the New England rustic and at the tradition of pastoral sentimentality which, however, the poet cannot entirely reject. In no other of the Wits' poems will we see so clearly the character of the colonial cosmopolitan, the American whose knowledge, only partly assimilated to be sure, of the great world across the ocean makes him unable to deal comfortably either with that world or with the world of his origins.

There is no space here to discuss Barlow's prose political works—*A Letter to the National Convention of France* (1791), *Advice to the Privileged Orders* (1792–93), *A Letter Adressed to the People of Piedmont* (1792), and *Two Letters to the Citizens of the United States, and One to General Washington* (1799), among other pieces—except to remark that the political philosophy often jumbled in the *Vision* and *The Columbiad* frequently finds eloquent expression in them. Barlow was also something of a critic, and in his prose prefaces and notes to *The Columbiad* often groped toward an awareness of the need for an American language, for modifications of Old World literary models, and for other innovations aimed at naturalizing and Americanizing literature. Despite the monumental failure of *The Columbiad*, Barlow must rank as the most accomplished of the Wits and the one whose influence upon American poetry, though perhaps transmitted indirectly, had most to do with the shape of things to come.

And yet, despite the modest successes of Barlow and Trumbull or the still more modest successes of Dwight, American poetry has gone its way almost as though the Wits had never existed, had never written a line. We come back in the end to Emerson, who pioneered on the frontiers of fact and symbol, testing and expanding the limitations of language, meter, and meaning in a way that exposes the narrowness of the couplet even if the Wits had been more often adept at its use. Barlow's democratic idealism and the dissenting voices raised by Trumbull and Dwight are perhaps their most important legacies to us, legacies involved in their verses and still somehow larger than the aggregate total of their poems. The voices which we hear in their best works— *M'Fingal*, "Columbia," *Greenfield Hill*, *The Hasty Pudding*, and "Advice to a Raven in Russia"—are part of an American colloquy of history and hope, despair and dream, and for that reason they can still speak to us in spite of the quaintness of their colonial accents. We understand ourselves better for understanding them.

SUGGESTIONS FOR FURTHER READING

Editions

Barlow, Joel. *The Works of Joel Barlow*. Edited by William K. Bottorf and Arthur L. Ford. 2 vols. Gainesville, Fla.: Scholars' Facsimiles & Reprints, 1970.

————, with Lemuel Hopkins, David Humphreys, and John Trumbull. *The Anarchiad: A New England Poem* (1786–87). Edited by William K. Bottorff. Gainesville, Fla.: Scholars' Facsimiles & Reprints, 1967.

Dwight, Timothy. *Columbia: An Ode*. Philadelphia: John McCullock?, 1794?

————. *The Conquest of Canäan; A Poem in Eleven Books*. Hartford, Conn.: Elisha Babcock, 1785.

————. *Greenfield Hill: A Poem in Seven Parts*. New York: Childs & Swaine, 1794.

————. *The Triumph of Infidelity: A Poem*. Printed in the world, 1788.

Parrington, Vernon Louis, ed. *The Connecticut Wits*. Hamden, Conn.: Archon, 1963.

Trumbull, John. *Address of the Carrier of the "Connecticut Courant," to His Patrons*. Hartford, Conn.: n.p., 1824.

————. *The Poetical Works of John Trumbull, LL.D*. 2 vols. in 1. Hartford, Conn.: Samuel G. Goodrich, 1820.

————. *The Satiric Poems of John Trumbull: The Progress of Dulness and M'Fingal*. Edited by Edwin T. Bowden. Austin: University of Texas Press, 1962.

————. "The Wedding: An Epithalamium." *The Columbian Magazine, or Monthly Miscellany*. June 1789.

Scholarship and Criticism

Ford, Arthur L. *Joel Barlow*. New York: Twayne, 1971.

Gimmestad, Victor E. *John Trumbull*. New York: Twayne, 1974.

Howard, Leon. *The Connecticut Wits*. Chicago: University of Chicago Press, 1943.

Pearce, Roy Harvey. *The Continuity of American Poetry*. Princeton, N.J.: Princeton University Press, 1961.

Silverman, Kenneth. *Timothy Dwight*. New York: Twayne, 1969.

Woodress, James. *A Yankee's Odyssey: The Life of Joel Barlow*. Philadelphia: J. B. Lippincott, 1958.

14

The Federalist

ROBERT BAIN

[*After the Revolution but before the shape of our nation's government had been decided, the United States suffered difficult years. It was only with the hammering out of the Constitution that stability and prosperity were held out to Americans. But first came the difficult task of ratification, of persuading the almost sovereign thirteen colonies to adopt federalism. This historical crisis was the occasion for the creation of a remarkable series of essays in political science.*]

Within months of the Minutemen's first volleys at Lexington and Concord, the Americans fired the opening shots of the Second Revolution. The weapons of the Second Revolution, wrote Richard Henry Lee, were "the tongue and the pen"; the first salvos were the Declaration of Independence, the Articles of Confederation, and the written constitutions of the thirteen states. When the battles of musket and sword ceased at Yorktown on October 18, 1781, skirmishes in the war of oratory and ink continued, culminating in the debates over the recommendations of the Constitutional Convention which met in Philadelphia from May 14 to September 17, 1787. No single work captures all the nuances of the millions of words spoken and written during this Second Revolution, but *The Federalist*, written by Alexander Hamilton, James Madison, and John Jay, provides the best explication of American political thought emerging from the experiments in revolution and republican government begun in the 1770s. These eighty-five essays, composed hurriedly between October 1787 and May 1788 and published anonymously in New York City newspapers over the pseudonym of Publius, also endure as a major achievement of American political journalism.

The Federalist develops in detail an observation made by Benjamin Rush, revolutionary physician and patriot, four months before the convention opened. In "An Address to the People of the United States," published in the

January 1787 *American Museum*, he expressed what had become for many citizens a commonplace: "There is nothing more common than to confound the terms of the *American revolution* with those of *the late American war*. The war is over: but this is far from being the case with the American revolution. On the contrary, nothing but the first act of the great drama is closed. It remains yet to establish and perfect our new forms of government; and to prepare the principles, morals, and manners of our citizens, for these forms of government, after they are established and brought to perfection." Rush concluded by reminding readers that "THE REVOLUTION IS NOT OVER!" The authors of *The Federalist* agreed. All three had played important parts in the "first act of the great drama"; all assumed decisive roles in the drama's second act—the writing and ratification of the Constitution.

What united Hamilton, Madison, and Jay as authors was their "unequivocal experience of the insufficiency of the subsisting Fœderal Government," as Hamilton wrote in the opening sentence of *The Federalist*. Both Federalists and Antifederalists, the name given to opponents of the Constitution, referred to events of the mid-1780s and "the present crisis." That crisis included the domestic strife of Shays's Rebellion in Massachusetts in 1786, the states' indiscriminate printing of paper money, the federal government's ineffective foreign policy, and the states' primacy over the general government's powers to tax, to regulate commerce, and to provide for the common defense. At stake was preservation of the Union.

I

By 1787 Hamilton, Madison, and Jay knew from firsthand experience the weaknesses of the revolutionary governments established, often hurriedly, during the exigencies of the war. Jay (1745–1829) had been an author of the New York state constitution, a chief justice of New York, and a delegate to the First and Second Continental Congresses, serving as president of the Congress in 1778. Appointed minister to Spain in 1779, he participated in the Paris peace negotiations with Britain, and on his return to America in 1784 Congress drafted him to serve as foreign secretary, a position he held until 1792. Jay's foreign service especially demonstrated the need for a stronger union. As early as August 1782 he observed, "Our power, respectability, and happiness will forever depend upon our Union. Many foreign nations would rejoice to see us split to pieces because we should then cease to be as formidable and such an event would afford a fine field for their intrigues." In December 1786 he wrote to George Read of Shays's Rebellion, "The late Revolution would lose much of its Glory as well as utility, if our Conduct should confirm the Tory Maxim, that 'Men are incapable of governing themselves.'"

Youngest and most flamboyant of *The Federalist* authors, Hamilton (1755?–1804) had published before he was twenty-one years old two remarkable and lengthy pamphlets—*A Full Vindication of the Measures of Congress* (December 1774) and *The Farmer Refuted* (February 1775)—attacking Parliament and defending the Americans' right to impose trade sanctions against England to redress grievances. During the war he was Washington's aide-de-camp and distinguished himself in the field at the Battle of Yorktown. As Washington's aide, Hamilton wrote important papers on the reorganization of the army and on federal finance; he also corresponded with influential patriots about the ills of the new government. Following the war, he was admitted to the bar, sat a term in Congress, and then retired to private practice. But he continued to support with tongue and pen reform of the Articles. Appointed a delegate to the September 1786 Annapolis Convention, which was a meeting of five states to discuss commerce, Hamilton joined the Virginians in proposing a constitutional convention. Strongly supported by Madison, Hamilton wrote the "Address of the Annapolis Convention," calling upon the states to convene a meeting in Philadelphia in May 1787 to "render the constitution of the Fœderal Government adequate to the exigencies of Union." He immediately won a seat in the New York legislature, where he convinced Governor George Clinton's faction to send a delegation to Philadelphia. Hamilton was one of the three New York delegates.

The most original thinker of *The Federalist* authors, Madison (1751–1836) had by 1787 studied history and government at the College of New Jersey (Princeton), served as a delegate to the convention writing the Virginia constitution, and been a member of the Continental Congress and the Virginia House of Delegates. He supported the Annapolis Convention's call for revision of the Articles, and in November of 1786 he won a seat in the Continental Congress. Virginia appointed Madison a delegate to the Philadelphia Convention.

During the mid-1780s Madison supplemented his broad experience in government with an intensive study of confederacies and of the weaknesses of the American system. To Kentuckian Caleb Wallace, who had requested advice on constitution-making, Madison wrote in August 1785 a short essay discussing the branches of government and singling out Virginia's weak executive as "the worst part of a bad Constitution." Between February and July 1786 Madison gathered extensive notes entitled "Of Ancient and Modern Confederacies," from which he concluded that these systems had failed because members would not submit to a general authority. In preparation for the convention he wrote in April 1787 "Vices of the Political System of the United States." The existing Confederation, he said, was "nothing more than a treaty of amity[,] of commerce and of alliance, between independent and Sovereign States." Listing eleven vices of the Confederation, Madison believed that "A sanction is essential to the idea of law, as coercion is to that of government. The federal system being destitute of both, wants the great vital principles of a Political Constitution." The solution to these vices was to give sufficient power to a national government.

When the convention began its secret deliberations in May, two of *The Federalist* authors, Hamilton and Madison, sat in its chambers and proposed reforms to the Articles. Madison's hand weighed heavily in the authorship of the large state or Virginia plan, submitted by Edmund Randolph on May 29. Strongly nationalistic, the Virginia plan recommended a federal executive, judiciary, and a two-house legislature, all with more power than the Articles granted. As the debates continued, major disagreements arose over Virginia's recommendation that representation in both houses of the national legislature be based on the states' populations. Fearful of such power in the hands of large states, William Paterson countered on June 15 with the New Jersey or small state plan, which advocated new authority for the central government, but which retained the unicameral Congress where each state had one vote.

Largely silent until June 18, Hamilton spoke most of that day opposing both the Virginia and New Jersey plans and outlining an even stronger central government, one stripping power from the states and providing for an executive and a senate to be elected "for life or at least during their good behaviour." Without debating Hamilton's suggestions, the convention voted the following day to scrap the New Jersey plan and to return to the Virginia proposals as a working paper. With Madison leading the opposition against the small states, the convention spent much of the next month working out the "Great Compromise" over large and small state representation in Congress. Other difficult hurdles remained, but with the problem of representation solved, the convention's work proceeded and its recommendations were signed and sent to Congress on September 17.

Historians have puzzled over reasons for the paucity of Hamilton's contributions to the convention debates; the New Yorker left Philadelphia on June 29 and returned only in September for the closing sessions. Madison, on the other hand, became the convention's central figure. Delegate William Pierce of Georgia wrote of Madison, "Every person seems to acknowledge his greatness. He blends together the profound politician with the scholar." Attending every session, Madison took extensive notes and spoke some 161 times during the debates. His *Notes of Debates in the Federal Convention of 1787*, published in 1840, remains the most complete contemporary account of the events at Philadelphia. His contributions to shaping the convention's recommendations have earned him the title "Father of the Constitution."

It should not be surprising that all three of *The Federalist* authors had doubts about the Constitution they were to defend, for the finished document was, as Jay noted, "the result of accommodation and compromise." Before the convention adjourned, Hamilton told delegates that "No man's ideas were more remote from the plan than his were known to be; but is it possible to deliberate between anarchy and Convulsion on one side, and the chance of good to be expected from the plan on the other." Broadus Mitchell, one of Hamilton's biographers, describes Hamilton's acceptance of the Constitution as an "act of self-abnegation" that was his "real triumph. Thenceforward he left off arrogance and took on maturity." To George Washington, Jay wrote that he favored adoption "less from an idea that it [the Constitution] will fully realize the sanguine expectations of many of its friends, than because it establishes some great points, and smooths the way for a system more adequate to our national objects." Madison mailed a copy of the Constitution to Edmund Pendleton with this remark: "I forbear to make any observations on it; either on the side of its merits or its faults." Madison had labored hard for many of the Constitution's merits, but he also knew its flaws.

II

Opposition to the convention had gathered long before delegates elected George Washington its presiding officer and began deliberations. In New York, Governor George Clinton's attempt to keep delegates at home would have succeeded had it not been for Hamilton and his friends. Two powerful Virginians, Richard Henry Lee and Patrick Henry, had declined to sit as delegates and were speaking against the Philadelphia meeting. Realizing that unanimous consent of the states would be impossible, the convention boldly prescribed that "ratification of the Conventions of nine States, shall be sufficient for the Establishment of the Constitution, between the States so ratifying the Same." This proviso would force a few recalcitrant states either to accept the sense of the majority or to shift for themselves.

As the secret sessions ended, it was also evident that two powerful states—New York and Virginia—might block ratification. Robert Yates and John Lansing, New York delegates sympathetic to Governor Clinton, left the convention on July 10 and did not return. At the end, Elbridge Gerry of Massachusetts and Edmund Randolph and George Mason, both of Virginia, refused to sign the document, despite Benjamin Franklin's plea for unanimity. When Congress approved the convention's recommendations and sent the Constitution to the states in September 1787, the war of words was on.

From New York City Madison reported to friends his impressions of the war of words. He wrote to Washington on October 18 that "The Newspapers here begin to teem with vehement & violent calumniations of the proposed Gov^t." On October 30, as the first *Federalist* essays were being published, he observed to Archibald Stuart that the danger of the controversy "is probably exaggeration on each side." Complaining that the opposition had falsely credited John Jay with authorship of an essay against the new plan, he told Washington, "Tricks of this sort are not uncommon among enemies of the new Constitution."

Antifederalist essays and pamphlets poured from the presses during the fall and winter of 1787 and the spring of 1788. Like *The Federalist*, most of these tracts appeared over such pseudonyms as "Cato," "Brutus," "Agrippa," "Centinel," "Philadelphiensis," and "A Federal Farmer." Though most Antifederalist writers have faded to obscurity, their ranks included such personages as George Mason, George Clinton, Robert Yates, and Richard Henry Lee. Elbridge Gerry's *Observations on the New Constitution* by "A Columbian Patriot" (February 1788) lists eighteen dangers of the Constitution and warns that adoption will result in "an immediate *aristocratic tyranny*" and "must soon terminate in the most *uncontrouled despotism*."

Lee's *Letters from the Federal Farmer* (October 1787), one of the most important Antifederalist pamphlets, went through four editions and circulated widely in the states. A thoughtful critic, Lee opposed the new plan because it abandoned federal and republican principles by aiming "strongly at one consolidated government." "The instability of our laws," wrote Lee, "increases my wishes for firm and steady government; but then, I can consent to no government, which, in my opinion, is not calculated to preserve the rights of all orders of men in the community." He exhorts his countrymen to examine "coolly every article, clause, and word in the proposed system" to guard against "abuse in the exercise of power." Once Americans examined the new plan, he thought, they would reject it.

Though Federalists and Antifederalists disagreed on many points, they shared some common assumptions. In 1787 most American political thinkers agreed that the Articles needed revising to prevent a crisis, that some form of union was necessary for the states, that a republican government best suited American society's aspirations, that government should rest on the consent of the people, that government's power should be limited, that men may be capable of reason but are more often ruled by their passions, and that power can corrupt.

What Federalists and Antifederalists disagreed upon was the best way of accommodating means and ends, and as the debates continued, the Antifederalist catalogue of fears and objections grew long. Some critics questioned the legitimacy of the convention, pointing to the secret sessions as a sign of conspiracy among "aristocratic" sympathizers. The most repeated and telling criticism was the absence of a bill of rights defining individual liberties. Echoing a political maxim of Montesquieu and other European thinkers, some believed the proposed system impractical in a territory as large as the United States. Others attacked the plan for violating "republican principles" by proposing a *national* or *consolidated* government rather than a *federal* or *confederated* system. Limiting the power of the states and investing the federal government with broad authority was dangerous to liberty, the Antifederalists argued. Still others objected because they thought the Senate, which was to be elected by the state legislatures, would become too aristocratic and might usurp the power of the House, the people's only directly elected representatives. Opponents also feared that the president might become as despotic as the British monarch. Another criticism was that the new plan had not sufficiently separated the powers of the three branches of government and had not provided adequate checks of one branch against another. Many opponents proposed a new convention; others, especially in New York and Virginia, offered amendments as conditions of ratification. Some Antifederalists of the northern and middle states objected to the continuance of slavery. Though Publius called the Antifederalist fears "airy phantoms that flit before [their] distempered imaginations," these critics pointed to obvious flaws that needed correcting.

I I I

To return the Antifederalist barrages and to overrun Governor Clinton's strongholds, Hamilton originated the idea of a series of essays whose "immediate object was to vindicate & recommend the New Constitution to the State of N.Y. whose ratification of the instrument, was doubtful, as well as important." Hamilton approached Jay, Gouverneur Morris, and William Duer before enlisting Madison, but Morris withdrew because of ill health and Duer "wrote two or more papers, which though intelligent and sprightly, were not continued." Ill health soon confined Jay, leaving most of the writing to Hamilton and Madison. Addressed "To the People of the State of New York," the first essay appeared on October 27, 1787, in *The Independent Journal* over the pseudonym of "Publius," a pen name Hamilton had used in 1778. They chose their pseudonym from Valerius Publicola, a sixth-century B.C. Roman writer known as "a friend of the people."

The complicated publishing history of Publius's letters dramatizes the urgency Hamilton and Madison felt about presenting their arguments to the people. Published in four New York newspapers, the essays did not, according to Jacob Cooke, "consistently first appear in any one," but "rather were first printed in one, then in another paper." John McLean's *The Independent*

Journal and Thomas Greenleaf's *The New-York Packet* "carried the entire series of essays, while *The Daily Advertiser* ceased to print them after number 51, and *The New-York Journal* carried only essays 23 through 39." Writing their essays at the rate of four a week, Hamilton and Madison both acknowledged "the haste with which many of the papers were penned in order to get through the subject while the Constitution was before the public." Madison wrote, "It frequently happened that, while the printer was putting into types parts of a number, the following parts were under the pen and to be furnished in time for the press." In the preface to volume one of the collected essays, Hamilton acknowledged that "The particular circumstances under which these Papers have been written, have rendered it impracticable to avoid violations of method and repetitions of ideas which cannot but displease the critical reader." It was, he said, "respect for public opinion, not anxiety for the literary character of the performance" that dictated the authors' motives.

As the letters were appearing in the press, Hamilton sought wider circulation by gathering the first thirty-six essays as volume one of *The Federalist*, published by John and Archibald McLean on March 22, 1788. Two months later, before the last eight essays had appeared in the newspapers, McLean published volume two (essays 37–85) on May 28. *The Independent Journal* and *The Packet* printed essays 78–85 between June 14 and August 16. As Hamilton and Madison hurried their work through the press, they dispatched individual papers and bound volumes to friends for ammunition in the conflict.

Publius's anonymity and the reluctance of the authors to identify their papers set off a 176-year controversy over authorship. A few close friends knew the authors' identities immediately, and in 1792 a French edition of *The Federalist* listed authors as "Mm. Hamilton, Maddisson e Gay, citoyens de l'Etat de New York," but did not specify who wrote what. Neither did the second or third American editions, published in 1799 and 1802. To complicate matters further, Hamilton and Madison had disagreed on interpretations of the Constitution by 1792, and as authors of *The Federalist*, both had taken positions they no longer held. Just before his death in 1804, Hamilton hurriedly listed authors of the individual papers, but his list conflicted with the one Madison made for the Gideon edition of 1818. The long controversy over authorship centered upon the so-called disputed papers: nos. 18–20, 49–58, and 62–63.

Largely through the research of Edward G. Bourne, Douglass Adair, and Jacob E. Cooke, scholars had by 1961 generally agreed that Madison wrote the disputed papers. These scholars argued for Madison's authorship from internal evidence and historical data. In 1964 Frederick Mosteller and David L. Wallace published an authorship study based on computer analysis. They concluded, "On the basis of our data alone, Madison is extremely likely . . .

to have written all the disputed *Federalists*: Nos. 49 through 58 and 62 and 63, with the possible exception of No. 55. For No. 55 our evidence is relatively weak because suitably deflated odds are about 90 to 1 in favor of Madison." They also found that Madison "wrote the lion's share of Nos. 18 and 19" and probably of no. 20. The best scholarship assigns Jay five papers (nos. 2–5, 64), Madison twenty-nine (nos. 10, 14, 18–20, 37–58, 62–63), and Hamilton fifty-one (nos. 1, 6–9, 11–13, 15–17, 21–36, 59–61, 65–85).

I V

Hamilton's prefatory remark that "a desire to throw full light upon so interesting a subject had led, in a great measure unavoidably, to a more copius discussion than was at first intended" suggests that the authors found the design of their argument as they wrote. Hamilton's revisions and rearrangements of the newspaper essays for volume one also indicate that, though pressed by deadlines, the authors paid attention to the shape of their argument. "Violations of method and repetitions of ideas" occur, but the design emerges clearly.

The design of Publius's argument falls into six parts. The opening section, nos. 1–14, argues "the importance of Union to your political safety and happiness." In part two, nos. 15–22, Hamilton and Madison show "the insufficiency of the present confederation to the preservation of Union." Then Hamilton writes in section three, nos. 23–36, about "the necessity of a Constitution, at least equally energetic with the one proposed, to the preservation of the Union." The design shifts in part four, nos. 37–51, where Madison takes a "more critical and thorough survey of the work of the Convention" and explores the theoretical assumptions of the new federalism. The fifth section, nos. 52–83, passes from "more general inquiries" to a "particular examination of the several parts of the government." This longest section of *The Federalist* describes the structure and powers of the House of Representatives (nos. 52–58), of the federal election system (nos. 59–61), of the Senate (nos. 62–66), of the executive (nos. 67–77), and of the judiciary (nos. 78–83). In the final section Hamilton argues in no. 84 that a bill of rights is unnecessary because the Constitution protects individual liberties; in no. 85 he appeals to the judgment, feeling, and experience of Americans to adopt the Constitution despite its imperfections.

In the first section (nos. 1–14) essays 1 and 2 establish the tone of the discourse by counseling moderation, by reminding readers of the important issues at stake, and by outlining a reasoned approach to the subject. In essay 1 Hamilton tells his readers that they are considering "the fate of an empire, in

many respects, the most interesting in the world.'' Appealing to his readers'
patriotism, reason, and sense of destiny, he continues: ''It has been frequently
remarked, that it seems to have been reserved to the people of this country, by
their conduct and example, to decide the important question, whether
societies of men are really capable or not, of establishing good government
from reflection and choice, or whether they are forever destined to depend, for
their political constitutions, on accident and force.'' After urging adoption of
the new plan, Hamilton outlines the design of the papers:

> I propose in a series of papers to discuss the following interesting
> particulars—*The utility of the UNION to your political prosperity*—*The in-
> sufficiency of the present Confederation to preserve that Union*—*The neces-
> sity of a government at least equally energetic with the one proposed to the
> attainment of this object*—*The conformity of the proposed constitution to the
> true principles of republican government*—*Its analogy to your own state
> constitution*—and lastly, *The additional security, which its adoption will
> afford to the preservation of that species of government, to liberty and to
> property.*[1]

Jay continues in no. 2 the appeal for adoption, stressing the unity of the people
and calling the Confederation an experiment ''greatly deficient and inadequate to the purpose it was intended to answer.''

Jay then turns in nos. 3–5 to the ways that union will protect the people and
the states ''from the arms and arts of foreign nations,'' and in nos. 6–8
Hamilton addresses the dangers ''from dissensions between the states themselves'' and the Constitution's provisions for lessening internal disorders.

Scholars have cited Hamilton's no. 9 and Madison's no. 10, both on the
subject of domestic factions, as proof of the ''split personality'' of Publius
because the two writers approach the problem from different premises. Hamilton argues that improvements in ''the science of politics'' have made it
possible for men to avoid the ''disorders that disfigure the annals'' of the
''petty Republics of Greece and Italy.'' These new discoveries lessen the
threats of factions by imposing ''powerful means'' of controlling them:

> The regular distribution of power into distinct departments—the introduction
> of legislative ballances and checks—the institution of courts composed of
> judges, holding their offices during good behaviour—the representation of
> the people in the legislature by deputies of their own election—these are
> either wholly new discoveries or have made their principal progress towards
> perfection in modern times. They are means, and powerful means, by which
> the excellencies of republican government may be retained and its imperfec-
> tions lessened or avoided.

1. All quotations are from the Jacob E. Cooke edition of *The Federalist*.

Contrary to opponents who believe that republican government can function only in a small republic, Hamilton argues that the "ENLARGEMENT of the ORBIT within which such systems are to revolve" illustrates the "tendency of the Union to repress domestic faction and insurrection." The *consolidation* proposed by the Constitution merely extends Montesquieu's definition of *confederate republic* and does not violate republican principles. Hamilton's case rests on the new discoveries of "checks and balances," which allow the whole greater force than any of its parts and therefore reduce the threat of internal disorder.

Madison's approach to factions in no. 10 is less scientific and more organic than Hamilton's. Madison defines faction as "a number of citizens, whether amounting to a majority or minority of the whole, who are united and actuated by some common impulse of passion, or of interest, adverse to the rights of other citizens, or to the permanent and aggregate interests of the community." He believes that "the diverse faculties of men" create differences in property and divide "society into different interests and parties." Man's nature and his attachment to property doom all civil societies to disruption from faction: "So strong is this propensity of mankind to fall into mutual animosities, that where no substantial occasion presents itself, the most frivolous and fanciful distinctions have been sufficient to kindle their unfriendly passions, and excite their most violent conflicts. But the most common and durable source of factions, has been the various and unequal distribution of property." Good government controls "these various and interfering interests" within society.

If the causes of faction lie in the nature of man and society, says Madison, the cure lies "in the means of controlling its *effects*." Experience shows that "neither moral nor religious motives can be relied on as an adequate control," and both history and experience demonstrate that "pure democracy . . . consisting of a small number of citizens, who assemble and administer the government in person, can admit of no cure for the mischiefs of faction." But an "extensive republic," one in "which a scheme of representation takes place," offers its citizens not only "a greater probability of fit choice" of representatives, but also "renders factious combinations" of interests less dreadful. "Extend the sphere," says Madison, "and you take in a greater variety of parties and interests; you make it less probable that a majority of the whole will have a common motive to invade the rights of other citizens; or if such a common motive exists, it will be more difficult for all who feel it to discover their own strength, and to act in unison with each other." The natural and republican remedy to faction lies in the people's representatives and in the variety of interests in the society. Madison shows that these remedies recognize man's corrupt nature and use to advantage his very weaknesses to protect him from his worst impulses. For two centuries readers have admired Madison's no. 10 because it incorporates much of his original thinking about men and governments.

Hamilton closes the first section of *The Federalist* by discussing in nos. 11–13 the importance to the Union of the federal government's power to regulate commerce and to impose taxes. Then in no. 14 Madison summarizes the arguments of the first thirteen essays and contrasts the Old World view of republican government with the New: "If Europe has the merit of discovering this great mechanical power in government, by the simple agency of which, the will of the largest political body may be concentred, and its force directed to any object, which the public good requires; America can claim the merit of making the discovery the basis of unmixed and extensive republics." Calling upon the Spirit of '76, Madison tells his countrymen that they should not fear the "experiment of an extended republic" because it is new. The "glory of the people of America" is that "they have not suffered a blind veneration for antiquity" and have displayed a "manly spirit" in the struggle for "private rights and public happiness." By implication, he suggests that the Constitution will realize and complete "a revolution which has no parallels in the annals of human society."

Part two (nos. 15–22) opens with three essays by Hamilton defining the principal flaws of the Articles. The existing Confederation's "great and radical vice," he writes, "is the principle of LEGISLATION for STATES or GOVERNMENTS in their CORPORATE or COLLECTIVE CAPACITIES and as contradistinguished from the INDIVIDUALS of whom they consist." To correct this vice, says Hamilton, "we must extend the authority of the Union to the persons of the citizens—the only proper objects of government." The whole, he argues, must be greater than the parts, and the Constitution remedies this defect without destroying the importance of the states. Then in nos. 18–20, Madison illustrates the ills of confederacies from Greek to modern times by tracing in detail the "melancholy and monitory lesson of history" taught by these forms of government. From ancient to modern times, these governments ended in anarchy, tyranny, and dissolution; the lesson was obvious: "The important truth, which it [experience] unequivocally pronounces in the present case, is, that a sovereignty over sovereigns, a government over governments, a legislation for communities, as contradistinguished from individuals; as it is a solecism in theory; so in practice, it is subversive of the order and ends of civil polity, by substituting *violence* in place of *law*, or the destructive *coertion* of the *sword*, in place of the mild and salutary *coertion* of the *magistracy*." Hamilton picks up this thread of the argument to point out that the "next most palpable defect of the subsisting Confederation is the total want of a SANCTION to its laws"; because the states can ignore federal laws, the Confederation does not even have the power to protect itself or to carry out its responsibilities.

Hamilton argues in section three (nos. 23–36) that the national government must have "without limitation" the power to achieve the goals for which it was created. Essays 23–29 define those powers as providing for the common defense, preservation of public peace, regulation of commerce, and conduct of foreign affairs. Hamilton bases his argument upon "axioms as simple as they are universal; the means ought to be proportioned to the end; the person, from whose agency the attainment of any end is expected, ought to possess the means by which it is to be attained." The Constitution gives the central government the "necessary and proper" powers to carry out its duties and makes the national document "the SUPREME LAW of the land." Antifederalists saw in these two ambiguous phrases an insidious threat to individual liberty, but Hamilton believes that "Wise politicians will be cautious about fettering the government with restrictions that cannot be observed." Essays 30–36 defend the Constitution's provision for "an indefinite power of taxation." Hamilton points out that state and federal governments share in some cases "concurrent jurisdiction" and that the power of internal taxation can be altered by amendment if it "should be discovered on experiment to be really inconvenient."

The essays in part four (nos. 37–51), all by Madison, define the "bold and radical innovations" of the convention and explicate the theoretical assumptions of the new federalism. A republican government, says Madison in essay 39,

> derives all its powers directly or indirectly from the great body of the people; and is administered by persons holding their offices during pleasure, for a limited period, or during good behaviour. It is *essential* to such a government, that it be derived from the great body of the society, not from an inconsiderable proportion, or a favored class of it; otherwise a handful of tyrannical nobles, exercising their oppressions by a delegation of their powers, might aspire to the rank of republicans, and claim for their government the honorable title of republic. It is *sufficient* for such a government, that the persons administering it be appointed, either directly or indirectly, by the people; and that they hold their appointments by either of the tenures just specified; otherwise every government in the United States, as well as every other popular government that has been or can be well organized or well executed, would be degraded from the republican character.

The Articles of Confederation did not recognize the complexities of representative government and thus erred by constructing a simple system upon fallacious principles. "The real character of republican government," says Madison, "may be considered in relation to the foundation on which it is to be established; to the sources from which its ordinary powers are to be drawn; to the operation of those powers; to the extent of them; and to the authority by which future changes in government are to be introduced." Ratification depends upon the assent of the people, who are to elect special deputies for this purpose and who are to vote as citizens of individual states, thus making establishment of the Constitution not "a *national*, but a *federal* act. Because the House of Representatives will derive its power directly from the people, its character will be *"national*, not *federal."* The Senate, however, will receive its power indirectly from the people through their elected representatives in the state legislatures and will therefore be *"federal*, not *national."* The people will choose the president indirectly through state electors, who then "form individual delegations, from so many distinct and coequal bodies politic," making selection of the executive "of a mixed character, presenting at least as many *federal* as *national* features." Because the government will exercise its power directly on the people, its make-up "falls under the *national*, not the *federal* character." Since the new government's powers are enumerated and thus limited, it "cannot be deemed a *national* one." The process of amending has both national and federal features.

For Madison and others, this mixture of forms in the Constitution represented the document's genius and originality. In the realm of government, the plan was wholly new and boldly experimental. The proposed government, says Madison, is "neither a national nor a federal Constitution, but a composition of both." This mixture of forms gave the new government sufficient authority to achieve its goals and adequate checks to prevent abuses of power and usurpation of the rights of the individuals.

In nos. 40–44 Madison reviews the six classes of powers given to the national government, and in nos. 45–46 he addresses the question of "whether the whole mass of them will be dangerous to the proportion of authority left in the several States." Madison argues that federal and state governments are "but different agents and trustees of the people, constituted with different powers, and designed for different purposes." He then turns in nos. 47–51 to the Constitution's "supposed violation of the political maxim, that the legislative, executive, and judiciary departments ought to be separate and distinct." He believes that this maxim "has been totally misconceived and misapplied." None of the state governments exhibits "a single instance in which the several departments of power have been kept absolutely distinct." Unlike European systems, which separate powers of monarch, the people, and the aristocracy, all branches in a representative republic derive their power from the people. The problem for a representative republic is not so much a separation of powers—all given by the people—but contriving "the interior structure of the government as that its several constituent parts may, by their mutual relations, be the means of keeping each other in their proper places." By mixing the powers of the three branches, the Constitution arranged "the several offices in such a manner as that each may provide a check on the other—that the private interests of every individual may be a sentinel over the public rights."

Because colonial Americans distrusted governors and upper councils, the state and federal constitutions of the 1770s had stripped the executive and often upper houses of most of their power. But the experience of the 1780s showed that legislatures and lower houses could also abuse power. Citing Jefferson's *Notes on Virginia*, Madison stated another commonplace of the day, "One hundred and seventy-three despots would surely be as oppressive as one." By mixing powers in the interior structure, the convention had guarded against such legislative despotism.

Passing from the general to the particular, Publius in section five (nos. 52–83) scrutinizes the Constitution article by article to explain the "interior structure " of the new plan. These thirty-one essays, most written by Hamilton, also refute specific Antifederalist criticisms published by Clinton, Lee, and others. For the most part, Publius follows the reasoning of the convention, but in essay 78 Hamilton boldly strikes out on his own to clarify a point the convention and the Constitution had left vague—the subject of judicial review of legislative acts by the Supreme Court. When Chief Justice John Marshall established the precedent of judicial review in the 1803 case of *Marbury* v. *Madison*, he cited Hamilton's essay 78. There Hamilton noted:

> If it be said that the legislative body are themselves the constitutional judges of their own powers, and that the construction they put upon them is conclusive upon the other departments, it may be answered, that this cannot be the natural presumption, where it is not to be collected from any particular provisions in the constitution. It is not otherwise to be supposed that the constitution could intend to enable the representatives of the people to substitute their *will* to that of their constituents. It is far more rational to suppose that the courts were designed to be an intermediate body between the people and the legislature, in order, among other things, to keep the latter within the limits assigned to their authority. The interpretation of the laws is the proper and peculiar province of the courts. A constitution is in fact, and must be, regarded by the judges as a fundamental law. It therefore belongs to them to ascertain its meaning as well as the meaning of any particular act proceeding from the legislative body.

Hamilton's interpretation of the Court's power prevailed and formed another important check in the interior structure.

When Hamilton argued in no. 84 that no bill of rights was necessary, he was merely following the consensus of the convention, which voted 10–0 against including such a bill. Fortunately, the Antifederalist critics in the state conventions won their point, and Madison, who told Jefferson he had favored such a bill in the convention, was instrumental in the passage of the first ten amendments limiting the power of the federal government over individuals. The Bill of Rights was adopted on December 15, 1791.

Hamilton completes the design of the argument in no. 85 by appealing for adoption of the new plan, which "though it may not be perfect in every part, is, on the whole, a good one." "I never expect," says Hamilton, "to see a perfect work from imperfect man." How could perfection spring from the compromises necessary to produce the document? And the Constitution's imperfections were evident to many of its friends. As delegates from North and South realized, the compromise on slavery was a costly one. In essay 54 Madison defends the convention's compromise, one he had disapproved, by creating the character of "one of our Southern brethern" to argue for the continuance of slavery. Though Americans Indians paying taxes and women were to be counted in apportionment, the convention was silent on suffrage for these groups. Other flaws would be apparent, but the convention's achievements were momentous. Near the end of his life Madison wrote, "The compound government of the United States is without a model, and to be explained by itself, not by similitudes or analogies." Americans had difficulty finding appropriate language to describe their creation. Publius uses such words as "mixed," "compound," "consolidated," "federal and national," and "republican" to characterize the new plan. Hamilton probably hit closer to the mark during the New York convention when he called the new government a *"representative democracy."* Commenting on the "representational consent of all parts of the government," Gordon S. Wood has observed: "No more revolutionary change in the history of politics could have been made: the rulers had become the ruled and the ruled the rulers." It was to advocate this Second Revolution that Hamilton and Madison designed their 175,000-word argument for the Constitution's adoption.

V

At the end of his *Notes of Debates* Madison gives Benjamin Franklin the final word about the proceedings. As the delegates signed the Constitution, Franklin commented on a rising sun painted at the back of the president's chair. Often during the sessions, said Franklin, he had puzzled over whether the sun "was rising or setting: But now at length I have the happiness to know that it is a rising and not a setting Sun." But the sun had not yet risen, for the struggle for ratification was difficult. Publius—in the persons of Hamilton, Madison, and Jay—would play a significant role in the final scenes of the drama.

By the time Hamilton published the last of *The Federalist* essays, seven states had ratified the Constitution.[2] South Carolina became the eighth on May 23, 1788, five days before volume two of *The Federalist* appeared.

---

2. Delaware, Pennsylvania, and New Jersey in December 1787; Georgia and Connecticut in January 1788; Massachusetts in February; and Maryland in April.

Hamilton corresponded regularly with Madison, who had gone home in March to stand for election to the Virginia Convention, about the gathering opposition in New York, and Madison replied about the growing Antifederalist strength in Virginia. In New York and Virginia Antifederalists had won enough seats to defeat ratification, and a union without these two states would be impossible.

The Virginia and New Hampshire conventions were meeting in June, and Hamilton waited impatiently for news of the results from these two states. Good news came from New Hampshire, the ninth state to ratify, where Federalists won by a vote of 57–47 on June 21. Antifederalists had about half of the Virginia seats, with such formidable men as George Mason and Patrick Henry leading the fight against approval. But with Madison managing the Federalist cause and convincing Edmund Randolph to support the Constitution, Virginia ratified on June 25 by a vote of 89–79.

Hamilton's situation in New York was even more precarious, for Governor Clinton's party claimed all but nineteen of the sixty-five delegates who gathered at Poughkeepsie on June 17. With John Jay and others as allies, Hamilton managed the floor fight brilliantly, allowing Antifederalist delays to work in his favor by holding off a vote until New Hampshire and Virginia had decided. Drawing upon the essays of Publius, Hamilton spoke eloquently for ratification, but as the debates continued, Clinton's forces proposed amendments as a condition for approval. When Hamilton read a letter from Madison stating that New York could not join the Union unless it adopted the Constitution "*in toto* and *for ever*," the Clinton faction pressed an immediate vote. With ten states having ratified and with Hamilton and his allies threatening secession of southern New York in order to join the Union, the Federalists carried the vote for ratification by 30–27 on July 26. Like Virginia and several other states, New York submitted a list of amendments to be considered by the new government at its earliest convenience.

Approval by Virginia and New York guaranteed establishment of the Union under the Constitution. Though North Carolina did not ratify until November 21, 1789, and Rhode Island held out until May 29, 1790, Congress had by September 1788 outlined the transition from the government of the Articles to that of the Constitution.

No one has studied in detail the immediate impact of *The Federalist* upon ratification. Many historians believe the essays had little direct influence upon the outcome of the state conventions because six states had ratified before volume one was in print. But Hamilton and Madison sent newspaper copies to friends, asking for distribution in Virginia and Pennsylvania, and copies of McLean's edition circulated widely in New York and Virginia. One Pennsylvania Antifederalist noted, "Get, if I can, the *Federalist*, without buying. It is not worth it." But he also admitted that *The Federalist* "truly was instrumental in procuring the adoption of the Constitution" in his state. Publius was present at the New York and Virginia conventions and drew upon his essays to argue for adoption. *The Federalist*, both directly and indirectly, influenced the outcomes of these two important deliberations.

Franklin may have been premature in his Philadelphia prediction that the sun of the republic was rising, but by the summer of 1788 advocates of the new plan could see more clearly the Union's course.

VI

Publius repeatedly asserts that men are depraved and ruled by their passions and self-interest. Madison says in no. 51, "It may be a reflection on human nature that such devices [checks] should be necessary to control the abuses of government. But what is government itself but the greatest of all reflections on human nature? If men were angels, no government would be necessary." Hamilton uses similar language in no. 15, where he states, "Why has government been instituted at all? Because the passions of men will not conform to the dictates of reason and justice, without constraint." For Publius, government must discover the means of controlling or redirecting the private and individual passions for the common or public good.

Madison's essay 37 develops explicitly the connection between language, human nature, and politics. The ostensible subject of this essay is the Constitution's establishment of boundaries "between the authority of the general and that of the State governments." The real subject is the obscurity, ambiguity, and indistinctness of human life and institutions. In the world of men, says Madison, "the most acute and metaphysical philosphers have been unable to distinguish and define the faculties of the mind." "Sense, perception, judgment, desire, volition, memory, imagination are found to be separated by such delicate shades and minute gradations that their boundaries have eluded the most subtle investigations, and remain a pregnant source of ingenious disquisition and controversy." This ambiguity extends to the "boundaries of the great kingdoms of nature," where the "most sagacious and laborious naturalists have never yet succeeded in tracing with certainty the line which separates the district of vegetable life from the neighboring region of unorganized matter." Because "obscurity arises as well from the object itself as from the organ by which it is contemplated," all the "efforts of human sagacity" have failed "to define with sufficient certainty" government's "three great provinces—the legislative, the executive, and judiciary." When men express their perceptions, they run aground upon another human limitation—language. "No language is so copious as to supply words and phrases for every complex idea, or so correct as not to include many equivo-

cally denoting different ideas.'' The result is ''unavoidable inaccuracy.''
''When the Almighty himself,'' says Madison, ''condescends to address
mankind in their own language, his meaning, luminous as it must be, is
rendered dim and doubtful by the cloudy medium through which it is com-
municated.'' As in human nature, nature, civil society, and language, the
boundaries between state and federal authority must be somewhat ambiguous.

Given the ambiguities of existence, Publius believed the Constitution responded to these human limitations by constructing a government that could
grow and amend itself peacefully as the needs of the people changed. If
through ''reason and choice'' men could devise a government possessing
stability and flexibility, they might hope for its life, growth, and orderly
change. Hamilton admits in no. 36 that the people's representatives will be
''almost entirely of proprietors of land, of merchants, and of members of the
learned professions,'' but he adds that ''the door ought to be equally open to
all; and I trust, for the credit of human nature, that we shall see examples of
such vigorous plants flourishing in the soil of federal as well as State legislation.'' Throughout the argument, Publius stresses the new plan's mixture of
stability and openness, of order and growth.

Repeatedly, Hamilton and Madison distinguish between the whole and its
parts, between fixity and flux. In their argument they regard the Articles of
Confederation as ''lifeless'' and describe that system in images of disease,
sickness, death, disorder, and impotence. Images of flux, flow, change,
openness, and life describe their hopes for the new form of government.
While they admitted the Constitution's imperfections, they believed that, given
the human limitations they perceived, the document offered the most hopeful
and original system men had yet devised for governing themselves.

Critics of *The Federalist* describe the book in a number of ways—from
hastily written popaganda to a ''classic of federalism'' and the ''Bible of
Republicanism.'' V. L. Parrington called the book ''a first line of defense
thrown up against the advancing democratic movement.'' For Charles Beard
The Federalist was ''the most instructive work on political science ever written in the United States'' and expressed the economic interests of its authors.
To some readers *The Federalist* asserts the political realism of postrevolutionary America; to others it records the triumph of reason during the American
Enlightenment; to still others the letters of Publius capture the beginnings of
''what might be called a romantic view of politics.'' For Thomas Jefferson
The Federalist was ''the best commentary on the principles of government
which was ever written.'' Washington, John Marshall, and other contemporaries praised the work highly, as have ensuing commentators of the last
187 years. Emphasizing the variety of the work, C. Carroll Hollis has characterized *The Federalist* as ''a curious conglomeration of tradition and originality, of classicism and romanticism, of conservatism and liberalism, of realism

and idealism, of aristocracy and democracy.'' While Americans still search for language to describe their government, *The Federalist* endures as a cogent explication of what happened in Philadelphia in the summer of 1787.

Writing more than forty years after the constitutional debates, Frenchman Alexis de Tocqueville marveled at the events of 1787–88. ''It is new in the history of society,'' he said, ''to see a great people turn a calm and scrutinizing eye upon itself when apprised by the legislature that the wheels of its government are stopped, and to see it carefully examine the extent of the evil, and patiently wait for two whole years until a remedy is discovered, to which it voluntarily submitted without its costing a tear or a drop of blood from mankind.'' De Tocqueville exaggerates, but the Second Revolution, fought with oratory and ink rather than sword and musket, was, to use his words, ''that lofty pinnacle of glory to which the proud imagination of its inhabitants is wont to point.''

SUGGESTIONS FOR FURTHER READING

Editions

The Federalist. Edited by Benjamin Fletcher Wright. Cambridge, Mass.: The Belknap Press of Harvard University Press, 1961. [Long and informative introduction.]

The Federalist. Edited by Jacob E. Cooke. Middletown, Conn.: Wesleyan University Press, 1961. [Excellent text and notes.]

The Federalist Papers. Edited by Clinton Rossiter. New York: The New American Library, 1961.

Madison, James. *Notes of Debates in the Federal Convention of 1787*. Edited by Adrienne Koch. Athens: Ohio University Press, 1966.

The Papers of Alexander Hamilton. Edited by Harold C. Syrett and Jacob E. Cooke. 19 vols. New York: Columbia University Press, 1961–73.

The Papers of James Madison. Edited by Robert A. Rutland. 9 vols. Chicago: University of Chicago Press, 1962–75.

The Records of the Federal Convention of 1787. Edited by Max Farrand. 4 vols. New Haven, Conn.: Yale University Press, 1911–37.

The Writings of James Madison. Edited by Gaillard Hund. 9 vols. New York: G. P. Putnam's Sons, 1900–1910.

Scholarship and Criticism

Adair, Douglass. *Fame and the Founding Fathers*. Edited by Trevor Colbourn. New York: W. W. Norton & Co., 1974.

Dietze, Gottfried. *The Federalist: A Classic on Federalism and Free Government*. Baltimore, Md.: The John Hopkins University Press, 1960.

Mason, Alpheus Thomas. "The Federalist—A Split Personality." *American Historical Review* 52 (April 1952): 625–43.

Mosteller, Frederick, and David L. Wallace. *Inference and Disputed Authorship: "The Federalist."* Reading, Mass.: Addison-Wesley Publishing Co., 1964.

Riemer, Neal. "James Madison's Theory of the Self-Destructive Features of Republican Government." *Ethics* 65 (October 1954): 34–43.

Rossiter, Clinton. *1787: The Grand Convention.* New York: The New American Library, 1966, 1968.

Scanlon, James P. *"The Federalist* and Human Nature." *The Review of Politics* 21 (October 1959): 657–77.

Smith, Maynard. "Reason, Passion, and Political Freedom in *The Federalist.*" *Journal of Politcs* 22 (August 1960): 525–44.

Swindler, William F. "The Letters of Publius." *American Heritage* 12 (June 1961): 4–7, 92–97.

Wood, Gordon S. *The Creation of the American Republic, 1776–1787.* Chapel Hill: University of North Carolina Press, 1969.

15

Worried Celebrants
of the American Revolution

CECELIA TICHI

[As we have now seen, the literature of the American revolutionary years is substantial and to a surprising degree still vital. These years and their events have been celebrated in much later literature that can also be called "the literature of the American Revolution": James Fenimore Cooper's first successful novel. The Spy *(1821), for example. More germane to our purposes is how the Revolution looked in retrospect to its most thoughtful observers. In the pages that follow we bring our account to a close with the consideration of three worried celebrants, as the writer of our chapter calls them, of the great events of the years 1764–89.]*

I

In 1815, eleven years before the jubilee of the American Revolution, John Adams began a letter to Jefferson with three crucial questions: "Who shall write the history of the American revolution? Who can write it? Who will ever be able to write it?" Adams probably expected the very answer he got from Monticello within a month. "Nobody," said Jefferson, arguing that because congressional proceedings on the Revolution had occurred *in camera* without extant records of participants, "the life and soul of history must for ever be unknown." Adams well knew how fragile, how ephemeral was that "life and soul of history." With regret he had heard his friend Benjamin Rush recount his own destruction in 1805 of documents and pamphlets once intended for a work entitled "Memoirs of the American Revolution," but incinerated and given away when Rush, repelled by nascent Toryism and by the canonization of Washington, decided his Philadelphia was "enemy's country" and determined to stay silent.

275

Adams rebuked him, reminding Rush that historical truth, itself the province of a very few, must be held in trust for the future. But on reflection Adams found himself equally remiss. Back in 1774 he had asked in his diary, "Have I patience, and Industry enough to write an History of the Contest between Britain and America?" By 1812 he confessed his sin of omission to Rush: "you and I have both been to blame. You, for destroying your notes of the Revolution; I, for keeping none and making very few." Nonetheless he was impatient for better accounts of the Revolution than those currently written by men who, as Rush said, "were children or not born in the memorable and eventful years which *preceded* the American Revolution," and whose motives Adams thought mercenary. Particularly Adams yearned in his old age for the appearance of a revolutionary history from the Loyalist point of view. He imagined the thousands of Loyalist letters "still concealed . . . which will one day see the light," and he "constantly expected that a Tory History of the Rise and progress of the Revolution would appear. And wished it."

While waiting he did not fail to make explicit in ten acerbic letters to Mercy Otis Warren just how deficient he thought was *her* three-volume *History of the Rise, Progress, and Termination of the American Revolution*. Warren's work, largely completed by 1791, had been put aside during the Federalist era politically repugnant to her. She claimed that virulent partisanship had then "shut up avenues of just information," and she waited for the time in which *"truth,"* meaning Jeffersonian republicanism, had its "chance for fair play." Claiming veracity and impartiality, Warren then came forward to say that as kin, confidante, and correspondent with "many of the first patriots," she was well qualified by her enforced (as she put it, providential) wartime leisure to collect the information that made her Clio's recording secretary of the American Revolution. Perhaps for the sake of their long-time, now-cooled friendship Adams often omitted her name from his catalog of historians *manqué*, though in recourse to private letters he sought redress of the injury he thought she had done him, and publicly dismissed her work with the line, "History is not the province of women."

Still, Adams resisted urgings of his friends to turn historian and deliver Americans "from the gross ignorance and errors which we daily hear and read." And finally in old age he granted to himself, to Benjamin Rush, and even to the errant Warren a kind of historian's amnesty when he declared Clio to be the muse not of history but of fiction. "I doubt whether faithful history ever was or ever can be written . . . . The world will go on always ignorant of itself, its past history and future destiny." Of the American Revolution itself, "no true history of it ever can be written."

Adams was, of course, wrong, for the history of the American Revolution had already been written, and by those same figures whose apparent silence, concealment, and distortion had provoked his self-recrimination and attack. It is true that of the revolutionary participants no intellectual ideal of the Enlightenment—a mind both encyclopedic and disinterested, virtually omniscient and possessed of unassailable Truth—had emerged to try to write *the* comprehensive account of the American Revolution. But Adams did not know how deeply inscribed the Revolution was in such diverse personal writings as his own diary and letters, in the autobiography and letters of Benjamin Rush, and, moreover, in Warren's history. Their Revolution—and by extension their ideas on the American experience—took shape in prose that was discursive and also figurative. For intuitively they sought images that conveyed their suspicions or convictions, yet whose import seems at times to have eluded the writers' consciousness. In diary, letter, autobiography, and history these three participants in the Revolution disclose disparate yet complementary visions rich in national myth and in the symbols that convey it. Adams said himself, "From the memoirs of individuals the true springs of events and the real motives of actions are to be made known to posterity." We have from him and from Rush and Warren just such a collective memoir.

For John Adams the American Revolution contained the Enlightenment version of an ideological paradox which Sacvan Bercovitch has traced back to New England Puritanism. That paradox embraced the English theological heritage of puissant nationalism along with that of atemporal sainthood. It was at once a conviction of the predestined election of a purely spiritual City of God outside human time, and yet also a belief in the earth-bound nation whose election depended upon fulfillment of its mission on earth. In Adams's eighteenth century both "nations" were sublunary but not fully reconciled with one another. The American Revolution in Adams's diary and letters is really an emblem of these two different ideas of the national experience.

In 1765 Adams had written in his diary, "I always consider the settlement of America with Reverence and Wonder—as the Opening of a grand scene and Design in Providence, for the Illumination of the Ignorant and the Emancipation of the slavish Part of Mankind all over the Earth." In his rhetoric is the certainty ("I always consider") of America's destiny as the world's "redeemer nation," to use Ernest Tuveson's phrase. Seldom inclined to write will-of-God, Adams favored the more comfortably contemporary "Design in [or "of"] Providence," terms equally assuring of movements historically predetermined. Yet he was continually dismayed by contrary evidence of public backsliding—for instance in what Adams thought to be regressive public idolatry of Washington—and he could be moved to write (as in this to Rush), "I do believe that both tradition and history are already corrupted in America as much as they ever were in the four of five centuries of Christianity, and as much as they ever were in any age or country in the whole history of mankind." These two disparate and contradictory views of America—both as the world's promised apotheosis, yet also as one more nation in a roll call of history's baleful degenerates—represent the love-have contraries of Adams's extremes of patriotic feeling, but convey as well the two strains of thought inherited from his New England forebears. The two essentially inform Adams's thinking on the American Revolution.

For Adams, as for the other colonial radicals, the motive for the Revolution (itself separate in his mind from the War for Independence) was liberty, which Bernard Bailyn has recognized as a virtually incantational term in the colonial prewar years. In the context of constitutional argument Adams defines it as the *sine qua non* of human happiness, a vital life force in a universe at once organic and mechanical. He calls the preservation and nurturance of liberty the "End, Use, Designation, Drift and scope" of the Constitution, "as much as Life and Health are the Ends of the Constitution of the human Body, as much as the Mensuration of Time is the End of the Constitution of a Watch, as much as the Grinding of Corn is the End of a Grist Mill, or the Transportation of Burdens the End of a Ship." Personally, for all his plaints in the diary on the tedium of legal studies, Adams finds commitment to the bar to be his way for self-identification with the cause of liberty. "Law is human reason," and its purpose nothing less than "the Preservation of the . . . Moralls and Liberties of Millions of the human species." His enlistment as a revolutionary made Adams no mere spokesman for liberty but its guardian and sponsor.

Adams's problem with liberty, however, was its inherent fluidity, its inclination to flourish or to wither. Although he regarded the American Revolution as a colonial conversion to the cause of liberty "in the fifteen years before a drop of blood was drawn at Lexington" and one which, as he told Rush, "continued till 1776, when on the fourth of July it was completed," Adams forever worried about the waxing and waning of libertarian motives. In 1765 he was heartened that "the People, even to the lowest Ranks, have become more attentive to their Liberties, more inquisitive about them, and more determined to defend them, than they were ever before known or had occasion to be." Moreover, Adams believed that liberty could be quickened in the public mind. To this end in 1769 he participated in a liberty party, an open-air gathering of 350 Sons of Liberty who after dinner and toasts "had the Liberty Song," thereby "cultivating the Sensations of Freedom." Adams concluded that such festivals "impregnate . . . the Minds of the People . . . with the sentiments of Liberty." The word is his invocation and convocation, defined by circling it back upon itself.

Of course liberty was threatened from without and, insidiously and more dangerously, from within. Not surprisingly, Adams called the Stamp Act "that enormous Engine fabricated by the british Parliament, for battering down all the Rights and Liberties of America." Should it succeed, it would probably "reduce the Body of the People to Ignorance, Poverty, Dependence." In 1772 Adams recorded "an unalterable Truth, that the People can never be enslaved but by their own Tameness, Pusillinamity, Sloth or Corruption." "The Preservation of Liberty depends, " he wrote, "upon the intellectual and moral Character of the People. As long as Knowledge and Virtue are diffused generally among the Body of a Nation, it is impossible they should be enslaved. This can be brought to pass only by debasing their Understandings, or by corrupting their hearts." It is this provisional and conditional nature of libertarian survival that is uppermost in Adams's mind and is always present in his recognizably Puritan Pattern of thought. For the Puritan nation being tried and tested in a wilderness survives in the revolutionary epoch in Adams's watchfulness over an America able to move forward in vigilant husbandry of liberty, yet susceptible to the torpor which could destroy it through acquiescence to those eighteenth-century devils, political despots. Through his diary and his letters Adams continuously graphs America's varying quotient of liberty.

Ultimately this conviction that America was ever in transit between libertarian ripeness or decay really made it impossible for John Adams to regard the Revolution as completed—ever. While he fixed its principal dates in an era when colonial conversion to liberty was incontrovertible and worked to dissociate mere military achievement from spiritual attainment, the intrinsic dynamism of liberty made the Revolution potentially, dreadfully ephemeral. Like Emerson a generation later, Adams worried even as a young man about metamorphosis and flux, about the Protean, Sphynx-like unfathomable *persona* of Nature. "Stability is no where to be found in that Part of the Universe that lies within our observation," he wrote. "The natural and moral World are continually changing." In this fearful flux Adams read a divine message that the world was designed, not for enduring human happiness, but "for a State of moral Discipline."

Yet moral discipline, certainly a prerequisite of liberty, remained elusive nearly thirty years later when, negotiating the Treaty of Paris, Adams agreed with a French nobleman that "universal History was but a Series of Revolutions," that "Nature delighted in Changes, and the World was but a String of them." He quipped that one was enough for the life of any man, that he hoped not to engage in another. But to Jefferson and to Rush he managed no such levity when in the early nineteenth century he measured the ebb of liberty in a nation as Rush said, "be-banked, bewhiskied, and bedollared." "Never," said Adams, punning unwittingly, "were three words better coined or applied." He feared that even the semantic basis of liberty had been subverted. "You ask [in 1808] how different were our feelings and conduct in 1774?," he wrote Rush. "Then liberty meant security for life, liberty, property, and character. Now the word has changed its meaning and signifies money, electioneering, tricks, and libels, and perhaps the protection of French armies and British fleets."

For all his lamentation Adams did not despair of the Revolution, principally because he was sustained by that part of the Puritan myth which, in the Enlightenment, counseled the predestined success of an independent, ascendant America "designed by Providence for the Theatre, on which man [is] to make his true figure, on which science, Virtue, Liberty, Happiness and Glory [are] to exist in Peace." To Rush he wrote in 1807 that no childhood memory was older "than the observation that arts, sciences, and empire had travelled westward" and that "their next leap would be over the Atlantic into America." On the subject of the Revolution we find throughout Adams's diary and letters an affirmation of the Puritan idea that America was predestined to inaugurate the global millennium.

The war especially fit this scheme of thought, despite Adams's subsequent dismissal of its revolutionary importance. True, his wartime letters best reveal the tug of his uxorious and paternal feelings against those of patriotic duty as he labored with the Continental Congress in Philadelphia and then struggled to learn French in order to help negotiate the treaty with Louis XVI. Instead of the long and moderate war toasted by army officers, Adams wished for "a short and violent war," though as late as 1781 urged Abigail "not to flatter [her]self with hopes of peace," since "there will be no such thing for several years." In Philadelphia, in Passy, and in Paris he suffered from the separation from his wife and children, from his garden and the goosequill of his leisure hours. Intermittently, too, the undisciplined Continental Army exasperated him, especially when regiments of his dear Massachusetts were thin of rank and succumbed psychologically to "the spleen, the vapors, the dismals, the horrors." "Do our people intend to leave the continent in the lurch?," he asked (not altogether rhetorically). "Do they mean to submit? or what fatality attends them? With the noblest prize in view that ever mortals contended for, . . . the people of the Massachusetts Bay are dead." He names his own anger ("More wrath than terror has seized me. I am very mad"), yet confides to his "Portia" that "this country knows not, and never can know, the torments I have endured for its sake."

Both personal and social privations of war, however, had for Adams an underside of redemptive reassurance. Though he afterward told Rush that those parts of the Revolution "acted from 1761 to 1776 were more difficult, more dangerous, and more disagreeable than all that happened afterward," he cast the war into a system of belief in America's divinely predestined, redemptive world role. Specifically he justified wartime privation and military setbacks as divine chastenings of the chosen people. On the eve of the issuance of the Declaration, Adams wrote to Abigail that to a people "addicted to corruption and venality," the imminent war will be "the furnace of affliction [that] produces refinement in states as well as in individuals." Confronting military defeats of 1778 he wrote that "it seems to be the intention of Heaven that we should be taught the full value of our liberty by the dearness of the purchase, and the importance of public virtue by the necessity of it." Moreover, Adams tried to see military defeats as inversely proportioned to America's spiritual gains:

> If it should be the will of Heaven that our army should be defeated, our artillery lost, our best generals killed, and Philadelphia fall into Mr. Howe's hands, still America is not conquered. America would yet be possessed of great resources, and, capable of many exertions, as mankind would see. It may for what I know, be the design of Providence that this should be the case. Because it would only lay the foundations of American independence deeper, and cement them stronger. It would cure Americans of their vicious and luxurious and effeminate habits, a more dangerous army to American liberty than Mr. Howe's.[1]

Years later, despite repudiation of the war as a salient part of the Revolution, Adams did bring it into revolutionary purview when he admitted to Rush his belief in the socially intrinsic value of wars. They are at times, he wrote, "as necessary for the preservation and perfection, the prosperity, liberty, happiness, virtue, and independence of nations as gales of wind to the salubrity of the atmosphere, or the agitations of the ocean to prevent its stagnation and putrefaction." The resonance from the 1770s cannot be gainsaid even though Adams spoke directly of the War of 1812.

Apart from the war, Adams found in scriptural phrophesy additional affirmation of America's predestined rise toward a redemptive world role. Ever his intellectual protégée, Abigail had written him in May 1775 that "the Lord will not cast off his people," that "great events are in the womb of futurity." "May their deliverance be wrought out" for the Americans, she implored, "as it was for the children of Israel." Adams did not himself seek out and explicate biblical texts in order to divine America's future, but he kept account of those who did, for instance the Philadelphia minister who about a year before the adoption of the Declaration preached "a kind of exposition on Isaiah. America was the wilderness, and the solitary place, and he said it would be glad, 'rejoice and blossom as the rose.' " Adams was assured that "God will come with vengeance, even God with a recompense," that untroubled by predators " 'the redeemed shall walk there.' " The minister "applied the whole prophesy to this country, and . . . . filled and swelled the bosom of every hearer."

Months later (May 1776) Adams heard the same minister parallel Pharaoh

---

1. *Familiar Letters of John Adams and His Wife Abigail Adams, During the Revolution,* ed. Charles Francis Adams, p. 306.

to George III, Egypt to Britain, Israel to America. To Abigail he told the prophetic theme, "that the course of events indicate[s] strongly the design of Providence that we should be separated from Great Britain." For himself, having observed how providential seemed his unusually robust health during congressional labors, Adams now broached in confidence to Abigail another bold scriptural parallel, that of Moses to John Adams. He dared to do so both from ambition and from conviction that his were notes for a brief on the divine will.

To Adams that will had been long apparent. For, knowing "that Liberty has been skulking about in Corners from the Creation and had been hunted and persecuted in all Countries by cruel Power," Americans now "think that the Liberties of Mankind and the Glory of Human Nature is in their keeping." Looking back he saw the colonial progenitors of the revolutionaries as "a Race which, in a Confidence in Providence, set the seas and skies, Monsters and savages, Tyrants and Devils at Defyance, for the sake of their Liberty and Religion." He would of course see the congressional resolve to enact a Declaration of Independence as "the most memorable epocha in the history of America," one deserving commemoration as "the day of deliverance," one warranting not only "solemn acts to God Almighty" but "pomp and parade, shows, games, sports, guns, bells, bonfires, and illuminations from one end of the continent to the other, from this time forward forevermore." Lest Abigail think him lost in transports of enthusiasm, Adams assured her that he knew the imminent cost in "blood and treasure," but added, "Through all the gloom I can see rays of ravishing light and glory."

With the wartime "gloom" largely in the past in 1781, Adams uttered from Amsterdam these millennial expostulations: "The great designs of Providence must be accomplished. Great indeed! The progress of society will be accelerated by centuries by this Revolution. The Emperor of Germany is adopting, as fast as he can, American ideas of toleration and religious liberty, and it will become the fashionable system of all Europe very soon. Light spreads from the dayspring in the west, and may it shine more and more until the perfect day." Never an enthusiast, Adams was nonetheless a kind of millennial rationalist whose ecstasies of rhetoric were infrequent, but whose faith in the global redemptive power of the American Revolution was adamant and constant. If he was barred by "reason and experience" from fatuous belief in a peaceable kindom of lion and lamb, of swords or musket barrels beaten to ploughshares and pruning hooks, Adams nonetheless foresaw a millennial epoch inaugurated by the Revolution and furthered by cosmopolitan access among men. It was to him "visible to the grossest eyesight that . . . from the North Pole to the South, . . . we are made for one another, that our destination is to be useful reciprocally, that we are members of the same body and children of the same family." The Revolution itself, though percussive of

Bonapartist Europe and foaling "this overgrown colt of a nation," will accomplish, Adams writes, "the ultimate good of the world, of the human race, and of our beloved country." He never retreated from that position.

II

Benjamin Rush, on the contrary, retreated *into* it. From his contentious and painful public career this innovative physician, writer, revolutionary doctor, and signer of the Declaration of Independence reverted, as Lyman Butterfield has said, "back to the religiosity of his youth." Gradually his sense of disillusionment with the American Revolution had grown until he divorced both the war and its national progeny, the United States, from the Christian future that became his solace. Uncorrupted by human intervention, the phrophesied Christian future held for Rush in late life all the libertarian promise he believed betrayed in the aftermath of the Revolution.

It is true that in the postrevolutionary (and pre-Napoleonic) years Rush saw a happy congruence of contemporary events with those of scriptural prophesy. Particularly in 1790–91 he read in contemporary history certain intimations of the Christian millennium. He divined in "the progress of reason and liberty in Europe" a forthcoming "manifestation of [the] power and influence [of the Gospel] upon the hearts of men." To Jeremy Belknap he quoted Revelation and anticipated the end of slavery, monarchic tyranny, ecclesiastical pride, and wars, and, concurrently, an edifying burgeoning "tenderness for human life." Conceding that his generation might not "live to witness the approaching regeneration of our world," he exhorted Belknap to join in readying God's world for the imminent millennial epoch.

By 1801, however, an embittered Rush had revised his schedule, convinced that "the present general prevalence of barbarism, ignorance, and slavery in the world" would require a least a century for extirpation by "civilization, human knowledge, and liberty," themselves the "heralds of religion." To John Montgomery he explained that, should the Messiah come in 1801, "he would not be welcome," that not only would Britain, France, Germany, northern Europe, Asia, and Africa prefer their benighted ways, but that "the citizens of the United States of America would probably concur with the ancient Jews, 'We will not have this man to reign over us.'" By including America in his roster of national delinquents, Rush severed God's prophesied events from those of America history. He willed himself to the pure City of God and repudiated his painful and disappointing involvement with the American Revolution. In so doing he disavowed some thirty-three years of his own life on earth.

According to his autobiography, *Travels through Life*, which was written in
1800 but not published until 1948, the physician who had first met John
Adams outside Philadelphia to escort him to the site of the Continental Congress had been converted to republican principles of government while in
Edinburgh as a medical student. (Just as Adams viewed the law as his revolutionary vocation, so Rush claimed that the intellectual ferment that shattered
his outmoded medical principles also converted him to republicanism.)
Though he claimed to have been an interested but uncommitted radical until
the battle at Lexington, Rush's earlier letters fix his empassioned determination to ally himself with the cause of the radical activists. From Edinburgh in
1768 he "resolved to devote head, heart, and pen entirely to the service of
America," which "will be revenged of the mother country." One month
from the adoption of the Declaration, Rush said the very spirit of God moved
him to declare, "I will never desert the cause I am [embar]ked in, till I see
the monster tyranny gnash [his] impotent teeth in the dust." "The declaration of independence," he wrote, "has produced a new era in this part of
America."

Unlike Adams, Rush often called the War for Independence the Revolutionary War, which he viewed as the inauguration, not the capstone, of the
American Revolution. In 1786 he called it the completed "first act of the great
drama," cautioning that while Americans had changed "forms of government, it remains yet to effect a revolution in our principles, opinions, and
manners so as to accommodate them to the forms of government we have
adopted." This next, contiguous phase of revolution would be for legislators
and patriots alike "the most difficult part," one requiring "more wisdom and
fortitude than to expel or to reduce armies into captivity." Five years earlier
Rush had warned that it would take America a half-century to cure itself of
monarchical habits and prejudices. He declared, "All will end well," and
counseled patience.

But Rush was not a patient man, and his ultimate disaffection from the
American Revolution may be traced to the consequences of his most human
*im*patience. Commissioned in 1777 as Washington's physician-general, he
had soon become agonizingly familiar with the mortality of hospital malad-
ministration. Battlefield medicine itself had not repelled him (though after
1800 he still recalled his first casualty, a young New Englander whose right
hand, broken by a cannon ball, "hung a little above his wrist by nothing but a
piece of skin.") The real source of his wartime outrage lay elsewhere. In 1812
he retold it to Adams: "I saw scenes of distress shocking to humanity and
disgraceful to a civilized country. I can never forget them. I still see the sons
of our yeomanry brought up in the law of plenty and domestic comforts of all
kinds, shivering with cold upon bare floors without a blanket to cover them,
calling for fire, for water, for suitable food, and for medicines—and calling in
vain." Caught in a corrupt hospital system that prevented his requisition of

needed stores and medicines, Rush twice wrote to Washington, and then, desperate, dispatched to Patrick Henry that unsigned letter impugning Washington's competence to lead the revolutionary army. Historians have never fully understood why Henry forwarded the letter to George Washington.

For his part Rush did not recant. Even in 1807 he scorned prudence as " 'a rascally virtue,' " one that "never achieved anything great in human affairs." Not *he* to be eulogized for prudence, no matter if the price was forced resignation from the army and subsequent ostracism from public life during Washington's administration. At third-hand he would learn, unsurprised, that Washington thought him *"the most black-hearted scoundrel he had ever known."* By then Rush had his own ledger of anti-Washington opinions and anecdotes, not to mention his ultimate consolation, that "there [was] not a single Washington among all the heroes of the Bible."

These consequences of Benjamin Rush's letter to Patrick Henry are crucial to an understanding of *his* American Revolution. It seemed to him at best quixotic and at worst fatally cruel that in the course of American history Washington should be venerated and Benjamin Rush neglected utterly. Infamy or anonymity seemed his hideous alternatives. Thus while the French Revolution gave "its *power* to a single man," Rush wrote, the American Revolution gave one man "all its *fame*." In autobiography and letters he uttered generalities and metaphors transparent of his plight. "In battle men kill, without hating each other; in political contests men hate without killing, but in that hatred they commit murder every hour of their lives." Again: "If fame is not thrown away upon the worthless part of mankind, it is certainly often given to those to whom it does not belong." On this basis could Rush concur with Adams that written history was but another word for romance.

Longing to affix himself to transcendent Christian history and thereby escape the judgmental vagaries of American history, Rush wished for a biographical metamorphosis. To Adams he wrote, "You charge me with feelings of *patriotism*. I grant that man is naturally a domestic, a social, and a political or rational animal . . . but those tribal passions have been and may be subdued. There are political . . . monks." In this sense his prose style in the autobiography is monkish. Insulated from the pain of recollection and guarded against the passions of his nature, Rush's language is bland, safe, constrained, his moments of deep depression and despair reported in sentences impersonal as statistics.

On the subject of the Revolution he yearns for retraction, for self-effacement. To his confidante Adams he admits, "I feel pain when I am reminded of my exertions in the cause of what we called liberty, and sometimes wish I could erase my name from the Declaration of Independence." "In looking back upon the years of our Revolution," he says, "I often wish for those ten thousand hours that I wasted in public pursuits." In religious diction of repentance he solicits from Adams the alien comforts of a mutual renunciation of revolutionary efforts. "From the present complexion of affairs in our country," Rush asked, "are you not disposed at times to repent of your solicitude and labors and sacrifices during our Revolutionary struggle for liberty and independence?" But repentance of that kind was apostasy to John Adams, who, though he understood the reasons for his friend's gall, never dissembled and in fact reminded Rush that patriotic duty ceased only at death.

For Rush, however, the American Revolution had died in the swamp city on the Potomac. The very site was one which a physician and Lockean environmentalist like Rush could but call "a place unfriendly to health, society, and instructing intercourse," one "calculated to foster party and malignant passions." He is bitter witness to "the downfall of the last and only free country in the world." In lines spaced to suggest a headstone Rush offers the epitaph: "Here lies interred the liberties of the United States." Instead of declaring war in 1812, he suggests sardonically, the Congress might advertise in European newspapers, "For *Sale* to the highest bidder. The United States of America." He sounds this knell: "A field of battle covered with dead bodies putrefying in the open air is an awful and distressing spectacle, but a nation debased by the love of money . . . is a spectacle far more awful, distressing, and offensive." The cranky obituary, the self-defensive withdrawal and renunciation—all have the ring of rhetorical palliatives, which John Adams recognized. "You pretend that you have outlived your patriotism," he wrote to Rush in 1809. "But you deceive yourself. Your feelings contradict your assertions."

In truth they did, and not only in pained discourse but in a cluster of images that reveal Rush's need to keep faith with the Revolution. In its service he writes in his autobiography, "I was animated by a belief that I was acting for the benefit of the whole world, and of future ages." Whether that ideal will be realized "is yet a secret in the womb of time," though "seeds" of cosmic moment "have been sowed years and centuries before [great progressive changes] came to pass." He concludes: "I still believe the American Revolution to be big with important consequences to the world." In all these figures of gestation Rush reveals that the significance of the American Revolution remains obscure to him, but that he means to suspend disbelief and skepticism and trust that his efforts will not be in vain. A hidden germination is his only approach towards optimism.

III

Like Rush, Mercy Otis Warren needed to keep faith in the Revolution whose aftermath was fraught with ominous signs for America's future. Had she confined her *History . . . of the American Revolution* (published in 1805) to the war, Warren would have left us a hymn to the insuperable American character triumphant in the crucible of military affliction. She, however, had some twenty additional years against which to test the premises of the Revolution, for the Treaty of 1783 was but one benchmark on the revolutionary continuum. The war was finished, but the Revolution uncomplete.

In large part Warren's *History* is a hymn to a fixed American character and a hagiography of the revolutionary leaders. On the eve of war when, as she writes, "the people trembled for their liberties, the merchant for his interest, the tories for their places, the whigs for their country, and the virtuous for the manners of society," Warren insists that "the genius of America was bold, resolute, and enterprising." Washington's surprise of the Hessians at Trenton demonstrates that the "spirit of enthusiastic zeal . . . enkindled [by] . . . any fortuitous circumstance that holds out the most distant promise of a completion of [the Americans'] wishes, is pushed with an ardor and unanimity that seldom fails of success." Then at Valley Forge the "nearly destitute" Americans "cheerfully erected themselves huts of timber and brush" and through the winter proved "their intrepidity in suffering, and their defiance of danger." When Charleston fell to the British, Warren asserted that neither the fallen capital, ravaged countryside, proscription of leading citizens, nor ruin of wealthy families "could subdue the spirit of independence . . . that had taken deep root in the bosoms of most of the inhabitants."

Writing her history after the war, Warren found in its campaigns, in its naval engagements, and even in local skirmishes a verification of an *a priori* American character she believed to be racially inbred since seventeenth-century settlement. Thus the war, which occupies some two-thirds of the work, is less a testing of the American will and public virtue than it is an exhibition of them. Her premises are verified deductively, and so it is no surprise to find at the close of the war a people whose spiritual biography points toward national election: "They had obtained their independence by a long and perilous struggle against a powerful nation. We now view them just emancipated from a foreign yoke, the blessings of peace restored upon honorable terms, with the liberty of forming their own governments, enacting their own laws, choosing their own magistrates, and adopting manners the most favorable to freedom and happiness."

For all this, Warren's is no work of flatulent optimism. All three volumes of the *History* are riddled with qualifications, provisos, grim doubts, above all by her fear that military victory may end in revolutionary defeat. Like Rush and Adams, Warren bore the heavy backpack of current events portending destruction of the new nation. She too worried about "a spirit of avarice and peculation" which as of 1780 had, she felt, "taken deep hold of the majority of the people" and which made her fretful about future public

"pursuit of the golden fleece." Too, she had particular postrevolutionary
bêtes noires. While Adams feared that every descendant of Washington would
be a genetically subversive neo-nobleman, Warren dreaded the power of
militarism and aristocracy combined in the fraternity of veteran revolutionary
war officers, the Order of the Cincinnati. While Rush saw in partisan politics
a mortal national malignancy, Warren was most appalled at the anarchy she
read in Shays's Rebellion that flouted the social compact.

Warren's anxieties about the so-called Whiskey Rebellion and about the
Order of the Cincinnati reveal attitudes that set *her* American Revolution apart
from those of Rush and Adams. She understood the war neither as culmina-
tion nor as inauguration of the Revolution, but as its premature birth made
necessary when Britain twisted the colonial umbilical into a Gordian knot.
This precipitate revolution and its consequent new nation troubled her deeply
because she feared the results of America's political and social immaturity.
On the one hand exultant that America was unfettered by centuries of serfdom
and vassalage, Warren found little comfort in the potential for growth by a
nation "untimely rip't."

This skepticism is consonant both with her belief in progressive evolution
of human enlightenment, which William R. Smith has discussed at length,
and with her personal distaste and suspicion of a gullible, credulous public.
Unswerving in faith that primitives (or dim yeomen) were capable of emerging through the years into socially responsible enlightenment, Warren
nonetheless suspected there would not be time enough—or rather, that the
necessary maturative years would be spoiled by political opportunists, corrup-
tive foreigners, or a greedy public blind to its own higher interest. Thus, while
she concedes that the people of the United States are better educated than "the
common classes of men in most other countries," she regrets that "many of
them ha[ve] but a superficial knowledge of mankind," being "ignorant of
the intrigues of courts" and of the "nature or origin" of government. Accordingly, she thinks them susceptible to "problematic characters which come
forward, the new-born offspring of confusion, and assume merit from the
novelty of their projects and the inscrutability of their designs." Such dem-
agogic "hot-bed plants . . . often hurry into irretrievable mischief, before
time has ripened the systems of men of more principle and judgment." Looking back at the war she reflects that the folk "had generally supposed there
was little to do, but to shake off the yoke of foreign dominion, and annihilate
the name of *king*." At the same time she fears that liberty is but a semantic
anodyne that "tickles the fond pride of man" and "is a jewel much oftener
the play-thing of his imagination, than a possession of real stability."

Warren's class biases reinforced her fears. Despite professed Jeffersonian
republicanism, her sympathies lie all with a cultivated respectable class.
Throughout her *History* it is apparent that Warren highly values the decorum

of officers on both sides, because she finds the highest standards of civilization to be represented in their codified gentlemanly behavior. And though she consistently portrays the British as the Hun of the Enlightenment and carefully includes such supportive evidence as that of the East India Bubble, Warren does refer sincerely to the "usual valor of British troops." She is far more at east reciting exemplary conduct (however sanguine) between honorable foes than reckoning with "the manners of the mountaineers and borderers of the Carolinas" who, though "descended from civilized ancestors" have sunk "into the habits of savages." Not motivated by snobbery, Warren's sense of need for social hierarchy is best revealed in her own observation that "it may be beyond the reach of human genius to construct a fabric so free as to release from subordination, nor in the present condition of mankind ought it ever to be wished. Authority and obedience are necessary to preserve social order, and to continue the prosperity or even the existence of nations."

The prosperity and the continued existence of the United States recur topically in Warren's *History* with that particular urgency of cosmic questions. Like Adams, she transcends nationalistic ardor to consider America's role as the redeemer nation of biblical prophesy. The Revolution has "awakened the attention and expectation of the millions among the nations beyond the Atlantic." It "may finally lead to the completion of prophetic predictions, and spread liberty and peace, as far at least as is compatible with the present state of human nature." She reminds skeptics that the world's confusion, begun with severance of the colonies from Britain, was divinely directed "in order finally to complete the beauty and harmony of the divine system." And she concludes her final volume with a millennial vision of the American West, "this last civilized quarter of the globe," which "may exhibit those striking traits of grandeur and magnificence, which the Divine Economist may have reserved to crown the closing scene."

For all the grandeur of possibility Warren cannot be assertive but only suggestive about America's destiny. The "prolific soil, abundant resources, commercial genius, and political principles" of America indicate a national rise "into eminence and consideration," but Warren is not confident of these indices. Her grammar becomes subjunctive and conditional as she ponders the future, and her grandest hopes rest upon a groundword of provisos. "From the accumulated blessings which are showered down on the United States," she writes, "there is reason to indulge the benign hope, that America may long stand a favored nation." Indulgence of "benign hope" is the extent of Warren's risk. She is a tenuous prophet.

Constrained empiricism and guarded optimism characterize Warren's work at the point of summation, which is itself protracted because, her story told, Warren was reluctant to stop. In efforts to be dignified and serious, she often became sententious and clumsy, her clauses as persistent and involuted as ground vines. Under the rubric of "Political and Moral Observations" she reviews endlessly her doubts and fears about America's future. This prolongation of the *History* suggests something other than Warren's uncertainties about literary pacing, namely her sense of political confinement in *belles lettres*. Unlike Adams or Rush, or the prolific Founding Fathers, Warren had only the printed page and the theater for her reformist political energies. She seems understandably reluctant to end the work whose directives and caveats, if heeded, could be instrumental in insuring the continuous success of the American Revolution. It seems that she too wished to be a Founder.

Mercy Warren's revolutionary aspirations dovetail with those of John Adams and Benjamin Rush because like them she shared passionately in the national vision of a redemptive America. In revolutionary context they all three revivified the visionary legacy of seventeenth-century Puritan thought by fitting it to a secular but fervid language of the Enlightenment and to a geography transcendent of, but specific to, the United States and the North American continent. Politically committed and unequivocating, at intervals self-pitying, baffled, or angry, these three figures year after year reassessed the Revolution compulsively in letters, diary, autobiography, and history. Conjointly over time they emerge as a chorus of worried celebrants, a troubled conscience of the Revolution afterward sullied in their interpretive doubt and fear, but embodying still their brightest hope for worldwide betterment of the human condition.

SUGGESTIONS FOR FURTHER READING

Editions

The Adams-Jefferson Letters. Edited by Lester J. Cappon. 2 vols. Chapel Hill: University of North Carolina Press, 1959.
The Autobiography of Benjamin Rush. Edited by George W. Corner. Princeton, N.J.: Princeton University Press, 1948.
Collections of the Massachusetts Historical Society. 5th ser., vol. 4. Boston, 1878. [Correspondence of John Adams and Mercy Otis Warren.]
Diary and Autobiography of John Adams. Edited by L. H. Butterfield et al. 4 vols. Cambridge, Mass.: Harvard University Press, 1961.
Familiar Letters of John Adams and His Wife Abigail Adams, During the Revolution. Edited by Charles Francis Adams. New York: Hurd and Houghton, 1876.
Letters of Benjamin Rush. Edited by L. H. Butterfield. 2 vols. Princeton, N.J.: Princeton University Press, 1951.
The Spur of Fame. Edited by John A. Schutz and Douglas Adair. San Marino, Calif.: The Huntington Library, 1966. [Correspondence of John Adams and Benjamin Rush.]

Warren, Mercy Otis. *History of the Rise, Progress, and Termination of the American Revolution*. 3 vols. Boston: E. Larkin, 1805.

Scholarship and Criticism

Bailyn, Bernard. *The Ideological Origins of the American Revolution*. Cambridge, Mass.: Harvard University Press, 1967.

Bercovitch, Sacvan. "Horologicals to Chronometricals: The Rhetoric of the Jeremiad." In *Literary Monographs*, ed. Eric Rothstein. Vol. 3, pp. 1–124. Madison: University of Wisconsin Press, 1970.

Binger, Carl. *Revolutionary Doctor: Benjamin Rush, 1746–1813*. New York: Norton, 1966.

Fritz, Jean. *Cast for a Revolution: Some American Friends and Enemies 1728–1814*. Boston: Houghton Mifflin, 1972. [Mercy Otis Warren's social ambiance.]

Hawke, David F. *Benjamin Rush: Revolutionary Gadfly*. Indianapolis, Ind.: Bobbs-Merrill, 1971.

Hutcheson, Maud M. "Mercy Warren 1728–1814." *William and Mary Quarterly*, 3d ser., 10 (1953): 378–402.

Smith, William R. *History as Argument: Three Patriot Historians of the American Revolution*. The Hague: Mouton, 1966. [Essays on Mercy Otis Warren, David Ramsay, and John Marshall.]

Tuveson, Ernest L. *Redeemer Nation: The Idea of America's Millennial Role*. Chicago: University of Chicago Press, 1968.

Notes on Contributors

WILLIAM D. ANDREWS, assistant professor of English, Ohio State University, has held a National Endowment for the Humanities Younger Humanist Fellowship. His publications include studies in cultural and intellectual history.

ROBERT D. ARNER, professor of English at the University of Cincinnati, is the author of numerous critical studies, especially in the field of early American comic writing, the subject of a forthcoming book. He has served as a research fellow at the Huntington Library.

ROBERT BAIN is associate professor of English at the University of North Carolina, Chapel Hill. Co-editor of *Colonial and Federalist American Writing* and *The Writer and the Worlds of Words*, he has been president of the North Carolina-Virginia College English Association and now serves on the editorial board of *The Southern Literary Journal*.

BERNARD W. BELL, assistant professor of English at the University of Massachusetts, Amherst, has edited *Modern and Contemporary Afro-American Poetry* and *The Folk Roots of Contemporary Afro-American Poetry*; forthcoming is his study of Jean Toomer. The recipient of a National Endowment for the Humanities Young Humanist Fellowship, he served as guest professor at the University of Freiburg, West Germany, in 1974–75.

ROBERT M. BENTON, associate professor of English, Central Washington State College, has divided his attention between early American literature and the writings of John Steinbeck, with publications in both fields.

EVERETT EMERSON, professor of English at the University of Massachusetts, Amherst, is editor of the journal *Early American Literature* and author of *John Cotton, English Puritanism from John Hooper to John Milton*, and *Captain John Smith*. He edited *Major Writers of Early American Literature* and *Letters from New England, 1629–1638*.

ELAINE K. GINSBERG is assistant professor of English at West Virginia University. Her research interests include early American literature and American fiction.

EVELYN J. HINZ, adjunct professor of English at the University of Manitoba, has published widely on such writers as D. H. Lawrence, Poe, James, Cather, and Anïas Nin (she is preparing the authorized biography). With John J. Teunissen she edited Roger Williams's *Key into the Language of America*.

PATRICIA M. MEDEIROS, director of the Report Writing Program, University of Western Ontario, is a specialist on American literature and contemporary Canadian novelists.

CHARLES E. MODLIN, assistant professor of English, Virginia Polytechnic Institute and State University, is preparing a study of political satire in the early republic.

THOMAS PHILBRICK, professor of English at the University of Pittsburgh, is author of *James Fenimore Cooper and the Development of American Sea Fiction* and *St. Jean de Crèvecoeur*. A member of the editorial board of the journal *Early American Literature*, he is currently at work on a study of the historical novel in America.

A. W. PLUMSTEAD, professor of English at the University of Massachusetts, Amherst, is the author of many studies in American literature and an editor of the journals of Ralph Waldo Emerson. Another of his publications is *The Wall and the Garden: Selected Massachusetts Elecion Sermons, 1670–1775*.

MARY E. RUCKER, assistant professor of English at the University of Michigan, has published studies of such writers as Henry James and Emerson; she is currently undertaking a study of Nathaniel Hawthorne.

CECELIA TICHI, associate professor of English, Boston University, has published widely on Puritan historiography and on Charles Brockden Brown and Melville. She has held fellowships of the Radcliffe Institute and the American Council of Learned Societies.

CALHOUN WINTON, professor of English at the University of Maryland, formerly served as coordinator of the Winterthur Program in Early American Culture and chairman of the English Department, University of South Carolina. His many publications include a two-volume biography of Sir Richard Steele.

Index